Desire, Faith, and the Darkness of God

DESIRE, FAITH, *and the* DARKNESS OF GOD

Essays in Honor of Denys Turner

Edited by

ERIC BUGYIS *and*
DAVID NEWHEISER

University of Notre Dame Press
Notre Dame, Indiana

University of Notre Dame Press
Notre Dame, Indiana 46556
undpress.nd.edu

Copyright © 2015 by the University of Notre Dame

Manufactured in the United States of America

Library of Congress Cataloging-in-Publication Data

Desire, faith, and the darkness of God :
essays in honor of Denys Turner /
edited by Eric Bugyis and David Newheiser.
pages   cm
Includes bibliographical references and index.
ISBN 978-0-268-02242-6 (pbk. : alk. paper)
ISBN 0-268-02242-9 (pbk. : alk. paper)
1. Christian theology. I. Turner, Denys, 1942–
II. Bugyis, Eric, 1980– editor.
BR118.D47   2015
230—dc23
2015031816

to
DENYS
the
Teacher

Contents

DISCOURSE AND AUTHORITY

MARXISM AND NEGATIVE THEOLOGY

Acknowledgments

This volume took shape at a conference hosted at Yale University in March 2012 that was generously supported by the Yale Divinity School, the Yale Institute of Sacred Music, the Martin Marty Center at the University of Chicago, the Yale Department of Religious Studies, the Saint Thomas More Catholic Chapel and Center at Yale, and the Yale Graduate School Dean's Fund. For providing practical support for the conference, the editors wish to thank Neil Arner, Fr. Robert Beloin, Anthony Domestico, T. J. Dumansky, Megan Eckerle, Rebecca Menning, Evan Morse, and Hannah Roh. We are grateful for the support of our editors at the University of Notre Dame Press and above all to the contributors for their extraordinary work.

Preface

To succeed in saying something about God is the
most elementary task of the theologian, as the word
"theologian" implies.
—Herbert McCabe, O.P., *God and Evil in the Theology
of St. Thomas Aquinas*

What is the theologian's task? In his *Thomas Aquinas: A Portrait*,
Denys Turner suggests that Thomas's ability to utterly disappear behind his texts, making the details of his own life and person irrelevant
to the truth that he is attempting to communicate, can serve as an
appropriate point of departure for reflecting on the theological calling. What Turner's Thomas shows us is that it belongs to the peculiar
vocation of the theologian to approximate, to the extent he or she is
able, the kind of egoless communication that makes real communion
possible. The theologian, then, is called on to perform a kind of linguistic martyrdom, whereby the greatest meaning is communicated
through a self-silencing that makes it possible for others to speak.
And, given the voluminous literature that the Angelic Doctor has inspired, it would seem that Thomas was such a martyr, writing more
in death than he wrote in life, which, as Turner points out, was quite
a lot.

The present volume, and the conference held in Turner's honor
at Yale University on March 22–24, 2012, whence it began to take
shape, is a testament to his ability to articulate a theological space
that is primarily concerned with creating the conditions that might

allow others to speak. To be sure, no one who has spent even a few minutes with Turner would describe him, as he describes Thomas, as laconic. And there is little to suggest that "the dumb ox," as Thomas's friends dubbed him, relished chance meetings with students and colleagues leading to lingering conversations and lively debates over lunch or while loitering on the quad of the University of Paris, as Turner still does on college lawns and in cafés across the United States and the United Kingdom. But, insofar as every caricature, which is what Turner freely calls his *Portrait*, is as much a product of the artist as it is of its subject, there are a few features that Turner as teacher and theologian does share with his Thomas.

The first of these is a desire to avoid the kind of hyperreflexive energy that tends to animate much academic discourse, especially in recent years. This manifests itself in the constant need to position oneself both within one's own work and vis-à-vis the work of other academics with the intention of ensuring one's proprietary claim to one's contributions to the field while shielding them from criticism under the cover of idiosyncrasy. Both in the classroom and in print, Turner is not interested in deploying such strategies of ownership. Unlike Augustine or Paul, whom he irreverently and playfully contrasts with Thomas, Turner would be somewhat embarrassed to offer his own life as proof of the existential relevance of the questions that most concern him. Much more interesting, rather, are the questions of his students and of the community of his fellow seekers, also known as the Church. This is why his books are often populated with insights and suggestions gleaned from direct conversations with students and colleagues. It is also probably why he enjoys trying out his ideas especially with master's degree candidates at Yale Divinity School, many of whom are planning to enter professional ministry and, like Thomas, are more concerned with whether some bit of theology "will preach" than whether it "will publish."

This brings us to a second trait that Turner shares with his Thomas, which perhaps belongs more properly to the theologian than it does to other intellectuals. Every good theologian knows that at some point his or her finite utterances will be inadequate to the infinite mystery of God, which is their proper object. But, in contrast to the preacher, who fervently hopes that he or she will not be so afflicted until the *end* of his or her remarks, some academic theologians *begin* speaking as if exploding like magicians from a flamboyant cloud of enigmatic apophasis. Of course, this can be intriguing and even entertaining on the page or from the lectern, but in everyday life it often functions to refuse conversation rather than to invite it. Turner writes in *A Portrait* that Thomas's fellow Dominican, Meister Eckhart, was just such a "fizzing show-off, just a bit too self-indulgently enjoying his own talent for paradox to be an entirely convincing preacher" (4). As a student of analytic philosophy, trained under R. M. Hare at Oxford, Turner understands that clarity is to the intellectual life as humility is to the moral life. This is not to say, as some analytically minded philosophers might, that one never trails off in silent *aporia* or prattles on in search of the right word. It does mean, however, that these forms of God-talk are neither to be offered for their own sake nor to be constructed to hide the insecurity of their author in the cloak of cleverness. They are simply to be endured as the necessary consequence of being confronted by an object that exceeds the capacities of our frail, human instrument.

This linguistic humility corresponds to the third and final quality that Turner shares with his Thomas. In joining the Dominican order, Thomas chose to give up a life of stability and self-sufficiency in the prestigious Benedictine abbey of Monte Cassino, for which his parents had prepared him since he was five, and threw in his lot with a relatively new group of wandering preachers, who lived by mooching off of the charity of others. It would most likely be saying too much to suggest that someone who has occupied academic chairs at Cambridge and Yale has experienced the same kind of material dependency. However, the conviction that our lives are not for ourselves alone and that the theologian serves at the pleasure of his or her audience is one that suffuses every line that Turner writes and every class that he teaches. He is acutely aware that the theological task is not necessary to modern society in the way that, say, industrial farming or investment banking might be. And because of this, theology has no instrumental value. Rather, like love and friendship, it is about finding people to waste precious time with you and, in the process, learning that time is most precious when it is so wasted.

This was the spirit when we gathered to honor our teacher, fellow seeker, and friend Denys Turner in 2012. Unfortunately, such things are difficult to translate into a volume like this, but it is our hope that there remains in these pages a glimmer of the gratuitous spirit that produced it.

Eric Bugyis
Lent 2015

Introduction

The Trials of Desire

DAVID NEWHEISER

Confronted by religious and cultural diversity, some doubt whether Christian faith remains possible today. There are times and places when commitment to a particular religious tradition seems almost automatic, but the modern West offers many possible forms of life, religious and otherwise. Yet although faith has become a tenuous possibility—appealing to some, perplexing to many—this ambivalence is rarely acknowledged in public debates over religion. Critics claim that religion is necessarily irrational and violent, and its loudest defenders are equally strident. This insistence masks an underlying anxiety, which stems from the half-conscious awareness that its bluster remains an unjustified bluff. Whether it supports or opposes religious commitment, dogmatic certainty is psychologically fragile, and in fact it frequently shatters.

This volume suggests that Christians need not lay claim to certainty, for faith is a matter of passion (which plays best in the dark). Drawing on classic Christian thought alongside modern philosophy and literature, these essays argue that language cannot capture divine transcendence, for the creator described in Christian discourse

1

is not an object in the world. This suggests that modern arguments about God's existence represent a dead end: in contrast to those who struggle to prove (or disprove) the existence of a divine being, Christian faith begins in a desire that outstrips itself, impassioned by the darkness of God.

THE ESSAYS gathered here are connected by four interrelated sets of questions. First, if God is the source of all things, God cannot be distinguished from the world in the way that two things are distinguished from each other, but this makes it difficult to avoid collapsing any difference between them. Augustine, Eckhart, and Nicholas of Cusa all affirm the ongoing importance of the created world, but their insistence upon divine transcendence risks dissolving God into creation—leaving one to worry that the value of either is lost. This theological tradition thus raises the question: If there is no common term on the basis of which God and creation could be opposed, how can God be differentiated from processes immanent to the natural order?

A second set of questions follows from the first: If the divine is no ordinary object, how can Christians speak of God? In order to explore possibilities for theological speech, these essays set Primo Levi's poetry and Jacques Derrida's deconstruction alongside Christian traditions of self-critique. In this way, they suggest that poetic expression converges with a strand of Christian thought which argues that theological affirmations require a corresponding unsaying (in Greek, *apophasis*). If descriptive discourse cannot capture a transcendent God, it may be that expressive speech can surpass predicative reference. Or, on the other hand, perhaps poetry embodies the self-critical openness that characterizes apophatic negativity.

Expanding the range of Christian discourse in this way raises a third question: If God cannot be captured discursively, how does Christian thought differ from atheism? The flexibility of theological speech could encourage apophatic traditions to embrace their similarity to a sophisticated atheism, but even the most mystical theologians have been known to draw the boundaries of orthodox doctrine.

The question comes to a head with Marx, whose atheism resembles apophatic negativity in more than one way. These essays explore the ways in which Christian thought may acknowledge its affinity with atheism while continuing to sustain Christian practice.

It might be tempting to resolve the difficulties that surround Christian discourse by appealing to love, but desire is equally problematic when directed toward the divine. Thus, a fourth set of questions emerges: What does divine desire suggest concerning the status of creaturely realities? What does it mean to desire a God who transcends knowledge and experience? How does the love of God relate to the love of others? Rather than settle the questions at stake (concerning the relation between God and the world, the character of Christian discourse, and the distinction between atheism and faith), the theme of desire only amplifies their intensity. Crucially, however, where reason reaches its limit in uncertainty, these essays suggest that desire may take divine darkness as the occasion for a passionate faith.

Each of the volume's four sections—Immanence and Transcendence, Discourse and Authority, Marxism and Negative Theology, and Revelations of Love—centers on one of the four sets of questions outlined above. However, these themes are so tightly connected that each runs through the collection as a whole.

IMMANENCE AND TRANSCENDENCE

Mary-Jane Rubenstein's essay, "End without End," reflects on the relation between God and creation by drawing together the love of God and the love of everything else. In Rubenstein's reading, where Augustine's introspective search for God returns him to all things (now encountered in God), Nicholas of Cusa comes to himself by finding God in all things. For Nicholas, the universe resembles God in its endlessness even as it differs from God as a created, contracted infinity. On account of this similarity-in-dissimilarity, the desire for any thing draws us to God, who is the ultimate object of every desire.

In "The Darkness of God and the Light of Life," Karl Hefty examines the function of the concept of life in negative theology against the background of modern phenomenology. Hefty argues that according to Augustine, Pseudo-Denys, and Meister Eckhart, life is not an empirical phenomenon but rather the form taken by union between God and humanity. For this reason, Hefty says, the path into divine darkness is illuminated by life, which is in fact the very content of that illumination. In this theological tradition, as for the phenomenologist Michel Henry, life is the source of everything, and it is the milieu of affectivity. Thus, Hefty provocatively concludes, perhaps reflection on life leads inevitably to theology.

In "Mysterious Reasons," Anna Williams observes that, although the Bible says that God is beautiful, it is not clear how this beauty relates to that of material creatures. Augustine claims in both cases that beauty is attractive insofar as it is rational, but he admits that aesthetic experience nevertheless precedes analysis. Williams argues that, although Edmund Burke's earthbound aesthetics differs from Augustine's, Burke helps us to imagine how the mind can be both drawn to and defeated by a mysterious object. In this, she suggests, the delight of the mind consists both in satisfaction and in the endless pursuit of deferred consummation.

In "Using Reason to Derive Mutual Illumination from Diverse Traditions," David Burrell argues that the insistence of some believers that "there is such a person as God" testifies to their idolatry, for such an assertion makes God into a thing (albeit a big one). Burrell claims that the postmodern and medieval are close insofar as they recognize that faith is a mode of knowing; from this perspective, theology provides a corrective to the modern assertion of superiority over supposedly regressive societies. According to Burrell, while reason is easily co-opted by power, theology models a form of reflection in which the positive and the negative intertwine in service of love.

DISCOURSE AND AUTHORITY

In "Assent to Thinking," Karmen MacKendrick describes a faith that is characterized by decentered unknowing. Against the widespread assumption that faith consists in propositional belief, MacKendrick argues that Augustine and Aquinas both describe faith as a thinking with assent that renounces security. There remains a place for propositions, but MacKendrick suggests that statements of faith deepen rather than dispel its mystery. This desirous inquiry is the converse of an apophatic negativity; in MacKendrick's account, the assent of faith aims to search rather than to declare, committed to a questioning that continues.

Katie Bugyis's essay, "Apian Transformations and the Paradoxes of Women's Authorial Personae in Late Medieval England," shows the way in which authors from Mechthild of Heckeborn to Julian of Norwich describe the fruitful chastity of women religious, often through the figure of the bee. According to Bugyis, the metaphor of the bee authorized women's voices, enabling them to defy the limits both of language as such and of the place of women in medieval society.

In "Academics and Mystics," Bernard McGinn examines Jean Gerson's evolving account of the relation between the academic and the mystical. Whereas his early mystical writings center on an affective reading of Dionysius the Areopagite, Gerson's later work qualifies this emphasis by articulating his suspicion of untutored lay mysticism. According to McGinn, although Gerson attends to the danger of academic pride, he suggests that mystical experience benefits from the scrupulous constraints of academic theology.

In "How Wrong Could Dante Be?," Robin Kirkpatrick argues that Dante devalues doctrinal purity, preferring instead to see error itself as part of the process of creation. Kirkpatrick traces the scathing wit with which Dante cuts self-important popes and academics down to size, and he suggests in this light that Dante's exhilarating comedy indicates that theological language functions as a sacramental sign which exceeds our command and understanding.

MARXISM AND NEGATIVE THEOLOGY

In "The Turning of Discourse," Cyril O'Regan argues that by cultivating a generous grammar Christian discourse avoids both the desire for overdetermined systematicity and the anxiety implicit in overwrought claims to orthodoxy. Such a grammar escapes the dialectic between system and fragment by emphasizing questions more than answers, and it recognizes that traditions are constituted by doctrinal contestation. In O'Regan's view, this grammar ultimately exists in order to give way to a silence that is more eloquent than even the most capable speech.

In "'Love was his meaning,'" Oliver Davies argues that medieval Christian thought and modern science share an analogous understanding of language and the self. In Davies's account, the performative use of language in Eckhart, Aquinas, and Dante approximates the modern emphasis on the materiality of the sign (which he associates with Karl Marx and Julia Kristeva). For this reason, Davies claims, reading premodern texts in light of modern science challenges the dualism naively presumed by some contemporary thinkers.

In "Ideology and Religion, Yet Again," Ludger Viefhues-Bailey argues that debates concerning the secular or religious origin of political power betray a desire for a single source of legitimation. In this, they mirror the polemic between theists and atheists, who seek a stable point on which meaning and value may be securely grounded. In response, Viefhues-Bailey argues that scholars of religion ought to reflect on how imperfect—even ideological—concepts allow particular contestations to be described even if language remains entangled in systems of power.

"Is Marxism a Theodicy?," Terry Eagleton asks. It could seem that Marx's historical materialism provides a justification of evil; as Eagleton observes, Marx sometimes suggests that some evils are necessary insofar as they are what enables good to follow. After all, it sometimes appears that the price of socialism is years of suffering under the evils of capitalism. Nonetheless, Eagleton argues, Marxism (like Christianity) is a tragic creed, for it acknowledges its own fragility and does not assume that a happy ending is worth the hell required.

"'If you do love, you'll certainly be killed'" records a conversation between Terry Eagleton and Denys Turner concerning the relation between Marxist theory and mystical theology. Expanding on his contribution to this volume, Eagleton suggests that the two traditions are close in their affirmation of the sacramental meaning of material things and in their relentlessly critical character. Turner agrees, connecting Marx with the emphasis on materiality in Thomas Aquinas. Turner goes so far as to suggest that Meister Eckhart's insistence on the dispossession of desire is the prerequisite of the transformative community that Marx describes. Turner and Eagleton thus come to agree that Christian sacramentality, like socialism, has a self-canceling character that anticipates its obsolescence.

In "As We Were Saying," Eric Bugyis places several Marxist theorists indebted to Christian thought into conversation with a number of Christian thinkers who draw on Marx. Bugyis argues that the latter group (which includes Eagleton, Turner, and Herbert McCabe) provides a better foundation for the hope that liberation can be achieved. In his account, the former group (which includes Alain Badiou, Antonio Negri, and Slavoj Žižek) lacks recourse to a theology of creation from nothing. For Bugyis, this theological trope is required for any revolution to avoid repeating the violence of the present order in a new context.

REVELATIONS OF LOVE

In "How to Say 'Thank You,'" Vittorio Montemaggi argues that the rejection of idolatry entails a willingness to learn through attention to the suffering of others. On the face of it, Primo Levi and Julian of Norwich would seem to be at odds, for Julian claims that evil is fitting insofar as it serves the divine plan while Levi insists that the existence of Auschwitz militates against belief in God. Montemaggi argues that the God Levi rejects is one who plays favorites, allowing some to live while condemning others to suffer, but on Julian's terms such a God would in fact be an idol. Montemaggi thus suggests that, despite his apparent atheism, Levi's open-minded gratitude for the world exemplifies a basic rule of theological grammar.

In "*Sitit Sitiri*," Philip McCosker distinguishes between varieties of apophaticism in terms of Christology, arguing that each corresponds to a logic of desire that either undermines or upholds the

Chalcedonian affirmation that Christ has two natures in one person. McCosker claims that Meister Eckhart sidelines Chalcedonian Christology by suggesting that God and creation displace each other, while Bonaventure strenuously attempts to maintain the balance between human and divine. According to McCosker, whereas the apophatic ascent described by Bonaventure is finally undone by the abandonment of creaturely desire, Maximus the Confessor effectively synthesizes negative theology and Christology by insisting that we can only journey to God as fully human.

In "Our Love and Our Knowledge of God," John Hare argues that our knowledge of God may be limited because God's relation to us is particular, unique in every case. Duns Scotus argues that we are each called to love God in a different way; according to Scotus (interpreted in light of Gerald Manley Hopkins), it is only through this particularity that we may contemplate the divine. Because we are in time while God is not, we cannot know God as God is in Godself, and yet for Scotus (as for Søren Kierkegaard), we may love that which we do not understand.

My own essay, "Eckhart, Derrida, and the Gift of Love," argues that Jacques Derrida and Meister Eckhart both construe love as a gift that is entirely free of economic exchange, and both conclude on this basis that love cannot be grasped or identified. In my reading, Eckhart and Derrida do not rule out consideration of one's own well-being, but their accounts do entail that calculated self-protection is external to love. For this reason, they suggest, lovers should not expect to balance love against prudential restraint: although both demands are indelible, they function at different levels. A gift of this sort is ineluctably dangerous, but Derrida and Eckhart suggest that unsettling darkness must be endured in order to preserve the possibility of love.

Denys Turner's concluding meditation, "How to Fail," ties together these themes by reflecting on anxiety and delight. In Turner's telling, obsessive critique characterizes life in the academy; in his view, a sophistic irony that he calls "deconstructive" drowns contemplative wonder. Turner contrasts self-satisfied cynicism with the delight in creation exemplified by Aquinas, Scotus, and Hopkins, each of whom acknowledge (in different ways) that amazement is the proper response to the gift of creation: that there is anything at all.

BECAUSE THESE essays are closely connected, they benefit from being read together. When the authors convened in 2012 for the conference in honor of Denys Turner's retirement, his work served as a guiding thread in our reflection on the issues at stake. Because the contributors were drawn from Turner's friends and former students, the gathering was characterized by a generous collegiality, and the participants devoted themselves with extraordinary sensitivity to creating a common conversation.

Each paper was circulated in advance of the conference, which meant that each benefited from a full hour of wide-ranging discussion. The essays in this volume have been revised in light of the other contributors' comments on the conference papers, and many of them explicitly describe their connection with the other essays. Although they disagree about many things, the essays trace a common trajectory insofar as they display their authors' commitment to reflection in community.

Together they suggest that the interplay between speech and unsaying opens the space in which an unknowing love may expand. Because faith is tenuous, some are tempted to retreat into dogmatic certainty, whether for or against religious commitment. However, the history of Christian thought opens the possibility of another response to uncertainty. Although dispassionate reason soon reaches its limit, Christian life may be understood as an ethical and political practice impassioned by a God who transcends understanding.

IMMANENCE
AND
TRANSCENDENCE

ONE

End without End

Cosmology and Infinity in Nicholas of Cusa

MARY-JANE RUBENSTEIN

> You, therefore, O God, are infinity itself, which alone
> I desire in every desiring.
> —Nicholas of Cusa, *On the Vision of God*

"A VAST AND INFINITE PROFUNDITY"

In preparation to pay tribute to the incomparable work of Denys
Turner, hoping among other things to express the profound effect it
has had on my own writing and thinking, I dug up my old notes from
a lecture series he delivered at Cambridge University at the turn of
the millennium titled "God and Creation in Mediaeval Theology."
There I found a number of recurring themes, like the tension between emanation and the ex nihilo, the manifold perils of volun-
tarism, and the difference between chalk and cheese. I also found
some classic Denysisms, such as "Psalm 88 is a great, *grumpy* prayer,"
"Zwingli is so hot on absence," and "theology is in constant danger

13

of reinventing its own wheel." But the phrase I found most often—which I had written down in nearly every lecture—was Saint Augustine's astonished exclamation, "You were within me, but I was outside myself (*intus eras et ego foris*)."[1]

Whether he was discussing Julian of Norwich, Marguerite Porete, or Meister Eckhart, Denys Turner's thoughts about creation always seemed to lead him back to this *intus eras*, to the God who dwells within the one who searches for God—specifically, within the very faculty that does the searching. For Augustine, this faculty is "memory" (*memoria*), the innermost part of him, which he at one point calls "a vast and *infinite* profundity (*penetrale amplum et infinitum*)."[2] The infinity of this inwardness is stated very quickly and not quite explained, but it seems to be a function of memory's ability to hold together contradictory states. Memory can remember red, for example, in a dark room. It can remember sadness with gladness.[3] And most strikingly for Augustine, memory can remember *forgetting*. I can remember having forgotten something, like my lunch or my keys; I can even remember that I am a generally forgetful person, and yet—this is what Augustine finds so amazing—I can remember all this forgetting without actually forgetting. When memory remembers forgetting, it makes present its own failure without itself failing, so that "both memory and forgetfulness are present."[4] And this *coincidentia oppositorum* plunges Augustine into a kind of astonished unknowing: "Who can find a solution to this problem?" he asks. "Who can grasp (*comprehendet*) what is going on?"[5]

What is most incomprehensible to Augustine is that this infinite memory is *within* him—in fact, it *is* him—and yet it exceeds him. How, he marvels, can a finite being contain infinity? "This power is that of my mind (*animus*)," he writes, "and it is a natural endowment, but *I myself cannot grasp the totality of what I am*."[6] As the faculty that both constitutes and exceeds him, memory becomes the "place" he finally finds God. Augustine's ungraspable God must dwell within the ungraspable core of the human subject, in the innermost part of him that is nevertheless beyond him.[7] What this means, Augustine comes to realize, is that throughout his protracted search for God, God was there all along—and not just sitting quietly, waiting to be found, but rather as the power fueling the search itself. As Turner explains in *The Darkness of God*, "It is I who am 'outside' myself and it is the God within who initiates, motivates and guides the seeking whereby and in which God is to be found."[8] And the mechanism by which God drives the self back to itself, back to God, is desire.

Desire appears early in the *Confessions*. It is, in fact, the first function—if one can call it that—that Augustine attributes to humanity. "Man desires to praise you (*laudare te vult homo*)," he writes, establishing humanity from the outset as the "little piece of creation" that *desires*.[9] More specifically, humanity is the little piece of creation that desires the *creator*, which is to say humanity desires its own unassimilable essence; humanity desires the God who both constitutes and exceeds it. This desire, moreover, is itself a gift of God: "*you* stir man to take pleasure in praising you," Augustine exclaims, signaling that God Godself instills the desire that God alone fulfills.[10]

Of course, God is not the only object of human desire; in fact, the first nine books of the *Confessions* chronicle Augustine's chasing after people and pleasures that lead him *from* God. Yet Augustine will eventually conclude that these were false desires: the soul may think it wants admiration and physical affection and entertainment, but what it really wants is God. Denys Turner, admitting this argument sounds a bit forced, explains Augustine's theological gymnastics in two ways. First, everything in the world reflects in some measure "the beauty and goodness of God"; therefore, the desire for anything "is always in some way a desire for God."[11] Second, everything other than God is finite and impermanent and therefore leaves the soul with a "dissatisfied longing" for something changeless and eternal.[12] This longing only increases as the soul flits from false desire to false desire, and so by means of a kind of universal repulsion everything in creation propels the soul to the God whom it truly desires; in better-known words, "our hearts are restless until they find rest (*requiem*) in you."[13] Now, at first blush, these two explanations may seem contradictory: the former asserts the reflection of God in all created things, whereas the latter asserts the difference of God from all created things. In the former, we are attracted *through* creatures to God; in the latter, we are repelled *from* creatures to God.[14] But we have already seen this sort of divine transimmanence at work in the infinite interiority of memory, which God at once constitutes and exceeds. There seems, therefore, to be a kind of structural homology between memory and creation: God's constitutive exceeding of the human subject recapitulates God's constitutive exceeding of the cosmos itself.

Following this lead, I would like to turn to the work of Nicholas of Cusa (1401–64), whose cosmology is strikingly redolent of Augustine's psychology. For the early Cusa, the infinite space that God both inhabits and exceeds is not memory but rather the universe itself: a boundless, ungraspable expanse whose centerless center is God.[15] I would therefore like to suggest that we can see in Cusa's cosmic meditations an "extrospective" ascent to God that mirrors Augustine's introspective ascent; while Augustine turns from all things to the God within him (and thus to all things), Cusa turns from himself to the God within all things (and thus to himself).

Standing in the way of this interpretation, however, is a dramatic but little-noted bifurcation in Cusa's work between the "mystical" and the cosmological. On the one hand, one hears about the Cusa who seeks learned ignorance, the coincidence of opposites, and the not-otherness of God; on the other hand, one hears about the Cusa who took the earth from the center of the universe one hundred years before Copernicus. Cusa himself is not much help in this regard, because as stunning as his cosmic vision is in *De docta ignorantia* (1440), it does not reappear in any of his later, more contemplative writings. This absence is puzzling: it might simply signal a shift in Cusa's interests, or it might be a consequence of Cusa's having been brought up on heresy charges for—among other things—pantheism. While he defended his position, reasserted the careful distinctions he had made between God and creation,[16] and was sufficiently cleared to be appointed a cardinal of the church in 1448, for one reason or another, Cusa rarely even mentions the universe in his later meditations on the soul's ascent to God.[17] The secondary literature tends to deepen this rift, focusing either on the theotic project or the proto-scientific project but rarely articulating their relationship to one another.[18] In the work at hand, then, I would like to try to weave these two strands back together, suggesting that there may be what Jeannette Winterson would call a "gut symmetry" in Cusa between the spiritual and the cosmic, that the path of desire is bound, and thus unbound, by both intensive and extensive infinities.[19]

IN SEARCH OF THE UNKNOWN GOD

If one is listening for such things, the first chapter of *De docta ignorantia* can be heard as an exceedingly wordy riff on the opening lines of the *Confessions*. "By a divine gift," Cusa writes, "there is within all things a certain natural desire (*desiderium*) to exist in the best manner which the condition of each thing's nature permits."[20] Like Augustine, then, Cusa begins with desire. One might notice, however, that he attributes this desire not to "man" but to "all things," not to "a little piece of your creation" but to creation itself. Nicholas continues: "toward this end (*finis*) all things work . . . so that their desire may not be frustrated but may be able to attain rest (*quietem attingere possit*) in that which is the inclination of each thing's natural desire."[21] Again, in this clunky prose we can detect a radical extension of the Augustinian person out to the universe: rather than "our hearts," it is "all things" that seek rest from their restlessness. All things desire—well, for the moment, all Cusa tells us is that all things desire that-which-all-things-naturally-desire and that this "end" will give them "rest."

But this progression from restlessness to rest begins to tremble toward the end of this chapter, when Cusa narrows down to what he calls the specific desire of humanity: the desire to *know*. "Since the desire in us for knowledge is not in vain," he reasons, "surely then it is our desire to know that we do not know."[22] Now, viewed in one light, Cusa is sticking to the Augustinian script; we may recall that after proclaiming "our hearts" to be "restless until they find rest in you," the *Confessions* dramatizes the inscrutability of this "you," tumbling in paradox until Augustine confesses he is not sure he has said anything at all.[23] Similarly, Cusa characterizes the "end" of human desire, in which it will finally "attain rest," as unknowable. One

considerable difference, however, is that Cusa still has not mentioned God, much less designated God the end of this desire. So
whereas Augustine desires an unknowable God, Cusa (in this passage, at least) desires unknowing *itself*: the desire to know desires to
know that it does not know.

There is, then, a kind of gratifying frustration built into the very
structure of Cusan desire: desire desires not to have the knowledge
it desires—and only thereby to have it. "One will be the more learned,"
Cusa concludes his introduction, "the more one knows that one is
ignorant. It is toward this end (*finis*) that I have undertaken the task
of writing a few words on learned ignorance."[24] But what sort of end
is this end? Can the "desire in us for knowledge," much less the desire of "all things," find its *rest* in learned ignorance? More precisely,
is learned ignorance an end at all? And how might the (un)learner
attain it? Frustratingly, although the introduction to the *De docta*
provokes these questions, the rest of the text never quite addresses
them. Apart from a brief appeal in a concluding letter to Christ as
"the end of all intellectual desires (*finis intellectualium desiderio-
rum*)," the treatise drops the language of ends and desire after the
first chapter.[25] It goes on to elucidate the infinity of God, the "contracted infinity" of the universe, and the unity of both in Christ, but
there is no explicit path through this theocosmology for the "intellectual desire" that begins and ends it.

Such a path begins to emerge in *De quaerendo Deum* (1445).
"The end toward which you have come into this world," Cusa tells
an unnamed "brother in Christ," "is to seek God."[26] This teleology,
he explains, is the "premise" of Paul's sermon on the unknown God
(*agnostos Theos/Deus ignotus*) (Acts 17:16–34): in the face of their
idols and shrines, Paul tells the Athenians that God has "appointed"
human beings "to seek God[,] . . . grope for God and find God."[27] So
where is God to be found? On the one hand, Paul assures us that
God is "not far from each one of us. For 'in him we live and move and
have our being.'"[28] On the other hand, he tells us "we ought not to
think that the deity is like gold, or silver, or stone," or anything in the
realm of human conception.[29] "Each time I read the Acts of the Apostles," Cusa confesses, "I marvel at this process of thought."[30] What

is marvelous is that God is both in everything and beyond everything; God is nearer than hands and feet and yet farther than our farthest imagination. What, then, are we to do? "If . . . the human being has come into this world (*mundus*) to seek God and . . . to find rest (*quiescevi*), and since in this sensible and corporeal world one can neither seek or grope for God . . . how . . . can God be sought in order to be found?"[31] The problem, in short, is that God has put us into a world full of things that are not God in order to find God. And the solution, Nicholas concludes, is that the world must reveal the God it also conceals: "Unless this world aided the seeker," he ventures, "humankind would have been sent into the world to seek God in vain. Therefore, this world must assist whoever seeks God, *and* the seeker must know that neither in the world nor in all that a human conceives is there anything similar to God."[32] The world, in other words, must somehow draw the seeker to itself beyond itself; the world must both attract the seeker by virtue of God's immanence to it and repel the seeker by virtue of God's transcendence of it.

The question, then, is how the seeker might find God through the world God both inhabits and transcends. What is the outward analogue of Augustinian inwardness? Different treatises offer different paths, but in each case Nicholas entreats the seeker to find something in the world that leads beyond the world. In *De quaerendo*, for example, this thing is the name *Theos*, which Paul proclaims to the Athenians. Of course, Nicholas is careful to say that "the name *Theos* is not itself the name of God, who surpasses every concept. Indeed, that which cannot be conceived remains ineffable." And yet, he continues, "in the name *Theos* there is enfolded a certain path of seeking God (*via quaedam quarendi complicatur*) on which God may be found so that God may be groped for."[33] The path in this case unfolds etymologically. "*Theos* is taken from *theoro*," Cusa tells us, "which means 'I see' and 'I run.' The seeker, therefore, has to run by means of seeing in order to be able to reach *Theos*, who sees all things."[34]

In order to run and see the God who sees all things (but who presumably does not run), the seeker must construct a "ladder of ascent" from sensible vision through all the senses to reason (*ratio*) and finally to the intellect (*intellectum*), whereupon she will realize that even intellectual vision falls short of the vision of God.[35] But at the same time, Cusa cautions, she should remember that intellectual vision functions *by means of* the vision of God. For just as human intellect is the "light" of human reason, God "is the light of the intellect."[36] God, in other words, is the medium in which the intellect operates; God, moreover, is the medium in which anything operates at all, for "it is God through whom the creature has what it is."[37] Inasmuch, then, as all human knowing knows in the light of God and every object of human knowledge *is* in the light of God, God can be said to be "Contemplation Itself (*ipsa speculatio*)."[38] In other words, Cusa concludes, in the work of contemplation, "it is not we ourselves who know, but rather it is God who knows in us."[39] Apart from the Pauline echo (Gal. 2:20), this passage recalls the Augustinian recognition that insofar as God is both in and beyond memory, God has been fueling the work of confession all along. Insofar as God is the light of the Cusan intellect, it is God who knows God when "we" ascend through God's creatures to God, although even in this knowing, God remains "unknown."[40] Thus it is that something in the world (in this case, a name of God) "enfolds" a path beyond the world to the God who inhabits and exceeds the world—a God who illumines the intellect by keeping it darkened.

In *De visione Dei* (1453), a different visual path unfolds, taking its leave from an image rather than a word. "In the effort to transport you to divine things by human means," Cusa begins, "I must use some kind of similitude. But among human works I have found no image more suitable for our purpose than that of an all-seeing figure."[41] Having sent an icon along with the letter that composes the treatise, Cusa walks "the abbot and brothers of Tegernsee" through a contemplative exercise. "Hang this up someplace," he instructs them, "perhaps on a north wall. And you brothers stand around it, equally distant from it, and gaze at it. And each of you will experience that from whatever place one observes it the face will seem to regard him alone."[42] Gazing upon everything with the same intensity and the same steadfastness, the brothers will see the icon as "an image of infinity."[43] Like God, its gaze moves without moving, sees all things simultaneously, and above all "deserts no one. . . . [I]t has the same very diligent concern for the least creature as for the greatest, and for the whole universe."[44] Unlike God, however, the icon's vision is limited (it cannot see behind itself), matter-bound, and impermanent (in fact, this particular icon seems to be "no longer extant").[45] By contemplating the icon, the brothers will therefore be stirred to address not the icon but God Godself, saying, "if you do not abandon me, the vilest of all, you will never abandon anyone."[46] The icon, in other words, leads the seeker *through* itself to the God it both resembles and falls short of.

As the treatise proceeds, however, it becomes clear that it is not just the icon that is an icon of God. A "lofty nut tree" provokes a similar ascent when Nicholas contemplates "this tree as a certain unfolding (*explicatio*) of the power of the seed and the seed as a certain unfolding of omnipotent power."[47] Just as the *De quaerendo* opens onto the realization that "God . . . is all that is in every existing thing," then, the *De visione* begins to imagine every existing thing as a possible path to God. In the vision that culminates and concludes the treatise, in fact, Nicholas imagines "this entire world (*universum hunc mundum*)" as a canvas on which God paints God's self-portrait. There is only one painter, he muses, "but the painter makes many images because the likeness of the painter's *infinite* power can be unfolded more perfectly only in many figures. . . . Moreover if they were not innumerable, you, O infinite God, could not be known in the best possible way."[48] The path to the infinite God, then, is not to be found in memory or a divine name or intellect or an icon alone but rather in the *innumerabilis* things of creation; in fact, if God were limited to a finite set of expressions, then our knowledge could never attain the unknowing that infinity provokes. "Therefore, by your gift, my God, I possess this whole visible world and all of scripture and all the ministering spirits in support of my advancing in the knowledge of you. *All things rouse me to turn toward you (Omnia me excitant, ut ad de converar)*."[49]

To summarize a bit before moving on, "all things" rouse Nicholas to turn toward God, first, because all things reflect God; second, because all things are not God; and third—this is where Nicholas moves beyond Paul—because all things are "innumerable." There is no end to the number of things the infinite God both is and is not. Indeed, this endlessness can *itself* be seen as a reflection and a falling short of divine infinity: it is like God insofar as it is endless but unlike God insofar as it is created. And yet in the reflection and the falling short alike, the endlessness of all things stirs the soul toward its infinite God. It is in this light, finally, that I propose to read Nicholas's radically post-Copernican, pre-Copernican cosmology. The boundless and omnicentric universe he imagines is structured in such a way that the whole thing constitutes a path—and arguably, the *greatest* path, because it enfolds all paths—to God.

CONTRACTING INFINITY

In his *De caelo* (On the Heavens) (ca. 335 BCE), Aristotle sets forth a spherical model of the cosmos, with earth at the center and progressive rings of water, air, and fire surrounding it.[50] Looking in particular to refute the atomist doctrine of an infinite universe filled with an infinite number of worlds,[51] Aristotle calls upon his layered arrangement of the elements to prove that the cosmos must be both singular and finite. This earth must be the only one, he argues, because it is the nature of earth to move "down" and the nature of fire to move "up."[52] If there were another earth outside our ring of fire, then in moving down with respect to its own world, it would be moving up with respect to ours (i.e., away from our earth). Similarly, in moving up with respect to its own center, the otherworldly fire would be moving down with respect to ours. "This, however, is impossible," Aristotle claims, because insofar as "moving downward" constitutes the essence of earth as such, its upward movement would make it not-earth. The same goes for fire: a downward-moving fire would not be fire at all. "It follows that there cannot be more worlds than one."[53] Moreover, this one world must be of limited extent because, as we can see, the "fixed stars" rotate around the earth once a day. Since they always return to the same place, they cannot extend out forever; as Aristotle puts it, "a body which moves in a circle must necessarily be finite."[54]

Thanks to Ptolemy's fine-tuning in the second century, this model held through the entire medieval period. When Cusa wrote his *De docta* in the mid-fifteenth century, Europe still imagined the world as a cosmic nesting doll with the earth at the center, the sun and planets in concentric circles around it, and a halo of fixed stars orbiting the circumference once a day. These stars were held to be the *Primum Mobile*, set in motion by the Prime Mover to confer movement upon the rest of the cosmic bodies. This motive gradation allowed the Aristotelian cosmos to be mapped onto the Neoplatonic "chain of being," so that physical position was thought to coincide with spiritual rank. "The higher an element [stood] in the cosmic stepladder," Ernst Cassirer explains, "the closer it [was] to the un-moved mover of the world, and the purer and more complete its nature."[55] The realm of the stars, made of an incorruptible "fifth essence" (*quinta essentia*), was thought to be nearest to God, while the corruptible earth was farthest away (here we might recall Dante's journey from the *inferno* at the center of the earth, up the purgatorial mountain, to the stars at the gates of paradise).[56]

This cosmological model is usually thought to have been overthrown by Copernicus, whose heliocentric universe would provoke Inquisitorial outrage at the dawn of the seventeenth century.[57] But for all the controversy it would generate, Copernicus's heliocentric model did not depart all that radically from the geocentric model because it retained a motionless center and periphery. Copernicus, in effect, put the sun where the earth had been but left the fixed stars in place, thereby reaffirming the singularity and finitude of the cosmos.[58] The thinker who genuinely abandoned Aristotelian cosmology was not Copernicus, who put the sun at the center of a bounded universe, but Nicholas of Cusa, who had declared one hundred years earlier that the universe had no center at all.

As do his other works, Cusa's cosmological writing draws us in with a contemplative exercise. Picture yourself on a boat, Cusa suggests, sailing through a vast ocean.[59] Unless you can see the shore recede behind you, or the waters rush beneath you, you will think you are at rest no matter how fast you may be moving. Indeed, even if you do gaze down at the waters flowing by, you may at first perceive that they are moving while you are standing still. So it is with our position in the universe. Although the earth moves through a vast expanse of space, we *perceive* ourselves to be at rest in the middle of the world because we lack an unmoved point of reference. Vaulting over Copernicus, Cusa goes on to say that the same holds for every other cosmic body: everything moves in imperfect circles around its neighbors (2.12.163–64).[60] And yet, precisely because nothing is at rest, "it always appears to every observer, whether on the earth, the sun, or another star, that one is . . . at an immovable center of things and that all else is being moved" (2.12.162). Nothing is at the center of the universe for Cusa, which means that everything is at the center—from its own perspective. Even those stars that we see at the outer edge of the universe occupy the center of creation from their own vantage point, so that their inhabitants will think that we orbit them.[61] Contra Aristotle, then, Cusa insisted that this world is not "the only one"; rather, there are a vast number of "earths," each of them full of inhabitants who think themselves at the center of what looks like a nesting-doll cosmos.

A mobile earth, elliptical orbits, the relativity of motion, extraterrestrial life, multiple worlds—each of these postulates is a feature of Cusa's systematic destruction of the tidy Aristotelian cosmos. But his most radical teaching, on which all the rest depend, is that this expanse of mobile bodies extends indefinitely. Of course, this remarkable new idea was not exactly new; Leucippus and Democritus had taught as much in the fifth century BCE. Four hundred years later, Lucretius would prove the infinity of the atomists' universe by entreating us to hurl a spear at whatever we might think to be its boundary. If nothing stops the spear, he argued, then there is no boundary; if something stops the spear, then there is something beyond the boundary. Either way, the boundary would not be a boundary, which means that the universe must be infinite.[62] Cusa offers a similar line of reasoning in the *De docta*, saying that "the universe (*universum*) is limitless (*interminatum*), for nothing actually greater than it, in relation to which it would be limited, can be given" (2.1.97). In other words, since the universe is all that *is*, there cannot be anything outside it to bind it.

That having been said, unlike the atomist universe, the Cusan universe is not *exactly* infinite. To be sure, Cusa reasons, the universe cannot be called finite, "since it lacks boundaries within which it is enclosed," but neither can it be called infinite, because unlike God, it is not "from itself" (2.11.156; 2.2.98). Since the source of its being lies beyond itself, the universe cannot, strictly speaking, be called infinite. And yet insofar as it "embraces all things that are not God," it is not finite either (2.1.97). To account for this finite sort of infinity, Cusa borrows some terminology from Thomas Aquinas, who distinguishes in his *Disputationes* between the "negative infinite which simply has no limit" and the "privative infinite . . . which should have limits naturally but which lacks them."[63] Cusa attributes the former to God and the latter to the universe: God has God's reason for being within Godself and is thus "negatively" infinite, whereas the universe has its reason for being outside itself and is thus "privatively" infinite.[64] In Cusa's own language, God is the "absolute" infinite, whereas the universe is a "contracted" infinite—a concrete, material, and for that reason restricted, infinite (2.4.113). But this very difference between God and the universe constitutes their inexorable relation: in its contracted infinity, the universe exists as a created reflection of God. Like God, it has no limits; like God, it contains everything that is, as well as the seeds of what might yet be. "It is as if the Creator had spoken, 'Let it be made,'" writes Cusa, "and because God, who is eternity itself, could not be made, that was made which could be made, which would be as much like God as possible" (2.2.104). Emerging from the very being of God, the universe is the fullest possible expression (*explicatio*) of the divine enfolding (*complicatio*), "a concrete likeness of God unfolded in the diversity and multiplicity of space and time."[65]

This likeness is perhaps nowhere more apparent than in the dizzying geometry of *De docta ignorantia*. As I have already mentioned, the Cusan universe has neither center nor circumference; rather, it appears to have its center wherever an observer finds herself, and its circumference as far as she can see. Our sense of the universe is thus irreducibly perspectival. And yet, Cusa promises, we can visualize the whole if we are willing to shatter our spatial sensibilities.

"You must make use of your imagination as much as possible," he advises, "and enfold the center with the poles" (2.11.161). The result will be something like a sphere whose center coincides with its periphery. Only if you can picture such an unpicturable thing, will you begin to "understand something about the [universal] motion of the universe" (2.11.161). Moreover, you will begin to understand the likeness between the universe and its creator. For insofar as God is both omnipresent and boundless, God Godself can be thought of as "*an infinite sphere*, whose center is everywhere, whose circumference is nowhere."[66]

This image of an infinite sphere is not new: it had appeared in the work of Alain de Lille, Saint Bonaventure, and Thomas Aquinas and throughout the sermons of Meister Eckhart (from whom Cusa most likely picked it up) to describe the ineffable being of God.[67] What *is* new is that Cusa is applying what had been a theological metaphor to the creation itself, thereby rendering the universe just as incomprehensible as its creator. "Therefore enfold these different images," he entreats us, "so that the center is the zenith and vice versa, and then . . . you come to see that the world and its motion and shape *cannot be grasped*, for it will . . . have its center and circumference nowhere" (2.11.161; emphasis added, translation altered slightly).[68] Yet even here, we should note, Cusa is careful not *quite* to identify the infinite sphere of the world with the infinite sphere of God: God, he has told us, is a sphere with its "center everywhere," whereas this passage calls the universe a sphere with its center *nowhere*.[69] And so just as we saw the universe's difference from God secure its resemblance to God, we now see the resemblance ratchet up the difference: both are infinite spheres, but God is omnicentric, whereas the universe has no center at all.

But then again, can the universe not be said to have as many centers as there are positions within it, and is it not in this sense omnicentric? The issue, once again, boils down to perspective. The universe has no absolute center *within itself* because there is no body in the universe that is equidistant to each of its "poles." "Precise equidistance to different points cannot be found outside God," Cusa explains, which is to say that God alone is equally proximate to all parts of creation (2.11.157). But insofar as God is equally proximate to all parts of creation, the universe does indeed have a center: "*God* is the center of the earth," Cusa proclaims, "of all the spheres, and of all things that are in the world." (2.11.157; emphasis added). And so in this very particular sense, the center of the world is not nowhere, but everywhere, because God is everywhere.

Even as he asserts this principle, however, Cusa adds a qualification—just in case we've missed the context: "the world machine will have, *one might say* (*quasi*), its center everywhere and its circumference nowhere, for its circumference and its center is God, who is everywhere and nowhere" (2.12.162; emphasis added). So just as the universe is finite in one respect and infinite in another, its center is nowhere on its own but everywhere "in God." This quasi-omnicentrism establishes the universe as the strongest possible *imago dei*, a concrete expression of divine being itself. Yet we should note that this likeness only holds insofar as God *occupies* the center(s) of the very universe that resembles God. Cusa, in other words, is shattering any simple mirror game between God and the universe by folding God *into* God's own image, as its omnicentric center. The world does not resemble a God that stands outside it; it resembles God only insofar as it embodies God, everywhere in the universe, equally.

It is with this insight that Cusa truly demolishes the graduated cosmos of his Aristotelian predecessors. God is not mediated down through the heavenly ranks to the lowly earth at its center; rather, God is directly present to every part of the boundless universe. As Cassirer explains it, "there is no absolute above and below, and . . . no body is closer or farther from the divine, original source of being than any other; rather, each is 'immediate to God.'"[70] For Cusa, there is no privileged place in the universe, no distinction between the astral and sublunar spheres. And so the order of things is not a static hierarchy under an extracosmic God; instead, it is a dynamic holography in which God is fully and equally present to everything in creation. This radical indwelling is, for Cusa, what it means for God to create in the first place: "creating," he ventures, "seems to be not other than God's being all things" (2.2.101). If all things exist as the image of God, then it is not the case that God is mediated by some things (intelligences, Reason, Man, etc.) to other things (matter, the passions, women, nonhuman animals). Rather, he writes, "God communicates without difference or envy," so that every creature becomes a "perfect" image of God: "every creature is, as it were, a finite infinity or created god, so that it exists in the way in which this could best be" (2.2.104). Precisely because God immediately communicates Godself to every creature, however, every creature also mediates God to every other creature. Because God is in each thing as the being of each thing, everything mediates God to everything. And insofar as "everything" as such is the universe itself, Cusa suggests, "God is in all things as if [*quasi*] by mediation of the universe" (2.5.117). "As if" by mediation of the universe, it is not just the case that God is in all things and all things are in God but also that "*all things are in all things*" (1.15.118; emphasis added).

DESIRING INFINITY

When Nicholas exclaims in the *De visione Dei* that "all things rouse me to turn toward you," we can therefore hear him saying not only that any thing (whether it be a name or a leafy nut tree) can be an icon of God but also that the endless run of "all things"—the universe itself—is an icon of God. Like the "all-seeing image," gazing equally upon each brother, the universe is equally present to every body within it: centered as much around poor demoted Pluto as it is around the earth or the sun. Like God Godself, the universe contains all that is and all that is to come, and like God, it has no boundaries, except God. Contemplating the universe, then, we are propelled both by its resemblance to God (in its boundless omnicentricity) and by its difference from God (who *is* its boundary and center). Drawn to the boundaries of the unbounded universe, we collide head-on with God Godself, the center and periphery of all things as such, and the "end" of all creaturely desire. But to circle back to the opening concerns of the *De docta* ("all theology is circular" [1.21.66], Nicholas will tell us, proleptically echoing Denys Turner and his reinvented wheels), how can desire find its end in such endlessness? Or as Nicholas exclaims in *De visione Dei*, "My God, you are absolute infinity itself, which I perceive to be the infinite end, but *I am unable to grasp how an end without an end is an end.*"[71]

Like Augustine, Nicholas figures the desire for *anything* as a desire for God because God is "the form of every desirable thing (*forma omnis desiderabilis*)," and as such both with and beyond every desirable thing.[72] Pushing far past Augustine, Nicholas will go on in *De li non aliud* (1461) to say that insofar as God is in each thing and each thing is in God, each thing in God *is God.*[73] But at the same time, insofar as God is the form of each thing, each thing in itself is nothing, and nothing is infinitely different from God. Therefore, all things exist in, through, *and as* the "infinite power" in whose image all things are made—and yet all things are irreducibly not-God. This, as we have seen, is particularly the case with the universe itself, whose "contracted" infinity falls infinitely short of the "uncontracted infinity" it nevertheless embodies most fully (insofar as it embraces all created things, each of which is a finite infinity). But for Nicholas, it is precisely this constitutive shortfall that sustains the desire that desires any "desirable thing." The farther the soul ascends in any given contemplation, "the more infinite [God] appears," which is to say the more incomprehensible it comprehends God to be.[74] And the more incomprehensible it comprehends God to be, the more it delights in the God whom it desires—precisely because there is always *more God* to desire. This, Nicholas ventures, could even be the *reason* God keeps Godself hidden: "the reason you, O God, are unknown to all creatures is so that they may have in this most sacred ignorance a greater rest (*quietus*) as if in an incalculable and inexhaustible treasure."[75] And here again, we find the Augustinian promise of rest, which again leaves us wondering, what kind of "rest" can the soul find in the incalculable and inexhaustible? How can an end without end be an end?

But then again, if the end *were* an end, that is, if desire desired something finite, then desire itself would come to an end once it attained its end. Desire would desire the end of desire, which Nicholas deems quite impossible, "for how could the appetite desire not to exist?"[76] Therefore, desire qua desire can *only* desire an end without end, which is once more to say that desire desires God alone. And God sustains this desire infinitely, by both giving and withholding Godself: "You come down, Lord, that you may be comprehended, *and* you remain incomprehensible and infinite, and unless you remained infinite, you would not be the end of desire."[77] In this sense, then, the task of desire is not to move from restlessness to rest but rather to move from "a certain determinable rest" in the finite to a restless rest in the infinite, where "the opposition of opposites is without opposition" and desire finds its end in an end without end.[78]

Insofar as the end of desire is endless, the path of desire is enfolded within the endless universe itself—both in the innumerable sum of things and in each thing insofar as it enfolds all things. There is, then, a kind of extrospective journey in Cusa that mirrors the introspective journey in Augustine: while Augustine moves from created things to the "vast and infinite profundity" within, Cusa moves from himself to the vast and infinite creation. But as Denys Turner would be the first to point out, a mirror image does not differ in kind *or* in magnitude from that which it mirrors; it is the same image, inverted. The only reason Cusa's "intellectual desire" is able to process cosmologically out to the infinite is that, like everything else in creation, the intellect bears the image of the cosmos that imperfectly images the God who dwells within it.

Cusa both suggests and covers over this connection between the intellect and the universe in *De quaerendo Deum*, saying that "our intellectual power embraces every corporeal and measurable nature"[79]—a function that the *De docta* attributed to the universe. And yet the *De quaerendo* goes on to say that human intellect "surpasses all capacity of the whole sensible world, and not only of this one world but also of an infinite number of worlds (*infinitorum mundorum*)."[80] Perhaps because he has changed his mind, or perhaps in an effort to avoid another accusation of pantheism, Cusa is now elevating human intellect over the universe, saying that insofar as it embraces all things (apart from God), it "surpasses" the capacity of even an infinite number of worlds and bears the image of God Godself.[81] But we will recall that in the *De docta*, the power that "embraces all things that are not God," contains an infinite number of worlds, and bears the fullest image of God, is the universe itself.[82] Regardless of the reason for Cusa's mysterious demotion of "the whole sensible world," we can nevertheless see a clear homology between the intellect and the universe it contemplates: each extends out boundlessly in a dazzling but imperfect *imitatio dei*. And if we recall that for the early Cusa "all things are in all things" and that for the late Cusa each thing in God is God, we can go even further and locate this homology in every creature (in fact, at the moment that the *De quaerendo* compares the human intellect to the divine intellect, it also compares it to a mustard seed).[83] Just as the icon gazes with equal care upon the Abbot and the gnat, just as the universe is as fully centered around Pluto as the sun, the image of God, and therefore the path to God, runs as surely through the mustard seed as it runs through the universe.

The trick, then, as it is for Augustine, is not to abandon created things for God—after all, God is the medium in which created things are—but rather to find a way through them to God, which is also to say more deeply into the world-in-God-in-the-world. More precisely, the work of desire is to allow *God* to draw us through God's boundless creation to the God who both constitutes and exceeds it—the God whom all things desire in the desire of all things. And for Nicholas, this is the point of the whole holographic cosmos: God has unfolded creation in such a way that anything and everything enfolds a path to God, leading desire "by the eternal beginning . . . to the end without end."[84] Or as Denys Turner might put it, in the desire of all things "there is some echo, however faint, of God."[85]

NOTES

1. Augustine of Hippo, *Confessions*, trans. Owen Chadwick (Oxford: Oxford University Press, 1991), 10.27.38. For the Latin text, I have consulted Augustine of Hippo, *Confessions*, trans. William Watts, 2 vols., Loeb Classical Library (Cambridge, MA: Harvard University Press, 2006). For Turner's own discussion of this passage, see Denys Turner, *The Darkness of God: Negativity in Christian Mysticism* (Cambridge: Cambridge University Press, 1995), 53, 70.

2. Augustine of Hippo, *Confessions*, 10.8.15; emphasis added.

3. Ibid., 10.14.21.

4. Ibid., 10.16.24. For a lengthier treatment of memory in the *Confessions*, see Mary-Jane Rubenstein, "Undone by Each Other: Interrupted Sovereignty in Augustine's *Confessions*," in *Polydoxy*, ed. Catherine Keller and Laurel Schneider (New York: Routledge, 2010), 120–23.

5. Augustine of Hippo, *Confessions*, 10.16.24.

6. Ibid., 10.8.15; emphasis added.

7. As Turner explains it, "the language of 'interiority' is, as it were, self-subverting: the more 'interior' we are, the more our interiority opens out to that which is inaccessibly 'above' and 'beyond' it" (Turner, *Darkness of God*, 69).

8. Ibid., 59.

9. Augustine of Hippo, *Confessions*, 1.1.1.

10. Ibid.; emphasis added.

11. Turner, *Darkness of God*, 65.

12. Ibid.

13. Augustine of Hippo, *Confessions*, 1.1.1; translation altered slightly.

14. This duplicity reflects a tension that runs throughout the *Confessions:* on the one hand, sin turns from God to "external things"; on the other hand, God is *in* all external things (which are also in God) (Augustine of Hippo, *Confessions*, 10.27.38; 2.1.1; 1.2.2–3). On the one hand, turning toward oneself is the root of all sin; on the other hand, turning toward oneself is the work of conversion (2.6.13–14; 10.27.38). The trick, for Augustine, is neither to fetishize nor to abandon created things but rather to love them in the right way, which is to say in God: "Let these transient things be the ground on which my soul praises you, 'God creator of all.' But let it not become stuck in them. . . . If physical objects give you pleasure, praise God for them and return love to their Maker. . . . If souls please you, they are being loved in God" (4.10.15–4.12.18).

15. Nicholas of Cusa, *On Learned Ignorance*, trans. H. Lawrence Bond, in *Nicholas of Cusa: Selected Writings* (New York: Paulist Press, 1997), 2.11.157; for the Latin text, I have consulted Nicholas of Cusa, *De docta ignorantia*, ed. Ernest Hoffman and Raymond Klibansky, 22 vols., vol. 1, *Nicolai de Cusa: Opera Omnia* (Leipzig: Felix Meiner, 1932).

16. See Jasper Hopkins and Nicholas of Cusa, *Nicholas of Cusa's Debate with John Wenck: A Translation and an Appraisal of "De ignota litteratura" and "Apologia doctae ignorantiae"* (Minneapolis: A. J. Banning Press, 1981).

17. A telling exception to this rule can be found in *De li non aliud* (1462), in which Cusa writes that "the universe must not be considered as the goal (*finis*) of all things; for were it the goal of all things, it would be God" (Nicholas of Cusa, *On Not Other*, in *Nicholas of Cusa on God as Not-Other:*

A Translation and an Appraisal of "De li non aliud" [Minneapolis: University of Minnesota Press, 1979], 77).

18. For the "mystical" Cusa, see Robert P. Scharlemann, "God as Not-Other: Nicholas of Cusa's *De le non aliud*," in *Naming God*, ed. Robert P. Scharlemann (New York: Paragon House, 1986); Burkard Mojsisch, "The Otherness of God as Coincidence, Negation, and Non-Otherness in Nicholas of Cusa: An Explication and Critique," in *The Otherness of God*, ed. Orin F. Summerell, Studies in Religion and Culture (Charlottesville: University Press of Virginia, 1998); and Nancy J. Hudson, *Becoming God: The Doctrine of Theosis in Nicholas of Cusa* (Washington, DC: Catholic University of America Press, 2007). For the scientific revolutionary Cusa, see Ernst Cassirer, *The Individual and the Cosmos in Renaissance Philosophy*, trans. Mario Domandi (New York: Harper Torchbooks, 1964); Hans Blumenberg, *The Legitimacy of the Modern Age*, trans. Robert M. Wallace (Cambridge, MA: MIT Press, 1983); and Alexander Koyre, *From the Closed World to the Infinite Universe* (Baltimore: Johns Hopkins University Press, 1957). Some of the few sources that engage both of these strands of Cusa's thought are Bernard McGinn, "Maximum Contractum et Absolutum: The Motive for the Incarnation in Nicholas of Cusanus and His Predecessors," in *Nicholas of Cusa and His Age: Intellect and Spirituality: Essays Dedicated to the Memory of F. Edward Cranz, Thomas P. McTighe and Charles Trinkaus*, ed. Thomas Izbicki and Christopher M. Bellitto, Studies in the History of Christian Thought (Boston: Brill, 2002); and Catherine Keller, "The Cloud of the Impossible: Embodiment and Apophasis," in *Apophatic Bodies: Negative Theology, Incarnation, and Relationality*, ed. Chris Boesel and Catherine Keller (New York: Fordham University Press, 2010).

19. Jeannette Winterson, *Gut Symmetries* (New York: Vintage, 1989).

20. Nicholas of Cusa, *On Learned Ignorance*, 1.1.2; translation altered slightly. Cf. Augustine of Hippo, *Confessions*, 1.1.1.

21. Nicholas of Cusa, *On Learned Ignorance*, 1.1.2.

22. Ibid., 1.1.4.

23. Augustine of Hippo, *Confessions*, 1.1.1–4.

24. Nicholas of Cusa, *On Learned Ignorance*, 1.1.4.

25. Ibid., 3.letter.264.

26. Nicholas of Cusa, *On Seeking God*, 3.43; viz., Acts 17:27. The Latin text can be found in Nicholas of Cusa, *De quaerendo Deum*, 22 vols., vol. 4, Opuscula I (Hamburg: Felix Meiner, 1959).

27. Nicholas of Cusa, *On Seeking God*, 1.17.

28. Acts 17:27–28.

29. Acts 17:29–30.

30. Nicholas of Cusa, *On Seeking God*, 1.18.

31. Ibid.

32. Ibid.; emphasis added.

33. Ibid., 1.19.

34. Ibid. Bond tells us that this derivation stems from Plato's *Cratylus* 379, "but here Cusa may be drawing from John Scotus Eriugena, *Periphyseon (De divisione naturae).*" See *Nicholas of Cusa: Selected Writings*, 320 n. 11.

35. Nicholas of Cusa, *On Seeking God*, 1.24–35.

36. Ibid., 2.36.

37. Ibid.

38. Ibid., 1.27. Nicholas combines these two points more explicitly in *De coniecturis* by means of the language of participation: "the intellect's partaking of that unimpartible, most actual Light *constitutes* the quiddity of created minds. Therefore the actuality of our intelligence consists in its partaking of the Divine Intellect" (Nicholas of Cusa, "On Surmises" [*De coniecturis*], in *Nicholas of Cusa: Metaphysical Speculations* [2000], 1.2.56).

39. Nicholas of Cusa, *On Seeking God*, 2.36.

40. Ibid.

41. Nicholas of Cusa, *On the Vision of God*, preface 2. The Latin text can be found in Nicholas of Cusa, *De visione Dei*, 22 vols., vol. 6, *Nicolai de Cusa: Opera Omnia* (Hamburg: Felix Meiner, 2000).

42. Nicholas of Cusa, *On the Vision of God*, preface 3.

43. Ibid., 15.61.

44. Ibid., preface 4.

45. Ibid., 234 n. 13.

46. Ibid., 4.9.

47. Ibid., 7.24. Cf. *De quaerendo*: "when we observe the smallest mustard seed and with the eye of our intellect contemplate its strength and its potency, we discover a vestige that stirs us in wonder at our God. For although it is so small in body, yet its power is without limitation. In this seed there is a large tree with leaves and small branches and many other seeds in which there also exists this same power beyond all reckoning" (Nicholas of Cusa, *On Seeking God*, 3.44).

48. Nicholas of Cusa, *On the Vision of God*, 25.117.

49. Ibid., 25.119.

50. Aristotle, "On the Heavens (*De Caelo*)," in *The Complete Works of Aristotle: The Revised Oxford Translation*, ed. Jonathan Barnes (Princeton: Princeton University Press, 1971), 287a31. Much of the material from this section finds greater elaboration in Mary-Jane Rubenstein, *Worlds without End: The Many Lives of the Multiverse* (New York: Columbia University Press, 2014).

51. As Diogenes Laertius explains it, Leucippus taught that a *kosmos* was just a small, bounded part of "the All" (*to pan*), which was "unlimited" (*apeiron*). Diogenes Laertius, *Lives of the Eminent Philosophers*, trans. R. D.

Hicks, 2 vols., Loeb Classical Library (Cambridge, MA: Harvard University Press, 1942), 9.6.31.

52. Aristotle, "On the Heavens," 269a31–35; 308b12–15.

53. Ibid., 276b12–17.

54. Ibid., 271b26.

55. Cassirer, *Individual and Cosmos*, 25.

56. On this connection, see Regine Kather, "'The Earth is a Noble Star': Arguments for the Relativity of Motion in the Cosmology of Nicholaus Cusanus and Their Transformation in Einstein's Theory of Relativity," in *Cusanus: The Legacy of Learned Ignorance*, ed. Peter J. Casarella (Washington, DC: Catholic University of America Press, 2006).

57. Giordano Bruno was burned at the stake for his Cusan-inflected, neoatomist Copernicanism in 1600, and Galileo was placed under house arrest for seeming to prefer the heliocentric model in 1633. See Maurice A. Finocchiaro, "Philosophy versus Religion and Science versus Religion: The Trials of Bruno and Galileo," in *Giordano Bruno: Philosopher of the Renaissance*, ed. Hilary Gatti (Burlington, VT: Ashgate, 2002).

58. Although Copernicus himself retained the "fixed stars" (fixing them even more, in fact, because if the *earth* turns once a day, then the stars must be motionless), those who followed him were quick to see that if the stars did not rotate, Aristotle's only argument for cosmic finitude was void. The first Copernican to ascribe infinity to the Copernican model was the English mathematician and astronomer Thomas Digges, whose translation of the *De revolutionibus* featured a diagram in which the stars, rather than being confined to a thin ring around the cosmos, were extended out indefinitely. See Hilary Gatti, "Giordano Bruno's Copernican Diagrams," *Filozofski vestnik* 25, no. 2 (2004).

59. Nicholas of Cusa, *On Learned Ignorance*, 2.12.162. Subsequent references are cited internally.

60. With his suggestion that planetary courses are not quite circular, Cusa anticipates Kepler's discovery of elliptical orbits. Like his other "discoveries," this was not based on observation but rather theological conviction; circular orbits would entail "precise equidistance" between a central body and its satellites, and "precise equidistance to different points cannot be found outside God, for God alone is infinite equality" (*On Learned Ignorance*, 2.11.157).

61. Cusa believed that all the "stellar regions" beyond our own were most likely "inhabited," imagining that the residents of the sun were likely to be "more solar, bright, illuminated, and intellectual, even more spiritual than those on the moon, who are more lunar, and than those on the earth, who are more weighty" (*On Learned Ignorance*, 2.12.172).

62. Lucretius, *The Nature of Things*, trans. A. E. Stallings (New York: Penguin, 2007), 1.980.

63. Cited in Tyrone Lai, "Nicholas of Cusa and the Finite Universe," *Journal of the History of Philosophy* 11, no. 2 (April 1973): 163.

64. "The universe cannot be negatively infinite, although it is boundless and thus privatively infinite, and in this respect neither finite nor infinite" (Nicholas of Cusa, *On Learned Ignorance*, 2.1.97).

65. Elizabeth Brient, "Transitions to a Modern Cosmology: Meister Eckhart and Nicholas of Cusa on the Intensive Infinite," *Journal of the History of Philosophy* 37, no. 4 (October 1999): 592.

66. "Deus est sphaera infinita, cuius centrum est ubique, circumferentia nusquam." This sentence can be traced back to the pseudo-Hermetic *Book of 24 Philosophers*. For an exhaustive history, see Karsten Harries, "The Infinite Sphere: Comments on the History of a Metaphor," *Journal of the History of Philosophy* 13, no. 1 (January 1975).

67. See Brient, "Intensive Infinite," 579.

68. Cf. Nicholas's statement earlier in the *De docta*: "derived being . . . is not understandable, since the being from which it exists is not understandable" (2.2.100).

69. See Brient, "Intensive Infinite," 592.

70. Cassirer, *Individual and Cosmos*, 28.

71. "Tu, deus meus, es ipsa infinitas absoluta, quam video esse finem infinitum, sed capere nequo, quomodo finis sit finis sine fine." Nicholas of Cusa, *On the Vision of God*, 13.53; emphasis added.

72. Ibid., 16.67.

73. Having established at great length that "in the sky . . . God is not other than the sky," Nicholas mentions briefly that the converse is also true: "the sky . . . in Not-other is not-other" (Nicholas of Cusa, *On Not Other*, 51).

74. Nicholas of Cusa, *On the Vision of God*, 16.67.

75. Ibid.

76. Ibid., 16.68.

77. Ibid.; emphasis added.

78. Cusa, "On Wisdom," in *On the Vision of God*, 13.55.

79. Nicholas of Cusa, *On Seeking God*, 3.45.

80. Ibid.

81. Cf. *De coniecturis* (1442–43), which calls "the human mind" a "lofty likeness of God" because it makes rational entities "just as the Divine Mind" makes "real" entities (Nicholas of Cusa, "On Surmises" [*De coniecturis*], 1.1.5). Here too there is no mention of the universe.

82. Nicholas of Cusa, *On Learned Ignorance*, 1.2.1.

83. Nicholas of Cusa, *On Seeking God*, 3.44.

84. Nicholas of Cusa, *On the Vision of God*, 16.69.

85. Turner, *Darkness of God*, 65.

TWO

The Darkness of God and the Light of Life

Augustine, Pseudo-Denys, and Eckhart

KARL HEFTY

If Christian theology speaks of what can be known of God, it does so in a way that also acknowledges the limits of this knowledge.[1] God can be known insofar as God has been revealed in scripture and creation, but as creator and source God remains unknown and infinitely surpasses all concepts and categories. The traditions of so-called negative theology go further, however, and affirm that God can be known even beyond these limits, since to know that God exceeds them, in a sense, is already to know something more of God. Whatever can be affirmed truthfully of God in a higher sense must also be denied truthfully of God, and these denials too must also finally be denied, so that the height of knowledge of God can also be called a form of darkness.[2] As the knowledge of God increases, so does the need to affirm that God exceeds all knowing.[3]

In the modern era, as the concept of experience comes to play a more prominent role in philosophy, another kind of limit to knowledge arrives on the scene. It is not a limit that follows from the transcendence of God as creator but a limit rooted in the very structure of human reason itself. Constrained by what can be given in space and time or thought by the categories of understanding, human knowledge simply has less of God available to it, and perhaps only the idea of God.[4] Philosophy struggles in various ways to adapt the historical event of Christian revelation to the limits of modern knowledge, and theology, for its part, in various ways accommodates or resists this struggle. Today, theology remains unsure of its status as knowledge, and philosophy is still looking for terms in which to admit it.[5]

As a way of navigating this terrain between philosophy and theology, this essay proposes to study the role of "life" as a name of God in key patristic and medieval texts that shape the genre of negative theology. Life's place in negative theology brings sources of Platonic and Aristotelian inspiration together with the foundational texts of Christianity. In this confluence, in a way that may seem surprising, the divine wisdom that is defined as the source of all things is everywhere identified with life. But this wisdom acquires a new inflection when it becomes incarnate in the person of Christ. When he gives his life for humanity, he offers a new horizon for human existence, giving it the capacity to receive divine life in the flesh. The negative theology that seeks to understand the event of incarnation conveys this new relationship between humanity and God in terms of life.

The limits modern forms of knowledge once placed on theology no longer hold the same force today, as the categories and concepts in which knowledge is defined have broadened and shifted. Possibilities lay open that once seemed foreclosed. Yet the modern limits are not the same as the limits theology itself has always admitted.[6] If the former are perhaps beginning to lift, the latter remain in place. God, as God, exceeds human knowledge to an infinite degree. But because Christian theology also affirms that the Christ is the fullness of revelation, that God has taken on human flesh and has given his body and blood for the life of the world, we are free to wonder what kind of knowledge of God this makes possible. If revelation is also a gift of life, then how far does life itself offer us a way to understand revelation?

My argument offers only a selective sketch of a more expansive picture and marks only the beginning of an agenda for further study. I begin by specifying what "life" has come to mean in philosophy today, notably in the field of study known as phenomenology. My purpose is not then to impose a foreign meaning on texts of a different genre and more ancient pedigree but merely to introduce the reader to a particular phenomenon before considering how that phenomenon might also "appear" in negative theology. I then examine the role "life" plays in the work of Augustine, in scripture, in Pseudo-Denys, and in Meister Eckhart. These texts do not define life as an empirical phenomenon but as the fruit of divine wisdom and as a form of union between humanity and God that wisdom brings about. On the path that leads to the darkness of God's infinite transcendence, life is both a source of illumination and the content of it.

"WHAT" IS LIFE? A PHILOSOPHICAL EXCURSION

In Anglophone countries today, where philosophy is practiced primarily as a form of conceptual analysis, "life" falls under the purview, not of philosophy, but of the biological sciences. In the biological sense, "living" beings can be defined descriptively in terms of organic physical and chemical processes, which are classified according to known properties. In keeping with the demands of scientific rigor, the conclusions of biology are of course bound to what in these processes can be observed and repeated, in a gradual and methodical accumulation of experimental knowledge. To the extent that these sciences are only at the beginning of their development, one might say that "life" in the biological sense of the term remains largely unknown and even mystifying. We must wait for the culmination and completion of biology and its supporting sciences before the secret of life is finally revealed.

For those unprepared to wait that long, in the broader field of European thought today "life" has a signification that is wider and more original than its biological meaning. It is true that the Aristotelian conception of life as a power of self-movement, though certainly still present in scholasticism, plays only an inexplicit role in the major problems that shape modern philosophy. But over the course of the twentieth century, and notably in the field of phenomenology, philosophy comes to regard life more profoundly, and as the source or foundation of a new method. In its phenomenological sense, "life" is not reducible to a set of attributes descriptive of a certain class of physical things or processes, nor is it to be found in a particular region of being, among "living things," for example. In a sense that is remarkable for its depth, life is *the original way in which being becomes phenomenal*.[7] For us to understand better what this may mean for theology, and to glimpse the magnitude of the transformation it implies for philosophy, let us notice first how life has come to play this new role.

As conceived by Edmund Husserl (1859–1938) and expounded by those following him, phenomenology is a form of science that is distinguished by the kind of object it studies. Unlike other sciences, it does not examine specific "phenomena" but considers instead what it calls their "givenness" or "phenomenality." Phenomenology is not a descriptive science of what appears in any given experience but a method of studying, according to strict evidential requirements, the original structures in which things become phenomenal. It quickly becomes clear that much is at stake in how basic terms are defined and understood. What does it mean for something to appear? What conditions have been imposed or presupposed? These questions are important because they pertain to essential conditions for all objects of human knowing, and also to the possibility of philosophy thinking the unconditioned. We can quickly see that these basic problems do not arise at random but respond to specific conceptual decisions rooted in the project of modern philosophy. These decisions are important for understanding the conceptual situation of theology in the modern period.

One way to approach the issues is to recall a historical sequence that surrounds the concept "appearance" and its related notions "affect" and "impression." For Hume or Locke, an appearance is the presence of an idea or object that exactly represents a simple impression.[8] Kant offers a formal definition: An appearance is an object that is "given" insofar as it affects the sensibility.[9] Although an appearance is only a representation, it is the anchor in reality that keeps philosophical objectivity from drifting into dogmatism. Yet the task of philosophy is to work out a priori, apart from any real appearance and according to categories it deduces transcendentally, what can be a possible experience.[10] If it was not already evident, the interpreters of Kant will come to regard the essence of appearance as purely formal, because it can be reduced to the pure forms of space and time.[11] Resisting any nonempirical conception of knowledge, the sciences by the end of the nineteenth century drift definitively away from philosophy, as the study of concrete appearances falls under the purview of the empirical sciences alone.[12]

Phenomenology emerges in this context. In response to what he eventually perceives as a crisis brought about by the separation of science from philosophy, Husserl envisions "phenomenology" as a new kind of science based on a new form of evidence that is made possible by a wider conception of givenness.[13] The given is not limited to what can be perceived "straightforwardly" in sensible intuition (e.g., this house, this animal, or that field). "States of affairs" (e.g., that this house is white) can also be brought to givenness—not directly in sensible intuition, but in new intuitions and new perceptual acts based on those straightforward intuitions.[14] This wider conception of givenness is so powerful that all kinds of formal relations, including universals and even being, can appear within it.[15] Essences have an existence that can be seen with evidence and known with certainty. Against all nominalism and skepticism, the breadth of human experience can be determined and described in its reality, as it is constituted in the active and passive syntheses of the ego.

Let us set aside certain important aspects of Husserl's work, and other significant ways he will be read and interpreted, in order to focus our attention on one that is decisive for the question of life, that of Michel Henry (1922–2002). Henry deepens Husserl's thought, but in a way that objects to its interpretation of how givenness is itself given. It is not a question of how, in an appearance that is taken in a specific way, an essence might be seen but rather of how to understand the essence of appearing. Henry approaches the problem as a question of the manifestation of the essence of appearing to itself, which then leads to the question of the possibility of the essence being affected by itself, and ultimately to the question of auto-affection. Here the essence of "appearance" is not an appearance of something else, the way intentionality makes thematic any eidetic essence; it is just appearing, in itself, qua appearing. The primacy of affectivity is not rooted in the desire for a formal explanation but in the requirement that the concept of givenness be brought to self-givenness: "A radical phenomenological thought must interrogate the manner in which the transcendental power which gives every thing, is itself given."[16]

Conceived as a power of givenness, "affectivity is not the abstract condition of affection; it is the event when everything which happens, happens and is gathered together."[17] One reason this shift is important is that it means affectivity cannot be defined in terms of sensibility, and thus not empirically.[18] Affectivity cannot be interpreted "as resulting from everything which affects our sensibility" because that would be to interpret a condition based on what it makes possible. For Henry, the question of the ontological possibility of affectivity must be approached the other way around. Because "affectivity is the condition for sensation,"[19] it cannot be interpreted starting from sensation: *It is not that which happens which determines affectivity, but affectivity makes possible the arrival of what happens and determines it, it determines that which happens as affective.*"[20]

When it comes time to name this unique source in which everything that appears, appears and is given as it is, this original essence that "moves" itself, nothing but "life" seems adequate. Affectivity is life: "Affectivity is not an empty structure—some abstraction which is nothing of itself[;] . . . it is life itself and its essence."[21] In the sense meant here, life is not an empirical reality of the kind studied in the biological sciences. To be alive is not to be given to oneself in that way, because life in its reality, as it is given, in which everything else arrives and is given, arrives well before the end of any ideal development of scientific knowledge. Nor is life some ideal that one can project for oneself as any imagined reality whatever, whether some religious or ethical ideal, or even some object of mystical experience. Life is not a property of a living being attributed with the power of self-movement; it is the reality of this power in its own effectiveness.

In its real and living actuality, life is a revelation of itself. In life, appearance and reality are one, just as, for example, the appearance joy or suffering is the living reality of joy or suffering. Affective tonalities may also be corporeal, as in the case of hunger or thirst or satiety, but in each case they are possible only in the living body itself, in flesh. Such phenomena are important (and not merely important for philosophy), because human reality—precisely its reality—is at stake in them. To grant affectivity and affective tonalities this status is not to reduce life to subjectivity but to found subjectivity on something prior, on life. "The living being is not founded on itself," as Henry puts it; "it has a basis in life."[22] Nor is affectivity something that would be individual in a way that could be opposed to what is communal. Both individual and community, far from being opposed or related hierarchically, are founded in life.[23]

The center of gravity and the method of philosophy have thus changed. In its reorientation in life, it is no longer a question of being, where "living" is only a subsequent and secondary determination. Rather it is a question of life, in which all being becomes phenomenal and is given. To the extent that "affect" is important for theology, and is a basic category for mysticism, this development is important. Theology, too, will have questions of its own; but if theology wishes to question the phenomenology of life, it must first recognize that not only have the acceptations of key terms changed (affectivity, subjectivity, ipseity, etc.), but the very status of philosophy itself has also changed. The antagonism of modernity is over.

Life, original plenitude, real temporality, all held together. For if an empirical given appears in space and time, one thing in front of the other, or beside it, another thing before, or after, or simultaneous with the other, it is not so with life. For if we ask how anything can acquire the status of being-now, or being-present, it would seem that nothing in the world and no act of the mind can make it so. In life, time is real, as a living present, the very life of which has no past or future. In life and thanks to life, the present is really present, not

some other time, which theoretically it could have been and an economic culture of alienation presumes it is. It may seem merely a poetic utterance or a conceptual confusion that would make life always,
always, always . . . now. Or perhaps we should instead affirm that in
life, as in the wisdom of which Augustine speaks, "there is no past
and future, but only being, since it is eternal."[24]

AUGUSTINE: ASCENT TO WISDOM AS
ASCENT TO LIFE

We cannot read back into a theological tradition a philosophical
development that is foreign to it, but we are now equipped with
a more rigorous determination of life that may help us to approach
more clearly the role it plays in negative theology. Augustine is far
more than a negative theologian, and his theological erudition and
suppleness cannot be reduced to any simple schematization, but the
place of life in his writing is significant and consistent and embraces
the breadth of his theology. In a way that is analogous to the philosophical history I have just put forth, Augustine's personal and theological itinerary also makes a turn explicitly toward life. It marks both
the beginning of his path of conversion and the end of this path, in
which wisdom itself is discovered to be life.

In the *Confessions*, life occurs frequently as name for God, and
often as an asyndeton alongside God. Augustine appeals to God as
the "fount of life,"[25] and invokes the title early and often: "True life,
my God . . . ";[26] "my God, my life, my holy sweetness . . . ";[27] "O God,
my life . . . ";[28] "God of my heart, my praise, and my life. . . ."[29] It can
easily pass unnoticed, but these invocations both speak to life in the
second person and modify that life with a possessive determiner, as
if the name were held in common. Life is at once personal, proper to
Augustine, and nevertheless a name for God. We must understand
better the justification for Augustine's use of the possessive adjective,
but the remarkable regularity of life as an appellation for God is
enough to secure its decisive place in Augustine's theology.

Far from being merely nominal, however, life is also in the strict sense appropriate to God, even while God remains ineffable. In *Teaching Christianity*, a text contemporaneous with the *Confessions*, Augustine acknowledges that any utterance of God, even a negative one, already implies a certain formal determination. "If I have spoken, I have not said what I wished to say. Whence do I know this, except because God is ineffable? If what I said were ineffable, it would not be said. And for this reason God should not be said to be ineffable, for when this is said, something is said."[30] Only pages later, however, Augustine writes that one can indeed, without the same absurdity, think of God as life itself. "Since *all those* who think of God think of something living, only they can think of Him without absurdity who think of Him as life itself."[31] The context leaves little doubt that Augustine has in mind not only the Christian but also anyone wishing to think of God. As we will see, it is an issue of an intelligibility that anticipates in a latent way what will become evident after his conversion.

In other texts, Augustine appeals to life as the basis for an incontestable argument against radical skepticism. In *De uita beata*, he asks, "Could you tell us one among the things you know? Yes. Say something. At least don't you know that you live? You know then that you have life, because no one can live without life."[32] It is not merely that if one is alive one has at one's disposal the true theoretical premise of a single argument against all doubt. Rather, it is the undeniable fact of living that implies always and everywhere that life itself is responsible for this condition. It is as though being alive, in a way that must still be understood, brings one into proximity with life itself, even before any explicit theological understanding of this has been attained, and even when its presence goes entirely unnoticed. A parallel argument appears in succinct form in *The Trinity*: "Even if the mind doubts, it lives."[33] In the very act of doubting, the mind proves it is alive.

In the *Confessions*, Augustine confirms that life, specifically the "happy life," was his aim even before it becomes thematic for him and even before he begins explicitly seeking for God, though perhaps this becomes evident only after his conversion and in retrospect. In

Book 10, after his conversion, he can still ask, "How am I to seek for you, Lord?" But even at this late point in the text, Augustine does not so much answer the question as specify what it is exactly that he seeks when he seeks God, and even why it is that he does so, as if he needed to remind himself: "When I seek for you, my God, my quest is for the happy life." But the object of his search is also, in another sense, the reason for his search: "I will seek you that my soul may live, for my body derives life from my soul, and my soul derives life from you."[34] He repeats the formula throughout the text. "You are the life of souls, the life of lives. You live in dependence only on yourself, and you never change, life of my soul."[35] As life itself, God does not merely give life to the soul; God is its very life.

Nevertheless, to speak of God as the life of lives is not only to distinguish God from visible matter, and therefore from the objective body, but also to distinguish him from the soul. Just as the body depends on the soul for its movement, so the life of the soul depends on life itself for its movement (while the life of God depends on nothing). It is not evidently an external relation between the soul and its life, and it is not even evident that two separate lives are in question, the life of the soul and the life of God. A different kind of relation is in play, between finite and infinite life, or in Augustine's lexicon, between mutable and immutable life. We have every reason to believe Augustine means that life itself moves the soul, and not some ideal or metaphorical life, for in another context, speaking now to the soul, he says, "your God is for you the life of your life."[36] The formulation is not poetic or propaedeutic but remarkably precise. It implies that the soul has its own proper life, but then equally denies this. It affirms that this life is proper to the soul, the soul's own life, but only insofar as what is life in it, its very life, is its God.

The growing recognition of God as life is a central theme of Augustine's conversion. Initially, his very idea of God was limited by his preoccupation with the visible, material world: "I conceived of you, life of my life, as a large being permeating infinite space on every side. . . . I thought simply not existent anything not extended in space, or diffused, or concentrated or expanding. . . . My eyes are accustomed to such images. My heart accepted the same structure."[37]

We may wonder why Augustine would describe images of visible things as a structure that his heart could accept, to which it could become habituated, but which ultimately would be foreign to it. We may also wonder what exactly is foreign about this structure, such that it could and would estrange the heart, the seat of affection, from itself, to the point of indeed alienating it from itself. It is not merely the representational character of the images that derive from visible things that Augustine laments; it is the presupposition that this reality is the only one there is. So long as the visible world is for him the sole reality, he is not merely blocked from finding God, he is equally and coextensively blocked from the happy life he seeks.

Life itself is the guiding clue that removes this obstacle and leads him in a direction of conversion. Augustine describes conversion as a turn toward life, but this cannot be understood as a turn from one aim or object to another, since the happy life was always and still remains the goal of his seeking. Rather, conversion marks a change in the place where he seeks and finds what he has always sought, the happy life.[38] This place is life, and is now defined in opposition to the visible world, which is then determined as a region of death. By turning to life he finds a place, a path with friction, so to speak, that allows this radical shift that can only be described as inward and upward. "Seek for what you seek, but it is not where you are looking for it. You seek the happy life in the region of death. It is not there. How can there be a happy life where there is not even life."[39] It is indeterminate whose life the happy life is; but if he starts from what he initially conceives as merely his own life, since it is his own happiness he seeks, he ultimately concludes that finding the happy life is finding his own life in God.

The significance of life for conversion is also confirmed in the opposite sense, where sinfulness and wickedness and pride are defined as turning away from life. "Our good is life with you forever, and because we turned away from that, we became twisted. Let us now return to you that we may not be overturned."[40] To the extent that fallen humanity is humanity turned away from life, Augustine can also say that it is turned away from itself, "toward inferior things, rejecting its *own* inner life and swelling with external matter."[41] Here, again, life is opposed to what is outside, external, and inferior. In a remarkable way, therefore, "life" comprehends both fallen and restored humanity, as the abiding truth in virtue of which both evil and good are what they are.[42] It is not life's absence from him but his absence from life that constitutes his fall. He was seduced because he was found, in his words, "living outside myself."[43] And yet, unfathomably, nothing about his life suffers loss during this period of prodigality: "Our good is life with you and suffers no deficiency, for you yourself are that good. . . . During our absence our house suffers no ruin; it is your eternity."[44] In other places he calls this good, not life with you, but "life in you."[45] To find the happy life is not merely to find life, but to find life in God, but to find life in God is to find true life.

We may be tempted to think that Augustine has only a theological ideal in mind, one that simply presupposes a dogmatic content far removed from an understanding of life that could be meant in a universal way, as it is actually lived here and now by everyone. But the text prohibits this conclusion, because Augustine also makes clear that he means the very life that begins with birth and that encompasses all the properties of a living being. He does not merely surmise that life is somehow present in him from birth, he makes the more radical assertion that life itself brings about his birth: "Where can a living being such as an infant come from if not from you, God? Or can anyone be the cause of his own making?"[46] Augustine does not appeal to an external force or cause as a principle of explanation, something asserted to be before or outside his birth that would bring it about. It is enough that he has life, and that this life is not self-caused. The text is clear, and rhetorically precise. "Is there any channel though which being and life can be drawn into us other than what you make us, Lord?"[47] It is not only a matter of birth, however, but also of all his real capacities as a living being. Though perhaps it becomes evident only in retrospect, and from the vantage point of conversion, even in his youth, while still far from God, the very unity of his life already evinces a latent integrity that is proper to it and not dependent on something extraneous. Simply when he "existed, and lived, and thought," the very integrity of his senses, his avoidance of pain and ignorance, and his delight in truth, were all marks, he says, of a "profound latent unity from which I derived my being."[48]

These significations of life and conversion come together in a conception of life as light, whose source is "above" the mind, yet nevertheless operative in the mind's own power of reason. The path on which the latent unity becomes a real, explicit, and lived unity is an ascent that involves reason and will in a judgment about the desirability of immutable life.[49] First, the path: "I was brought up to your light by the fact that I knew myself both to have a will and to be alive."[50] Once the mind passes through all living things that it finds vivified by life, it comes upon life itself, and discovers, "above" mutable life, an immutable life that it holds as "better." The mind makes a judgment that is within its power, though it is a power it does not give to itself. It is a judgment that provides a certainty: immutable life is intrinsically more desirable than mutable life. Why? Because mutable life can change from better to worse—and he knows his own life is mutable, since his condition was one of being turned away from life—while immutable life is always life, can never change from this condition, and depends on nothing. It is rational for the mind to judge that this immutable life is the true object of its desire.

Augustine ultimately identifies this life as wisdom itself. Just as his seduction—which in the language of wisdom literature is the seduction of the fool—was a turning away from his own life, so now turning toward life is tantamount to turning toward wisdom. And insofar as the life now in question is immutable, this wisdom is also immutable. Like life, it can simply be defined as wisdom in the true sense, which it would be redundant to call immutable. It "is not sometimes foolish and sometimes wise but is rather Wisdom itself." Unlike the wisdom that was foolish before discovering this, the wisdom it discovers "was never foolish and can never be."[51] The rule of truth that makes possible the transition from the first to the second, from mutable life to immutable life, is above the mind. Yet it is a rule that everyone follows when they hold immutable life as better. Speaking of the interior, Augustine says, "I entered, and *with* my soul's eye, *such as it was*, saw above that same eye of my soul that illuminative light higher than my mind. . . . It was superior because it made me. I was inferior because I was made by it."[52] The ascent to life and wisdom is not a human achievement, nor is it an achievement of reason strictly speaking.[53] "It was you, entirely you, who brought this about. For no other could recall us from all deadly error than the life that knows no death, and the wisdom which itself needs no light, illuminating needy minds."[54]

Augustine repeats this same ascent in another way with his mother, Monica, shortly before her death. It is affection for life itself that brings this ascent about. The text, for which the preceding remarks can serve as commentary, confirms and reinforces our itinerary to this point.

> Our minds were lifted up by an ardent affection. . . . We moved up beyond them [created things] so as to attain to the region of inexhaustible abundance where you feed Israel eternally with truth for food. There life is the wisdom by which all creatures come into being, both things which were and which will be. But wisdom itself is not brought into being, but is as it was and always will be. Furthermore, in this wisdom, there is no past and future, but only being, since it is eternal. . . . But what is to be compared with your word, Lord of our lives?[55]

If confession is a work of memory, are all these recollections merely memories of past events no longer real, but recalled, and perhaps even misremembered? A final dependence on memory would seem to be an insurmountable limitation, a finite achievement of a finite capacity, whatever may be the force of its strength. But the ascent to life as wisdom is an ascent that passes through memory, and memory itself is another term for the force of life. It is memory that recalls Augustine to the present and gathers him together, but this act leads him ultimately to go beyond memory itself: "So great is the power of memory, so great is the force of life in a human being whose life is mortal. What then ought I to do, my God? You are my true life. I will transcend beyond even this my power which is called memory."[56] It is as though memory is a name for the finite life Augustine passes beyond in his ascent to his own true life in God.

But any account of conversion and ascent in Augustine must finally admit that Christ's own life and death plays the leading role. We have seen Augustine affirm that life itself brings his conversion about, and yet we have also seen that his own life is incapable of doing this. Once turned toward the region of death, the soul has no power to take itself up again, or to bring itself back to life. Christ is the one who "had the power to lay down his soul and the power to take it back again."[57] He restores to Augustine his own life by giving his own life to him. It cannot be overemphasized that it is real life in question, and not a mere metaphor or concept. Here faith takes on a determinate meaning as that which confirms the truth and reality of the life in question. Augustine's formulation is pristine: "In so far as the death of his flesh was in my opinion unreal, the death of my soul was real. And in so far as the death of his flesh was authentic, to that extent the life of my soul, which disbelieved that, was inauthentic."[58] In a radical sense, then, faith means life, for without it the soul is really dead; or in other terms, unbelief is the guarantee that the life of the soul is unreal.

THE LIVING WORD: SCRIPTURE AND KENOSIS

In order to ratify the central role of life in Augustine's thought, and to broaden the basis on which we approach the medieval traditions of negative theology, we may confirm our reading by turning back to Augustine's primary textual source, which is scripture. Life's essential link with beatitude is not his invention but a theme he finds first in scripture. Yet life is not merely one theme among all the others; it has a superlative status, since it is what scripture as a whole, centered on the words and works of Christ, points to and brings about in its true hearers, in all those who receive it in faith. The life of which it speaks, or more precisely, the life that it speaks, is not a vague and indeterminate idea beyond the horizon of intelligibility; it is rigorously specified as the very wisdom of God, his "living word."[59]

The historical and spiritual themes of the Hebrew Bible and the New Testament accentuate life in many ways but always as having its source in God. It is found in the breath of Yahweh given to Adam at the creation, making him a living being;[60] in the covenant with Abraham as the promise of an impossible son, beyond any human power of generation;[61] in the law of Moses, not only as the explicit prohibition of killing and in the sacrificial economy, but as what the Psalmist will call the "path to life" and Ben Sira the "law of life";[62] in the prohibitions against idolatry, defined as the worship of dead idols in place of the one, true and living God;[63] as the life through Christ that the Gospel proclaims;[64] in the gift of the Holy Spirit, whom the Nicene Creed calls "the Lord, the giver of life";[65] in the centrality of the resurrection for faith; and finally, in the very understanding of the human being as a child of God.[66]

The place of life is pronounced in the wisdom literature of the ancient Near East, much of which is collected in scripture, and which Jewish tradition makes increasingly its own.[67] These texts describe life not merely as the fruit of wisdom, but as the very meaning of wisdom, to the point of being identified with it, so that wisdom personified can say, "Whoever finds me finds life";[68] "Hear, my son, and receive my words, and the years of your life shall be many. . . . Hold fast to instruction, never let it go; keep it, for it is your life. . . . My son, to my words be attentive, to my sayings incline your ear . . . for they are life to those who find them. . . . With all vigilance guard your heart, for in it are the sources of life."[69] Further: "Wisdom teaches her children. . . . Those who love her love life";[70] "She is a tree of life to those who grasp her";[71] "Death and life are in the gift of the tongue, those who indulge it must eat the fruit it yields."[72] In a way that will also be important for the development of negative theology, other texts refer to wisdom as an illumination and form of speech that give rise to praise. Here praise is not only for creation, but for the light that allows it to be seen as a divine work: "He put his own light in their hearts to show them the magnificence of his works, so that they would praise his holy name as they told of his magnificent works. He set knowledge before them, he endowed them with the law of life."[73]

To the extent that life can be found in wisdom's own words, and can be defined as a form of speech and even as *logos*, it is not difficult to notice the resonance of these themes in the Gospel of John, for which life is a source of illumination and a form of speech, now fully manifest in the person of Christ. In the famous prologue, the *logos* is not only with God in the beginning, but is also identified as God. In a remarkably condensed way, the text states that in him, in the *logos*, was life, and then in turn identifies this life as the light of humanity.[74] Jesus speaks of himself as this light, which he also calls the "light of the world."[75] In a similar manner, the first Epistle of John places *logos* and life in an essential relation, for it is now the "Word of life" that is fully manifest in the Son and proclaimed by all who have witnessed him.[76] The same verb for this manifestation, which occurs frequently in the first letter of John, also appears in the Gospel of Mark, notably in the long ending, when after the resurrection Jesus appears to two unknown people on the way into the desert.[77]

Together with this "positive" meaning of light and life in the New Testament, as that which must be affirmed and proclaimed, we find a "negative" meaning, as that which must be denied, and denied as a condition for the manifestation of the life of Christ—in oneself! In his second Epistle to the Corinthians, and speaking in the name of all believers, Paul claims to carry the death of Jesus in his body, *so that* the life of Jesus can be manifest. Speaking of himself and his followers, Paul says we are "always carrying in the body the death of Jesus, so that the life of Jesus may also be manifested in our bodies. For while we live we are always being given up to death for Jesus' sake, so that the life of Jesus may be manifested in our mortal flesh."[78] But then a strange shift occurs, for Paul immediately displaces this manifestation in his own body to locate it in his auditors, for the text continues, "So death is at work in us, but life in you." It is as though a double condition is in operation: first one's own life must be denied, so that the life of Christ can be manifest instead; then it must be denied again, so that it can be manifest in an other, in a continual reception that is also a gift.

Paul's rigorous logic is repeated equally succinctly in John, where it receives the shorthand name "love": "We know that we have passed from death to life because we love our brothers. Whoever does not love remains in death. Everyone who hates his brother is a murderer, and you know that no murderer has eternal life remaining in him. The way we came to know love was that he laid down his life for us; so we ought to lay down our lives for our brothers."[79] Neither Paul nor John is inventing Christianity. On the contrary, their refusal to separate the words of Christ from his life-giving action is a refusal out of fidelity to the original unity of those words and action. The synoptic Gospels all place these words in the mouth of Jesus: "For whoever wishes to save his life will lose it, but whoever loses his life for my sake will find it."[80] And then, as if it were obvious that it is a question of giving and receiving life: "Whoever receives you receives me, and whoever receives me receives the one who sent me."[81]

Paul also ratifies the strong identification between wisdom and life that I have already established. He is perfectly aware that his words will seem foolish to the Greeks, and he embraces the implication. It is in reference exactly to the absurdity of the cross that he writes: "For since in the wisdom of God the world did not come to know God through wisdom, it was the will of God through the foolishness of the proclamation to save those who have faith."[82] Only on the basis of a presumed identity of wisdom and life would the death of Christ appear foolish. Why, then, does Paul not object to the identification of wisdom and life, perhaps by claiming that wisdom goes beyond life, so as to cast Christ's death in a more appealing light? Instead, he accepts the more radical option, and is more prepared to call the proclamation foolishness than he is to disassociate wisdom from life. He knows it is foolishness only to the Greeks, but accepting this is the price of the proclamation itself: Christ is the wisdom of God and therefore the life and the power of God. Though it is foolish to the Greeks, to all "those who are called, Jews and Greeks alike, Christ is the power of God and the wisdom of God."[83]

The significations of life as wisdom in scripture, along with their Christological implications, do not exactly amount to a negative theology, but they do anticipate the motifs that recur in the theology of Pseudo-Denys and Eckhart. The medieval theologians concerned to hold negative theology together with moral practice will indeed emphasize the ascetic dimension of negativity, where denying one's life operates as a kind of condition for the manifestation of divine life, as a kind of kenosis or dispossession in which nothing is left but the life of God.[84] But another way of saying this is that God alone is life and gives life, and the denial of one's own life is better expressed as a denial that life is one's own. In this sense, contemplation is not separable from practice, "a practice which was expected to be embodied in a life."[85]

FROM DIVINE WISDOM TO NEGATIVE THEOLOGY: LIFE IN PSEUDO-DENYS AND ECKHART

When Pseudo-Denys appropriates life as a name of God, he does so in a way that is consistent with a long and well-established tradition that holds wisdom as the path to life. Together with Augustine, he becomes a key source for various forms of negative theology that develop in the medieval period. Like the Neoplatonists, Denys considers life as both a source from which all things originate and an end to which they return, and life is a paradigmatic case of the power of this source to remain itself while going out into all things. Eckhart then develops the theology of Denys in a radical way that places an even more pronounced emphasis on life, where life itself is the very form of ultimate union with God.

Let us recall that for Denys, as for the Fathers, scripture is identified with divine wisdom. Taking the form of speech, this wisdom is what the source and end of all things has revealed about itself.[86] The procession of divine wisdom is creation. When spoken, it is a source of light that illuminates for the just soul a path of ascent toward union with God. This light does not merely illuminate from the outside and leave the soul indifferent to what it reveals, however. When returned to God as true praise, these spoken words, the divine names, truly bring about the ascent of the soul and return it to its source in God. Praise thus accomplishes a real union of the soul with God that gives form to human existence.[87] This circuitous movement originates and culminates in the "real yearning" of God, as the power of his word that goes out into all things and nevertheless remains in itself. Though the soul's ascent culminates in darkness and silence, beyond all knowledge and activity of the intellect, this real yearning never ceases.

The names Denys calls "divine" are "conceptual names."[88] It is not a question of affirming epistemic truths but of praising God in a way that is supremely attentive to the appropriateness, and also the final inadequacy, of all speech to God. Speech is ultimately inadequate not because it is speech in human language; it is ultimately inadequate because it can be spoken in human language only insofar as God has revealed himself in scripture and creation, both of which are first spoken by God. The words are thus not only appropriate of him, but are precisely and justly due him. To utter the divine names, then, is to return these words to God as praise, to admit that the only affirmation of God that can be appropriate is God's own. "We can use only what scripture has disclosed,"[89] and can ascend only "as far upward as the light of sacred scripture will allow,"[90] simply because the cause of all existence "alone could give an authoritative account of what it really is."[91]

But it would be incorrect to conclude that Denys is so blinded by his faith that he simply asserts that these words are appropriate of God without offering any demonstration why they are. If "wisdom becomes known through speech,"[92] then to become known, this wisdom must first be spoken; and in being spoken, it becomes known. To speak truthfully of the divine, in turn, is to participate in the speech of its wisdom in a way that brings about a union with it, in a way that reunites it with itself.[93] A union of this form presupposes the original unity of the Word with God, a unity far beyond any human power to achieve. But it is not beyond the power of the divine names themselves to achieve, and in this sense their power demonstrates itself. To be more precise, their *meaning* in each case *is* their power to enact a union.[94] "If we may trust the superlative wisdom and truth of scripture," the very act of hearing and speaking the divine names, in proportion to the capacities of each illuminated mind, accomplishes a union with God far "superior to anything available to us by way of our own abilities in the realm of discourse or intellect."[95]

For Denys, life is a prime name of God, as it was for Augustine.[96] Aquinas cites Denys as the authority for his famous notion of God as "subsisting being itself,"[97] but Denys also speaks of the transcendent source as "life itself" and the "subsistence of life itself." Explaining the distinction between these two locutions, Denys says that the "supra-divine life" is the "originating Cause of all living beings and of life itself."[98] Thus life is at once predicated of the one transcendent "source beyond source" of all things and of the "provident acts of power," which come forth from that God.[99] An infinite distance separates created and uncreated life, and only the latter can be called life in the true sense. Yet the "provident acts of power" are also called "life itself," and any human participation in life is spoken of in this sense.[100] One might say that Denys maintains a distinction between the "transcendent" life above what is living and the life within what is living, operating as a source that is "immanent" within what is living insofar as it is alive. Nevertheless, as transcendent source beyond source, life "is something beyond words, something unknown, and something wholly unrevealed."[101]

As a "being-making procession," however, the appropriateness of life as a name of God stems from life's role as source that bestows on life the power to be what it is. In Denys's words, it "gives to life itself the capacity to be life, and gives to everything alive and to every form of life the existence appropriate to it."[102] "Life itself is the source of everything alive."[103] Though it may seem redundant, the logic is rigorous. Life gives to life the capacity to be life. But life itself is from God. We are not permitted to conclude that there are two kinds of life, one that would be supernatural and one that would be merely natural. Rather, all life is of the same nature: "the mighty nature of Divine life . . . is the nature of all lives . . . and insofar as it is concerned there is no life which is contrary to nature or supernatural."[104] Denys can still call life supernatural, but he does so only "because it rises above the visible order of things," not because it would have a nature that is distinct from divine life. Life itself, he says in a way that provokes wonder, "does not transcend the mighty nature of divine Life."[105]

We might be inclined to stop with the observation that because all divine processions are illuminating, life too is illuminating in its own particular way. But Denys also makes the more radical claim that illumination in general is life. Divine illumination is life in the sense that it truly makes alive. It is not an abstract, formal, or independent life, but real life that vivifies. Not only do "they call him source of life,"[106] but: "To sum up," Denys says of divine illumination, "it is the life of the living."[107] An immediate relationship and inextricable bond is established between the living and life, from which they can never be separated so long as they are alive. It is possible to turn away from life, as we saw in the case of Augustine, but even so, life is "overflowing with love for mankind" and "returns us and calls us back to itself after we have strayed."[108] "To those who fall away it is the voice calling, 'Come back!' and is the power which raises them up again."[109] But it is not as though the power that returns the soul back to life does so in a one-sided way, from the outside, for it is a power that also works in some way within the soul. The effort to understand more clearly the form of union that brings this about leads us back to the concept of real yearning.

In response to an objection that his use of the term *yearning* in reference to God is at odds with scripture, Denys responds that we must be attentive not to words but to their meanings, and even more precisely, to "the power of the meanings," if we wish to understand how divine wisdom signifies.[110] But what, one might ask, is the power of the *meaning* of yearning? In a condensed turn of words, Denys says, "The divine longing is Good seeking good for the sake of the Good."[111] What is signified by yearning, Denys says, "is a capacity to effect a unity."[112] Yearning, longing, *eros*, desire, love—these are all synonyms for the power of the divine Word that accomplishes human redemption. But how this power operates, notably in the case of a word that is also life, remains unclear. If, when the Good, or "superabundant Life," bestows existence on all things and makes them good, it also makes them desirable, then in a nascent way, the very desire to live already illuminates a path of return.[113] *Exitus* and *reditus*, emanation and return, creation and redemption, all depend upon a real longing that brings about a unity. The effective power that unites the just soul with God is an affective power.

When it comes time to offer an instance of this union with God beyond speech, Denys simply points to Paul—and to life. Since it is a question of ascent, one might have assumed that the obvious illustration to select would have been Paul's reference to the man caught up to the third heaven, but this is not what Denys cites.[114] Instead, he brings us back to the words we have already considered, in which "the great Paul, swept along by his yearning for God," writes, "It is no longer I who live, but Christ who lives in me."[115] Denys elaborates on Paul's utterance in a way that brings it more fully into the lexicon of negative theology: "Paul was truly a lover and, as he says, he was beside himself for God, possessing not his own life but the life of the One for whom he yearned, as exceptionally beloved."[116] This description of union in terms of life might seem to suggest that it is an ecstatic union: Paul is "beside himself," and Denys at first seems to confirm such an interpretation, but the context indicates otherwise.

Immediately following his reference to Paul's yearning, Denys predicates this same yearning of the "cause of the universe." Much like Paul is, the cause of the universe "is also carried outside of himself in the loving care he has for everything."[117] The cause of this cause spilling over into the universe and becoming the cause of everything is simply the "superabundance of his benign yearning for all."[118] It may seem as though life, as transcendent source, becomes ecstatic too, since Denys says this source is carried outside of himself. In one sense, the source must be "carried out of himself" in yearning for all things, "beguiled by goodness, by love, and by yearning." But Denys ultimately denies this is an ecstasy, or rather, he affirms it while redefining what ecstasy means, so that it has exactly the opposite sense. The transcendent source "comes to *abide* within all things . . . by virtue of his supernatural and *ecstatic capacity to remain, nevertheless, within himself*."[119] When the divine yearning goes out from God to restore all things to himself, it does not leave God.[120] Indeed, its power to remain in God in an original unity is the condition for its power to reestablish the union of the soul with it. If the ecstasy of divine yearning is its capacity to remain in itself, must we conclude that the human yearning that responds to it is also a capacity to remain in itself, since its yearning and the goal of yearning are one?

Meister Eckhart takes up this question in a radical way that he also develops in terms of life. Eckhart understands life, as the source of all things, also as a ground, and as a form of oneness that qualifies the union of the soul with God. Eckhart does claim, "Only between equals can unity be produced."[121] But as his *Commentary on John* makes clear, he also conceives of unity in terms of generation: "What is born of God is God, God's son."[122] Because generation means generation of life, it is life itself that allows us to understand what, in this union, belongs to God and what is proper to the soul. Eckhart professes that life is proper to both God and the soul, insofar as God alone is life, yet life is truly given to the soul as its own. As he puts it, "What is without principle lives in the proper sense, for everything that has its principle of operation from another *insofar as it is other* does not live in the proper sense."[123] In giving life to the soul, God does not give it in a way that could be separated from himself. On the other hand, to be alive is to have one's principle of motion within oneself, as a power of self-movement. Much as Denys defines ecstasy, if God truly gives real life to the soul, then the soul's own life, proper to it, also remains in God and proper to God alone. "God alone, insofar as he is Final End and First Mover lives and is life."[124] But at the same time, "the blessedness he brought us was *ours*," so that we are not merely "called" sons but also can "truly be" sons.[125]

As for both Augustine and Denys, life for Eckhart is also an illuminating source. This does not mean merely that "life and existence are light"[126] but also and more radically that "those he does not enlighten *insofar as he is life* do not live and are not living beings."[127] The soul is illuminated, then, insofar as it has life. To be alive and living, in the sense in which Eckhart understands it, is truly and really to have one's life from God. But his claim is also more radical. All who pretend to live but live as though life were not from God do not "have" life in the sense Eckhart means it, because they fail to know the reason for their living. It is not possible to live for oneself, because life does not come from oneself and one cannot give life to oneself. "Man . . . receives his total existence from God," he says, and "existence for him is not 'existence-for-himself,' but 'existence-for-God.'"[128] Existence-for-God means that God is the source and end "for which man exists and lives."[129]

But in another sense, life has no reason beyond itself, because life itself is the reason for living. Since life has no prior reason to obey, it is its own ground. That is why, Eckhart says, "If anyone went on for a thousand years asking of life: 'Why are you living?' life if it could answer would only say: 'I live so that I may live.' That is because life lives out of its own ground and springs from its own source, and so it lives without asking why it is itself living."[130] "Why do you live? So as to live; and still you do not know why you live." So, much like Augustine, for whom the happy life is the finality of all desire, for Eckhart too, "Life in itself is so desirable that we desire it for its own sake."[131] Here the object of desire is not the idea of life, in the end an empty ideal, but true life in its living reality. Only "what is in life is life."[132]

Eckhart thus makes life the principle in which the just soul is united with God, as the common ground, so to speak, that gives form to their union: "Here God's ground is my ground, and my ground is God's ground." "Here I live from what is my own, as God lives from what is his own."[133] And at the same time: "What is life? God's being is my life. . . . He gives birth not only to me, his Son, but he gives birth to me as himself and himself as me."[134] This is not to say that Eckhart defines the self in its difference from God and then asserts a subsequent unity. Rather, in all these ways, life is the ground of a union that unites as one giver, gift, and recipient. The life given to the soul is given as its own, but it can be its own only insofar as it is true life, the only life there is, the life proper to God alone. To be oneself is to belong to God.

It is thus no surprise if Eckhart's strongest claims about the soul and God sharing the same ground occur in a context of dispossession, in which the soul denies its claim to anything. Here Eckhart makes an essential link between justice and life, with justice defined in the classical sense as giving to each their due.[135] Eckhart can affirm that the relation of the soul to God in its ground is the relation of the soul to its own life, precisely insofar as its life is not its own. Life belongs to God, and so life is due him. "Honor belongs to God. Who are those who honor God? . . . Those who . . . do not seek for what is theirs in anything[,] . . . who are not looking beneath themselves or above themselves or beside themselves or at themselves[,] . . . who have gone out from all this[,] . . . *from everything that is theirs.*"[136]

Eckhart's word for the state of the soul that honors God in this way is *"detachment."* He explains its meaning in affective terms. In the detachment that manifests life, "no transient thing" moves the soul. The one moved only by life "experiences nothing of whatever is bodily, and he calls the world dead, because nothing earthly has any savor for him."[137] This is in no way to deny the world or creation but rather finally to let it be what it is in life, nothing less, but also nothing more. It is striking that to illustrate this detachment, Eckhart, like Denys before him, cites Paul: "I live by faith in the Son of God" and "for to me life is Christ, and death is gain."[138] In another context, precisely when explaining the affective meaning of detachment, Eckhart again refers to Paul. It is an affirmation, followed by the denial and then another affirmation, and together they secure the place of life in negative theology: "I live, and yet I do not; Christ lives in me."[139]

Life itself then becomes a norm of action in which the soul is united to God. "If you want to know whether your work has been done in God, see if it is living. If you want to know whether your work has been done in God, see if it is your life. . . . My message is: If you want to act justly and well . . . be like your life is to you, indeed, may it be dearer and more precious than your life is."[140] What can it mean for someone to be like her life is to her? And how can the answer to this question then satisfy the conditional "if you want to know"? If life gives me to myself by giving life to me, then for me to be like life is to me is not merely to receive my givenness from life's givenness to me but also to prove this life is my own by giving it in return. The Christ shows me this for the first time, by giving life back to me a second time, in the gift of his own life to me.

ALTHOUGH IT is beyond the scope of this essay to demonstrate methodologically or historically any specific connection between the role of "life" in negative theology and "life" as it appears in contemporary philosophy, certain parallels do suggest themselves. In both cases, it is a question of life itself, as it is really lived; in both cases, life plays the role of an absolute source of everything; in both cases, life is radically distinguished from an empirical object in the world; and in both cases, life is the milieu of affectivity. Whether its own affirmations cohere with or confirm those of philosophy is a question for theology to ask and answer; and philosophy, for its part, can also pose the same questions of theology.

But an initial conjecture can be offered. The conceptual battle that takes place on the terrain of the modern world and leads to a massive cultural and cognitive displacement of the *theological* is not simply a story for the history of epistemology to recount. It is also a question of the subject matter of theology itself. The task is not only to understand the historical and conceptual reasons for its reduced stature in the modern West but also to identify the reasons why contemporary thought is returning to theology today. Is it possible that when thought returns to life, it also and necessarily returns to theology? If "the sole criterion for an interpretation is its fecundity,"[141] the final test of our reading is that the words of the texts speak for themselves, and if the life they name has given itself to us, then the contemplation it elicits is our own.

NOTES

1. As the First Vatican Council (1869–70) puts it, God is both "incomprehensible" and "ineffably exalted above all things which exist, or are conceivable, except himself." At the same time, God "may be certainly known by the natural light of human reason, by means of created things" (cf. Rom. 1:20). Yet the things God has in store for those who love him "utterly exceed the intelligence of the human mind," and the "Divine mysteries by their own nature so far transcend the created intelligence that, even when delivered by revelation and received by faith, they remain covered with the veil of faith

itself, and shrouded in a certain degree of darkness" (Heinrich Denzinger, *Enchiridion Symbolorum* [San Francisco: Ignatius Press, 2012], 1782 ff.).

2. In *The Darkness of God: Negativity in Christian Mysticism* (Cambridge: Cambridge University Press, 1995), Denys Turner shows the great difference between the epistemology of negative theology as a positive form of speech in praise of the divine and more recent, reduced conceptions of "mysticism." Cf. Denys Turner, "The Darkness of God and the Light of Christ: Negative Theology and Eucharistic Presence," *Modern Theology* 15, no. 2 (April 1999); and "Apophaticism, Idolatry, and the Claims of Reason," in *Silence and the Word: Negative Theology and Incarnation*, ed. Oliver Davies and Denys Turner (Cambridge: Cambridge University Press, 2004), 11–34.

3. As the Fourth Lateran Council (1215) puts it, "Between creator and creature there can be noted no similarity so great that a greater dissimilarity cannot be seen between them" (Denzinger, *Enchiridion Symbolorum*, 431 ff.).

4. See especially Immanuel Kant, *Religion within the Boundaries of Mere Reason*, trans. George di Giovanni, in *Religion and Rational Theology*, ed. Allen W. Wood (Cambridge: Cambridge University Press, 1996), 39 ff.

5. Examples of these efforts include the classical formulation of William James, who makes the "mystical states of consciousness" a privileged class of (ineffable, noetic, transient, and passive) experience, which can be empirically enumerated and studied; the work of Rudolf Otto, where the mystical is finally nonrational and analyzed in terms of the "numenous" (holy, *qddosh*, *aiyos, sanctus/sacer* . . .), which, strikingly, is "pre-eminently a living force in the Semitic religions"; and the work of William Alston, who argues that the predicative logic of religious "perception" involves the same structure of doxastic commitment that other forms of perception do (William James, *The Varieties of Religious Experience* [1902] [New York: Penguin, 1982], 379 ff.; Rudolf Otto, *Das Heilige: Über das Irrationale in der Idee des Göttlichen und sein Verhältnis zum Rationalen* [1917] [Munich: C. H. Beck, 2014]; William Alston, *Perceiving God: The Epistemology of Religious Experience* [Ithaca, NY: Cornell University Press, 1991]). One does not need to ignore the merits of these studies to recognize the methodological difficulty of aligning their results with the interests and achievements of historical theology.

6. Medieval apophaticism involves a rationality that embraces both the necessity and the limitations of speaking praise to God, because it admits both a God that has been revealed and a God absolutely beyond the categories of human speech and experience. The tendency of modern thinking, by contrast, is to test how far a God may or may not fit within its own categories, often without questioning the very terms in which the question is posed. The veneer of a common vocabulary conceals what in modern thought is antithetical to the ideas and practices whose language it borrows.

7. As Michel Henry puts it, "What could I know about a being that could not appear? Because life is the original phenomenalization at the core of being and thus what makes it be, one must reverse the traditional hierarchy that subordinates life to being under the pretext that it would be necessary for life itself 'to be'" (*Material Phenomenology*, trans. Scott Davidson [New York: Fordham University Press, 2008], 3; French edition: *Phénoménologie matérielle* [Paris: Presses Universitaires de France, 1990], 7. Hereafter *MP*).

8. David Hume, *Treatise of Human Nature* (Oxford: Oxford University Press, 2000), 1.1.1.7/4. Thomas Hobbes quite literally reduces life to motion in matter: *Leviathan* (Cambridge: Cambridge University Press, 1996), 9 ff.

9. Immanuel Kant, *Critique of Pure Reason* (Cambridge: Cambridge University Press, 1998), 155; German edition: *Kritik der reinen Vernunft* (Hamburg: Felix Meiner, 1960), A20/B34.

10. Even as it is understood in Kant, "real experience" more broadly understood always unites the conceptual and the sensible.

11. See Hermann Cohen, *Kants Theorie der Erfahrung* (Berlin: Dümmler, 1871).

12. Nevertheless, the sciences generally have no interest in sensibility, and in fact tend to rely on new ways for appearances to be given—telescopes, brain scans, hadron colliders, etc.—which then imply new or more visible causal relationships that can lead to new forms of knowledge, to which unaided senses have no access.

13. If Heidegger says, "Phenomenology as the science of the *a priori* phenomena of intentionality . . . never has anything to do with appearances and even less with mere appearances," he means only to say there is nothing "behind" a phenomenon, of which it would be an appearance. So confident is he that the phenomenon has delivered being, it no longer makes sense to talk of appearance. See his *History of the Concept of Time*, trans. Theodore Kisiel (Bloomington: Indiana University Press, 1985), 86; German edition: *Prolegomena zur Geschichte des Zeitbegriffs*, GA 20 (Frankfurt am Main: Vittorio Klostermann, 1979), 118.

14. "If 'being' is taken to mean predicative being, some *state of affairs* must be given to us, and this by way of an *act which gives it, an analogue of common sensuous intuition*." Edmund Husserl, *Logical Investigations*, vol. 2, trans. J. N. Findley (London: Routledge, 1970), § 44, 279; German edition: *Logische Untersuchungen: Zweiter Teil: Untersuchungen zur Phänomenologie und Theorie der Erkenntnis* (The Hague: Martinus Nijhoff, 1984), Hua 19.

15. The categories of logic are not purely ideal; they are operative "synthetically" in every act of perception and on this basis can become a new object of perception that is self-given and can be studied and understood. Thus the acts of the mind that in every perception constitute a real state of affairs can themselves be perceived in new acts.

16. *MP* 22.

17. Michel Henry, *The Essence of Manifestation*, trans. Girard Etzkorn (Dordrecht: Kluwer, 1973), 489; French edition: *L'Essence de la manifestation* (Paris: Presses Universitaires de France, 1st ed., 1963; 3rd ed., 2003), 611, 612; Hereafter *EM*.

18. *EM* 498 / 622, 623.

19. *EM* 501 / 626.

20. *EM* 489 / 611.

21. *EM* 519 / 649.

22. *MP* 132.

23. See especially Michel Henry, *Incarnation: A Philosophy of Flesh*, trans. Karl Hefty (Evanston, IL: Northwestern University Press, 2015) §§33–48; French edition: *Incarnation: Une philosophie de la chair* (Paris: Seuil, 2000).

24. St. Augustine, *Confessions*, trans. Henry Chadwick (Oxford: Oxford University Press, 2008) IX.x.24, 171 (*Patrologia Latina* 32:659–868). Hereafter *Conf.*

25. *Conf.* III.viii.16, 47.

26. *Conf.* I.xvii.27, 20.

27. *Conf.* I.iv.4, 5.

28. *Conf.* I.xiii.20, 15.

29. *Conf.* IX.xiii.35, 177.

30. St. Augustine, *Teaching Christianity*, trans. Edmund Hill, O.P. (Hyde Park, NY: New City Press, 1996) I.vi (*Patrologia Latina* 34:15–122). Hereafter, *Christ. doct.*

31. *Christ. doct.* I.viii; my emphasis. The context for these statements is not part of a doctrinal formulation but rather a broader discussion of the subject matter of scripture.

32. "Scis ergo habere tu vitam, si quidem vivere nemo nisi vita potest." St. Augustine, *On the Happy Life*, trans. L. Schopp (Washington, DC: Catholic University of America Press, 1948), 2.7 (*Patrologia Latina* 32:959–76).

33. St. Augustine, *The Trinity*, trans. Edmund Hill, O.P. (Hyde Park, NY: New City Press, 1991), 10.10.14 (*Patrologia Latina* 42:819–1098), 10.10.14.

34. *Conf.* X.xx.29, 196.

35. *Conf.* III.iv.10, 42.

36. *Conf.* X.vi.9, 184.

37. *Conf.* VII.i.2, 112.

38. For the development of a related point, see Jean-Luc Marion, *In the Self's Place: The Approach of Saint Augustine*, trans. Jeffrey L. Kosky (Stanford: Stanford University Press, 2012); French edition: *Au lieu de soi: L'Approche de saint Augustin* (Paris: Presses Universitaires de France, 2008).

39. *Conf.* IV.xi.18, 64.

40. *Conf.* IV.xvi.31, 71.

41. *Conf.* VII.xvi.22, 126; my emphasis.

42. This is not to suggest that evil has its own being but that evil is not merely a turn away from being but a turn away from life.

43. *Conf.* III.iv.11, 43.

44. *Conf.* IV.xvi.31, 71.

45. *Conf.* VI.xi.19, 106.

46. *Conf.* I.vi.10, 8.

47. *Conf.* I.vi.10, 8.

48. *Conf.* I.xx.31, 22.

49. It is an ascent "first supporting itself on the created order, and then passing on to you yourself who wonderfully made it" (*Conf.* V.i.1, 72).

50. *Conf.* VII.iii.5, 114.

51. *Conf.* VII.iii.5, 114.

52. *Conf.* VII.vi.16; my emphasis.

53. *Conf.* VII.xi.3.

54. *Conf.* VII.vi.8, 116, 117.

55. *Conf.* IX.x.24, 171.

56. *Conf.* X.xvii.26, 194.

57. "He had the power to lay down his soul and the power to take it back again. . . . For us before you he is priest and sacrifice, and priest because he is sacrifice. Before you he makes us sons instead of servants by being born of you and being servant to us" (*Conf.* X.xliii.69, 220).

58. *Conf.* V.ix.16, 82, here echoing Paul: "I live by faith in the Son of God who has loved me and given himself up for me" (Gal. 2:20).

59. The author of Hebrews proposes a rigorous description of God's word that the Johannine conception confirms and accentuates: "Indeed, the word of God is living and effective, sharper than any two-edged sword, penetrating even between soul and spirit, joints and marrow, and able to discern reflections and thoughts of the heart" (Heb. 4:12).

60. "Then the LORD God formed the man out of the dust of the ground and blew into his nostrils the breath of life, and the man became a living being" (Gen. 2:7).

61. "Abraham fell face down and laughed as he said to himself, 'Can a child be born to a man who is a hundred years old? Can Sarah give birth at ninety?'" (Gen. 17:17). And Yahweh's reply: "Is anything too marvelous for the LORD to do?" (Gen. 18:14).

62. Ps. 16:11. Cf. "He set before them knowledge, and allotted to them the law of life" (Ecclus. 17:9).

63. "Their idols are silver and gold, the work of human hands. They have mouths but do not speak, eyes but do not see. They have ears but do not

hear, noses but do not smell. They have hands but do not feel, feet but do not walk; they produce no sound from their throats. Their makers will be like them, and anyone who trusts in them" (Ps. 115:4–8; cf. Isa. 44, 46, Wisd. 15).

64. "Through him was life, and this life was the light of the human race" (John 1:4).

65. Cf. John 20:22.

66. "The Spirit itself bears witness with our spirit that we are children of God" (Rom. 8:16); "So you are no longer a slave but a child, and if a child then also an heir, through God" (Gal. 4:7).

67. See e.g., Ecclus. 24:1–12 ff., "Wisdom speaks her own praises, in the midst of her people she glories in herself. She opens her mouth in the assembly of the Most High." And Wisdom 10, which makes wisdom the constitutive principle of everything and ultimately of Israelite history.

68. Prov. 8:35.

69. Prov. 4:10, 13, 20–23.

70. Ecclus. 4:12.

71. Prov. 3:18, 22.

72. Prov. 18:21.

73. Ecclus. 17:8–11.

74. "*In ipso vita erat . . .* ," as the Vulgate puts it (John 1:4).

75. John 1:4; 8:12.

76. Λόγου τῆς ζωῆς—καί ἡ ζωή (1 John 1:1, 2).

77. It is striking to note that here, however, he appears in "another form" (ἑτέρᾳ μορφῇ); Mark 16:12.

78. "For it is the God who said, 'Let light shine out of darkness,' who has shone in our hearts to give the light of the knowledge of the glory of God in the face of Christ. But we have this treasure in earthen vessels, to show that the transcendent power belongs to God and not to us. We are afflicted in every way, but not crushed; perplexed, but not driven to despair; persecuted, but not forsaken; struck down, but not destroyed; always carrying in the body the death of Jesus, so that the life of Jesus may also be manifested in our bodies. For while we live we are always being given up to death for Jesus' sake, so that the life of Jesus may be manifested in our mortal flesh. So death is at work in us, but life in you. Since we have the same spirit of faith as he had who wrote, 'I believed, and so I spoke,' we too believe, and so we speak, knowing that he who raised the Lord Jesus will raise us also with Jesus and bring us with you into his presence" (2 Cor. 2:10–14).

79. 1 John 3:14–16.

80. Matt. 16:25; cf. Luke 9:24, Mark 8:35.

81. Matt. 10:39, 40.

82. 1 Cor. 1:21.

83. 1 Cor. 1:24; cf. 1:30, "It is due to him [to God] that you are in Christ Jesus, who became for us wisdom from God, as well as righteousness, sanctification, and redemption."

84. Henri de Lubac, in *Théologie dans l'histoire 1, La Lumière du Christ* (Paris: Desclée du Brouwer, 1990), II.4.ii, separates the philosophical-theoretical interest in twofold distinctions, such as *ratio-intellectus* in Thomas, from the tendency toward threefold distinctions in the spiritual writers. De Lubac gives emphasis to a Catholic equilibrium of religious, moral, and spiritual levels of mysticism, and takes care, with Paul (1 Thess. 5:22), Theresa, and others, not to reduce spirit (*pneuma/animus*) to soul (*psyche/anima*) but also not to separate them. Though he can cite Theresa, who says, "in reality they are but one."

85. Turner, *The Darkness of God*, 8. By framing the question of life in terms of wisdom, we place ourselves within the ambit of the very limited sense in which the term *mysticism* occurs in scripture. For as Hans Urs von Balthasar notes, a favorable use of the term μύστες in scripture is to be found only once, in the Greek Septuagint (Wisd. 8:4). There speaking of "God's way of 'reaching from one end to the other, mightily and sweetly ordering all things,'" it says that she is "privy [μύστις] to all the secrets of God's knowledge" (Hans Urs von Balthasar, "Understanding Christian Mysticism," in *Explorations in Theology*, vol. 4, *Spirit and Institution*, trans. Edward T. Oakes [San Francisco: Ignatius Press, 1995], 309).

86. "The Source that has told us about itself in the holy words of scripture," citing the English edition, *Pseudo-Dionysius: The Complete Works*, trans. Colm Luibheid (New York: Paulist Press, 1987), which preserves the Greek column pagination in B. Corderius, *Patrologia Graece* (Paris: Migne, 1857), DN 1 589B. Hereafter DN.

87. With "our beings shaped by songs of praise." "What I wish to do is to sing a hymn of praise for the being-making procession of the absolute divine Source" (DN 5 816B).

88. DN 13 981C.

89. DN 1 588C.

90. DN 1 589A.

91. DN 1 588B.

92. Sir. 4:24.

93. "If he thinks nothing of the divine wisdom of the scriptures, how can I introduce him to a real understanding of the Word of God" (DN 2 640A).

94. We see this perhaps above all in the case of the Good, which he calls an "agent of cohesion" (DN 4 710A).

95. DN 1 585B–588A, and citing his master, Paul, at 1 Cor. 2:4.

96. "Life" receives its own heading, placed after the Good and Being, and before the "wisdom," "mind," "word," faith," and "truth" of the following chapter.

97. Thomas Aquinas, *Summa theologiae*, Ia, q. 4, a. 3.

98. DN 11 953C–D.

99. "Being itself," "life itself," "divinity itself," are names signifying source, divinity, and cause, and these are applied to the one transcendent cause and source beyond source of all things. But we use the same terms in a derivative fashion, and we apply them to the provident acts of power, which come forth from that God in whom nothing at all participates. I am talking here of being itself, of life itself, of divinity itself which shapes things in a way that each creature, according to capacity, has his share of these. From the fact of such sharing come the qualities and the names "existing," "living," "possessed by divinity," and suchlike (DN 11 953D–956A).

100. Denys also predicates life of the Godhead as such. For "if they do not accept that the whole Godhead is life," he says, "what truth can there be in the holy words 'As the Father raises the dead and gives them life, so also the Son gives life to whom he will,' and 'It is the spirit that gives life'" (DN 2 637A).

101. DN 5 816B.

102. DN 6 856C.

103. DN 5 820B.

104. DN 6 857A.

105. DN 6 857A.

106. DN 1 596B.

107. DN 1 589C.

108. DN 4 856D.

109. DN 1 589C.

110. "It would be unreasonable and silly to look at words rather than at the power of the meanings" (DN 4 708B).

111. DN 4 708A. "In this divine yearning shows especially its unbeginning and unending nature circle through the Good, from the Good, in the Good and to the Good, unerringly turning, ever on the same center, ever in the same direction, always proceeding, always remaining, always being restored to itself" (DN 4 712D, 713A).

112. DN 4 709B.

113. DN 4 696B. "Whatever is, is from the Good, and desires the beautiful and the good, by desiring to exist, to live, and to think" (DN 4 725C).

114. Cf. 2 Cor. 12:2–4.

115. DN 4 712A, citing Gal. 2:20.

116. DN 4 712A.

117. DN 4 712A.

118. DN 4 712A.

119. DN 4 712B; my emphasis.

120. Since "on the one hand he causes, produces, and generates what is being referred to, and, on the other hand, he is the thing itself" (DN 4 712B).

121. *Sermon* 2, 177. All citations follow Edmund Colledge and Bernard McGinn, *Meister Eckhart: The Essential Sermons, Commentaries, Treatises, and Defense* (New York: Paulist Press, 1981).

122. *Comm. Jn.* n. 110, 164.

123. *Comm. Jn.* n. 10, 125; my emphasis.

124. *Comm. Jn.* n. 62, 144.

125. *Sermon* 5b, 182; *Comm. Jn.* n. 120, 169.

126. *Comm. Jn.* n. 93, 157.

127. *Comm. Jn.* n. 91, 156.

128. *Comm. Jn.* n. 107, 163.

129. *Comm. Jn.* n. 107, 163.

130. *Sermon* 5b, 184.

131. *Sermon* 6, 186.

132. *Comm. Jn.* n. 66, 146.

133. *Sermon* 5b, 183.

134. *Sermon* 6, 187.

135. *Sermon* 6, 185.

136. *Sermon* 6, 186; my emphasis. In this sense, as Eckhart claims, in his *Commentary on John*, "the meanings of the categories are determined by their contingent subjects" (n. 61, 144).

137. "On Detachment," 288.

138. Gal. 2:20; Phil. 1:21.

139. "On Detachment," 288, citing Gal. 2:20.

140. *Comm. Jn.* n. 68, 146.

141. Jean-Luc Marion, *The Idol and Distance: Five Studies* (New York: Fordham University Press, 2001), xxxvii; French edition: *L'Idole et la distance* (Paris: Grasset, 1977).

THREE

Mysterious Reasons

The Rationality and Ineffability of Divine Beauty

A. N. WILLIAMS

Standard Western treatments of aesthetics tend to give accounts of beauty that either focus on Christian aesthetics' indebtedness (one might say enslavement) to Platonic conceptualities or ignore the possibility of divine involvement in the matter altogether, passing over in curious silence the long pre-Enlightenment tradition of aesthetics, which resolutely connected beauty to God.[1] Beauty seems at best a foreign import into Christian discourse, available only for borrowing by the theologian, and then solely on the terms dictated by the secular world. The oddity of this situation is attested in the first instance by the fact that beauty is attributed to God in the Bible. This scriptural attestation demands that divine beauty be neither ignored nor dismissed as a Platonic interloper into Christian thought.

The biblical warrant for the connection between beauty and divine nature authorizes theological reflection on beauty but equally cautions against taking the history of such reflection as the mere refrain of Platonic commonplaces. Nevertheless the biblical grounding for the notion that God is beauty (or that divine nature is beautiful) is not extensive: there are only two unmistakable references to God as beauty (Ps. 27:4; Zech. 9:17). Other texts propose a close association of God with beauty (Pss. 50:2, 96:6) or attribute created beauty to God (Wisd. of Sol. 13:3).[2] Given the paucity of references, one can scarcely claim divine beauty is one of the Bible's larger themes, though it remains that the identification of God with beauty is clearly scriptural. Just as it would be absurd to pretend the biblical grounding for beauty as an attribute of God is either very wide or very deep, it makes equally little sense, in the face of the scriptural affirmations, to assign the Christian tradition's identification of beauty as an attribute of God to Platonic influence—certainly not alone, and perhaps not even in significant part. Although one of the Christian theologians who reflected most deeply on beauty, Augustine, has sometimes been characterized as a belatedly and barely baptized Neoplatonist, others could not be so described: Jonathan Edwards, for example, is not generally accused of intoxication from drinking too deeply at the well of Platonism, and since his conception of divine beauty seems little dependent on Augustine, he cannot even be charged with influence once removed, yet his theology is charged with the conviction that divine nature is beautiful.[3] Likewise, although John of the Cross no doubt knew Augustine's works, nothing about the structure or content of his theology smacks of Neoplatonism; yet it, too, is drenched with references to divine beauty.[4] Regardless of the case to be made for Christian aesthetics' debt to Platonism, it must equally be acknowledged to be the legacy of the Bible, taken up by Christians pondering the sacred page, representing modes of biblical engagement from the mystical and apophatic John to the Calvinist Edwards. If beauty figures not much more pervasively in the Christian tradition than in the Bible, it figures in both in a way that argues against dismissing it as an insignificant attribute of God.[5]

The Bible however bequeaths, as it often does, not only an affirmation but also a problem. If God is beauty, what exactly does it mean to assert divine beauty? The Bible attests the beauty of created things, but God's beauty cannot possibly be of the same kind, since the beauty of creatures is generally perceptible to the senses and thus presupposes material instantiation while the Bible insists God is not only beauty but also immaterial spirit. If beauty is to be predicated of both God and creatures, then either it means something quite different in each case or there is a root meaning of "beauty" which can be separated out from material instantiation and sense perception, in which case, we would need to specify what this is, precisely. To this conundrum, Augustine offers a potential answer.

Augustine's aesthetics is heavily dependent on a numerical base.[6] His high esteem for music as one of the highest forms of art, if not the highest, reflects his arithmetical preoccupations. The numerical base essentially suggests beauty is about proportion, notably, the relation of parts to each other and to the whole in which they subsist. While this kind of proportionality might seem to pertain solely to the material world (describing the dimensions of buildings or the composition of paintings, for example), it also describes the relation of musical systems to each other (such as the different parts of a vocal score). Proportion of this latter kind is more obviously grounded in sheerly mathematical relations. Although the numerical base and the appeal to proportion go some way toward dislodging the concept of beauty from the more overt forms of attachment to the material world, they entail problems of their own when applied to divine nature, notably, potential collision with the doctrine of divine simplicity. One might get around this problem by jettisoning simplicity as an attribute of God, but neither Augustine nor any other patristic theologian (to my knowledge) does so. Despite its lack of any indisputable biblical pedigree, simplicity ensconced itself early and firmly in Christian theology.[7]

Augustine's theology does not lack for resources to address this issue, though he himself does not do so in quite the terms I will suggest.[8] One of Augustine's most potent suggestions is that "beauty" names the power to attract;[9] that which is beautiful is, quite simply, attractive, not in the sense of being merely appealing in some vague or bland way, but in the sense of drawing others to itself, we might even say, arousing desire for itself. If what it means to be beautiful is to possess the power to attract, then beauty must be said to have an inherently relational quality. This relational dimension is implicit in Augustine's aesthetics, though he does not allude to it as such. Picking up on this latent element in his thought, we could view beauty as a dynamic bond between perceiver and perceived, forged by this quality. Beauty might therefore be conceived of not only as a quality inhering in objects or entities labeled "beauty" or "beautiful" but also as a transaction between two entities, and what subsists between them in virtue of their relation to each other.[10]

In *Confessions*, Augustine does not precisely specify what it is that might attract, but his arithmetical predilections suggest that the qualities of the material things we deem beautiful reduce to abstract principles: "proportion" can label the relation of lines, masses, or sounds. Inasmuch as we could call the harmony of a piece of music or of the dimensions of a building well proportioned, we are saying that such different entities as sounds and stones might have at their root a commonality, namely, their reducibility to numerical expression, indeed their instantiation of numerical values. Extending a little further, we might say that the arithmetical proportionality familiar to us from its instantiation in material things, including the evanescent materiality of music, expresses a rationally perceptible relationality, a set of relations which are satisfying to the intellect and attract the intellect to the ground of all relation, the supremely intelligible divine nature.[11] (This is not to say, of course, that we *only* find music or architecture beautiful when we have analyzed it down to its basic proportions and are explicitly aware of these.) If we pursue this line of thinking, we could say that "beauty" labels the power of that which is rationally intelligible to attract other rational entities to itself, thereby forging a relationship between itself and them, a relationship profoundly shaped by the intellectual structures inherent in perceiver and perceived and the transaction between them. Or to state the matter a little differently, beauty could be parsed as the attractive force of rationality, that which explains why the intelligible is desirable.

The relationality just posited does not match Augustine's conception of the numerical basis of beauty in one important respect: on Augustine's account, the proportions in question are those of the beautiful thing itself, rather than a relation between perceiver and perceived, so the constituents of proportionality—rationality and relationality—seem now to have been teased out from each other, one being allocated to divine nature and the other to the bond between that nature and creatures. The estrangement of the constituents is not as complete as it might seem, however, for beauty could be taken not only as the fact but also the power of attraction, a power that is the condition of the possibility of relationality, even if no relation is actually forged. For this reason, divine nature could be said to be beautiful *in se*, even in the absence of creatures to be attracted to it. It is the attractive *capacity* of that which is supremely rational, or rationality as inherently adorable, adorable even in the absence of any who actually adore.

Here we approach one of the most important broad themes in Augustine's theology: the nature of intellect and will, knowledge and love, and the relations subsisting between these. The faculties of intellect and will and their fruits of knowledge and love are the prime constituents of Augustine's doctrine of God, as well as of his theological anthropology, but he explores them most fully in the context of the doctrine of the Trinity. The latter has the potential to supply many seeds of an Augustinian aesthetic but is too large a subject to be broached here. Instead, I shall focus on the nontrinitarian implications of Augustine's view of intellect and will. When, in the *De Trinitate*, Augustine "appropriates" intellect or knowledge to the second person of the Trinity and will or love to the third (XV.29, 30, 37), he is engaging in a form of speculative rumination rather than dogmatic theology. That is, he is exploring a means of more deeply understanding the doctrine of the Trinity, by understanding the relations of the persons in terms of faculties basic to both the human person and divine nature. He is not, of course, identifying intellect with the Word in some way that would imply that the Father and the Spirit are devoid of it, or asserting love as somehow the exclusive property of the Spirit. The point of appropriating these faculties or qualities to one of the persons is to understand relationality: the relation of the persons to each other, their relation to human persons, and the relations of these faculties in the human soul. The exercise is pursued on the assumption that the soul is the created entity that most closely resembles God and that therefore offers the best heuristic device for helping us to understand the divine Other. The heuristic device can only function as such, however, if the relation of intellect and will from which Augustine reasons is necessary, not merely something that often happens to be the case in the human sphere. The ultimate grounding of the position is the doctrine of God undergirding the whole, a doctrine which assumes divine nature is both intellectual and volitional. This point is generally missed in the flurry of controversy over the work's anthropological speculations, the exploration of *vestigia Trinitatis*, which have often been taken as the attempt to prove divine triunity by reasoning from the tripartite nature of the human soul. What the *vestigia* in fact illuminate is the multifaceted relationality of intellect and will, a relationality that obtains, in the first instance, in divine nature, and which from this basis grounds, not only the created likeness of humankind to God, but also the creature's rapprochement to God. The issue is not solely the one pursued at length in the *De Trinitate*—the chicken-and-egg question of which faculty is logically and chronologically prior[12]—but the way in which the two faculties work together to draw the rational creature toward the Trinity. The priority question asks whether knowledge incites desire (i.e., whether we first know something, and this knowledge attracts us to it) or whether love spurs us to acquire knowledge (loving something, we desire to know it better). There is a good case to be made for either, as Augustine acknowledges, but what is significant for the present purposes is simply how thoroughly entangled knowledge and love are taken to be, and how their entangling serves to draw us more deeply into the "thicket" of divine life.[13]

The notion that knowledge and love, much less intellect and will, are necessarily related is not self-evident. A lot of the mythological and literary tradition dealing with romantic love, for example, portrays love (or what passes for love) as often based on delusion or self-deception.[14] Augustine's schema, in contrast, insists that real love is always based on knowledge of love's object; love can increase the desire to know, but some real knowledge of a thing is necessary before it can be loved in any meaningful way. This is not the same as love of knowledge for its own sake but love based on and then prompting knowledge of the beloved. The catch is that in Augustine's scheme, the Beloved is rationality itself, Logos.

With this insight in mind we may return to reflect on the notion of beauty as the power of attraction. If divine nature is beautiful, then, on Augustinian reasoning, it is attractive. To what, though, does it attract? Is there any quality denoted by "beauty" or "beautiful" that explains why the attractive is able to attract? The answer, I would suggest, is *ratio*. "Beauty" labels the power of *ratio* to draw and hold our attention; its power to delight suggests the sheer desirability of what is susceptible of caress by the mind's lingering gaze. This suggestion correlates to other elements of Augustine's aesthetics ("correlates" is important: it does not restate anything Augustine himself explicitly claims). The strongly numerical basis of Augustine's aesthetic is problematic if applied at the divine level inasmuch as it implies the relation of parts to a whole. The numerical element of the theory can be viewed at a more fundamental level, however: rather than expressing some form of proportionality that assumes composition, it can be taken as articulating the principle of intelligibility, and indeed intelligence itself, the quality of being perceptible to the mind, the capacity for being appreciated by the mind. *Ratio* in this sense is not solely the power *to* think, but the power of delighting the mind. Here, then, lies one form of the relationality of intellect and will, of the mind and desire. The perceiver's delighting in the mind's object indicates two forms of relationality: the knowledgeable and affectionate bond between perceiver and perceived but also a relation within the perceived, in the intertwining of the faculties of intellect and will. That pure rationality or reason (Logos) should be desirable, should invite our devoted attention, is not self-evident: there are more obvious candidates for the object of human aspiration toward the transcendent—love itself, for example. "Beauty" may, however, be taken as naming the desirability of the rational in a way that parses such attraction and makes the very desire for the intelligible itself intelligible to us. Moreover, the act of apprehending beauty unites intellect and will within the one who experiences love for the intelligible. Experiencing beauty may then be seen as the salutary exercise of intellect and will in tandem, the harmonizing of the self. Attempts to specify beauty's qualities in terms of some notion of proportion or harmony that is ultimately mathematical or quasi-mathematical may then be taken as constituting no more than a quest after some means of stipulating the notions of rationality and relationality in their barest form. The qualification offered from the side of the *De Trinitate* is that the relations in question lie not only within the beautiful object, or between the object and the one who views it as beautiful, but also within the perceiver, in the entangling of knowledge and love, analysis and desire.

These realizations, however, form only part of the aesthetics proposed here. To sketch another side of the picture, we return to Augustine, this time picking up an opposing strand of his thought. Alongside his numerical rumination, we find some blunt admissions of the limitations of reason. We do not, after all, he reminds us, sniff a rose and exclaim "how reasonable it is!"[15] Its fragrance can be enjoyed and appreciated specifically as beautiful without our analyzing it, or even being able to analyze it (as a professional "nose" might be able to specify the constituents of its scent). Part of Augustine's point arises from the fact that he has greater regard for some of the physical senses than others. Smell does not rate as highly in his esteem as sight or hearing,[16] so it is significant that he chose the rose's scent as an example of the nonrational dimension of beauty. Whether or not we choose to concur with his hierarchy of senses, his essential point seems unassailable: beauty cannot *only* be a matter of reason, surely? Is there not some element of aesthetic experience that defies explanation, or at the very least does not require some form of analysis as its basis?

Aside from any thesis deriving from a hierarchical ranking of senses, Augustine surely has a point about the immediacy of aesthetic experience. We may be helped to deeper appreciation of the beautiful by engaging in rigorous analysis of its qualities, or even simply because having developed the facility for such analysis, our capacity to appreciate has been formed in such a way that we grasp the "structure" of beauty prior to any formal analyzing. Even so, there are obviously occasions when analysis of any kind is unlikely to be a factor in the experience of beauty: someone can know nothing of music theory and yet find a piece of music beautiful; people without any kind of training in art history still appreciate paintings, and so

on. Even if we were to say that in such cases some inchoate or sub-
conscious discernment of *ratio* comes into play, to the extent that this
is ill-formed or untutored we must acknowledge some factor other
than sheer intellectual acumen to be at work. Rationality may be a
component of the appreciation of beauty, perhaps even its core or
foundation, but it surely cannot be the whole.

Although Augustine beckons us down this path, the numerical
emphasis of his aesthetic may not make him the most fruitful dialogue partner from here on, and so we turn to a thinker who had a
great deal to say about the suprarational and its relation to beauty,
Edmund Burke, one of a clutch of Enlightenment thinkers interested
in the sublime. While one might anticipate an Enlightenment aesthetic could be too strongly marked by deism to serve the purposes
of a Christian account of beauty, and specifically the beauty of the
triune God, in fact Burke's thought marries with that of Augustine in
fruitful ways. One immediate reason that Burke's thought helpfully
complements Augustine's is that he, too, balances the role of reason
with something beyond reason: his appeal to the sublime is not a plea
for irrationality, nor is his appeal to reason based on the naive over-
estimation of human capacities, but he fleshes out the role of the
suprarational in ways Augustine does not.

Burke begins his treatise on the sublime and the beautiful with
a contentious volley: the vast differences in taste that supposedly prevail are more apparent than real, the standard for both reason and
taste being the same in all human beings.[17] This counterintuitive position is based on the assumption that there is far greater agreement
among people about matters of taste than reason.[18] According to
Burke, we are more likely to agree on "the excellence of a description
in Virgil, than on the truth or falshood [*sic*] of a theory of Aristotle"
(207). Perhaps we might incline to say that Burke inhabited a more
culturally and intellectually homogeneous world than we do, and his
confidence in the uniformity of judgments about Virgil is based on
blithe cultural chauvinism. The specifics of Burke's examples perhaps distract us from the force of his point, however. Instead of assuming too much of the uniformity of human taste, Burke might be

taken as anticipating modern debates over the cultural specificity of reasoning;[19] perhaps reason is not so universal after all.

The complexity of reason's role in Burke's aesthetics emerges even more pointedly in the tension he posits between beauty and the sublime. Beauty in his view is mostly a matter of sensible qualities: being small, smooth, varied, not angular, delicate, clearly and brightly colored, with no glaring colors except those that blend into neighboring hues so as to mitigate their harsh effect (276–77). This notion of beauty bears little resemblance to earlier aesthetics, especially since Burke specifically rejects the idea that beauty has anything to do with the proportion of parts (255). Burke's notions of beauty are so idiosyncratic that it might be hard to press them into use in formulating an aesthetic or in understanding the Western tradition of aesthetics, but for the way his concept of beauty contrasts with that of the sublime. While he deems things beautiful because of their delicacy, sublime things inspire terror (216, 289) to the extent that the fear so inspired robs the mind of its power of reasoning (230). Beauty seems therefore quite distinct from the sublime as far as Burke is concerned, a point he makes explicit when he claims an "eternal distinction" between the two (282).[20] The sublime is founded on pain, beauty on pleasure. Ne'er the twain shall meet, it would seem, except that Burke concedes they are sometimes found united. This union does not necessarily mean they are "in any way allied" to Burke's mind; in fact, it might confirm they are opposites, as black and white may blend, even though they are not at all the same (282). The last point constitutes an important qualification in Burke's framework. He is at pains to distinguish, indeed distinguish sharply, the beautiful and the sublime, yet he acknowledges they may be found conjoined,[21] a conjunction already implied in the fact that he chose to treat the two in tandem. It is in the conjunction of these two that the power of Burke's aesthetic lies.

Although Burke's insistence on the terrifying aspect of the sublime may seem to sit ill with any theory that purports to account for beauty as an attribute of God, key elements of it accord fruitfully with a theological aesthetic. For Burke, the sublime is terrifying in large part because of its magnitude: one source of the sublime is infinity (243, 246), although the operative notion of infinity (what he calls "the artificial infinite" [244]) has more in common with mathematical notions of infinity than any theological one. This artificial infinite consists in an uninterrupted progression of uniform elements (244) and is exemplified by the circle or sphere. It is the criterion of uniformity, drawn from his notion of infinity, that causes Burke to judge buildings with a multiplicity of angles to lack in grandeur: their displeasing design stems from "an inordinate thirst for variety" (245). Profusion of a different kind, however, contributes to magnificence, which is another source of the sublime. A starry sky, for example, consists in a great number of things which are splendid or valuable in themselves, and the sight of them therefore "never fails to excite an idea of grandeur" (247). Here the connection between terror and the sublime recedes, terror being replaced by a form of awe less tinged by fear. As secondary effects, the sublime prompts admiration, reverence, and respect (230). Most significantly, for Burke, the fact that the sublime inspires astonishment and some degree of horror (230) means it has a virtually mesmerizing effect, such that "the mind is so entirely filled with its object, that it cannot entertain any other, nor by consequence reason on that object which employs it" (230). The power of the sublime is such that it does not spur the mind to cogitation, but rather "anticipates our reasonings, and hurries us on by an irresistible force" (230). Whether the sublime is seen as evoking fear or reverence, therefore, it has the same effect, urging the mind beyond its own limitations. Burke is here quite close to the sensibilities of both the Bible and older Christian theology and piety, in all of which references to the fear of God abound. The notion that reverence differs fundamentally from fear, or to put the matter more positively, that reverence implies a cozy, trusting relationship antithetical to feeling fear, is a modern one, perhaps tied to the "domestication of transcendence" (to use William Placher's phrase).[22] Although Burke's discussion of the sublime does not edge into explicitly theological territory, his positing of fear and awe as responses to the sublime is at least compatible with what the Bible and the Christian tradition have described as a human response to the divine: an awe in the face of what transcends us, that which unseats our natural capacities.

Although Burke is concerned to separate the sublime from the beautiful, his account of each suggests greater similarity than he himself explicitly allows, specifically, in the relation between object and subject suggested by his scheme. Beauty has, in Burke's view, a social quality, since it gives joy or pleasure in beholding (219; again, he seems to be thinking of beauty largely in visual terms). Beautiful entities inspire tenderness and affection, so that we "willingly enter into a kind of relation with them" (219). We are close here to Augustine's notion of beauty as attraction, a power that forges a relation between object and subject, inspiring as it does so desire on the part of the perceiver. The relation Burke suggests is created by beauty and therefore differs from that created by the sublime in that beauty prompts tenderness and perhaps a certain familiarity, while the sublime seems to distance the apprehender. Although Burke does not explicitly stipulate a relation between perceiving subject and sublime object, as he does with beauty, the reverence or terror the subject is said to feel still implies a bond, albeit a bond of a rather different kind from that which Burke posits of beauty. Reverence, and even terror, need not imply the subject inclines to turn away from the sublime: that which inspires awe may compel the attention (as Rudolf Otto suggested with his notion of *mysterium tremendum et fascinans*). Moreover, Burke's own notion that the sublime moves us by an irresistible force beyond our own capacity to reason suggests one form of attention, if an apparently involuntary one. His notion of movement toward the attractor differs from Augustine's in that the latter seems to be thinking of perceivers moving of their own accord, although drawn by the intrinsic appeal of the perceived. Burke seems to put the impetus more firmly—perhaps exclusively—on the side of the perceived, which pulls the perceiver almost against the latter's own will. In either case, nonetheless, the bond between attractive object and attracted subject is both powerful and dynamic.

If for Burke the relation between the sublime and its perceiver is rational or suprarational, the relation between beauty and its perceiver is more a matter of the heart (Burke's term, 271) than the mind. Although, as we have seen, Burke thinks that we are carried away by the sublime, it is our "reasonings" that are anticipated, and so it would seem he associates the sublime with mental activity, despite the obvious correlation of terror with emotion.[23] Beauty and the sublime are therefore distinct, on Burke's account, not only with respect to the quality of response they evoke but also in terms of what faculty or dimension of the human personality they engage. Nevertheless, as noted earlier, Burke concedes that beauty and the sublime can be conjoined. This point is significant, because in granting it, Burke opens the way to envisaging an entity's being both sublime and beautiful, inspiring both affection and reverence, engaging both the mind and the heart. Such an entity would attract through its approachability and yet exceed the perceivers' grasp, and in exceeding their capacities, confound their own faculties while drawing them beyond.

Burke's aesthetic, at first glance so different from Augustine's, especially in the way it exiles elements of the aesthetic to a supposedly distinct space labeled "the sublime," in fact complements and supplements it. The notion of the sublimely beautiful suggests the possibility that we might be drawn to something that nevertheless inspires awe, even terror, in virtue of its magnitude and magnificence. Burke's idea of the sublime's racing ahead of the mind proposes that the mind might be simultaneously engaged and defeated, its autonomy routed as it continues to be drawn to that which surpasses it. Burke does not use the term *mystery* to denote the quality in the perceived that is capable of both attracting and defeating, but his insistence that the sublime inspires both reverence and terror is formally similar to the idea of mystery, in the way it suggests both the rapprochement of adoration and the distancing of awe. Although neither Augustine's nor Burke's aesthetic leans on the category of mystery, we might ask if the latter does not provide a helpful gloss on the terrain each has traced, as well as indicate a means by which the insight of each aesthetic might be yoked together and harnessed for new ends.

First, however, it might be as well to clear away a preliminary objection to the category "mystery." The chief of these is that "mystery" is merely a dodge, the refuge of bad theology when it can no longer provide an adequate account of itself. In this case, the culpable vagueness might consist in refusing to specify content for the notions of beauty or the sublime. The answer to this charge is that in this instance the appeal to the category of mystery serves not to foreclose reflection on the content of the attendant concepts but quite the opposite: to show how, in an Augustinian-Burkean aesthetic, "mystery" labels beauty's power to appeal to the mind and transcend its limitations.

To sketch such an aesthetic, let's begin from the Augustinian assumption that beauty appeals to the mind and not only to the senses. In following this suggestion, we fall in line with a broad trajectory of Western aesthetics but differ from Burke. Beauty's appeal to the mind, which Augustine conceives of chiefly as a matter of the appreciation of proportion, can be understood in slightly broader terms as the perception of relationality. The notion of relationality appears in Augustine's aesthetic in the suggestion that beauty is a matter of the interrelation of parts to each other and to the whole that is the beautiful itself, but also in the notion that "beauty" labels what attracts a perceiver. For Augustine, the beautiful attractor would above all be God, since divine nature is not only beautiful, but the most perfect form of beauty, the ground of all other beauties. For Burke, in contrast, the beautiful may attract, but the sublime distances the perceiver by inspiring awe and even terror, and he identifies neither the beautiful nor the sublime explicitly with God. The distancing he proposes, however, still implies relationality. If the relations Burke posits between the beautiful and its perceiver, and the sublime and its perceiver, differ markedly from each other, his acknowledgment that the beautiful and the sublime may be found combined allows that the same entity could inspire both tender attraction and awe. The relation between perceiver and perceived would then be construed as both complex with respect to the response evoked in the perceiver and complex in terms of the faculties engaged in the experience of apprehending beauty. Augustine's account stresses the motion of the will as it is attracted, but even more, the mind's activity and subsequent rest in contemplation. Burke's denial of the mind's involvement in the appreciation of beauty is counterbalanced by his acknowledgment of its soaring to reverence and terror before the sublime. The introduction of the category "mystery" here expresses the creative tensions arising from this combination. The mind could be viewed as at once engaged and attracted, and yet dwarfed, by the enormity of that which it contemplates, trembling before that which it seeks, loves, and reveres. It can both operate by its own power and be empowered by the object of its attention, which draws it inexorably toward that which it does not, and of its own accord cannot, attain. If Burke's notion of terror suggests retreat and withdrawal but also impulsion toward the perceived, his concept of awe suggests tarrying before what surpasses the revering subject's every attempt to grasp. In this respect, he approaches the Augustinian notion of contemplation.[24]

The relationality proposed in this schema is therefore of simultaneous attraction and the averting of a bedazzled gaze, of the simultaneous apprehension and evanescence of the object of the mind's desire. Just so, mystery can be read as the intellect's defeat, but a defeat in which the mind's gaze is not deflected but enthralled. "Mystery" here does not denote the mind's foreclosure but its soaring in wonder, impelled by a force greater than itself, a force that draws perceivers onward, even if almost in spite of themselves. The mind's defeat, therefore, is not in this instance its undoing. Indeed, quite the opposite: when the mind's own powers prove inadequate to its aspirations, it is drawn all the more surely toward its object, lured and borne by the power of that object itself, the perceived's desire for the perceiver. The synthesis of Augustine and Burke results in a scheme in which the mind is viewed as engaged, both actively and passively, in both what it attains by its own effort and what it attains to through the ravishing of its faculties and the vanquishing of its autonomy. Surprisingly, perhaps, it is Burke's notion of the mind's being drawn by a force greater than itself that correlates to a Christian doctrine of grace, much more so than any element of Augustine's aesthetics, although Burke himself does not speak in such terms.

"Mystery" can therefore be taken as labeling one element of the intricate web of relations wrought by the apprehension of the sublimely beautiful. "Mystery" denotes the power of beauty to engage the faculties of intellect and will by both satisfying them and leaving them desiring more from the object of their attention. The ultimately but mysteriously beautiful can therefore be conceived as that which exceeds the possibility of consummation, yet without frustrating desire. To envisage how desire might not be extinguished, even in the face of the postponement of consummation, we might turn to a different well of the Christian tradition, and replace Burke's "artificial infinity" of a never-ending sequence with a notion of infinity drawn from the Cappadocian Fathers. Here the infinite denotes that which is boundless and unconditioned, rather than Burke's interminable iteration of finite elements. This boundlessness is conceived in the theology of Gregory Nyssen as a governing attribute, that is, one which stipulates the quality of other attributes, since for Nyssen divine infinity indicates the character of holiness. Because divine holiness is unlimited, what it means for humankind to be sanctified is to embark on a process of transformation which must be never-ending because the nature that is perfect holiness is itself infinite. The conjunction of holiness and infinity is, however, in one respect more straightforward to assert than predicating both beauty and infinity of divine nature. Beauty seems to require form, and if infinity is taken as boundlessness, there would appear to be little possibility of the same entity's being both beautiful and infinite. Nyssen's working out of the anthropological ramifications of infinite holiness may, however, provide a helpful paradigm.[25] On his account, the saints are in a state of continual sanctification, and remain in this state of spiritual growth everlastingly, because the telos of sanctification is participation in the infinitely holy. "Telos" in this instance therefore ironically denotes that which is without term, although this state of perpetual motion toward the divine is also a state of union with God; it denotes what has been attained, yet remains ever beyond our possessing.

An Augustinian-Burkean aesthetic, qualified or extended by a Cappadocian concept of infinity, might propose that beauty satisfies the mind's desire for rational order or intellectual structure while simultaneously and endlessly drawing it beyond its own capacity to understand, because the ultimately beautiful is the Infinite. The mind's delight would be taken as consisting neither solely in satisfaction, nor in the pursuit of an ever fugitive consummation, but in both. Inasmuch as this pattern of simultaneous attainment and non-attainment, apprehension without comprehension, is that of an ancient Christian understanding of union with divine nature, a theological aesthetic has now been sketched which accords with and is illuminated by a doctrine of sanctification. So we are led back to the traditional conjunction of beauty and holiness found in writers like Edwards, and to the ancient Christian assertion of simplicity, or the indivisibility of divine attributes, in virtue of which divine beauty is just what God is, as is divine holiness: the exhaustible well, the summit which only discloses the vista of yet higher peaks.

This assertion of simplicity, at first glance so troublesome for a Christian aesthetic, now may aid in showing the unity of divine attributes grounded in scripture. As divine beauty, holiness and infinity are identical in divine nature—simply what that nature is, in essence—so human persons who are ordered to the divine source and ground of their being will find that their relation to beauty formally resembles their relation to holiness. Both patterns of relationality are conditioned by divine infinity and the mystery of life in the Trinity—a life in which we know and yet do not comprehend, attain, only to find we have reached out to touch an *au-delà* that lies ever beyond our grasp. This beauty satisfies *because* it is inexhaustible, and while its very limitlessness is terrifying to the finite creature, it tenders its own consolations, precisely because it assures us that our smallness is not the final word: the horizons our minds can almost envisage are not entirely beyond us, despite the finitude of our capacities. It is in the nature of aesthetic experience, grounded in the awareness that true beauty is divine, both to feel dwarfed by the immensity of that beauty and yet to yearn to know it, and seized by this yearning, to love. It is the pattern Rilke envisaged in his portrayal of the Annunciation, the encounter of two creatures in a numinous moment bearing tidings of a new advent of the divine into the world of finitude, a moment of fearful apprehension of beauty, crystallized in the confines of poetic form:

Not that he entered, the angel,
But that he so inclined
The face of a youth to her, closely,
That his glance and hers,
As she looked up, collided,
As if all outside were suddenly void,
And what millions looked at, pursued, bore,
Pressed into her; only she and he;
Beholding and Beheld, Eye and Eye's Feast,[26]
Nowhere else but in this place—: see,
This startles. And both started.

Then the angel sang his melody.[27]

NOTES

1. Andrew Ashfield and Peter de Bolla concur with what they see as the standard reading of the history of aesthetics, which elevates the eighteenth-century tradition of the sublime to the supreme moment in that history, on the ground that this was the era when there was a change in epistemology from one based in "the old certainties" of a predominantly religious culture to one in which "man must find from within himself the grounds of knowledge" (Introduction to *The Sublime: A Reader in British Eighteenth-Century Aesthetic Theory*, ed. Andrew Ashfield and Peter de Bolla [Cambridge: Cambridge University Press, 1996], 1). On this account, the definitive moment in aesthetics is when it finally dispenses with God. Adam Phillips claims that Burke's *Enquiry*, which will be examined later in this essay, offers "the beginnings of a secular language of profound human experience" of the sublime and the beautiful (Introduction to *A Philosophical Enquiry into the Origins of Our Ideas of the Sublime and the Beautiful* [Oxford: Oxford University Press, 1998], xi), and Carol Harrison considers that even the Christian theological tradition neglected beauty (*Beauty and Revelation in the Thought of Saint Augustine* [Oxford: Clarendon Press, 1992], 270).

2. Speakers of English may be surprised that there are so few references to God as beauty, if they know the Authorized Version of the Bible or the Coverdale translation of the Psalms used in the Book of Common Prayer. For Ps. 96:9, both of the latter read "worship the Lord in the beauty of holiness" (cp. AV Ps. 29:2; 1 Chron. 16:29; 2 Chron. 20:21), wording which, by identifying

beauty with holiness, incontestably an attribute of God, implies that beauty is itself divine. The relevant Hebrew word in these verses does not, however, really denote beauty, and later versions have corrected the AV with translations of "holy array" (RSV), "holy splendor" (NLT, NRSV), "splendor of holiness" (NJB, NLT, REB, TNIV), or "holy attire" (ESV, NET, REB) or in some completely different rendering altogether (GNB, NJB, NET, Tanakh).

3. Robert Jenson makes passing reference to Edwards's "Platonizing warrants of thought" but himself gives no justification for this assumption of Platonic influence (*America's Theologian: A Recommendation of Jonathan Edwards* [New York: Oxford University Press, 1988], 170).

4. For just a few examples, see *Subida del monte Carmelo* I.4; the commentary on *Cántico spiritual* 5–6, 11, 24; *Llama de amor viva* 3.14, in *S. Juan de la Cruz obras completas*, 8th ed., ed. Eulogio Pacho (Burgos: Editorial Monte Carmelo, 2003).

5. One could query whether *any* attribute of God could be considered insignificant: if scripture is taken as divine self-disclosure, then what would warrant our ignoring any part of what it reveals about the God we worship?

6. Harrison makes this clear (*Beauty and Revelation*, 22), as does Montague Brown ("Augustine on Beauty, Number and Form," *Studia Patristica* 43 [2006]: 33), although he dislodges Augustine's thought from a sheerly arithmetical preoccupation when he claims that for the latter, number is "the intrinsic intelligibility of things" (33).

7. Simplicity is not, as Nicholas Wolterstorff asserts, a medieval import into Christian theology. See "Divine Simplicity," in "Philosophy of Religion," ed. James E. Tomberlin, special issue, *Philosophical Perspectives* 5, (Atascadero, CA: Ridgeview, 1991), 531–52. For a convenient (though brief) discussion and collection of references to simplicity in patristic theology, see G. L. Prestige, *God in Patristic Thought*, 2nd ed. (London: SPCK, 1952), especially 9–11 on indivisibility. His examples are by no means exhaustive.

8. Harrison associates Augustine's conception of beauty wholly with matter and the senses and claims this as the reason beauty is the most ambivalent of the transcendentals (*Beauty and Revelation*, 270, 271). Robert J. O'Connell, in contrast, considers that for Augustine the beauties of the sense world are all derived beauties (*Art and the Christian Intelligence in St Augustine* [Oxford: Blackwell, 1978], 55) and that divine beauty is therefore beauty in its prime form.

9. *Conf.* I.i.1 and II.v.10.

10. This is not the only kind of relationality to which one might appeal in constructing an aesthetic along Augustinian lines, since there are also possible Christological and trinitarian approaches that could prove fruitful, but considerations of space forbid my broaching those here. Others have looked to Augustine's trinitarian theology as a source for his aesthetics: Maarten

Wisse holds that the *De Trinitate* is Augustine's most significant work of aesthetics ("Augustine's Trinitarian Aesthetics in *De Trinitate*," in *Aesthetics as a Religious Factor in Eastern and Western Christianity*, ed. Will van der Bercken and Jonathan Sutton [Leuven: Peeters, 2005], 405), though he is taking aesthetics in a narrow (but quite legitimate) sense.

11. Here I am leaning on Aquinas's notion of divine nature as supremely intelligible. By this, he of course does not mean that God is somehow utterly transparent to created minds: what is in itself intelligible may not be so to a particular intellect (*Summa theologiae*, I.12, 1 resp.).

12. Augustine dwells on this issue repeatedly in Books VII–X of *De Trinitate*. His basic answer is that some sort of knowledge always precedes love (see, e.g., VIII.6, 8; IX.3; X.2, 15).

13. I am here borrowing an image from John of the Cross (*Cántico spiritual* B, 36; commentary 36.9–11).

14. There are examples in various mythologies, from Oedipus's unwitting marriage to his mother to Kullervo's unwitting seduction of his sister in the *Kalevala*. The theme of misguided love figures in *A Midsummer Night's Dream* (Helena's hopeless infatuation with Demetrius and Titania's fairy potion–induced passion for Bottom); in *War and Peace* (Pierre's becoming enamored of Hélène, only to find her soul is not as beautiful as her shoulders); in *Middlemarch* (Dorothea's falling for Casaubon and her gradual discovery that he is neither as high-minded nor as scholarly as she imagined); in *Faust*, Part I (Marguerite's seduction by Faust); and in *Don Quixote* (the Don's love for Dulcinea, who is neither the great lady nor the blonde of his fantasies). Deception and awakening to truth both figure in Dante's dream of the Siren in Purgatorio 19.

15. *De ordine* II.32–35.

16. *De ordine* II.32; and *De libero arbitrio* II.16–19, 38.

17. Edmund Burke, *A Philosophical Enquiry into the Origin of Our Ideas of the Sublime and the Beautiful*, in *The Writings and Speeches of Edmund Burke*, vol. 1: *The Early Writings*, ed. T. O. McLoughlin and James T. Boulton (Oxford: Clarendon Press, 1997), 196. Subsequent citations given in the text in parenthesis.

18. Burke's view of taste is complex, however. Taste is, he maintains (noting in an aside "whatever it is"), improved by good judgment, by extending our knowledge, through attention to the object and frequent exercise (209). Taste therefore seems to be very much a matter of the mind, its conscientious and tutored use.

19. See, e.g., Paul Feyerabend, *Against Method*, rev. ed. (London: Verso, 1988), 231, 243. Skeptical modern views about the universality of any one rationality are expressed by Richard J. Bernstein, *Beyond Objectivism and Relativism: Science, Hermeneutics and Praxis* (Oxford: Blackwell, 1983); and

Robert Audi, *The Architecture of Reason: The Structure and Substance of Rationality* (Oxford: Oxford University Press, 2001), among others.

20. Tom Furniss goes so far as to claim Burke holds the sublime and the beautiful to be utterly opposed to one another (*Edmund Burke's Aesthetic Ideology: Language, Gender and Political Economy in Revolution* [Cambridge: Cambridge University Press, 1993], 19). The central task of the *Enquiry*, on his reading, is "to develop a set of principles which will demonstrate this mutual repugnance" (8). Furniss does not take adequate account of the qualification which Burke makes later in the treatise. His claim that the sublime's importance for Burke is that it acts as a means of "staving off the devastating effects of beauty" (38) is also contestable.

21. One way of accounting for the simultaneous rift between and conjunction of the beautiful and the sublime in Burke's thought is to deem it "dichotomized," as Carsten Zelle does, a tendency he sees not only in Burke but also in Boileau and various German writers ("Beauty and Horror: On the Dichotomy of Beauty and the Sublime in Eighteenth-Century Aesthetics," *Studies in Voltaire and the Eighteenth Century* 305 [1992]: 1542–45). He sees a "dual aesthetic" reaching from Burke perhaps even to Lyotard (1544) and asks whether Klopstock's rejection of the beautiful in favor of the sublime could be connected to George Steiner's resacralized view of the arts (1545).

22. See William Placher, *The Domestication of Transcendence: How Modern Thinking about God Went Wrong* (Louisville, KY: Westminster John Knox), 1996.

23. Thus I differ from Phillips, who interprets Burke as holding that the sublime makes reasoning altogether impossible (Introduction, xxii).

24. For just a few examples, see *Conf.* IX.10; XII.15; and *De Trinitate* I.20, 27, 31; IV.24; VII.6; XII.22; XIII.2, 24; XV.45.

25. See *De vita Moysis* PG 44.401A–B; 404.B ff.; *In Cantica Cantorum* VIII (PG 44.940D–941C); and Jean Daniélou's account of "epectasis" in his Introduction to *From Glory to Glory: Texts from Gregory of Nyssa's Mystical Writings* (Crestwood, NY: St. Vladimir's Seminary Press, 1995), 46–71.

26. A rather free rendering of "*Augenweide.*"

27. The translation is my own. The German, "Mariä Verkündigung," may be found in *Das Marien-Leben*, a public domain edition of which is available at www.amazon.de/Das-Marien-Leben-Rainer-Maria-Rilke-ebook/dp/B004SYA1SU/ref=sr_1_1?s=digital-text&ie=UTF8&qid=1399640532&sr=1–1&keywords=Rilke+das+marienleben.

FOUR

Using Reason to Derive Mutual Illumination from Diverse Traditions

DAVID BURRELL, C.S.C.

I would like to illustrate medieval dialectics between faith and reason by more contemporary inquiry relating different faiths to one another, as a way of mining the major theme of Benedict's Regensburg address (minus the extraneous and distracting asides about Islam) to show how it encapsulates Denys Turner's artful exposition of the fruitful range of human reason.[1] In the process I shall employ Deirdre Carabine's masterful interweaving of the church fathers' use of the negative valence of human reason to display its potentially infinite reach—a cognate theme of Turner's work. These two themes converge in Nicholas of Cusa's animadversions about *docta ignorantia* to celebrate the way liminal reaches of reason surpass any pretense of "figuring things out" or offer a definitive articulation of the kind which some philosophers deem to be their office to accomplish.[2] For both Carabine and Turner remind us vividly how jejune it is baldly to oppose "negative" to "positive" attempts to state anything truthfully about the God we worship as "creator of heaven and earth and all that is between them."[3]

Our guide here will be Proclus as Deirdre Carabine encapsulates him: in attempting to speak of God, our positive intent may have to be rendered negatively to retain its force.[4] Aquinas articulates the reason for this by noting laconically that human language can at best "imperfectly signify" divinity (*ST* 1.13.3). Expanded slightly, that observation warns that we will get it wrong much of the time, as the glass half full will also be half empty. More analytically, we are reminded that human language directed to divinity, used straight off, as it were, cannot help pretending to be adequate to the task, so will invariably falsify its subject. That caveat will operate to discriminate sheep from goats among philosophical theologians, separating those judicious in their choice of idiom from those heedless enough about history and hermeneutics to unwittingly presume prevailing philosophical categories to be adequate in this domain. Here our guide will be Olivier-Thomas Venard, O.P., as he delineates the artful way Thomas Aquinas displays the inadequacy of human language to articulate divinity, as Denys Turner calls our attention to cognate yet quite different strategies employed by Meister Eckhart.[5] All this should recall the counsel of Wittgenstein—that reason display its virtuosity by carefully attending to the language we employ, in this case regarding divinity, as will emerge tellingly in comparative theological inquiry.

But first let us explore what is wrong with an uncritical use of current philosophical strategies to amplify what analytic philosophers call "our intuitions" when assessing attempts to speak of God, thereby unwittingly broadcasting their cultural myopia. Aristotle regularly begins with our shared speech, of course, yet invariably submits it to searching comparative criticism. A particularly egregious example is the way Alvin Plantinga can blithely invoke the "existential operator" to insist "there is such a person as God." Recalling how often his discourse is in the service of apologetics, this is as if to say, is this what atheists pretend to deny? Anyone classically trained would have to respond thus: if they were to deny the person so picked out, they could hardly qualify as atheists, for one so identified could never count as creator of heaven and earth. On the contrary, in pretending to identify the God they worship in so crude a fashion—"there is such a person as God"—believers offer unwitting testimony to their own idolatry.[6] For one so identified could be nothing more than "the biggest things around," as Barry Miller has decisively shown with regard to "perfect being theology."[7]

Yet it is hardly surprising, in so privileged yet restricted a milieu as academe, that prevailing strategies would prevail over critical discernment, despite the watchword "critical thinking." We might well expect one engaged in the inquiry called philosophy of religion to privilege philosophical categories in a way that minimizes or even deliberately overlooks the variety of ways in which revelation challenges those very categories, for that discipline was constructed in the full light of modernity. Yet when a group trained in that manner begins, for whatever reasons, to style themselves as "philosophical theologians," their insouciance regarding issues critical to that classical discipline cannot but show their inadequacy to the task. Take, for example, the key issue of divine *simpleness*. I endorse the term employed by Timothy McDermott to render *simplicitas* for the Blackfriars edition of Aquinas's *Summa theologiae* because the convenient English term *simplicity* might connote that we are speaking directly of a *feature* of divinity. I say "might connote," for a perusal of "simplicity" as a criterion for choice among theories in scientific inquiry would quickly disabuse us of that presumption: "simplicity" cannot be reduced to a sense sufficiently univocal to name a feature. The constructed term *simpleness*, however, can remind us that we are speaking here of a "formal feature" of divinity: that is, a linguistic warning to alert us to metaphysical difference.[8] Indeed, both David Braine and Brian Davies have reminded us how our insisting that the God we worship, the creator of heaven and earth, must be *simple* introduces a corollary of what Robert Sokolowski calls "the distinction of creator from creation."[9] For what distinguishes creatures from their creator is precisely that they are *composed* of *essence* and *existing* (*esse*), whereas God, to be creator, cannot but be that One whose essence is simply to be. The metaphysical distinction between *essence* and *existing*, articulated by Avicenna and elaborated by Aquinas, offers a succinct way of articulating how things in the world display their constitutive relation to their source by way of their *composition*, so showing themselves to be creatures.

Yet if this reasoning can be both elegant and persuasive to those like Avicenna and Maimonides, formed in classical thought while steeped in a revelatory tradition grounded in free creation, it regularly eludes moderns in an intellectual milieu quite oblivious of creation. This observation suggests the first reason that adopting current philosophical strategies with regard to divinity will inevitably falsify the subject intended, for those very strategies were constructed to facilitate inquiry into a universe from which creation had effectively been bracketed: "we have no need of that hypothesis." For what it may be worth, let me offer a schematic defense of that contention, recalling the usual division, redolent of Hegel: premodern, modern, postmodern, which readily identified "modern" with "critical," and "premodern" with "precritical," so leaving "postmodern" quite up in the air—indeed, open to the trivial "anything goes." So let us rather offer a new periodization of philosophy, promising a proper sense to "postmodern" as well as showing how contemporary (rather than "premodern" or "precritical") are the Jewish, Christian, Muslim reflections on creation initiated in the medieval period. Instead of the vague "premodern," we begin with the acknowledged beginnings of Western philosophy, using the variable *post-* to mark succeeding stages:

> Hellenic
> Medieval = post-Hellenic (by introduction of a free creator)
> Modern = postmedieval (by removing the creator), that is: post (post-Hellenic)
> Postmodern = post (postmedieval), that is: post (post [post-Hellenic])

Here the various uses of "post-" will differ, either by adding or subtracting to the previous configuration, yet the upshot suggests that the "postmodern" context in which we find ourselves bears startling affinities with the "post-Hellenic" (or medieval) context of Jewish, Christian, and Islamic attempts to introduce a free creator into the seamless garment of Hellenic philosophy.

Note how this fresh periodization works by decentering *modernity* from the customary "premodern, modern, postmodern" triad, wherein medieval thought is identified with both the "premodern" and "precritical," while respectable philosophy is identified with the "modern" and "critical." Yet this very configuration, so long in possession, would prove unstable once its foundation in "self-evident truths" began to dissolve—negatively with Richard Rorty, who signaled the "end of philosophy [so conceived]," yet positively with Hans-Georg Gadamer. To discern the difference and to illuminate the references to these two persons, let us try the new scheme. The affinity between *postmodern* and *medieval* turns on *modernity's* rejection of a creator, and with it, faith as a mode of knowing. Cultural reasons for having rejected a creator abound, usually coalescing around Europe's exhaustion with the prolonged and acerbic religious conflict in the wake of the Reformation. Philosophically, the foundational rationalism of Descartes removed any fiduciary element from knowing, rendering *knowledge* and *faith* mutually exclusive, whereas Gadamer illustrated how reason in its multifarious uses inevitably presumes a constituent trust. Moreover, this opposition marked early twentieth-century Thomism as well, revealing how much it embodied the culture of its times, in stark contrast to the appropriately "postmodern" presentation of the mutuality of faith and reason in John Paul II's encyclical appropriately named *Fides et Ratio*.[10]

For those who might find it perspicuous, a scheme like this one can show how it comes about that modern categories prove to be insufficient in articulating a creator, so have spawned a perplexing variety of counterpositions known as "postmodern." Yet another feature of modernity, however, has not merely proved insufficient for theology, but in fact lethal to countless human beings and to the earth, though it is still operative among us. It is epitomized in the same penchant to divide "modern" from "premodern," where "modern" is presumed to exemplify the unprecedented human achievement of critical thought, otherwise known as "the Enlightenment." Recent residence in Israel-Palestine and in East Africa has brought me to make Foucault's analysis my own: reason so conceived easily transmogrifies into power, or perhaps better: reason so delineated has little or no capacity to resist being co-opted in the service of power, as it serves to justify using power to our advantage while unable to temper the destructive effects of that use. And as the geographic distribution of humanity and human resources seemed to ordain, "the Enlightenment" justified the systemic practice of enslaving one portion of humanity to serve another portion (the "enlightened" part), while that practice itself (called "colonization") financed the Enlightenment.

Now I am hardly alone in suggesting the collusion between *enlightenment* and *colonization* is the "dirty little secret" of so-called Western civilization (which Gandhi suggested "would be a good idea"). Europeans found it convenient to engage in this practice when that other portion of humanity was separated by extensive oceans and so only recently "discovered," but Brits had only to traverse the Irish Sea to engage in practices designed to turn an entire people into "internally displaced persons"—hardly a contemporary category. But you ask, what can we do besides regret what happened? The answer is, we can reflect on what constitutes the "we" in that innocent query. For if we are inclined to think of all inhabitants of the earth as human beings, then how could *we* act as we did, in a prolonged and systemic fashion? Quite obviously we thought of ourselves as superior, and superior precisely in our way of using reason. So what had "reason" become if that same reason could justify untold horrors against others presumed to be human and so rational? Yet it takes more than logical reflection on varieties of rationality; it takes intercultural experiences to further enlighten those of us trained in Enlightenment ways of knowing to see how power-laden is the facile periodization into premodern and modern and so suggest why the following postmodern phase would inevitably be (for the most part) wild and wooly.

I propose this critical aperture on *our* characteristic practices—both intellectual and exploitative—in the face of Charles Taylor's long-standing and articulate reminders to those inclined to emphasize the downsides of the Enlightenment: we are all its children. Yet I also see in his most recent extensive exploration of "the secular age," notably in the sections offering alternatives (by way of heroic individuals), a decidedly critical reassessment of his earlier reminders to Enlightenment critics, though now proceeding at an irenic and stately pace.[11] Yet as extensive as it is, that work bears no reference to the still-colonized portions of humanity, and little reference to the practice itself. Yet "colonization" offers a pregnant metaphor for a distortion of reason peculiar to modernity to which Taylor and others have called attention: "knowledge as representation." For so long as one contends that to know something, we must first *represent* that object to ourselves, then whatever we know will necessarily be refracted through the practices endemic to our intellectual formation, with little chance of learning anything new, as the only way we have of knowing "the other" will be by colonizing them. Yet the Aristotelian tradition, as assimilated and developed by Islamic, Jewish, and finally Christian thinkers, rather espoused "knowledge by identity," and we shall see how this difference can offer a staunch alterative to Enlightenment reason as it has played itself out.

The path I shall propose to an alternative use and understanding of reason is one which Denys Turner has long traversed as well as illuminated via reflections at once historical and philosophical. Yet it has been explicitly opened to me in a recent collection of essays exploring "theology as poetry" in Dante's *Commedia*, which seeks, in the contribution of its editor, Vittorio Montemaggi, to show how for Dante "to be human, to speak, to love, and to be related to God, are, if properly conceived, one and the same thing."[12] One way of suggesting the power of this reading of Dante is to recall how the attention to language which poetry demands can serve as a healthy antidote to various forms of "conceptualism" we have seen bedevil academic philosophical treatments of the subject of divinity, especially in criticizing what some take to be "negative theology." Nor will it be surprising to find that a volume of incisive authors presenting "theology as poetry" will help ease, if not dissolve, a purported opposition between *cataphatic* and *apophatic* theologies. In fact, the title of Montemaggi's own contribution, "In Unknowability as Love," recalls the way Proclus encloses "the whole process of negation as a preparation for the ultimate goal of unification."[13] If discourse regarding divinity must inevitably be couched in negative terms, that is because it partakes of a movement of desire calling us beyond our selves to the One itself: "the love which moves the sun and the moon and all the stars."

Montemaggi identifies the "theological principle underlying the writing of the *Commedia*: [human beings] ultimately cannot and will not, even in Heaven, fully come to know God; what [human beings] can do and ought to do, and most perfectly will do in Heaven, is to participate in the love which God is" (62). He continues:

> For Dante, the love which God is, and through which everything that is has its being, reflects itself into creation, finding new and particular expression in creatures capable of loving [63–64]. . . . All being, for Dante, originates in God and is constantly sustained in existence by God who is existence itself. As such, full comprehension of God ultimately eludes the grasp of all created beings—angelic or human—since that which is the ground of all existence cannot itself ultimately be reduced to an object of intellectual comprehension [64]. . . . [Yet] this does not . . . imply that for Dante, human beings cannot meaningfully speak about God [but] that the meaning of theological utterances always lies in more than their objective accuracy. To speak meaningfully about God, for Dante, is also always to convey an invitation to others to consider what it might mean to think of one's being as intimately related to the unfathomable and ultimately non-objectifiable love that sets the universe in motion and sustains it in existence [65]. . . . For Dante, then, it is in the nature of the truth which God is, that such a truth cannot be fully comprehended *and* that it can be fully participated in [66].

I have quoted extensively to give a flavor of this remarkable volume, subtitled *Theology as Poetry*, as well as a taste of the way doing theology as poetry can effectively neutralize recurrent antinomies in purported "theology as *scientia*," a strategy which Olivier-Thomas Venard uses extensively in each of his three volumes—*Littérature et théologie: Une saison en enfer* (2002), *La langue de l'ineffable: Essai sur le fondement théologique de la métaphysique* (2004), *Pagina sacra: Le passage de l'Ecriture sainte à l'écriture thélogique* (2009)—and effectively introduces in the first by illustrating the affinities between Aquinas's deft use of prose and Rimbaud's poetry. These remarkable literary-philosophical explorations reveal a vast chasm between a conceptual "Thomism" inattentive to the nuances of language and the keen linguistic genius of Thomas. Moreover, as we are invited to walk through selected cantos with Vittorio, we come to realize how "one's understanding of truth will always be put into question and redefined by one's encounter with other people" (75): theology as a journey of understanding in a community of discourse, where our modes of expression ever remain open to challenge, so that our understanding might be enhanced as we come to recognize how deficient articulation will always be *in divinis*.

Denys Turner's contribution to *Theology as Poetry* presses Montemaggi's keen sense of linguistic potency a further step, to the "performative": "precisely as poetic, the language of the *Commedia* creates and transforms the realities of interaction of which it speaks—it enacts that of which it speaks" (287).[14] To illustrate how prose needs to be modified as well when addressing issues *in divinis*, he details the relevant strategies operative in the preaching of Meister Eckhart, in a manner similar to Venard's delineation of Aquinas's linguistic skills. Moreover, Eckhart's virtuosity represents "a marked shift towards a new self-conscious cultivation of a distinctive theological rhetoric" (288). As readers of Eckhart experience, and Turner avows: "Eckhart the preacher wants theological language in some way to participate, as one might put it, in the event of its own failure, [so that] negativity . . . is a living, organizing feature of the language itself and intrinsic to its compositional style as theological writing" (293). Yet his rhetorical byplay itself depends integrally on the metaphysical framework it expressly challenges: "'How should I love God?' . . . as he is non-God, a nonspirit, a nonperson, a nonimage, but as he is pure, unmixed, bright 'One,' separated from all duality; and in that One we should eternally sink down, out of 'something' into 'nothing'" (192).[15] Yet despite the vast rhetorical difference in their prose, we should also note how Aquinas repeatedly fractures grammar, notably in elucidating the formal demands of *simpleness* by insisting "that nothing can properly be said of God except that 'to be God is to be to-be': that in God essence and *esse* are identical. God is his own being (*suum esse*) (ST 1.10.2), he is subsistent existence itself (*ipsum esse subsistens*) (*ST* 1.11.4), so that to be God is simply to-be (*ST* 1.3.4)."[16] It can hardly be wondered that anyone trained in ordinary English grammar, reinforced by Aristotelian logic, would balk at these assertions. My cryptic formula—"to be God is to be to-be"—is so presented as to display that "to-be" expresses what the formula itself shows we cannot know, the nature of God, since we cannot properly express it. So once again, a binary "positive/negative" test is pointless: the apparently "positive assertions" show by their fractured grammar our inability properly to express the nature of divinity. Aquinas knew what he was doing, for philosophical grammar had become second nature to him.

In a similar vein, a recent study of Moses Maimonides's *Guide for the Perplexed* argues persuasively that Maimonides's predilection for negation in speaking of God results from the semantic sophistication I have noted—statements are composite while the subject in question cannot but be simple—without in any way derogating from our attribution of perfections to divinity.[17] Daniel Davis develops Joel Kraemer's reading of the *Guide* as primarily *dialectical*, explicating just how that approach mediates between the dichotomy Maimonides himself will often invoke between *knowledge* and *opinion*.[18] And in the Islamic tradition, Cécile Bonmariage's study of Mulla Sadra details the linguistic dance which Mulla Sadra consistently executes to show how the existence of any existent is rendered nugatory once one ceases to consider its dependence on the Real Existent. Whether addressing human acts or the reality of particular existence, Mulla Sadra is ever at work to show that we must invoke a specific denial to execute the kind of affirmation which will be able to incorporate inherent reference to the creator who makes all things to be.[19]

Finally, to bring these extensive reflections on language and theology to a dénouement, let me recommend Paul Griffiths's pithy inquiry, *Intellectual Appetite: A Theological Grammar*, for a model exposition reminding us how there can be no viable theology without careful and critical attention to language.[20] Framed, to be sure, by an astute intelligence, the structure of these reflections is effectively internalized so as not to distract the reader with apparatus. So what results? Try the image of a series of exercises to improve the skills needed to find our way through life's obstacle course, or of a scalpel deftly used to lay bare the sinews we exercise in our daily activity. The first image focuses on practice, to which a plethora of examples constantly recalls us; the second alerts us to the fine-grained analysis we will often encounter as well. Both images call attention to the grammar announced in the title. We seldom welcome grammatical corrections until we have come to be grateful for the way they have saved us from gaffes we can observe others make. Appeals to grammar are meant to be liberating rather than dominating, however, and this guidebook into ways of knowing and loving uses careful analysis to liberate us from sentimentality, to realize a healthy relationship to what is good and true in God's creation by offering a "properly Christian account of what it is to want to know" (52), depicting "the way in which you ought to see the world if you are a Christian" (30). His skillful analysis proceeds by way of examples to alert us to healthy or to *damaging* ways we attempt to engage our *world*, focusing on creation as an unmerited *gift* in which creatures are called to *participate* through an *appetite* for *wonder*, yet always ready to be subverted by our tendency to *kidnap* beautiful things which face us so as to *own* them or turn them into titillating *spectacles* to feed our need for *novelty*, stoking our *loquacity* rather than nourishing our *gratitude* (where italics signal the table of contents.)

Griffiths defines the "the principal topic of this book [as] the rational creature's knowing response to the world" (76), or more pointedly: "a depiction of the way you ought to see the world if you are a Christian" (30). By eschewing reliance on modern epistemology (which rather takes its knocks herein), his optic on knowing is far more down to earth, along the lines of Jung's apparently banal "what we do not know, we fear," or Kierkegaard's "children fear the dark; adults know what really to fear." So our need to know, our "wanting to know," as he puts it, is primary, as well as the admonitions about knowing found in biblical wisdom literature, especially Luke 14:33, which admonishes those who would prepare for the real battle of life to "renounce all their possessions." Indeed, this admonition will guide the way he helps us discriminate ersatz from authentic knowing.

Griffiths explores this elementary human need topically by calling on refined discussions which have shaped the Christian tradition over the centuries, beginning each chapter with a pithy quote from Augustine. Yet his treatment of these pregnant issues is also shaped by current debate in philosophical or theological circles, yet sparing readers the usual footnotes. While that strategy is explicitly defended in the final chapter, readers by that time will have come to realize that it displays the principal point of this illuminating journey: contrasting *curiosity* with *studiousness*, or better: *mathesis* with a mode of inquiry which attends to creatures as creatures. "Advocates of mathesis seek, and often take themselves to have found the perfect method of an ensemble of spatialized, discrete objects" (149); where the "magical key is method" (148), with mastery if not ownership the goal, like the skilled seducer who views victims as replaceable objects for his insatiable appetite. Yet "the studious Christian, seeking participatory intimacy driven by wonder and riven by lament, cannot coherently seek ownership" (154), since what is brought into being and sustained by God can only be shared. Lament affects these seekers not simply because they cannot attain what they are after, but because their own propensity to grasp and to possess can bring their original desire to naught. So we are presented with a searing critique, not just of the "entertainment industry" diverting our natural zest for wonder into a feeding frenzy for novelty, but of any form of schooling which hones our skills for knowing in order to satisfy a yearning for power. We are constantly faced with "if the shoe fits, wear it" by an unabashed "Christian advocate of gift, participation, and wonder" (151) toward a universe freely created by a loving God.

So this work is to be pondered, as befits its elaboration, as it traces those propensities, shaped by our culture, which so easily captivate our appetites and distort them. What is at stake is the operative sense faith can give us of ourselves: "A Christian understanding of creatures as *imagines dei*, especially intimate participants in divine gift, is different in almost every interesting respect from an understanding of humans as autonomous beings possessed of a rational will capable of universal species-wide legislation. And each is equally though differently different from an understanding of humans as desire-driven congeries of causally connected event-continua" (116). What marks the principal difference from a Kantian morality or a materialist ideology, and the only thing that can, lies in realizing the implications of avowing the universe to be freely created by a loving God. Yet that is hardly pollyannic but rather utterly realistic: "Our pride, complacency, violence, fear, and so forth, are like . . . a genetic defect or an infection[;] we tend towards these like second nature, whether we like it or not. [Yet] this damage is not restricted to sentient creatures, much less to rational ones. It afflicts the entire cosmos, as Christians should never forget: the cosmos in its entirety groans in anticipation of its salvation to come" (90–91).

The difference which Griffiths is intent on articulating finds primary expression in our characteristic ways of knowing: "Thinking and speaking of creation as the gift of being from nothing, and of creatures as recipients of and participants in that gift, suggest some things to say about what it is for creatures to . . . perform the act of knowing. By definition, this act must establish a relation between knower and known, and this relation will inevitably be . . . a relation between one participant in God and another [since] knower and known share a fundamental likeness and intimacy because each participates in God" (129). Griffiths acknowledges that "participation" is not a *category* but a *figure*, the point of which "is to indicate that it is part of the grammar of the Christian account of things to say that no account of what it is for things to be can be given that does not begin and end with God. This is exactly to reject ontological system and to place ontology where it belongs, which is a part—and always a derived and subsidiary part—of theology" (87). He displays that he knows his "ontology" by showing how those who propose to think "about God in terms of existential quantification and necessity, . . . when pressed tend exactly in the direction of participation, [maybe even sensing] that [their] thinking does not suggest, and tends to contradict, the intimacy between God and creatures intimated by talk of creaturely participation in God, and along with it, an understanding of the intrinsic goodness of creation" (84, 85).

These illustrations are offered to help us taste how the prose this work exhibits is itself an icon of the *intimacy* associated with a conception of knowing which has deliberately replaced a modern fascination with *representation* with a classical predilection for *participation*. And that move is executed by an exacting analysis of what it means to be *gift*, enabling us to approach gingerly and modestly the daunting task of speaking of the universe as gift. For "thinking analogously about God's being is more difficult than any other intellectual enterprise: we grope, we fail, and our failures are magnified by our unwillingness to recognize the depth and scope of what we do not know and of the errors in whose truth we have confidence" (69). Philosophers of religion, take note: this extended essay reads like a meditation of one who has come to appreciate the limits of academic study of religion, and would initiate others into the set of attitudes and practices which can nurture wonder and even intimacy with God. So it can only be read in the spirit of Griffiths's earlier *Religious Reading* (1999), offering academics a challenging transition to *lectio divina*.

Perhaps the best way to prepare readers for this mode of inquiry (if the author will forgive me) is to compare it to Wittgenstein's *Philosophical Investigations*, as one might liken some of Griffiths's earlier work (to continue the trope) to the *Tractatus Logico-Philosophicus*. Nor is the comparison as outrageous as first one might feel. Indeed, a transformation of this sort might even be expected of those reflecting on "things divine" (*in divinis*), much as (reaching for yet another touchstone) John of the Cross signals a normal development toward a more intimate mode of knowing on the part of those who are brought to levels of detachment which foster it. Yet such detachment is not something we undertake but something which happens to us, the very etymology of *suffer*. Here the cumulative images suggesting the intimacy of this mode of knowing certainly move in this direction, as opposed to the ordinary Western metaphor of "dealing with" things. I am often reminded of Aquinas's prescient statement that our best efforts to speak of God amount to "imperfectly signifying divinity" (*ST* 1.13), which means that most of the time we get it wrong. That is the quality of intellectual humility which this inquiry into intellectual appetite intends to foster. Yet the work is hardly limited to or even primarily directed to philosophers of religion. For we are offered a guidebook inviting mature and searching human beings into attitudes appropriate to a universe said to be good by its gracious author, yet one which our possessive propensities ever seek to own and exploit for our own ends, leaving us all face-to-face with what we have come to call "the ecological crisis," yet now become painfully aware of its source. So we are invited on a journey not unlike Dante's, designed to purify our perceptions on the way to clarifying our judgments, and leading us to a conviction similar to the one with which we began, from Vittorio Montemaggi summarizing Dante: manifesting how "to be human, to speak, to love, and to be related to God, are, if properly conceived, one and the same thing."

NOTES

1. Benedict XVI's Regensburg Lecture can be found on the Vatican website, www.vatican.va/holy_father/benedict_xvi/speeches/2006/september/documents/hf_ben-xvi_spe_20060912_university-regensburg_en.html. Denys Turner, *Faith, Reason and Existence of God* (Cambridge: Cambridge University Press, 2004); see review in *Modern Theology* 21 (2005): 686–88.

2. Deirdre Carabine, *The Unknown God: Negative Theology in the Platonic Tradition: Plato to Eriugena* (Louvain: Peeters; Grand Rapids, MI: Eerdmans, 1995); Nicholas of Cusa's *De docta ignorantia* (1440), English translation by Lawrence Bond in *Nicholas of Cusa: Selected Writings* (New York: Paulist Press, 1997); also see James Heft, S.M., Reuven Firestone, and Omid Safi, eds., *Learned Ignorance: Intellectual Humility among Jews, Christians and Muslims* (Oxford: Oxford University Press, 2011).

3. See my review of Thomas Joseph White, O.P., *Wisdom in the Face of Modernity: A Study in Thomistic Natural Theology* (Ave Maria, FL: Sapientia Press of Ave Maria University, 2009), in *Nova et Vetera* (2010).

4. Carabine, *Unknown God*, 171.

5. Olivier-Thomas Venard, O.P., *Littérature et théologie: Une saison en enfer* (Geneva: Ad Solem, 2002); *La langue de l'ineffable: Essai sur le fondement théologique de la métaphysique* (Geneva: Ad Solem, 2004); *Pagina sacra: Le passage de l'Ecriture sainte à l'écriture thélogique* (Paris: Cerf; Geneva: Ad Solem, 2009). Bruce Marshall makes the argument in his contribution to Thomas Joseph White's collection, *The Analogy of Being: Invention of the Antichrist or the Wisdom of God?* (Grand Rapids, MI: Eerdmans, 2011): "Christ the End of Analogy," 280–313.

6. See my extended debate with William Hasker and Richard Cross: "Creator/Creatures Relation: 'The Distinction' vs. 'Onto-theology,'" *Faith and Philosophy* 25 (2008): 177–212.

7. See my review of *A Most Unlikely God* (1992) and *From Existence to God: A Most Unlikely God* (1996), in *Faith and Philosophy* (2001): 123–27, which also covers *The Fullness of Being* (2002), to which I had access in manuscript. Elmar Kremer is at work on an extended analysis and appraisal of this oeuvre.

8. I have employed this strategy of Wittgenstein to elucidate the properly metaphysical moves Aquinas makes in questions 3–11 of the *Summa theologiae*. See *Aquinas: God and Action* (Notre Dame: University of Notre Dame Press, 1979; Scranton, PA: University of Scranton Press, 2008), 16.

9. See David Braine, *The Reality of Time and the Existence of God* (Oxford: Oxford University Press, 1988); Robert Sokolowski, *The God of Faith and Reason* (Washington, DC: Catholic University of America Press, 1983).

10. For an appreciation of that encyclical along these lines, see my "Philosophy," in *Blackwell Companion to Modern Theology*, ed. Gareth Jones (Oxford: Blackwell, 2004), 34–46.

11. Charles Taylor, *A Secular Age* (Cambridge MA: Belknap Press, 2007).

12. Vittorio Montemaggi and Matthew Traherne, eds., *Dante's "Commedia": Thelogy as Poetry* (Notre Dame: University of Notre Dame Press, 2010), citation at 60. Subsequent citations of this volume appear in parenthesis in the text.

13. Carabine, *Unknown God*, 182–83.

14. Denys Turner, "How to Do Things with Words: Poetry as Sacrament," in Montemaggi and Trahern, *Dante's "Commedia,"* 286–305.

15. Eckhart, *Sermon* 83, *Renovamini Spiritu*, in *Meister Eckhart: The Essential Sermons, Commentaries, Treatises, and Defense*, ed. Edmund Colledge and Bernard McGinn (New York: Paulist Press, 1981), 208.

16. See my summary of these fractures in *Aquinas: God and Action*, 48.

17. Daniel Davies, *Method and Metaphysics in Maimonides' "Guide for the Perplexed"* (Oxford: Oxford University Press, 2011); see review by John Inglis in *Notre Dame Philosophical Reviews* (2012).

18. Joel Kraemerr, "Maimonides' Use of (Aristotelian) Dialectic," in *Maimonides and the Sciences*, ed. Robert S. Cohen and Hillel Levine (Dordrecht: Kluwer Academic, 2000), 111–30.

19. Cécile Bonmariage, *Le réel et les réalités: Mulla Sadra Shirazi et la structure de la réalité* (Paris: J. Vrin, 2007), 133.

20. Paul Griffiths, *Intellectual Appetite: A Theological Grammar* (Washington DC: Catholic University of America Press, 2009). Subsequent citations of this work appear in the text in parenthesis.

DISCOURSE
AND
AUTHORITY

FIVE

Assent to Thinking

KARMEN MacKENDRICK

In *The Darkness of God*, Denys Turner provocatively writes of faith as "the darkness of unknowing," as "the conviction that our deepest centre . . . is in us, but not of us, is not 'ours' to possess, but only to be possessed by." And so faith, he adds, "at once 'decentres' us, for it disintegrates the experiential structures of selfhood on which, in experience, we centre ourselves, and at the same time draws us into divine love where we are 'recentred' upon a ground beyond any possibility of experience."[1] This dark, divine decentering and recentering unknowing—an importantly knowing unknowing—conflicts with some popular versions of faith, from many who would call themselves faithful and from many more who are impatient to rid humanity of what they understand to be a set of old and pointless—even dangerous—superstitions. Both groups argue that faith means a belief in scriptural inerrancy and that inerrancy means truth in a mode exactly coincident with that of science or history (which, of course, have identical senses of what truth is). In this belief the faithful can rest secure.

David Carr, in the introduction to Genesis in the *Oxford Study Bible*, finds such beliefs sufficiently widespread to require response. "Some believers," he writes, " . . . insist on the importance of affirming the historical accuracy of every part of Genesis, and have come

111

to see such belief as a defining characteristic of what it means to be truly faithful. This definition is relatively new: the historicity of Genesis was not a significant concern prior to the rise of modern science and the historical method."[2] Once history and science gain this methodological firmness and wide respectability, the urge to fit myth into them begins to take hold. This relatively new version of faith seems to have a much more direct relation to a particular kind of propositional belief than to anything that might accommodate unknowing and decentering. Either one believes it firmly, evidence notwithstanding, or one rolls one's eyes and sighs at its foolishness. Such "faith" is a belief in "facts" that is nonetheless oddly divorced from the intellectual and empirical means by which we ordinarily determine what is factual.

One can cling to such belief by declaring those ordinary means inessential, and reason inferior to commitment. However, in both *The Darkness of God* and *Faith, Reason and the Existence of God*, Turner reminds us that faith is not somehow opposed to intellect. To make sense of this, we need to complicate our understandings both of faith—it must already be clear that the propositional version is not very workable—and of the intellect's workings.

In keeping with Turner's nonopposition, I would like here to draw out a little the epistemology of a kind of complex apophatic faith, a faith of acquired ignorance, of deliberate unknowing, of centering on what decenters us.[3] In this sense, faith is a deep intellectual investment and entails an intense intellectual hunger, one not satisfiable by unsupported propositions. I will not be able to help much with the frustration that all of us face when asked by those outside theology, "So, what do you believe?," but perhaps I can give reasons that the question itself is in error.

There is a classical formulation of faith in this sense. In both Augustine and Thomas Aquinas, we find faith described by the phrase "thinking with assent."[4] I intend not to explore carefully the details of these complex thinkers' use of the phrase but instead to extrapolate from it in a manner I hope they would find not entirely disagreeable (though I'm certain they would give me strange looks now and then). In agreeing with the Augustinian formulation, Thomas remarks that the kind of belief appropriate to faith "is distinguished from all the other acts of the intellect, which are about the true or the false."[5] If, like those I have almost caricatured above, we would prefer to think quickly and reductively, this distinction from other intellectual modes is both irritating and suspicious: it makes of faith "that fluffy stuff," as I was once informed by an irritated young man who clutched his copy of Richard Dawkins as he spoke.[6] But it reminds us that theological thought must be willing to be nonreductive even with regard to truth-value (thus distinctly unfluffy) and, if not patient, at least very stubborn and persistent. "Thinking with assent" is (at best) intellectually problematic if we assent a priori not to *thinking* but to particular *thoughts*—if we have already agreed to believe in a way that actually forestalls thoughtfulness or open exploration. Neither Augustine nor Thomas thought that clumsily.

The notion that assent *could* overcome thinking presupposes a split between intellect and desire. One *wants* to believe, reason be damned. Turner has long problematized that very division. He writes of Pseudo-Dionysius, for instance, "It is . . . the *eros* of knowing, the passion and yearning for the vision of the One, which projects the mind up the scale. . . . Nor . . . is Denys' 'cloud of unknowing' a vehicle for anti-intellectualism, for a displacement of the role of intellect, at least ultimately, in favour of that of love in the making of the ecstatic union of the soul with God."[7] By the late Middle Ages, however, the gap between love and knowledge will have already opened, such that Denys the Carthusian will have to worry about whether he can effect "a reconciliation on the issue which had so often preoccupied late medieval mystics, and so often distracted them from their main purposes: the issue of 'intellectualist' as against 'voluntarist' accounts of 'union with God.'"[8] Opposing intellect and love, knowledge and desire, we also oppose the mystical and the theological, rendering problematic a pretty significant (and interesting) portion of Christian theological history.[9] A more interesting option is to continue to seek to understand faith as a kind of knowing that remains desirous throughout. Obviously, this is not the declaration of truth as a set of propositions.

Faith as a priori assent to particular propositions is tenaciously opposed not only to intellectual desire and to opposing beliefs[10] but to doubt as well. Doubt may be regarded as the lack of faith or, in more thoughtful versions, as a sort of strengthening test, or as a pain by which the faithful are able to identify with passionate suffering. The latter mode of doubt is a step on the way to making faith stronger. This allows a little more flexibility into the concept of faith, but faith is still identified with certainty, or at any rate steadiness of belief, belief accompanied affectively by security and trust. Doubt is not a necessary *part of* such faith, just something that will probably emerge in struggling for it. Certainty is still the goal and the ideal. The appeal of this kind of security, whether in belief or in affect, is self-evident.[11] By secure belief we are spared not only uncertainty, but a lot of mental effort. Faith as stubborn belief offers the security of knowledge, again, without the pesky evidentiary requirements usually attached. This is the version of faith on which critics of "religion," usually treated sweepingly as a whole, tend to focus.

It would not be quite fair to dismiss this version out of hand as absurd. After all, theological thinkers have for millennia linked God to truth, and we believe what we consider to be true. The creedal claim to "believe in one God" seems to provide further evidence for faith as belief. However, both the sense of what it is to "believe" and the sense of what "truth" as the object of belief might have undergone historical change in ways that may be relevant. The notion that belief must be a propositional attitude, that is, that it consists in regarding a particular proposition as having the logical value "true," takes its firmest hold in the Enlightenment, and while such thinking has been immensely useful, it has also been overuniversalized. The "truth" with which early Christianity identifies its God is not so much the truth of a proposition as Platonic Truth as such; not something which is *true*, as propositions can be, but as something which is *truth*, from which all other truths of the world derive their veracity. One believes that a proposition is true, but not a god—not, at any rate, in the propositional sense.[12]

The creeds' "We believe in . . . " is actually not the same sort of claim as "We hold these truths to be self-evident," no matter how many people in how many ways do their very best to conflate them. Wilfred Cantwell Smith writes that in classical use the primary meaning of the term *credo*, with which the Latin church begins the Nicene Creed, is "to entrust, to commit, to trust something to someone"—also "to lend," as in money. He adds, "A secondary meaning in secular usage was 'to trust in,' 'to rely upon.' . . . There had also developed a derivative usage wherein *credo* meant 'to believe' (usually a person); but that was tertiary. To believe a proposition was quaternary and relatively rare."[13] The creeds' earliest use, he argues, is to mark a conversionary commitment to a new way of living, not to a new set of beliefs; they do not declare "we believe that there is" but rather "we believe *in*." The English word *believe*, says Smith, similarly begins as a verb of allegiance and dedication,[14] related to words for love and devotion. Our problem would not be poor translation as such, then, but a semantic shift and concomitant epistemological transition. One does not believe in one God as an act of accepting a proposition but rather as a devotion or commitment.

Simply to declare the problem solved would be a bit too easy, though. After all, devotion may not be the same as propositional sureness, but it still seems to imply some propositions, such as that its object exists. Staunch believers and devout atheists alike err, I suspect, not so much in the propositions they affirm as in their certainly that those propositions, notably "God exists" or "God does not exist," have ready, familiar, easily definable meanings; that whatever is called "God" exists or fails to exist, like a rosebush or a unicorn. The point here is not that we do not know enough of the details about God to be confident in what sort of being God is, or what sort of attributes God has, which we might with proper information affirm or disavow. It is rather, and more deeply, that we do not know what *existence* is in this instance, and that will mess thoroughly with the notion of truth claims. As Turner points out, "In the sense in which atheists . . . say God 'does not exist,' the atheist has merely arrived at the theological starting point" from which Augustine, Thomas Aquinas, and quite a few more theologians begin.[15]

If we were affirming propositions, this would be a problem. If we were devoting ourselves clearly to a figure of power or authority, it would remain a problem: one likes the presence of one's authority figures to be fairly clearly defined, if only so as to keep an eye on them. So we need to think about a sense of belief and devotion in which this is not a problem, or at least in which it might be an *interesting* problem, rather than a counterargument. This entails a shift in our sense of the right ways of saying, so that we speak to search and not simply to declare—though we must do the latter as well. No small part of the problem of contemporary popular conceptions of faith is the extent to which our search for verifiable truths has excluded us from the kind of truths found in myth, or from poetry, where language is at its most evocative, its most deliberately aporetic, and yet its most rigorous. Religious faith seems to me less a matter of tidy propositions and more a matter of the kind of truth that poetry is, with its spaces and silences, its openings and interruptions. (Several essays in the present volume make both the connections and the rigor very clear.) The difficulty is all the more pronounced because we conflate evocation with obscurity and obscurity with downright malicious confusion. Reason as fact-finding is meant to liberate us from just such obfuscation. As I have noted, this rational view of light and truth is immensely valuable, but it becomes a problem when we assume that it is the *only* right thinking. And it often assumes that faith too has claimed the possession of such truth, is engaged in such reasoning, but is doing very badly. Instead, as Lewis Mackey argues, "faith . . . is inherently and essentially . . . a self-critical stance."[16] It is self-critical not simply because it is willing to alter its answers, but because it is inherently *about* questions. So whatever faith may be, it is not an answer accomplished in which the intellect and desire rest but a question that impels them both. This is not a truth that establishes and settles; it is a truth that unsettles and opens. In thinking theologically, we might do well to treat words as openings and provocations. In this sense, the language of faith is poetic—evocative, invocative, provocative, and decentering. Even what the faithful seem to believe—to affirm propositionally— turns out to render its propositions so strange that it becomes not a declaration but an inquiry. The propositions of faith deepen mystery, as Turner notes, rather than tidy it away.[17]

The reduction of the mystery of faith to immysterious fact seems so painfully dull that we must wonder at its persistence. Clearly one reason faith is so readily linked to stubborn and ill-grounded belief is that it participates in will as well as in intellect.[18] The senses of *believe* brought out in Smith's work emphasize the willful aspect, as does the "assent" of thinking-with. The other traditional senses of faith on which I want to touch here also emphasize the involvement of the will, as either fidelity (being faithful to) or trust (having faith in) or some combination of both. But these senses will help us to bring out just what is both peculiar and delightful in the faith of a central decentering that recenters without bypassing the intellect.

Let us take trust first. It is a reasonable alternative to other senses of belief, especially where devotion is concerned. If I say to someone, "I have faith in you," it is quite unlikely that I mean, "I affirm the truth of the proposition that you exist." In fact, it is pretty unlikely that I even mean "You exist." Rather, I am likely to mean something like "I trust you" or "I believe that you can accomplish what you intend to." This faith as trust generally plays out as a sense of the rightness and the power of divine will and action.[19] Such faith is often a source of great comfort to those who hold it. This view is most strongly associated with Luther, for whom a deeply trusting faith is also a primary source of justification—an association so profound that the Council of Trent, deeply irritated with all things Lutheran, declared the emphasis on trust (or, to be fair, the emphasis on trust as solely constitutive of faith) anathema.[20] Of course, at its extreme, this slides into a more worrisome fatalism or even quietism, excusing us from further action once our trust is engaged.

Is this "thinking with assent"? The elements of will—desire and (an initial) decision—are clear enough. But the intellectual component of trust is harder to ascertain, unless we want to make of it a trust in a certain kind of knowing. John Calvin does something like this: "Now we shall have a right definition of faith if we say that it is a steady and certain knowledge of the divine benevolence towards us, which is founded upon the truth of the gracious promise of God in Christ, and is both revealed to our minds and sealed in our hearts by the Holy Spirit."[21] This seems, however, only to combine trust with unquestioning belief—though it is not so troubling a belief as that of, say, creationism, since it need not directly defy other evidentiary modes.

If we understand trust as faith-in, its flipside is fidelity-to. Jean-Luc Nancy notes the connection: "Christian faith is distinguished precisely and absolutely from all belief. It is a category sui generis, which is . . . faithfulness in its own right, confidence, and openness to the possibility of what it is confidence in. What I am saying here would be perfectly suitable to our modern definition of faithfulness in love."[22]

Religious faith as fidelity would be the direction of desire to God—an active attentiveness and an absence of (intentional) rejection. It appears to be something like fidelity for which Augustine struggles in the famous prelude to his conversion, as he attempts to direct and unify his scattered desires.[23] But either to assent in trust to such thinking or to be faithful to it is to be willing to follow the openness of the question, not to assume an answer.

We still, however, must think about the question itself. Jacques Ellul, as he worries about "belief and doubt in a perilous world," declares that faith is not what provides answers but rather what questions us; it is meant "to confront us with questions . . . to get us to listen to questions."[24] He adds that faith *knows*, by revelation, the existence and power of its God; what it *doubts*, under that same revelation, is the rightness of its own acts and knowledge.[25] This gives new sense to the link between faith and doubt. Here doubt is not merely a contrary of faith, not even one that can function as a strengthening test of it. Rather, at least some kinds of self-doubt *are* faith. But I hesitate to embrace this view entirely; it is promising to find an open question here, but unless we are careful in our sense of *exists*, the question of God is foreclosed.

And God is indeed the question, but just as we need to pay some subtle attention to what counts as truth, what counts as an answer, so too we need to think about questioning carefully. Augustine will once more be helpful. Seeking God, Augustine notices worldly beauties, and inquires of them regarding God's whereabouts. "My question was the attention I gave them," he says, "and their answer was their beauty."[26] Such inquiry is answered by exactly what calls it forth. Inquisitive attention always opens further questions—and the divine is the most open, the most reversible, question of all.[27]

In one of my favorite passages in his work, Turner writes that the theologian, like the child,

> asks the question 'why?' once too often, where 'once too often' means; when there is no intellectual possibility of understanding an answer[,] . . . where language itself has run out. And that, for Thomas [Aquinas], is where theology begins. . . . Philosophers seem happy enough to say, after Aristotle, that philosophy begins in wonder. Alas, all too often their philosophy ends with its elimination. Instead of leaving us, as it were, in a condition of *instructed awe*—what Nicholas of Cusa called a *docta ignorantia*—it leaves us instead with Russell's blank and indifferent stare: that there is anything at all is just a brute fact.[28]

Such blankness is created by the incapacity to recognize the unique existential nature of the question, "Why anything?"[29] Nicholas, with his instructed ignorance, must be among our exemplars for such recognition. For him, God's ineffability arises from divine infinitude: "Sacred ignorance has taught us that God is ineffable. He is so because he is infinitely greater than all nameable things."[30] "For you," he says to God, "have shown me that you cannot be seen elsewhere than where impossibility confronts and obstructs me."[31] Faith is just this confrontation—and the willingness not to avoid it. Just this, but with an important inclusion: the child's *delight* in the question, the thinker's delighted assent when an answer arrives and bears with it new queries.

To question and be questioned is neither to apprehend with confidence nor to relax in easy ignorance. It is, rather, to think with assent by way of assenting to thinking, which is not nearly as easy as it sounds. The desire for knowledge that takes the infinite as its object is itself an infinite desire. Turner even argues that, for Augustine, "the love of learning *is* the desire for God."[32] The truth revealed in theological wonder is a revelation not of fact but of mystery. We seek the mysterious, the infinite. But if we think that we have found it, that we have stripped away its veils and seen its secrets, then we have not, in fact, found the mystery at all; we have, instead, destroyed it. To seek mystery must be not only to wonder, but to continue to seek to wonder, to seek to continue to wonder—not by refusing answers, but by pursuing what remains unanswered and even unanswerable.[33] It must mean to seek questions *and* answers, because the desire to find answers is no small part of what it is to ask questions in the first place.

The open query, attention to wonder and the entanglement of beauty with truth, demands a poetic theology, one that sustains possibility in a way that more straightforward discourse does not. Affirmations and negations of faith become poetic statements—statements that, like T. S. Eliot's "three white leopards sat under a juniper tree," mean just what they say, yet the meaning of which is perpetually elusive.[34]

It seems a foundational difference between atheism, on the one hand, and a mystically inflected theism (or perhaps even agnosticism), on the other, whether one finds poetic questions interesting and is drawn by them, or instead finds them irritatingly and quickly dismissible, a pathetic effort to cling to belief by redefining the most basic of terms, such as "is." "What the atheist has to deny," Turner rightly notes, "is the legitimacy of a certain kind of question, to deny which requires setting *a priori* limits to a capacity which is, as Aristotle says, potentially infinite; which being so, Thomas Aquinas adds, is not going to be satisfied by—that is, enjoy any question-stopping complacency in—even an infinite object."[35] It is easy to dismiss as illogical these claims of mystery and desire, but that assumes that they were meant, in the first place, to be logical propositions. In fact, they seem rather more to be *dialogical*: their open spaces, their elusive meanings, invite a speaking back, an inquiry.

Retaining our sense of a knowing more interrogative than declarative, let us further consider divine existence in a conversational mode, in the play between wonder and ineffability, question and answer, call and response. Immediately upon asking the question of God, we are confronted by the most puzzling of responses—by poetry and indirection, and within them also by silence. Beth Hawkins writes in *Reluctant Theologians* of the poet Paul Celan: "All at once the speaking God of the covenant is superseded by the mystical, silent God, but a trace remains, a longing for a dialogical relationship."[36] Ours too is a God of traces, a name written in the world; our dialogue speaks with silence—by engaging the silence within speaking.[37] We enter this dialogue in questioning and in question, gradually realizing that the only trace of an answer leads us into further query. Here, as Maurice Blanchot notes, we are in relation with what properly excludes all relationality: "What we owe to Jewish monotheism is not the revelation of the one God, but the revelation of speech as the place where men hold themselves in relation with what excludes all relation: the infinitely Distant. . . . God speaks, and man speaks to him."[38] But how can this God, traced in withdrawal and exile, be the God of Augustine's exuberantly overflowing beauty, a divinity of delight and not only of sorrowful bewilderment? How, that is, can the assent to thinking affirm anything other than negation?

We find the divine doubly in the world, where it speaks to us and where there is silence—and it speaks to us of silence, and the silences intercut and resonate within all theological speaking. Theological language means right up to its incomprehensible edge, where it opens onto other questions. The openness to the question is not about indeterminacy alone; it is an openness to mystery. Paradox, suggests Mark McIntosh, "might recall a way of speaking about and understanding God that seemed to have been lost among the deists and free-thinkers, a way of living in relationship with mystery that patiently exposes the mind to what it cannot grasp."[39] McIntosh characterizes this as a difference in epistemic cultures: "In such a culture of knowledge, there is no real room for the radically new or other or incomprehensible; everything is massively clear, explicable, quantifiably appreciable. . . . This kind of formation does not *really* have a use for the ability to encounter the unknowable."[40] This ability is constitutive of faith.

The encounter with mystery is forestalled if we read "thinking with assent" as not really thinking at all but rather, at most, presenting a proposition to oneself as something prejudged to be true or real.

When assent to truth-value has already been given, thinking is narrowly constrained. Thinking with assent is not providing in advance the answers to one's questions (thus keeping them from being questions at all) but assenting to thinking—whatever we may call it. "God" is the name of the question, a name that calls when it is called. It calls to language; it calls to thinking. And sometimes thinking says *yes*, answers to that call with assent; says yes to the name of the question, not as an answer to abolish it. Intellect, as Turner notes, must include not just discursive reason, but "the non-discursive act of *seeing* a truth as such or the desirability of some good."[41] It is to this that we assent. Apophasis, as Turner has reminded us, says yes as much as it says no, affirms as much as negates: "It is of the greatest consequence to see that negative language about God is no more apophatic in itself than is affirmative language."[42]

Like other pleasures, the delights of the assenting intellect bring with them a desire for repetition. But, to remind us of the obvious, we can't have more of them without going back to the question, without descending again into the obscure. When we assent to thinking, when we assent in thinking, we assent as well—indeed, we demand—questioning, and puzzlement, and doubt. The link between questioning and negation, between infinite inquiry and negative theology, is mirrored by the question's link to affirmation. Assent is the converse, not the antithesis, of negation.

Faith becomes, then, a faith in the worth of questioning, a belief—or a conviction deeper than belief—that such questioning matters. The delight of thinking with assent is complicated by and implicated within the struggle, the darkness, of its own necessary and negative condition. There is trust here as well but, again, not in the sense in which we might most readily think it. It is oddly popular to assume that if one believes in just the right God, one will get prizes, ranging from riches to weight loss to inner peace to eternal salvation.[43] This is a crude reduction of trust. Equally crude is the blithe assumption that all proceeds according to divine plan, that everything is under control however little it may so appear. An epistemological trust must emphasize trust's element of openness—the element that precisely does *not* guarantee outcomes and answers. We are faithful not to a truth already seized upon as authoritative but to the pursuit itself. And because, again, questions are about something, this is also a fidelity to the object of inquiry, to its value. Affirmation is essential to this sense of faith as fidelity, including fidelity to thinking, where commitment is maintained and reasserted.

This is faith's founding paradox: in all of this questioning, in order to believe that it is worthwhile to ask, in order to trust that inquiry leads us and does not merely scatter us randomly, in order to be true to the object of our asking, faith demands as well what cannot be questioned. It demands an unquestionable and perhaps an ineluctable. I suspect that Lewis Mackey is right when he remarks, using *believe* in its more complex sense, "I have spoken as if there were a choice: to believe or not to believe. . . . The most abstemious rational inquiry is inevitably guided by commitments of which it may or may not be aware. Faith only makes these commitments explicit."[44] Faith is neither belief nor hope, nor precisely the fidelity and trust they inspire, yet it is not entirely disconnected from any of them. It is rather the willingness—more strongly, the will—to dwell in question, in mystery, and so, paradoxically, in the pursuit of answers. It is thus learning's constant enticement. It has, of course, parallels in any kind of knowing. What characterizes *faith* as the term is religiously used is the deeper inherence of the question in every one of its answers. Its answers precisely *are* questions; the answer is questioning, wonder, absence and excess, and knowledge at its most restless.

This could seem to leave faith peculiarly aimless, and to strip it entirely of its commitment to any given tradition. But what traditions give us is precisely their questions. Perhaps an example will serve. The Christian tradition most directly considered here begins its question where it begins itself—in Incarnation. Augustine writes of his near-conviction by Plotinus, and the rightness of much that he found in Platonic texts. Then he adds, "But that 'The Word was made flesh, and dwelt among us,' I find nowhere else" than in Christian scripture—and the same for several other points pertaining particularly to the Incarnation.[45] This might not have the grammatical form of a question, but it is certainly a puzzle, even a paradox. The particular readiness with which the Incarnation, precisely because of its paradoxical elements, is provocative to query thus becomes part of its value. It also reminds us, especially in the Johannine formulation that links it to word and to principles, of how bodily thinking is. As poetry likewise reminds us, an attention to the notion of word made flesh must also mean attending to the fleshy sensuality of words. A faith that starts with a divine embodiment is particularly fascinating as the "object" of a desirous knowing that cannot be divorced from the flesh—and not only, though certainly also, from the flesh of the brain.

Such faith holds not that the answers end somewhere but that the questions start somewhere. Faith traditions do not offer us pseudoscience or sloppy history but the enticing possibilities of inquiry at the edge of knowing. For the Christian version of a decentering faith I would say not, as a once-popular bumper sticker had it, that Jesus is the answer but that incarnation, as the Incarnation reminds us, is a very good, a rich and an infinite, question.

NOTES

1. Denys Turner, *The Darkness of God: Negativity in Christian Mysticism* (Cambridge: Cambridge University Press, 1998), 251. I should note that this essay shares material and argument with the chapter bearing the same name as its subtitle in *Divine Enticement: Theological Seductions* (New York: Fordham University Press, 2013) but is not identical to it in either respect.

2. David M. Carr, Introduction to Genesis, in *The New Oxford Annotated Bible*, 4th ed. (Oxford: Oxford University Press, 2010), 7–11, at 10.

3. See, e.g., the claim that apophaticism "is the conception of theology not as a naïve *pre*-critical ignorance of God, but as a kind of acquired ignorance, a *docta ignorantia* as Nicholas of Cues called it in the fifteenth century. It is the conception of theology as a strategy and practice of unknowing, as the fourteenth century English mystic called it, who, we might say, invented the transitive verb-form 'to unknow' in order to describe theological knowledge, in this its deconstructive mode" (Turner, *Darkness of God*, 19). Turner is making reference to *The Cloud of Unknowing*, esp. chaps. 4–7. See also: "We can, of course, *know* that God is present to us. We can struggle to say what we mean by this. We can live a life centered upon that knowledge. We can experience the world in all sorts of ways consequent upon that knowledge, which would not be available to our experience if we lacked the knowledge of God. And so we can, in a sense, be aware of God, even be 'conscious'

of God; but only in that sense in which we can be conscious of the failure of our knowledge, not knowing what it is that our knowledge fails to reach. This is not the same thing as being conscious of the absence of God in any sense which entails that we are conscious of what it is that is absent. God cannot be the object of any consciousness whatsoever" (264–65; original emphasis).

4. Augustine, "The Predestination of the Saints," in *Four Anti-Pelagian Writings*, trans. John Arthur Mourant and William J. Collinge (Washington, DC: Catholic University of America Press, 1992), 218–70, at 222. Thomas Aquinas, *The Summa Theologica of St. Thomas Aquinas*, 2nd rev. ed., trans. Fathers of the English Dominican Province (Notre Dame: Christian Classics, 1981), IIa–IIae, q. 2, a. 1, http://newadvent.org/summa/3002.htm#article2/.

5. Thomas Aquinas, *Summa Theologica*, IIa–IIae, q. 2, a. 1, *corp*.

6. I believe it was Richard Dawkins, *The God Delusion* (New York: Mariner Books, 2008).

7. Turner, *Darkness of God*, 47. Granted, this unity doesn't hold invariably; we read that for Bonaventure, for instance, intellect and love are united only until "the final *excessus* into which only love can proceed" (131).

8. Turner, *Darkness of God*, 211. Cf. "It is within the fragmentations of the mystical and the theological, of loving and knowing, of experience and speculation that we today, scholars or practicing Christians, generally stand. Where the Middle Ages end, we begin. As Denys the Carthusian was compelled to read the history of medieval mystical theology, *malgré lui*, in terms of these bifurcations, so do we, though, unlike Denys, we need not do so. Nor do we appear to have any conception of why we should resist that reading" (225).

9. See, e.g., the discussion of Eckhart in Turner, *Darkness of God*, 168.

10. James Carse notes how strongly dependent on a defined enemy or opposition most belief systems are in the interview, "Religion Is Poetry," *Salon*, July 21, 2008, www.salon.com/books/atoms_eden/2008/07/21/james _carse/index1.html.

11. Ibid., 4: "In one respect, it is not a mistake to associate religion with belief. Mystery is difficult to live with, and for some even terrifying. It can often be of great comfort to hide our unknowing behind the veil of a well-articulated belief system." Compare Turner on our sometimes frantic efforts to rid ourselves of temptation, a description readily applied to desperate belief: "Much of what we call 'spirituality' seems to issue from this anxious, threatened condition of soul. . . . Let us at least acknowledge in ourselves the anxiety to become as temptationless as possible, invulnerable to weakness and failure; and let us look, from time to time, at how much work, how much fretting, how much anxiety we invest in the futile pursuit of this invulnerability" (Denys Turner, "How to Be Tempted: A Homily," in *Faith Seeking* [London: SCM Press, 2002], 101–3, at 102).

12. Wilfred Cantwell Smith writes of "the Platonic, rather than the propositional, sense of truth, comparable to our speaking of a true note in music[,] . . . a man's being true to his word, not logically true, as a statement." See his *Faith and Belief* (Princeton: Princeton University Press, 1979), 109.

13. Ibid., 76.

14. Ibid., 105–27.

15. Denys Turner, "How to Be an Atheist," in *Faith Seeking*, 3–22, at 8. Augustine in his second homily on the Gospel of John, sec. 2, identifies the Word with being, as other than *a* being. See Augustine, "Tractates on the Gospel of John," trans. John Gibb, in *Nicene and Post-Nicene Fathers*, 1st ser., vol. 7, ed. Philip Schaff (Buffalo, NY: Christian Literature Publishing Co., 1888), www.newadvent.org/fathers/1701002.htm.

16. Lewis Mackey, *Peregrinations of the Word* (Ann Arbor: University of Michigan Press, 1997), 3.

17. "The believer has a stronger sense of mystery than the philosopher, not a weaker," a sense of the "darkness of God" that "is deepened, not relieved, by the Trinity, intensified by the incarnation, not dispelled" (Turner, *Faith, Reason and the Existence of God*, 43).

18. Thomas was aware that some might find this element of assent intellectually objectionable. Thomas Aquinas, *Summa Theologica*, IIa–IIae, q. 2, a. 1, ad. 3: "Further, to believe is an act of the intellect, since its object is truth. But assent seems to be an act not of the intellect, but of the will, even as consent is, as stated above [*ST* Ia–IIae, q. 15, a. 1, ad. 3]. Therefore to believe is not to think with assent."

19. H. Richard Niebuhr, *The Responsible Self: An Essay in Christian Moral Philosophy* (New York: Harper and Row, 1963), 118: "When we say that the interpretation of the radical action is made in faith, we use the word, faith, not as meaning some set of beliefs that must take the place of knowledge until knowledge is possible. The aspect of faith we have here in mind is simply that trust or distrust . . . to which theologians, notably Luther, have pointed as the fundamental element in religion. Faith is the attitude of the self in its existence toward all the existences that surround it, as beings to be relied upon or to be suspected. . . . Such faith is an ingredient in all knowing."

20. See Richard Swinburne, *Faith and Reason* (Oxford: Oxford University Press, 2005), 142. Swinburne cites Martin Luther, "The Freedom of a Christian," in *Reformation Writings of Martin Luther*, vol. 1, trans. B. L. Woolf (Cambridge: Lutterworth Press, 1952), sec. 11.

21. John Calvin, *Institutes of the Christian Religion*, trans. Henry Beveridge (Edinburgh: Calvin Translation Society, 1845), 4.14.22.

22. Jean-Luc Nancy, *Dis-Enclosure: The Deconstruction of Christianity*, trans. Bettina Bergo, Gabriel Malenfant, and Michael B. Smith (New York: Fordham University Press, 2008), 153. Ellipses original.

23. Augustine, *Confessions*, trans. Henry Chadwick (Oxford: Oxford University Press, 1991), 8.7–12.

24. Jacques Ellul, *Living Faith: Belief and Doubt in a Perilous World*, trans. Peter Heinegg (San Francisco: Harper and Row, 1983), 100.

25. "Belief is reassuring. People who live in the world of belief feel safe; God is their protector. On the contrary, faith is forever placing us on the razor's edge. Though it knows that God is the Father, it never minimizes his power. . . . [T]his doubt concerns myself, *not* God's revelation or his love or the presence of Jesus Christ. It is thus the clean contrary of belief" (Ellul, *Living Faith*, 112–13).

26. Augustine, *Confessions*, 10.6.

27. For the Jewish as well as Christian roots of such thought, note, e.g., Beth Hawkins's remarks on Franz Kafka in *Reluctant Theologians: Kafka, Celan, Jabès* (New York: Fordham University Press, 2003), 65: "Kafka provides the capacity for a faith circumscribed by the question, a faith that is a condition, a way of being-in-the-world, rather than a prescribed set of behaviors." She also comments on Edmond Jabès: "the question is exploded; it becomes the symbol of faith par excellence in a world where answers no longer apply" (167). Other, still more obvious, thinkers of the question in more or less Jewish terms include Derrida and, in the realm of ethics, Levinas.

28. Turner, "How to Be an Atheist," 20.

29. "But we are able to grasp this 'proto-sacramentality' of reason only if we grasp what is different about this question, 'why anything?'" (Turner, *Faith, Reason and the Existence of God*, 257).

30. Nicholas of Cusa, *De docta ignorantia* 1, 26, in *A Concise Introduction to the Philosophy of Nicholas of Cusa*, ed. and trans. Jasper Hopkins (Indianapolis: University of Indiana Press, 1986), 45.

31. Nicholas of Cusa, *De visione Dei*, in *Nicholas of Cusa: Selected Spiritual Writings*, trans. H. Lawrence Bond (Mahwah, NJ: Paulist Press, 1997), 252. As cited in Catherine Keller, "The Cloud of the Impossible: Feminist Theology, Cosmology and Cusa," presentation at Harvard University, March 22, 2007, http://users.drew.edu/ckeller/essays-download.html.

32. Denys Turner, "Dominus Illuminatio Mea," in *Faith Seeking*, 128–38, at 135; original emphasis. More completely: "Augustine knew . . . well . . . that to love learning is to be in love with love. For learning is a kind of loving, a desire whose object is an *infinite* truth and an *infinite* beauty. . . . [T]he love of learning *is* the desire for God. For sure, a teaching and a learning which lacks that 'infinity' to it, are nothing but forms of pedantry." Original emphasis.

33. There is no small resonance here with Mary-Jane Rubenstein's elegant exploration of wonder throughout *Strange Wonder: The Closure of Metaphysics and the Opening of Awe* (New York: Columbia University Press, 2010).

34. According to the poet Stephen Spender in "Remembering Eliot," an Oxford undergraduate asked the meaning of a line in Eliot's "Ash Wednesday": "Lady, three white leopards sat under a juniper tree." And Eliot replied, "I mean, 'Lady, three white leopards sat under a juniper tree.'" Stephen Spender, "Remembering Eliot," in *T. S. Eliot: The Man and His Work*, ed. Allen Tate (New York: Delacorte Press, 1966), 42.

35. Turner, *Faith, Reason and the Existence of God*, 258. In an observation that my own experience has borne out beautifully, Turner also remarks that a fairly thoughtful atheist, having listened to apophatic arguments, "may well be experiencing some degree of exasperation at what he will perceive to be the theist's evasiveness as to what he is now expected to deny" (235).

36. Hawkins, *Reluctant Theologians*, 106.

37. Such a seduction appears even within strongly protested atheism. Thus, Blanchot disagrees with Pierre Klossowski's claims about Sade: "Klossowski seems to think that such burning hatred testifies to a faith that has forgotten its name and has recourse to blasphemy to force God to break his silence." Blanchot argues instead that Sade has infinite hate and fury and so seeks an infinite object. But both may be true; fury, like joy, hate, like love, demand a response to their call. Maurice Blanchot, "Sade's Reason," in *The Blanchot Reader*, ed. Michael Holland (Oxford: Blackwell, 1995), 74–100, at 91.

38. Maurice Blanchot, *The Infinite Conversation*, trans. Susan Hanson (Minneapolis: University of Minnesota Press, 1993), 249. As cited in Lars Iyer, "The Movement of Testimony: Suffering and Speech in Blanchot and Antelme," www.yorku.ca/jspot/5/liyer.htm.

39. Mark A. McIntosh, "Trinity and Understanding in Newman," in *Silence and the Word: Negative Theology and Incarnation*, ed. Oliver Davies and Denys Turner (Cambridge: Cambridge University Press, 2002), 136–58, at 138.

40. Ibid., 145.

41. Turner, *Faith, Reason and the Existence of God*, 80; original emphasis.

42. Turner, *Darkness of God*, 34. Cf. Turner's observation on Augustine: "This is what Augustine, upon his conversion, so emotionally 'recognizes'— that the God he had always been seeking was familiar to him as having always been in his seeking" (66).

43. It was my intent to provide representative URLs, but the websites are simply too numerous. I urge readers to do a Google search for hours of fascinating and somewhat frightening entertainment.

44. Mackey, *Peregrinations of the Word*, 3. Mackey, it is clear in context, does not use *believe* in the reductive sense I have criticized here.

45. Augustine, *Confessions*, 7.14.

SIX

Apian Transformations and the Paradoxes of Women's Authorial Personae in Late Medieval England

KATIE ANN-MARIE BUGYIS

The topic of the metaphorization of medieval women's authorial agency and productivity as beelike may seem an unlikely one in a collection of essays dedicated to the *problemata* of desire in their many literary, philosophical, and theological incarnations. For the bee, most notably eulogized in Virgil's *Georgics*, was perfectly virginal and reproduced without copulation: she did not indulge in sexual union, idle her body in love, or bring forth her young in labor but autogenerated in the blood of dead cattle.[1] Yet this chaste bee, in concert with the fellow members of her hive, produced the sweetest of foods, exceeding all earthly delicacies. Her surpassing fruitfulness was attributed to her participation in the divine mind and the heavenly draughts that she received therein.[2] To the metaphorizing mind, especially to many later Christian ones, the bee, in the very paradox of her virginal fecundity, was a fertile site for polyphonic troping.[3]

The oral and textual productions of medieval women religious, both in their fictional and in their more "historical" manifestations, frequently deployed this metaphor,[4] especially to authorize those utterances that aspired to embody the Word-made-flesh. From preaching the scriptures to relating divine revelations, their words sought to defy the very limits of human language, and, even more transgressively, those limits imposed on the discourses of women. Barred from the roles of preacher and public teacher, denied the sacramental agencies of proclaiming and confecting the Word, these women and their scribes, translators, and hagiographers had to sanction the transmission of their words in creative ways.[5] Very often, they had to become bees, because through their apian metamorphoses they were able to make their female bodies, the very barriers to their possessing sacerdotal power, materialize otherwise. The figure of the bee became the body through which these women could bear the Word beyond the bounds of any cloister or private female or familial relationship. More important, this figure pointed beyond the immediate oral or written production that it signified to the most improbable and paradoxical act of verbal enfleshment—the Incarnation. If the Virgin Mary, virgin though she was, could not only conceive but also give birth to the Word without any violation to her virginity, then any women, similarly overshadowed by the Spirit, could become authorized Word-bearers. Indeed, invocations of Mary and the annunciation of the Word to her frequently attend upon authorial identifications with the bee or her honeyed production, thus signaling that no impediment of the flesh could prevent the irruption of the Word into human history: something new was happening again, and no man could silence it.

The pervasive presence of the apian metaphor in texts authored by, for, and about medieval women religious makes an exhaustive genealogy of it impossible within the confines of this essay. Instead, in what follows, I focus on two late medieval Middle English appearances of it in order to shed light on the authorial strategies that may have been at the disposal of Julian of Norwich, the theologian who lately has busied the mind of Denys Turner. The first exemplum is found in Geoffrey Chaucer's *Canterbury Tales*, in the unnamed pilgrim-nun's telling of the Life of Saint Cecilia in "The Second

Nun's Tale." Though there is no evidence that Julian ever read Chaucer, we do know that she heard the tale that his Nun tells in a homily. In the Short Text of her *Revelation*, she writes that she once "harde a man telle of halye kyrke of the storye of Sainte Cecille."[6] The three deathblows to the neck that the saint received inspired Julian to pray for the spiritual wounds of contrition, compassion, and willful longing to God.

The second exemplum is the early-fifteenth-century Middle English translation of Mechthild of Hackeborn's *Booke of Gostlye Grace*. Mechthild (1241–ca. 1298) was a nun at and eventually the *cantrix* of the convent of Helfta in Saxony. At Helfta, she received many revelations, which, at the age of fifty-one, while seriously ill, she related to two nuns. These nuns recorded her visions without Mechthild's knowledge. When she finally learned of their scribal activities, she was initially distressed by the thought of the textual transmission of her revelations; however, despite her protestations, God assured her that her revelations were to be disseminated for the edification of others and gave the book its title, *Liber specialis gratiae*.[7] The original version of Mechthild's *Liber* contained a prologue and seven parts, the first five of which related her revelations and the last two of which recounted her death. By the mid-fourteenth century, various abridgements of her text were in circulation on the Continent, most of which included only the first five parts. The Middle English translation of Mechthild's *Liber* was based on one such Latin abridgement and also includes the translator's prologue and epilogue. It was likely made in the first quarter of the fifteenth century, possibly at an English Carthusian charterhouse.[8] Two manuscript copies of Mechthild's *Booke* survive: Oxford, Bodleian Library, MS Bodley 220; and London, British Library, MS Egerton 2006.

Theresa Halligan speculates, on the basis of the concluding line of the Bodley MS, that its scribe may have been John Wells, a monk at the London charterhouse in 1425, then at Hull in 1427, at Mount Grace in 1439, and, at the time of his death, at Hinton in 1445.[9] The scribe of the Egerton MS is unknown, but on the basis of unique, orthographic features, Ian Doyle locates the scribe in Lincolnshire.[10]

Halligan even offers the "cautious suggestion" that the manuscript was written at the Carthusian charterhouse at Axholme.[11] More intriguingly, this scribe also copied the only surviving copy of Julian's Short Text, found in London, British Library, MS Additional 37790.[12] Given that the terminus ante quem of the Additional MS is 1435,[13] and that most datings of the Long Text antedate this, Julian was likely not exposed to this manuscript prior to the completion of her *Revelation*. However, the fact that both Julian's Short Text and Mechthild's *Booke* passed through the hands of the same scribe potentially reveals how their texts may have circulated among similar reading circles. Though Mechthild's *Booke* may not have served as a model for Julian's *Revelation*, their visionary and authorial personae may have been interrelated in the minds of late medieval English readers.[14]

"WHAT MANER WOMMAN ARTOW?": CHAUCER'S BISY BEE[15]

Chaucer's *Lyf of Seynt Cecile* is ambiguously situated within the poet's canon. It was originally authored as a freestanding translation of Jacobus de Voragine's Life of Saint Cecilia, found in his *Legenda Aurea*, but it was later retold in the *Canterbury Tales* by the unnamed Nun on the pilgrims' way.[16] Only the latter version of Chaucer's translation survives, but mention of the former is made in both versions of the prologue to *The Legend of Good Women* (F.426; G.416).[17] Once a male poet's textual offering to the god of love, Cecilia's *Lyf* becomes more than a work of hagiography in the mouth of the heretofore silent Nun: it becomes the matrix within which a cloistered woman religious is transformed into the saintly subject of her textual production, the mellifluous Cecilia. The radicality of the saint's conversionary efforts, public denunciation of Roman cultic practice, and pastoral care of her followers at her Life's end take on new meaning when voiced by the Nun. So told, both the saint and the Nun chafe against the limits imposed on female speech by the church of Chaucer's day. Mutually incorporated, they become more than they could become on their own: together, they become authorized preachers.

The textual incarnation of the Nun into Cecilia is annunciated early in the Nun's prologue to her tale, and, more significantly, it is mediated by the Virgin Mary herself. Within the very paradoxical space of Mary's chaste, yet fecund, womb, the Nun locates the paradox of her narrator's "I," for as she is figured in her prologue, she is simultaneously neither oralized nor textualized, neither cloistered nor uncloistered, neither embodied nor disembodied, neither male nor female. She becomes the perfect word that is able to materialize into any/body—the body of Cecilia, a "bisy bee," even the Word-made-flesh. For it is in the Nun's "feithful bisynesse" of translating the saint's Life, her apian *imitatio* of Cecilia, that she becomes a "sower of chaast conseil," an *incarnatrix Verbi Dei* (CT, VIII.24, 192).

Astride her horse, directed toward the words that she so impassionedly delivers to her pilgrim congregation, the Nun was illustrated by the illuminator of San Marino, California, Huntington Library, MS EL 26 C9, fol. 187r, and one can see her now as Chaucer may have imagined her during his authoring.[18] She begins her prologue with a fiery sermon against idleness and asserts that the tale she will tell, presumably unlike the tales told by the other pilgrims thus far, will try "to putte [them] fro swich ydelnesse" (VIII.22). Moreover, not only do her words seek to keep them from such sin, but in the very act of speaking (and translating) against it, she also hopes to keep herself faithfully occupied. She proclaims:

> I have *heer* doon my feithful bisynesse
> After the legende in translacioun
> Right of thy glorious lif and passioun,
> Thou with thy gerland wroght with rose and lilie–
> Thee meene I, mayde and martyr, Seint Cecilie.
>
> (VIII.24–28; emphasis mine)

The Nun is clear that her present, preacherly activity is not without historical or, to anticipate her tale-telling enterprise, textual precedent. She models her own holy occupation "after" the Life of Cecilia and thus prefigures the very tale that she is about to tell with her public reenactment. For as she notes, "feith is deed withouten werkis"

(VIII.64). In her analysis of the Nun's "ethical repetition" of Cecilia's preaching, Catherine Sanok argues, "The apparent modesty and conventionality of the prologue obscures the affinity between the Second Nun's performance and the heterodox positions on women's preaching and other devotional practices."[19] Consequently, we fail to see how the Nun's *imitatio sanctae Ceciliae* "authorizes a woman's public voice, her right to preach to the assembled company in order to turn them away from idleness and its attendant dangers."[20]

Likely aware of the church's prohibition against women's public preaching when he imagined his sermonizing Nun, Chaucer deftly thwarts any neat identification of her speech-act with a more heterodox performance not only through her appeal to the textual precedent of Cecilia's *vita* but also through her persistent textuality. Twice in her prologue, the Nun refers to the writtenness of her performance. After her condemnation of idleness, she invokes the intercession of the Virgin Mary. At both the beginning and the end of her prayer, she asks the "flour of virgines" to guide her in her writing (VIII.29). In the first verse of her invocation, she prays:

> Thou confort of us wrecches, do me endite
> Thy maydens deeth, that wan thurgh hire merite
> The eterneel lyf and of the feend victorie,
> As man may after reden in hire storie.
>
> (VIII.32–35)

And at the end of her supplication, she begs her readers:

> Yet preye I yow that reden that I write,
> Foryeve me that I do no diligence
> This ilke storie subtilly to endite,
> For bothe have I the wordes and sentence
> Of hym that at the seintes reverence
> The storie wroot, and folwen hire legende,
> And pray yow that ye wole my werk amende.
>
> (VIII.78–84)

In both passages, the Nun emphasizes her hope to *write* the story of Cecilia effectively, so that it will be of spiritual benefit to those who *read* her text. She seeks to do justice to the lived testimony of the saint's Life with her hagiography by carefully attending to the words and meaning of him who originally wrote it. Moreover, she does not set her work above the reproach of its future readers; she humbly admits the inadequacy of her words and opens them up to critical emendation.[21] Some scholars have argued that the Nun's references to the writtenness of her tale reveal the carelessness of Chaucer's edition of his earlier *Lyf of Seynt Cecile*, but I believe that Chaucer's preservation of the *Lyf*'s textuality safeguards the Nun's words from being condemned as an act of preaching. So related, they are written, not spoken; translated from Jacobus de Voragine's, not created; exposed to readerly correction, not dogmatically imposed. But are they really? Chaucer's Nun refuses to sit comfortably within either her vocal or her textual frame; she is always already in both.

Further complicating any univocal definition of the Nun's speech-act as either preacherly or not is the seeming bilocation of her authorial voice. Especially after reading her rousing harangue against idleness at the beginning of her prologue, with its pointed references to her assembled congregation, we are tempted to locate her speaking body *only* on the road to Canterbury, that is, in a very public, uncloistered domain. However, in her invocation to Mary she complicates the locative source of her authority; we hear (or read) the Nun's exalted praise of the fair maiden's womb: "Withinne the cloistre blisful of thy sydis / Took mannes shap the eterneel love and pees" (VIII.42–43). She locates the salvific speech-act of the Incarnation in the humble enclosure of Mary's womb, and in metaphorically equating this sacred space to a cloister, she also locates her own spiritual authority within Mary's keeping. Sanok argues that this metaphoric equation, "the Second Nun's strongest argument for women's performance of sacred speech itself[,] recalls the restriction of that speech to the intensely private space of a womblike cloister."[22] While I do agree with Sanok that here, in the Nun's use of the metaphor of the cloister for Mary's womb, she legitimates her public performance, I believe that her analysis fails to recognize that the Nun is *only* able to find both authorization and an authorized space for her performance within such an "intensely private" enclosure given the constraints of her historical situation. In 1298 Pope Boniface VIII issued the decretal *Periculoso* to extend the rule of cloister to all nuns in the church; that is, nuns were not permitted to leave the confines of their nunneries without the permission of their local bishop.[23] Though, as Henry Kelly emphasizes, the efforts to enforce *Periculoso* in England were not entirely successful, the perpetual enclosure of nuns was nevertheless the expressed ideal of the church into the time that Chaucer wrote "The Second Nun's Tale."[24] And though the Nun, as the chaplain of her nunnery, may have had the authority to orate publicly to her conventual sisters on liturgical occasions such as reading from hagiographic exempla during the lessons at Matins,[25] she was not authorized to speak publicly to an assembly outside the walls of her cloister. So, necessarily, the Nun has to encloister her voice if she is to speak with authority before the party of pilgrims, and quite remarkably, she does so by in-wombing her words with the divine Logos. But far from restricting her voice to a "private space," Mary's "cloistre" provides the very space in which the kind of daring, public speech that the Nun performs is made possible. For it is within the sides of Mary's womb, joined to and, most boldly read, transformed into the Word, that the Nun can speak freely as a woman endowed with the grace of speech. For only enfleshed there can she become a preacher both in and out of the cloister.

The Nun's dramatic enfleshment within the Virgin's womb, however, does not result in the kind of embodied presence that we might expect. In fact, Chaucer's construction of her lively, vocal personality seems to resist the very embodiment that he gives to most all of the other tale-telling pilgrims and thereby allows her to overcome any attempt to deny her voice authority on the basis of its associations with woman's allegedly, inherently sinful bodiliness.[26] Though the Nun tells her company that her soul "troubled is by the contagioun / Of [her] body, and also by the wighte / Of erthely lust and fals affeccioun," we never see the bodily "prison" within which her soul labors, because she is neither burdened with nor bolstered by a detailed portrait from the Chaucer-like narrator of *The Canterbury Tales* in the

"General Prologue" (VIII.72–74, 71). We are simply told, after the lengthy description of the Prioress, that "Another Nonne with hire hadde she, / That was hir chapeleyne, and preestes thre" (I.163–64). Quite misleadingly, the illuminator of the Ellesmere MS took great liberties with the narrator's nearly nonexistent verbal portrait in order to create his vivid rendering of the Nun. In contrast to his lurid descriptions of other pilgrims, he only names the Nun's position in her convent. Interestingly, scholars rarely read her indistinct form as ultimately intended by Chaucer.[27] But what if, in the poet's final imagining, she was complete in her seeming incompleteness? So unfigured, she would not have to bear the weight of the body that the narrator sees; freed from his interpellation, her body would be able to materialize with her own words. Her no-bodiness would allow her to take on any/body, even that of a man.

In her *Invocatio ad Mariam*, the Nun implores the Virgin to help her, "flemed wrecche," that she is "in this desert of galle," for she is as desperate as "the womman Cananee, that sayde / That whelpes eten somme of the crommes alle / That from hir lordes table been yfalle" (VIII.58–61). The Nun's references to both the exiled Eve and the Canaanite woman, whose request for her daughter's healing Jesus initially dismissed, seem to invite the reader to identify the Nun with these outcast women.[28] However, such an identification is disturbed by the lines that immediately follow: "And though that I, unworthy *sone* of Eve, / Be synful, yet accepte my bileve" (VIII.62–63; emphasis mine). The unexpected self-appellation "sone of Eve" troubles the female body that any reader or illuminator may want to give her. And though as before we may be tempted to read this intrusion of the male body into the Nun's prayer as just another one of Chaucer's editorial oversights, this reading appears in an overwhelming majority of the surviving manuscript copies of Chaucer's *Canterbury Tales*, including the Ellesmere MS.[29] And though the ambiguity of the Nun's sexed body may simply reveal the authorial kinship that Chaucer felt toward her, the poet's skill as master craftsmen of authorial personae should not be underestimated. Did Chaucer intentionally give his Nun a body that could be read as neither male nor female? If so, to what end did he do so? To allay the fears of his more doctrinaire readers by entertaining the possibility that a male body, concealed under a nun's habit, was really preaching? Or to give her a body that embodied the early Christian baptismal formula found in Paul's letter to the Galatians,[30] a body that could resist circumscription by the liturgical codes found in other Pauline epistles?[31] Chaucer's poetic play teasingly leaves such questions unanswerable. He makes her body porous to multiple inhabitations, including one by the unlikeliest of creatures—a honeybee.[32]

In the Nun's tale itself, we hear Pope Urban I's offertory prayer for Cecilia's newly converted, chaste spouse, Valerian:

> "Almyghty Lord, O Jhesu Crist," quod he,
> "Sower of chaast conseil, hierde of us alle,
> The fruyt of thilke seed of chastitee
> That thou hast sowe in Cecile, taak to thee!
> Lo, lyk a bisy bee, withouten gile,
> Thee serveth ay thyn owene thral Cecile."
>
> (VIII.191–96)

Urban's prayer acknowledges that from birth Cecilia was brought up in the Christian faith and ever sought to "bar his gospel in hir mynde" (VIII.123). She prayed ceaselessly to God, whom she loved and feared, "bisekynge hym to kepe hir maydenhede" (VIII.126). God, in turn, rewarded her faithful prayers by sowing in her his seed of right counsel, the very wisdom of his salvation, and it was this "conseil" that Cecilia in turn sowed in Valerian during her wedding night catechesis (VIII.145). She was a busy bee that spread the productive pollen of God's Word to all souls in need of regeneration. More suggestively, Urban's prayer likens Cecilia to the Virgin Mary and her chaste impregnation with the Word. Valerian is the fruit of the seed that was implanted in Cecilia. Thus, Urban rightfully offers Valerian to God as the bounty of her virginal womb, or hive.

Like Cecilia, the Nun metaphorically incarnates the "feithful bisynesse" of the bee in her sermon-giving and tale-telling (VIII.24). But more significantly, the very words that she both speaks and writes drip with the very mellifluence of her tale's saintly subject: the Nun's performance is an apian *imitatio Ceciliae*. And in imitating the saint's beelike labors, in seeking to convert idle wanderers to the righteous way, the Nun creates not only a holy hive into which she gathers her spiritual offspring to nourish them with her honeyed wisdom but also a sacred space very much like Mary's womb in which she can safely act as an *incarnatrix Verbi Dei*. As a bee, she assumes a body that is not only freed from the church's prohibition against women's preaching in public but also able to become a prophet of the heavenly mysteries.

MECHTHILD OF HACKEBORN'S EUCHARISTIC "HONYCOMBE"

The second prologue to Mechthild of Hackeborn's *Booke of Gostlye Grace* supplies the contents of the five parts of the book: (1) revelations that occurred on feast days of saints and Mary throughout the year, (2) revelations that concern Mechthild herself, (3) teachings that belong to the worship of God and to the health of human beings' souls, (4) revelations that belong to the health of human beings' souls, and (5) revelations that concern some human beings' souls. Thus in the first four parts of her *Booke* we hear of Mechthild's own visions and in the final part of those received by others that relate to the seer and the spiritual benefits transmitted by her *Booke*. Included among the recipients of special revelations in the fifth part are Mechthild's two scribes, who, in the original Latin *Liber*, are two sisters in her community, one possibly being Gertrude the Great (1256–ca. 1302), but who, in the Middle English translation, become Mechthild's two male confessors. Their clerical presence in the *Booke* is by no means incidental to its authorization. As the second prologue further relates, this *Booke* may contain a "sentence," or teaching, that is not found in the scriptures, but if the reader encounters such a passage, she should commit it to Christ's grace, which shows "new things" of his wisdom and goodness that are secret and uncertain to his "lovers," as he did for others in "olde tyme" (69/10–16). The recognition of Mechthild's inheritance of the biblical prophetic tradition is given greater legitimacy through the sacerdotal power of her "male" scribes. Far from threatening the reader with unorthodox teachings, her extrascriptural revelations offer new testaments of God's love, and by the *Booke*'s end, we learn that her words were graced with the power to become more than textual offerings. Rightly received, they become eucharistic.

In the sixteenth chapter of the fifth part, one of the scribes records a vision that "he" had while he was asleep, three years before he wrote down Mechthild's revelations. In his vision, he found himself at Mass standing with the nuns of Helfta in the choir of their church. He saw Mechthild receive communion and return to the choir. Upon returning, she began to sing, "Domine, quinque talenta" (590/1–2).[33] After she finished singing, she turned to the choir and asked, "Who wille haffe of þe honye of heuenlye Ierusalem?" (590/4–5). Whereupon, as the scribe recounts,

> sche profryde a honycombe owte of a vesselle þat sche hadde to alle þe sustrene in the qweere whiche come to here. Ande þat same persone þat sawe [alle þis] as by vysioun [went] to here also, als hym thow3t, ande sche gaffe hym a gobette of brede owte fro þe honye. Ande while sche helde þat breede in here handdys, wonderfullye þat gobette of breede with þe honye both togydders bygane to wexe owte into a loofe so þat the gobette of breede wexe owte in a hoole loofe ande the honycombe persede þe lofe withyn ande withowte, ande þorowe here handdis. Whilys sche helde þat loofe itt droppede in so moche plenteuosnes ande habundaunce þat itt wette alle here lappe ande so ranne forth ande moystede alle the erth abowte þem. (590/6–18)

Here the scribe's vision breaks off, but the chapter further relates "anoþer tokynne of þis booke" that was received by those who worthily read it (590/19).

On an unspecified feast day, a certain nun was about to read from Mechthild's *Booke*, but before she could do so, another nun "with a stronge spyritte" said to her: "A sustere, what goodenesse ande frewte es in þis booke, for þe furste tyme þat euere I lokede þareopoun, my herte felte suche a wonderfulle ande a luffynge styrrynge þat itt wente þoroweowte alle the partyes of my bodye" (591/3–7). This occurrence, the scribe notes, proved, yet again, the fittingness of the *Booke*'s title: "þe Booke of Spyrytualle Grace" (591/8–9). Both "the fygour of swa swete a lykoure" and the fact that "itt peersede so lyȝtlye ande so softelye þare hertys þat lokede þareopoun" reveal the abundant spiritual fruit that the *Booke* yielded for the entire community at Helfta, even her "male confessors" (591/10–12). Nothing is "swettere" than God's grace, for it comforts, instructs, and enlightens the human soul, thereby leading it to "alle goodenes" (591/12, 15).

The inclusion of both of these "tokynne[s]" in the same chapter textually materializes the book of Mechthild's revelations that her sisters read into the very honeycomb-bread that she offered them in the scribe's vision. Both stand as *sacramenta* of the *res* of God's grace contained within. In the scribe's vision, Mechthild appeared before her community, after having received communion, singing the words of Jesus's parable of the talents. Seemingly a *nova figura* of the servant who multiplied his five talents into ten, Mechthild made a rich offering from the abundance of her harvest, using well the spiritual gifts given to her. Her honeycomb offering was taken out of a vessel, whose origin is not revealed. In her brief treatment of this scene, Heather Reid, I think convincingly, has linked it to a similar one found in the fifteenth-century Middle English translation of *The Storie of Asneth*, which recounts the Life of the Egyptian wife of the Old Testament patriarch Joseph.[34]

While locked in her room during a period of self-imposed penance, Asneth was visited by an angel, who asked her to bring him a honeycomb for his repast. She was dismayed by the request because she did not have any honeycombs in her "celer," but the angel commanded her still: "Entre into thi celer . . . And thu schalt fynde an honycomb redy on the bord, / Take and brynge yt to me."[35] Asneth doubted the angel's words a second time, but he again insisted that a honeycomb would be waiting for her in her cellar. To Asneth's wonderment, when she entered her "celer," she found a honeycomb "of a gret assise, / Also white as the snowe, clene and pure in kynde, / Of odour swete."[36] Given other Mariological figurations of Asneth found in her *Storie*, Reid argues that Asneth's "celer" should be read as a type of Mary's womb.[37] Like Mary, Asneth had to be assured by the angel that her womb, though virginal, could indeed bring forth great fruit, and the fruit that would be brought forth from both of their wombs would truly be the sweetest of foods to be broken and shared for the nourishment of all.[38] Like Mary and Asneth, so too Mechthild. Her offering was the fruit of the spiritual graces that had been placed within her; she brought forth the Word-made-honey for all to share.

In several earlier visions of Mechthild's own, found in the first part of the *Booke*, she is recurrently figured in sacerdotal roles, performing various eucharistic acts. All these acts are authorized by and flow out of Mechthild's first vision recorded in the *Booke*. In chapter 2, on the feast of the Annunciation, while thinking on her past sins with great bitterness, she was given a "gostelye syght" of herself clothed "with a fowle garmente" (74/19–20). This vision made her feel even more keenly the weight of her conscience, moving her to greater contrition for her past negligence in the love of God. Suddenly, from this state of dread, her vision was elevated to a more glorious scene. She was taken before the throne of the Son, and "with that delectabylle syght sche felle into noȝt fro hereselfe als brennede woode tornede to askes" (75/18–19). When she regained consciousness, she was made to know that all the good deeds that she neglected "were perfourmyde ande made perfyte in the hoolye conuersacion of Cryste ande in his holye and perfyte werkes, ande þat alle here perfeccion and affeccion was perfitlye reformede in the perfeccion of Goddys sonne" (76/1–5). Secure in the knowledge of God's unfailing, grace-filled productivity within her, she boldly rose up to rest "opoun the lappe of Ihesu, here dere lovere" (75/14–15). Here she received many "tokenges of love," including a pipe of gold from Jesus's heart through which she could "gyffe worscheppes, thankkynges, and lawdeys to God" (75/16, 21–22).

Later in this same vision, Christ grasped Mechthild's hands in his own and "gaffe here parte of that trauayle ande excercyses of alle hys werkes whiche he perfytelye wrought in his humanyte" (78/20–22). He then blessed her sense organs with his own: he pressed his eyes, ears, and mouth to hers, so that she could see, hear, and speak as he did, giving worship and thanksgiving to the Father and teaching and preaching to the people.[39] All these gifts were given to her so that she could "make aseth ande satisfaccion for here negligencez in his seruyce" (79/10–11). After this sensual blessing, Christ then joined Mechthild's heart to his own, "whiche passede honye in swetnesse" (79/13). It seemed to her that her soul was "fullye" incorporated into Christ's, so "softenede ande liquifiede" had it become in his love (79/17–19). Like soft wax that is impressed with a seal and then bears the "lyknes" of the seal, her soul was made "alle oone ande [onede] with here dere love" (79/20, 22).

In this initial vision, Mechthild was given the great commission not to be like Christ's disciples but to become like Christ himself in her ministry. To carry out this mission, Christ transformed her with and into his very body. She took on his eyes, ears, mouth, and very heart to reincarnate the Word in her own day. So inter-corporated do their bodies, souls, and words become that by the vision's end, Mechthild no longer seemed to be able to distinguish herself from Christ. She completely identified herself with the Word and, thus, was truly able to become that Word for others. What is more, her very body and soul became the authorizing charter on which Christ affixed his seal, bearing his own image, licensing her to be his very presence in the world, and on this charter, he inscribed his Word for the edification of all.

In subsequent visions, Mechthild lived out the radical calling Christ authorized in the eucharistic acts that she performed at his bidding. In chapter 4, the scribe relates a time when Mechthild was to receive the Eucharist and, instead, owing to her great desire to give thanks and worship to God, was taken up into a vision in which Christ "gaffe here his herte of the godhede in the lyknes of a cuppe of golde" and told her, "Be myne herte ande þorowe myne herte of godhede, þowe schalte alwaye worschepe me. Tharefore goo furthe ande make redye ande bere the wyne of myne herte in this cuppe to alle sayntys" (82/16–17, 18–21). Beginning first with the angels, then patriarchs, prophets, apostles, martyrs, confessors, and virgins, Mechthild brought the cup filled with the wine of the divine heart to the entire communion of angels and saints, and at the end of her service, she returned to Christ who "toke that cuppe ande putt hitt in here herte, ande so sche was blesfullye oonyde to God" (84/19–20). The reward that Mechthild received for her service again re-created the very union that we saw her enjoy in the earlier vision: it seems to have bestowed upon her the office of his cupbearer. Her heart became the tabernacle in which the cup containing the eucharistic offering of Christ's blood was concealed. More significantly, this cup bears a striking resemblance to the vessel from which Mechthild procured and distributed the honeycomb-bread in the vision that her one scribe beheld.[40]

Chapter 27 of part 1 relates another vision in which Mechthild performed a eucharistic act, but in this vision she served Christ himself. On Palm Sunday, Mechthild desired to know more about "whate Martha ande Maria ordeynede to oure lorde Ihesu whene he was herborede with thame" (150/10–12). So consumed by this desire, she was given a vision in which she found herself in the sisters' house in Bethany. Sitting at table, Christ greeted her and said, "Suche ane howse þowe schalte make to me in þyne sawle wharein þowe schalte *mynistre* me ande do me seruyse" (150/20–22; emphasis mine). Then Mechthild saw Christ "atte a borde" again, but this time the table seemed to be within her very soul (150/23). Here she served him seven dishes: platters of honey, violets, lamb, fatted calf, fawn, Christ's own roasted flesh, and his sacred heart. Each of these dishes signified a different aspect of Christ's love for humanity. Notably, for this essay, the platter of honey signified "that blessede luffe swettere þan anye honye whiche made hym come fro the faderes lappe ande reste hym in ane erthlye crache, whenne þorowe alle the worlde heuyns were made fulle of ioy and swetnesse" (151/3–6). After serving all seven dishes, Mechthild offered him three drinks: "a fulle goode drynke"; a red wine, "whiche betokenede Crystes passyoun ande his deyde"; and a clear wine, "whiche betokenede þe inwarde gostelye infucioun of swetnes þat he puttys in a mannys sawle" (152/5, 8–9, 10–12). Mechthild's vision, according to the scribe, reveals the "gostelye mynystreys" that every devout soul performs when it gives thanks and worship to God for the grace that it has received (152/12–13).

The scribe's inclusion of the universal significance of Mechthild's vision is essential to the agenda of the *Booke* as a whole. Every reader is called to perform the same ministries that Mechthild performed in her visions, but the reader's soul will only be empowered by the Word to live out this calling if it desires to receive and be transformed into it just as Mechthild did. More significantly, the reader will be enabled to imitate Mechthild by the very grace that the *Booke* itself supplies. Her words become the eucharistic offering partaken of by the reader that arouses her or his soul's desire for God. As the scribe relates, one nun professed that Mechthild's *Booke* had so moved her that "[her] herte felte suche a wonderfulle ande a luffynge styrrynge þat itt wente þoroweowte alle the partyes of [her] bodye" (591/5–7). Mechthild's words, wholly joined to God's through a union more penetrating than any sexual one, were and still are capable of inseminating the hearts of her readers in turn.

Mechthild's transformation from Word bearer to Word scatterer is signified in the scribe's own vision. The honeycomb that she proffered from her vessel was transformed into a eucharistic host from which she could extract pieces of bread for the sisters who came forward to receive the heavenly offering. When she was about to give a piece to her scribe, the bread and honeycomb began to grow together into a larger loaf, the one element completely interpenetrated with and nearly indistinguishable from the other. The loaf became so plentiful and abundant that it spilled out of Mechthild's hands and soaked her lap and moistened all the earth about her. So figured, Mechthild stood before her community as a new Aaron, with honeyed bread, rather than oil, running down and anointing her body and everything surrounding her,[41] and as a new Levite, she was given the ministry of sharing her Word-made-bread with others. Quite surprisingly in the Middle English translation, and seemingly unbeknownst to the translator, she distributed this eucharistic offering to a male cleric, who desired to receive "þe honye of heuenlye Ierusalem" from her hands. She both bore and scattered the Word, sowing the ground with the seed of the Word that had truly become her own. Her words were her *Booke*; her *Booke* was God's Word, new scriptures and new sacrament. In her *Booke*, the sacraments of word and Eucharist perfectly commune; the one cannot be distinguished from the other. It is a vessel of God's grace.

CONCLUSION

The bee served as a significant exemplum of virginal fertility, communal concord, and spiritual busyness in other fourteenth- and fifteenth-century Middle English texts authored for and by women religious.[42] Despite its seeming ubiquity in closely neighboring texts, however, it neither appears as a spiritual model nor as an authorizing trope in the writings of Julian of Norwich. As mentioned above, Julian invokes the name of Saint Cecilia as the model for her threefold prayer in her Short Text, but in the process of expanding that text into her Long Text, the explicit reference to Cecilia was taken out. There Julian still prays for the three wounds of contrition, compassion, and willful longing to God, but she removed her description of the context that gave rise to such a prayer: we no longer hear of the sermon on the Life of Cecilia that she heard in church.[43] Such an excision seems to accord with Julian's overall editorial strategy. Many other personal references found in her Short Text, like the mention made of a "childe" brought to her bedside when she was believed to be near death, are absent from her Long Text.[44] Elsewhere, I have argued that the stripping of such markers of personal identification reveals Julian's radical conversion of her authorial "I" into a more capacious "we," a voice that is inclusive of all her "evene cristen."[45] But other scholars, most notably Kathryn Kerby-Fulton, have argued that Julian's removal of her invocation of Cecilia may have been motivated by the changed ecclesiastical context in which she wrote her Long Text.[46] Interestingly, though, Julian did not completely erase Cecilia from that text. Her three wounds still remain and could lead the intrepid reader back to her "gostly," authorizing presence.

Although the bee does not explicitly figure into Julian's writings and nearly all potential associations with it were expunged from her Long Text, it is nevertheless striking that Julian located her authorial voice in numerous hive- or womblike spaces, from her anchorhold to Christ's side wound to the city in her soul where Christ sat enthroned to Mary, whose receptive posture at the Annunciation was mirrored by her seer in the first revelation. And though the bee may not have busied Julian's mind, as it did those of Chaucer's Nun or Mechthild of Hackeborn, the spaces in which she authorized her theology were not at a far remove from the beehives populated by other medieval women writers and preachers. Thus we cannot rule out the possibility that their mellifluous labors may have inspired Julian's own. Indeed, Cecilia's did. As in Christ's side, perhaps also in their texts, Julian learned how to create with her words "a fair, delectable place, and large inow for alle mankinde that shalle be saved to rest in pees and in love."[47]

NOTES

This essay is dedicated to my teacher Denys Turner, who always indulged this medievalist's persistent fascination with the bee in her many textual and artistic incarnations and metamorphoses. He will ever be my *Doctor Mellifluus*.

1. Virgil, *Georgics*, ed. R. A. B. Mynors (Oxford: Clarendon Press, 1990), IV.197–99, 281–314.

2. Ibid., IV.219–21.

3. For early, influential witnesses, see especially Ambrose of Milan, *De virginibus*, ed. F. Gori, Biblioteca Ambrosiana 14.1 (Rome: Città nuova, 1989), I.viii.40; and Aldhelm of Malmesbury, *Prosa de Virginitate cum Glosa Latina atque Anglosaxonica*, ed. Scott Gwara, CCSL 124A (Turnhout: Brepols, 2001), cc. IV–VI. For a helpful overview of these witnesses, see Augustine Casiday, "St Aldhelm's Bees (*De uirginitate prosa* cc. IV–VI): Some Observations on a Literary Tradition," *Anglo-Saxon England* 33 (2004): 1–22.

4. For more on the significance of the bee in classical and medieval metaphors of authorship, see Fiona Griffiths, *The Garden of Delights: Reform and Renaissance for Women in the Twelfth Century* (Philadelphia: University of Pennsylvania Press, 2007), 82–107.

5. See Alcuin Blamires, "Women and Preaching in Medieval Orthodoxy, Heresy, and Saints' Lives," *Viator* 26 (1995): 135–52; and Alastair Minnis,

Fallible Authors: Chaucer's Pardoner and Wife of Bath (Philadelphia: University of Pennsylvania Press, 2008), chaps. 3 and 4.

6. Nicholas Watson and Jacqueline Jenkins, eds., *The Writings of Julian of Norwich: "A Vision Showed to a Devout Woman" and "A Revelation of Love"* (University Park: Pennsylvania State University Press, 2006), ST, 1.36, 65.

7. Mechthild of Hackeborn, *The Booke of Gostlye Grace*, ed. Theresa Halligan (Toronto: Pontifical Institute of Medieval Studies, 1979), 406/13–407/7; 586/21–587/15. Subsequent citations of Mechthild's *Booke* are cited parenthetically in the text with page and line numbers from Halligan's edition.

8. For scholars who advance such an origin for the *Booke*, see Halligan, *The Booke of Gostlye Grace*, 47–59; Rosalynn Voaden, "The Company She Keeps: Mechthild of Hackeborn in Late-Medieval Devotional Compilations," in *Prophets Abroad: The Reception of Continental Holy Women in Late-Medieval England*, ed. Rosalynn Voaden (Cambridge: Cambridge University Press, 1996), 51–69, at 53; and Alexandra Barratt, "Continental Women Mystics and English Readers," in *The Cambridge Companion to Medieval Women's Writing*, ed. Carolyn Dinshaw and David Wallace (Cambridge: Cambridge University Press, 1999), 240–55, at 245.

9. Halligan, *The Booke of Gostlye Grace*, 2 n. 4. The line reads: "Deo gracias Amen. quod Wellys I. et cetera" (fol. 103r).

10. Ian Doyle, "English Carthusian Books Not Yet Linked with a Charterhouse," in *A Miracle of Learning: Studies in Manuscripts and Irish Learning in Honour of William O'Sullivan*, ed. Toby Barnard (Aldershot: Ashgate, 1998), 123–35, at 127.

11. Halligan, *The Booke of Gostlye Grace*, 22.

12. Doyle, "English Carthusian Books," 126–27. See also Marleen Cré, *Vernacular Mysticism in the Charterhouse: A Study of London, British Library, MS Additional 37790* (Turnhout: Brepols, 2006), 50–59.

13. This dating is based on the inclusion of Richard Misyn's translations of Richard Rolle's *Emendatio vitae* and *Incendium amoris* in the manuscript.

14. On the front flyleaf of London, British Library, MS Egerton 2006, the names "Anne Warrewyk" and "R. Gloucestre" appear. "R. Gloucestre" also appears on the back flyleaf. The latter name refers to Richard, duke of Gloucester (1452–85), who would become Richard III, and the first name refers to his wife, Anne (1456–85). Another name also appears in the manuscript, on fol. 127v, that of "Marget Thorpe," the daughter of a gentry family in York affiliated with Richard III. In her study of the ownership of the Egerton MS, Rosalynn Voaden notes that the manuscript containing Julian's Short Text was owned in the late eighteenth century by William Constable, a descendant of Marget Thorpe's family. Though the evidence for this later

historical connection between Julian's and Mechthild's texts cannot be used to argue for an earlier one, it is suggestive. See Rosalynn Voaden, "Who Was Marget Thorpe? Reading Mechthild of Hackeborn in Fifteenth-Century England," *Religion & Literature* 37 (2005): 9–25.

15. All quotations from Chaucer are taken from *The Riverside Chaucer*, ed. Larry Benson (Oxford: Oxford Paperbacks, 1988), and are subsequently cited parenthetically in the text (*CT*, VIII.424). A similar question is asked by the Host of the Chaucer-like narrator in the prologue to "The Tale of Sir Thopas": "What man artow?" (VII.695).

16. Sherry Reames provides the most exhaustive analysis of the sources of Chaucer's "The Second Nun's Tale." See both her early article on the subject, "The Sources of Chaucer's 'Second Nun's Tale,'" *Modern Philology* 76 (1978): 111–35, and her later article, which revises her earlier conclusions, "A Recent Discovery Concerning the Sources of Chaucer's 'Second Nun's Tale,'" *Modern Philology* 87 (1990): 337–61.

17. In her explanatory notes to "The Second Nun's Tale" in *The Riverside Chaucer*, Florence Ridley states that Chaucer's reference to his *Lyf of Seinte Cecile* in the prologue to *The Legend of Good Women* places the terminus ad quem for his initial authoring of the saint's Life at 1386/7 (942).

18. The authority of the Ellesmere MS, with respect to both its order of the tales and its compositions of the individual tales, has recently been bolstered by Linne Mooney's alleged discovery of Chaucer's own scribe, Adam Pinkhurst, whose hand prominently appears in the two earliest manuscripts of *The Canterbury Tales*, the Ellesmere MS and the Hengwrt MS (Aberystwyth, National Library of Wales, MS Hengwrt 392 D), both produced in the late fourteenth to early fifteenth century. Pinkhurst's close scribal relationship with Chaucer, as argued by Mooney, certainly begs the question of how much of the production of the Ellesmere MS, particularly the portraits of the pilgrims, reflects Chaucer's own authorial direction. See Linne Mooney, "Chaucer's Scribe," *Speculum* 81 (2006): 97–138.

19. Catherine Sanok, "Performing Feminine Sanctity in Late Medieval England: Parish Guilds, Saints' Plays, and the *Second Nun's Tale*," *Journal of Medieval and Early Modern Studies* 32 (2002): 269–303, 291; see also Catherine Sanok, *Her Life Historical: Exemplarity and Female Saints' Lives in Late Medieval England* (Philadelphia: University of Pennsylvania Press, 2007), 167–68.

20. Sanok, "Performing Feminine Sanctity in Late Medieval England," 291.

21. Here, the words from the closing chapter of Julian's Long Text echo the Nun's call to her readers well: "This boke is begonne by Goddes gifte and his grace, but it is not yet performed, as to my sight. For charite pray we alle

togeder, with Goddes wurking: thanking, trusting, and enjoyeng" (LT, 86.1–3, 379). Like the Nun, Julian stresses the necessarily communal and ongoing nature of theological performance.

22. Sanok, "Performing Feminine Sanctity in Late Medieval England," 291.

23. For an accessible edition and translation of *Periculoso*, see Elizabeth Makowski, *Canon Law and Cloistered Women: "Periculoso" and Its Commentators, 1298–1545* (Washington, DC: Catholic University of America Press, 1997), App. 1.

24. Henry Kelly, "A Neo-Revisionist Look at Chaucer's Nuns," *Chaucer Review* 31 (1996): 115–32, 120.

25. For more on the liturgical lives of late medieval English nuns, see Anne Bagnall Yardley, *Performing Piety: Musical Culture in Medieval English Nunneries* (New York: Palgrave Macmillan, 2006).

26. My reading of the Nun's performance challenges Alastair Minnis's, which argues that her tale "seems to support the orthodox consensus that it is impossible for a woman to go beyond her female body (in this life at least), inasmuch as the impediment of sex is always there, barring her from the priestly prerogative of consecration (whether of sacramentals or sacraments) and ensuring that any preaching she undertakes is fully justified by special circumstances" (*Fallible Authors*, 336). While the Nun's no-bodiness may trouble modern, feminist readers, it should be remembered that she could not have performed an "orthodox" act of public preaching otherwise.

27. A notable exception to the scholarly silence on the issue of the absence of the Nun's portrait from the "General Prologue" is Karen Arthur's "Equivocal Subjectivities in Chaucer's *Second Nun's Prologue* and *Tale*," *Chaucer Review* 32 (1998): 217–31. While I agree with Arthur's explanation of why Chaucer did not include the portrait of the Nun, I do not think that she sufficiently considers the historical context in which Chaucer was writing. I believe that the scholastic debates on women's preaching that were taking place around the time that Chaucer was writing "The Second Nun's Tale" may have influenced how he chose to figure his Nun. For a study of such debates, see Alcuin Blamires and C. W. Marx, "Woman Not to Preach: A Disputation in British Library MS Harley 31," *Journal of Medieval Latin* 3 (1993): 34–63. For a more recent assessment of this issue, see the exchange between Fiona Somerset and Kathryn Kerby-Fulton in *Voices in Dialogue: Reading Women in the Middle Ages*, ed. Linda Olson and Kathryn Kerby-Fulton (Notre Dame: University of Notre Dame Press, 2005).

28. Gen. 3; Mark 7:25–30; Matt. 15:22–28.

29. The noun "*sone*" appears in all the eighty-four manuscripts of the *Canterbury Tales* consulted by Manly and Rickert except for two: London, British Library, MS Lansdowne 851 and MS Sloane 1686, which contain the

reading "douhter"; *The Text of the Canterbury Tales*, vol. 8 (Chicago: University of Chicago Press, 1940), 9.

30. Gal. 3:26–28.

31. Cf. 1 Cor. 14:34–35; 1 Tim. 2:11–14.

32. So interpreted, Chaucer's citation of apian *imitatio* may provide a model for performing theology nonideologically, set free from the phallic epistemological framework critiqued in Ludger Viefhues-Bailey's contribution to this volume.

33. Cf. Matt. 25:14–30.

34. Heather Reid, "*The Storie of Asneth* and Its Literary Relations: The Bride of Christ Tradition in Late Medieval England" (PhD diss., University of Victoria, 2011), 189.

35. "The Storie of Asneth," in *Heroic Women from the Old Testament in Middle English Verse*, ed. Russel A. Peck (Kalamazoo, MI: Medieval Institute Publications, 1991), 38/521–23.

36. Ibid., 38/526–28.

37. Reid, "*The Storie of Asneth* and Its Literary Relations," 189. For Reid's fuller exposition of the Mariological associations in the *Storie*, see chap. 4.

38. After Asneth procured the honeycomb, the angel proclaimed: "And blessed be thei that come to God in holy penance, / For thei schul ete of this comb, that bees made of Paradise" (39/545–46). He then broke the honeycomb, ate part of it, and placed the remnant in her mouth.

39. When Christ granted Mechthild's the "excercyse of his holye mowthe," the scribe explains that his mouth "gave worscheppys ande thankkynges to his fadere, wharewith also he taught his dysciples ande prechede to the pepylle" (79/7–9).

40. See Reid, "*The Storie of Asneth* and Its Literary Relations," 182. Reid draws a connection between Mechthild's vessel and the tabernacle of Mary's womb, but given that the focus of her work is on *The Storie of Asneth*, her analysis of the scribe's vision does not elaborate on the sacerdotal significance of this vision, examine the preceding visions that authorize her to perform this eucharistic action, or flesh out the figuration of Mechthild's textual acts as eucharistic ones.

41. Ps. 132:2: "Like the precious ointment on the head, that ran down upon the beard, the beard of Aaron, Which ran down to the skirt of his garment."

42. See the early-fourteenth-century English hermit Richard Rolle's *De natura apis*, a tropological reading of the virtues of the bee, written for a female recluse, and his *Meditatio de Passione Domini*, as found in Cambridge University Library, MS Additional 3042, a tropological reading of Christ's Passion, in which he likens Christ's scourged body to a honeycomb; Carl

Horstmann, ed., *Yorkshire Writers: Richard Rolle of Hampole, an English Father of the Church and His Followers*, 2 vols. (Woodbridge: Brewer, 1999), i.96–97. Also, the late-fourteenth-century Middle English *Chastising of God's Children*, likely authored for the nuns of Barking Abbey, allegorizes the bee in order to exemplify proper spiritual discretion; Joyce Bazire and Edmund Colledge, eds., *The Chastising of God's Children and the Treatise on the Perfection of the Sons of God* (Oxford: Blackwell, 1957), chap. 3. Finally, in the Middle English translation of Bridget of Sweden's *Liber Celestis*, which was likely made at Syon Abbey in the early fifteenth century, the *figura* of the bee makes several striking appearances. Not only does Bridget offer the bee as an example of Spirit-filled productivity, but two important interlocutors in her revelations, Mary and Christ, also describe themselves as a beehive and bee, respectively; *The Liber Celestis of St. Bridget of Sweden*, vol. 1, ed. Roger Ellis, EETS, o.s., 291 (London, 1987), II.19, IV.86, VI.12, 44.

43. LT, 2.33–38, 129.

44. ST, 2.20, 65.

45. This is in an article titled "Writing Theology in Christ's 'stede': Julian of Norwich's *Revelation* and Sarah Coakley's *théologie totale*," which is currently in preparation.

46. Kathryn Kerby-Fulton argues that the downfall of Adam Easton (d. 1397) may have motivated Julian to distance herself from the English cardinal of Santa Cecilia in Trastevere; *Books under Suspicion: Censorship and Tolerance of Revelatory Writing in Late Medieval England* (Notre Dame: University of Notre Dame Press, 2006), chap. 8.

47. LT, 24.3–4, 201.

SEVEN

Academics and Mystics

The Case of Jean Gerson

BERNARD McGINN

Jean Gerson (1363–1429) was among the most influential figures of his era.[1] As chancellor of the University of Paris, he was perhaps the most important academic of the fifteenth century. He was a man of tremendous energy as well as wide interests.[2] He was also a prolific writer, leaving about five hundred works, short and long.[3] Even a brief look at these writings shows he had an abiding interest in mystical theology. Although Gerson wrote mostly in Latin, he was concerned with the dissemination of mystical teaching in his French vernacular and in other languages, as his attack on the Flemish mystic Jan van Ruusbroec (1293–1381) demonstrates. What follows is an examination of the relation between the academic and the mystical dimensions of Gerson's life,[4] in terms of the mutual enrichment of these aspects of his career as well as the tensions between the two. I do not pretend to give a full account of Gerson's view of mystical theology, which would be the task of a book and not an essay, but I hope to highlight some of the major themes of his evolving view of the significance of the forms of direct experience of God available in this life (*experientia* was one of Gerson's favorite words).

Gerson was born into a modest family on the border of Champagne and the Ardennes and came to Paris as a student in 1377.[5] He studied under Pierre d'Ailly and received his *magister theologiae* degree in 1394, succeeding his master as chancellor in 1395. The young Gerson thus had attained the pinnacle of academic success and embarked on an important ecclesiastical career as a proponent of church reform. Due to a vocational crisis, Gerson withdrew to Bruges in 1399, but he returned to Paris in late 1400 to plunge into a decade of great activity and writing. A moderate conciliarist, he became a major figure at the Council of Constance (1415–18). Political difficulties prevented him from returning to Paris, so he spent time in Austria and eventually settled at Lyon during the last decade of his life (1419–29), engaged in writing on theological, pastoral, and spiritual issues. It is impossible here to give a full picture of Gerson's multifaceted career as academic, theologian, conciliarist,[6] humanist, polemicist, preacher, biblical commentator,[7] spokesman for the French monarchy, and more. Some consideration of his view of mystical theology, however, is important for understanding late medieval mysticism, as are some of the tensions between his academic and mystical interests.[8]

Gerson was a complex and ambivalent figure, not least in his treatment of mysticism. Like a number of other ecclesiastical figures (e.g., Gregory the Great, a favorite authority), the chancellor felt called to the life of silence and contemplation but spent much of his life active in many different pursuits. Deeply interested in conveying sound devotional and mystical teaching to a lay audience, he was nervous about the dangers of unregulated devotional and mystical ideas and practices, both in terms of visionary claims and in terms of accounts of union with God. Surveying Gerson's spiritual writings, Daniel Hobbins makes the observation, "After inviting the laity to a spiritual banquet, he grew skeptical when his guests started to arrive."[9] Furthermore, Gerson's view of the nature of mystical theology is not always easy to unravel. Although he insisted on the roles of both knowing and loving in the *preparatory* stages of the path to God, like many late medieval thinkers (at least in his earlier works) he ad-

hered to what has been called "affective Dionysianism," the view that
the height of union with God can only be found in the highest aspect
of affectivity, the *synderesis*, in a form of loving darkness.[10] André
Combes and a number of later students of Gerson, however, see a
major change in Gerson's late writings (from ca. 1425 on), away from
the affective reading of the Dionysian writings.[11] Jeffrey Fisher, for
example, has recently argued that in his later works Gerson moved
to a full-fledged apophaticism that placed attaining God beyond all
human knowing *and* loving, a view that would bring him closer to
mystics like Meister Eckhart, if in his own way.[12]

During his retreat at Bruges, probably in April and May 1400,
Gerson wrote his most important vernacular mystical treatise, the
Mountain of Contemplation (*La montagne de contemplation*), which
was directed to his sisters, who lived as house beguines.[13] The work
was designed for a wide audience, and it is significant that the chancellor's first major writing on mysticism was in the vernacular. The
Mountain consists of forty-five sections in two parts: why he is writing (1–8); and the path to contemplation (9–45). The latter is set out
in terms of a stairway with three steps: humble penance and work in
the active life (Sec. 17–20); secrecy of place and silence (Sec. 21–
32); and the perseverance that enables one to reach the summit of
the mountain of contemplation (Sec. 33–45). The organization of
the treatise, lively writing, and use of images from daily life testify to
Gerson's desire to instruct a lay audience of "ordinary people, and
especially . . . my sisters" (Sec. 1; trans. 75). At the outset, Gerson
introduces a major theme in his writings: though scholarship and
learning may be suitable for attaining contemplation, the temptations to pride and arrogance that come with learning can destroy the
humility that is the necessary foundation for all progress. Therefore,
laity, and especially women, often attain the heights of contemplation more easily than the learned (Sec. 2).[14] In other words, the academic life appears to be more of an obstacle than an aid to attaining
mystical contemplation.

A crucial distinction introduced in Section 4 appears in many of
Gerson's early writings on mysticism. He distinguishes that form of

contemplation that "seeks through reasons based on the true faith the nature of God and his being and also his works" (i.e., the contemplation of the theologians) from that "which concentrates principally on loving God and enjoying his goodness without trying to acquire clearer knowledge than that which faith has inspired and given" (Sec. 4; trans. 78). This is the contemplation open to ordinary people and, according to Gerson, the wisdom that "Saint Denis of France taught in his books of mystical theology" (Sec. 4; trans. 78). This point makes Gerson's adherence to the affective reading of the Dionysian corpus clear, though one wonders what most "ordinary people" would have gotten out of reading Denys's *Mystical Theology*. Love of God is both the beginning and the end of the contemplative life, according to Gerson, although he admits that "this spiritual taste or sensation [of love] can be considered a mode of knowledge. As Saint Augustine says, love is knowledge."[15]

Most of the teaching Gerson provides in the *Mountain* is unexceptional: the value of sober pious practices, the need for balancing the active and the contemplative lives (Sec. 18), and the need for interior and exterior silence and solitude (Sec. 22–24). He defends the contemplative life against its opponents (Sec. 26–29), he speaks of the need for both God's grace and "doing what is in one" (the Scholastic adage *facere quod in se est*; Sec. 30, 35, 36), and he gives advice on prayer (Sec. 39–43).[16] The chancellor does not neglect the higher stages of contemplation, but he treats them cautiously. For example, Section 31 discusses "elevation of soul," or ecstasy, when the operations of the soul are stilled through "holy meditation and burning love" but explains that his audience must not think of this as the soul leaving the body.[17] Section 33 speaks of three states of burning love— winter, spring, and summer—the third of which features the greatest light and heat but can also bring grave temptations and storms. The most detailed discussions come in the two final sections. Section 44 speaks of three dwelling places on the ascent of the mountain, identifying these with the theological virtues of faith, hope, and charity. Following Augustine (*Conf.* 7.9–11), Gerson says that in the final stage love can bring the soul to a sudden breakthrough in which God is briefly attained, though this is not a clear vision, as in heaven. After once again mentioning "Saint Denis," he says, "Those who know God in this way sense and know what it is they perceive, as in grasping a sweetness, a fullness, a taste, a melody, and such sensations that we cannot adequately describe by anything similar."[18] And Section 45 speaks of three ways of possessing grace: by justification; by feeling and comfort, such as in spiritual intoxication; and by the union experienced by Paul. "But," says Gerson, "concerning this matter I am not worthy to open my mouth. I will leave it to the great" (trans. 125). Thus, the chancellor distances himself from any personal claim to such experience of God. All in all, the *Mountain of Contemplation* is more original in its mode of presentation than in its content.

During the following productive decade back in Paris (1400–1410), Gerson continued his interest in mysticism but now more specifically directed to the nature of mystical theology, writing in Latin with a clerical audience in mind. A number of his sermons from this time bear on mystical themes,[19] but his main concern was to convey doctrinal teaching *about* mystical theology. The first focus of his efforts was the campaign against Jan van Ruusbroec. This dispute between Gerson and Ruusbroec and his followers has attracted considerable literature, especially the lengthy study by André Combes.[20] The basic facts and issues at stake can be presented fairly succinctly.[21] Late in the 1390s the Carthusian Bartholomew Clantier sent Gerson a copy of Willem Jordaen's Latin translation of Ruusbroec's central mystical text, the *Spiritual Espousals* (*Die geestelike brulocht*), asking for his opinion. Gerson became convinced that the third book of Ruusbroec's work was heretical, so in March 1402 he wrote a letter-treatise to Bartholomew spelling out his objections. This epistle is an important source for late medieval debates over mystical union and its relation to heavenly beatitude.[22] Gerson expressed admiration for much of Ruusbroec's teaching in Books 1 and 2 of the *Spiritual Espousals*,[23] but he took a strong stand against the account of union with God found in Book 3.

Gerson attacked on several fronts. First of all, he appears to have been legitimately confused about the status of the author, mistaking Jordaens's unsigned prefatory letter in Latin for a missive from Ruusbroec himself, thus leading him to deny that an author who could pen such elegant Latin was "unlearned" and therefore writing under divine inspiration (Combes, 617.5–618.3). The issue of divine inspiration in mystical teaching remained important during the controversy. The chancellor concentrated his attack on the doctrinal problems of the third book, which, he says, "does not agree with the clear decision expressed in the decree (*cum determinatione expressa decretalis*) setting forth how our beatitude consists in two actions, vision and enjoyment, with the light of glory."[24] Gerson demonstrates this lack of agreement by citing seven passages from the Latin version of the *Spiritual Espousals* and analyzing their errors.[25] He also raises two issues that were to become a continuing part of the debate: the relation between intention and expression in mystical discourse; and the status of unlearned vernacular theology based on affectivity and personal experience.

The question of the relation between intention and expressed statement had already surfaced in Eckhart's trial in 1326,[26] and it was to continue to be an important factor in later investigations of mystical error and commentaries on mystical writings.[27] What are the hermeneutics appropriate to interpreting mystical texts? Can a good intention excuse daring or theologically questionable statements? Like Eckhart's judges, Gerson answered with a resounding no. At the end of his citations from Ruusbroec, he says that it is only on the basis of written texts that we can make a judgment about the author's intention, because "certitude about his intention cannot be taken from what he implies, but from the writings themselves."[28] The letter then sets forth an important principle of Gerson's view of mysticism: the difference between what is known by affective experience and what is known to holy persons by "inspired understanding." His basic claim is that Book 3 of Ruusbroec's treatise deals with the second set of issues, namely, those relating to understanding, and that they therefore must by judged by people who are "well-exercised in biblical learning" (622.7–623.3), that is, those who possess the requisite theological understanding, whether inspired or not. As a representative of Scholastic theology, the chancellor will return to this point several times in his attacks on Ruusbroec.

Gerson's case against Ruusbroec proceeds in three stages. The first is a treatment of the nature of beatitude; the second, a consideration of mystical union; and the third, a brief attempt to show that Ruusbroec's view of union does not differ from that of the Beghards condemned in the conciliar decree *Ad Nostrum* of 1312. The key issue is the correct understanding of union. Gerson is aware that some theologians claimed that it was not impossible that beatitude could be realized by God uniting with the soul to become its very knowledge and enjoyment, "not as its object but as its form." Be that as it may, he insists that no theologian ever advanced the position he ascribes to Ruusbroec, namely, that in beatitude "the soul ceases to exist in its own being (*in esse proprio*) and is transformed into that divine ideal being it had from eternity in God" (623.18–19).[29] Gerson notes some of the "innumerable absurdities" that would follow from such a claim of annihilation and absorption into God. He next lays out his own understanding of mystical union, citing two of the most popular scriptural proof-texts for union, 1 Corinthians 6:17 (Paul's *unitas spiritus*) and John 17:21–22, Jesus's prayer that his disciples may share in the unity that binds Father and Son, a text that mystics like Eckhart employed to defend a union of identity. Gerson explains these texts by saying that the "holy fathers" make it clear that the unity spoken of in such passages "is not essential, nor does it exist through a precise likeness, but only assimilation and participation are meant there, just as Luke says that the assembly of the believers was of one heart and one mind" (Acts 4:32). In other words, all traditional expressions and metaphors used for uniting with God are to be understood "in terms of participation and assimilation, in imitation and appellation."[30] Here Gerson reflects the traditional monastic notion of loving union of spirits that had been challenged by those late medieval mystics, like Eckhart and Ruusbroec, who insisted that on some level at least a deeper union involving identity with God could be attained, even in this life. How could Ruusbroec have fallen into so grave an error, Gerson wonders. Although he notes that the Flemish canon had condemned false mystics at the end of the second book of his work, Gerson says that because Ruusbroec lived close in time to the Beghards he appears (to Gerson at least) to have shared their view of union. He even opines that the "decree" that beatitude comes in two acts may have been drawn up against Ruusbroec's view, "which by chance he then held in common with many." Gerson was obviously confused about the early fourteenth-century debates over mysticism, but he was correct in discerning that Ruusbroec used language of indistinction between God and the soul that was also found among his heretical opponents. What Gerson did not advert to was Ruusbroec's attempt to incorporate this language within a broader and more complex teaching on three coexisting levels of mystical union: union with intermediary, union without intermediary, and union without difference or distinction.[31]

The final part of Gerson's letter (Combes, 628.11–635.6) sets out his view of the relation of affective and intellective knowledge of God and reveals some of the key elements of his own mystical teaching. In order to judge rightly about "these difficult matters of theology," Gerson says, it is not enough to be devout and adept at affective contemplation, because "even little women and the uneducated" (*etiam mulierculae et idiotae sine litteris*) can attain this—indeed, often more easily than the learned. Trained theologians, however, excel in intellectual contemplation, and although the affective contemplation that comes from experience is higher, the truly wise person should have "both types of contemplation, namely that of affectivity which gives taste, and that of intellect, which provides the brightness of knowledge" (631.9–11).[32] In deciding about the truths of faith, learned theologians need to be consulted, though even they can fall into error, especially if they lead sinful lives. Those who have only "small intellectual light and small learning, even in secular studies" (among whom Gerson probably numbered Ruusbroec), should be careful about writing and teaching, because while their works may contain "many divine and very deep things" (*in multis divina altissimaque sint*), there is also much that is "false or badly explained" and that can lead the simple into error. Gerson was conscious of the growing split between scholastic theology and the vernacular mystical theology in his time, and he sought various ways to bridge the growing divide, as shown by the *Mountain of Contemplation*. Despite his praise for affective contemplation, however, there is a strong element of suspicion of vernacular mysticism in his Latin writings and an insistence on the priority of academic judgment. This attitude appears in other sermons and writings from the period around 1402–8, where he also criticizes the Flemish mystic's treatise.[33]

It is not clear when Gerson's attack came to the attention of Ruusbroec's community of Augustinian canons at Groenendaal, but it must have been relatively quickly. The community commissioned Jan van Schoonhoven, who had studied at Paris, to reply to the chancellor.[34] His two works defending Ruusbroec, the *Commendation or Defense* and the *Letter of Response*, date to about 1402–8.[35] Gerson, however, did not yield an inch. About the middle of 1408 he wrote a second public letter to Bartholomew Clantier reiterating his rejection of Ruusbroec's teaching on union.[36] The letter unfolds according to eight theological principles that Gerson says were violated in Book 3 of the *Spiritual Espousals*. The first is that "we should always speak according to a certain rule," so that considering nouns as arbitrary is against the practice of the Fathers. The second principle declares that an "unsuitable and metaphorical, or unusual and figurative," theological statement ought not become common but should rather be reduced to a proper and accepted usage, as one finds in the theology of Thomas Aquinas and Bonaventure. Thus, says Gerson, "we ought to find the greatest security in a theology that is both practical and speculative, when it brings all previous doctors of theology back to one proper and safe way of expression."[37] Theological uniformity is Gerson's ideal. The third principle is that we should put our trust only in a person who is expert in his art. Since the objectionable part of Ruusbroec's treatise considers "the highest theology, which is called mystical," it should be investigated only by established experts, like Albert the Great, who treated these matters in his commentaries on Dionysius. Gerson is indignant at van Schoonhoven's claim that such matters could be discussed, not only in the schools, but also by the ignorant laity.

Gerson's fourth principle comes to the heart of the controversy. He once again quotes 1 Corinthians 6:17 as teaching that the only correct understanding of union is one of assimilation, saying that "any other manner of speaking in the holy doctors, as in Dionysius and others, is metaphorical and figurative, hyperbolic or emphatic, and if it is not related to this rule, it is to be rejected."[38] He cites as examples not only the doctrine of personal annihilation of the heretic Amaury of Bene (d. ca. 1207), with its teaching on our absorption into our own "first ideal existence," but also the likeness (*similitudo*) adduced by "a certain doctor," who had compared union to a drop of water being immersed in a jug of wine. This doctor is none other than Bernard of Clairvaux, who had used this metaphor in his treatise *On Loving God* (as had many other mystics). Gerson's stringent view of union and the rules for expressing it thus led him to attack even Bernard (one of his prime authorities in other contexts), both here and in his 1402 treatise, *On Speculative Mystical Theology*, which provides the source of this passage.[39]

The last four principles are meant to cut the ground out from under Jan van Schoonhoven's defense of Ruusbroec. According to the fifth principle, we should reject the devotion of those who mix up their theological conclusions with "statements that are unlearned, alien, and unusual." Gerson illustrates this principle with a contemporary example. In the sixth principle, Gerson cites the philosophical adage, "Plato is a friend, Socrates a friend, but the truth is more a friend." The seventh principle is similar: "Those who love are making up dreams for themselves" (Vergil, *Bucolics* 8:108); that is, even learned theologians in their enthusiasms can make mistakes.[40] Finally, again quoting a Roman poet (Horace, *Ars poetica*, 438–44), the eighth principle states that a person who defends a manifest error rather than trying to correct it is not to be instructed or warned but rather should be censured by the judgment of bishop or inquisitor or the action of the faculty of theology of the University of Paris. This reiteration of opposition to Ruusbroec's view of union from the perspective of academic theology was to last for the rest of Gerson's life.[41]

The other focus of Gerson's interests in the decade 1400–1410 was also doctrinal and closely connected with the attack on Ruusbroec. This is expressed in the twin treatises he called *On Mystical Theology* (*De mystica theologia*), divided into the *First Speculative*

Treatise (*Tractatus primus speculativus*), written in 1402 (revised in 1422), and the *Second Practical Treatise* (*Tractatus secundus practicus*), dating from 1407–8.[42] These dual treatises are the earliest fifteenth-century examples of a mystical handbook, a type of literature that, while not new, experienced a florescence in the era.[43] Gerson's aim had switched from making mystical theology available to the laity to ensuring that the clergy knew what was *real* as opposed to false mystical theology.

The range of topics treated in the two treatises is large, but a look at the structure and a few major issues reveals Gerson's perspective. In the prologue to the *SMT* he once again identifies Dionysius's "mystical, or hidden theology" with knowledge of God attained "through repentant affectivity" (*per penitentem affectum*). He says that he will try to show that the things the "lofty teachers" (*doctores elevati*), or mystics, have left in their writings, such things as "contemplation, meditation, rapture, ecstasy, passing beyond the mind, the division of spirit and soul, and the like," can be communicated to people who have not experienced them.[44] In other words, although mystical theology is higher than rational theology and depends on experience, if the practitioner of rational theology approaches the topic with the proper humility and prayer for divine aid, he can, and indeed should, investigate, clarify, and even judge aspects of the message of the mystical writers. Finally, Gerson honestly admits that he is not going to say anything that cannot be found in "the books of the saints," though, he adds, "I will explain their views in my own order and words" (Combes, 6).

In a careful scholastic manner Gerson divides the treatise into eight parts with forty-four considerations. The first part consists of nine considerations on preliminary questions about mystical theology, such as the proper Dionysian understanding of the term (Consid. 1),[45] the importance of experience as the basis for mystical theology (Consid. 2–5),[46] the inexpressibility of mystical theology (Consid. 6), and the role of scholastic theology in relation to mystical theology (Consid. 7–8). "In order to acquire speculative knowledge of mystical theology," Gerson says at the beginning of the second part, "it is necessary to know the nature of the rational soul and its cognitive and affective powers" (Consid. 9; Combes, 22).[47] Hence Considerations 9–17 set out Gerson's rational psychology, which distinguishes three cognitive powers (sense knowledge, reason, simple understanding)[48] and three affective powers (animal appetite, the rational will, and what he calls the *apex mentis*, or *synteresis*). Given Gerson's affective Dionysianism, *synteresis*, which he calls "an appetitive power of the soul that comes directly from God, receiving a certain natural inclination to the good" (Consid. 14; Combes 33), is crucial for mystical theology.

Part 3 (Consid. 17–20) deals with the six powers as illuminative faculties and the necessary interaction of cognition and affectivity. Part 4 (Consid. 20–25) treats the activities of the cognitive powers: sense knowledge as producing thought (*cogitatio*), reason as giving rise to meditation (*meditatio*), and simple intelligence as the source of contemplation (*contemplatio*). This is matched in Part 5 (Consid. 26–28) by a treatment of the three eyes of the soul (*oculus carnis*, *oculus rationis*, *oculus contemplationis*) and the three corresponding activities, concupiscence, devotion, and love, as the products of animal appetite, rational will, and *synteresis*. This discussion is important for attaining a clear notion of mystical theology, because "just as contemplation is in the cognitive power of understanding, so too mystical theology resides in the affective power of *synteresis*" (Consid. 21; Combes, 51). The love produced in the *synteresis*, according to Gerson, "is not any kind of love, but ecstatic and anagogic love, that is, leading above and rapturing into things divine" (Consid. 27; Combes, 67–68). Part 6 (Consid. 29–34) turns to the investigation of the ways of acquiring mystical theology and ten differences between mystical and speculative theology, a constant theme in Gerson's thought.[49] One of the most famous passages in Gerson's writings occurs in Consideration 28, where he gives five definitions of mystical theology, each stressing its experiential, affective, and anagogic nature. The third is the most noted, often cited by later authors: "Mystical theology is experiential knowledge of God gained through the embrace of unitive love."[50]

Two important issues in medieval mystical theology were the nature of ecstasy and union with God, so it is no surprise that Gerson concludes the speculative treatise with a treatment of each. Part 7 (Consid. 35–39) takes up the triple property of love and the kinds of ecstasy. It is "loving affection" (*amorosa affectio*) that brings us to God, not knowledge, and such love has three characteristics: "First, love raptures the soul to the beloved and hence creates ecstasy; second, love joins with the beloved and makes it as if it were one; and third, love suffices unto itself and does not seek anything save loving" (Consid. 35; Combes, 94). In Consideration 36 Gerson distinguishes between rapture (*raptus*) and ecstasy (*ecstasis*), rapture being every elevation of mind and the superior powers above the inferior powers in the actualization of their operation, while "ecstasy is a kind of rapture which takes place more appropriately in the superior portion of the rational soul, which is called spirit or mind or intelligence, while the mind is so suspended in its action that the inferior powers cease from acting" (Combes, 96).[51] In identifying ecstasy as higher than rapture, Gerson appeals to Paul being raised up to the third heaven in 2 Corinthians 12:2–4 as signifying the elevation of the highest powers (= the third heaven) and the cessation of the activity of all lower powers (i.e., the apostle not knowing if he was in or out of the body).[52] The final part, the eighth (Consid. 40–44), takes up the issue of union with God, beginning by distinguishing various kinds of "spiritual unions" before focusing on "the loving union of the mind with God, which happens through mystical theology, fittingly called transformation, as the divine Dionysius and the holy fathers have said, although it is now expressed in a variety of ways."[53] Gerson's treatment of union shows his solid grounding in scripture and tradition, as well as his abhorrence of any teaching or even metaphors that might suggest a merging of identity between God and human. All union with God is perfect conformity of wills based on the fact that the human person is created *like* God but always remains essentially different.

In the shorter *Practical Mystical Theology* (PMT) written some five years later Gerson the pastor and guide of souls comes to the fore. The treatise is organized according to twelve Considerations, or forms of activity, because, as the prologue says, "it is proper to this science above all others that speculation about it cannot be perfectly handed on or fully understood unless practical use has gone before" (Combes, 125). Presumably, Gerson is advising confessors and spiritual directors about how to guide souls about the higher forms of contact with God. Again, his advice is traditional,[54] sane, and sober, touching on such practical issues as the different forms of calling to salvation (Consid. 1), the role of natural dispositions and various vocations and states of life (Consid. 2–3), the importance of perseverance (Consid. 7), and concrete advice about spiritual practices and the need for moderation (Consid. 9–11). Along the way, issues of importance in mystical teaching come up for discussion, such as the role of our own efforts (although mystical experience is always a gift of God)[55] and the relation of the active and contemplative lives.[56] Considerations 5 and 12 touch on speculative issues, since Gerson admits it is impossible to keep the speculative and practical sides of mystical theology apart. Consideration 5 reprises the teaching of the *SMT* on preparing for contemplation, but this time in the context of psalmody and sacred song as an apt setting for "perceiving ecstasies above the mind" (*sentire supermentales excessus*). Consideration 12 also repeats previous teaching about the process of gradual spiritualization and stripping away by which "the spirit lifts itself up through love into the divine cloud, where God is known in an ineffable way above the mind."[57] What is new in the *PMT* appears in the discussion in Consideration 12.6–10 concerning the knowledge given in loving union. Gerson recognizes that different interpretations of Dionysius have been given. Some authorities say that the knowledge gained in union is only "experiential" (*expermentalis*), while others say that "it can be called intellectual, not intuitive, but abstractive or 'evening knowledge,' not only connotative but absolute knowledge."[58] What the chancellor is referring to here is the difference between the "affective Dionysian" interpretation with which he was familiar through Hugh of Balma and the "intellectual Dionysian" view that was available through the commentaries of Albert the Great.[59] He does not decide between these two approaches, and his view of an intellectual knowledge of God as a concept (*conceptus absolutus*) raises serious questions that he does not address (Can we have an absolute concept of God? What does Gerson mean by *conceptus*?).

Gerson's two treatises witness his concern that clerics have correct knowledge of *mystica theologia* for themselves and the souls they guide, as well as to his growing nervousness about how easy it is for the laity to fall into error in mystical matters. Both the *SMT* and the *PMT* also reveal his ambivalence about claims to have attained union with God.

A similar ambivalence is found in his attitude toward the spiritual charisms allied with mystical states of consciousness, especially visionary claims. The late Middle Ages saw a visionary explosion and a growing concern on the part of ecclesiastical authority with how to deal with visions and visionaries. This is evident in the many discussions about the discernment of spirits (*discretio spirituum*) needed to judge which revelations come from God and which are either dangerous delusions or diabolical deceptions, especially in the case of women.[60] Gerson was not alone in addressing this challenge, but he was unusual in writing more than one treatise on the topic, beginning with *On Distinguishing True from False Revelations*, an overview published in 1402.[61] At the time of the Council of Constance he composed a treatise expressing suspicion about visionaries, including Birgitta of Sweden, titled *On Proving Spirits*.[62] And in 1423, during his Lyon period, he issued *On the Examination of Teachings*.[63] His last work on the topic was a defense of Joan of Arc, *About the Issue of the Maid and the Credence to Be Accorded Her*, published in May 1429.[64] Considerable literature has been devoted to these tracts and what they say about Gerson's attitude toward visionary women, so I will not treat them here.[65] Suffice it to say that Gerson, like others, found it difficult to provide clear and consistent theological criteria for distinguishing between true and false visionary claims.

A number of Gerson's later works demonstrate his continued interest in mysticism. The most important mystical work of the Conciliar period is the Pentecost sermon "Spiritus Domini" that he preached to the assembled council fathers on June 7, 1416. It shows the intimate bond between reform, conciliarism, and mysticism in his thought.[66] Here Gerson distinguishes three modes of the Spirit's filling (*repletio*) of the earth (Wisd. 1:7). The first is the "filling of sufficiency" in which the Spirit provides all people with the grace sufficient for salvation. The second is the "filling of abundance" which empowers progress toward union with God. Third and finally comes the "filling of redundance or overflowing," which enables prelates to become "ambidextrous" (*ambidextri*), that is, able to unite both the active and contemplative lives, thus possessing "the stability of contemplation in action and of action in contemplation."[67]

In the *Consolation of Theology*, written in exile in 1418 after the conflicts at Constance, Gerson steps back to meditate on the trials and tragedies of the life of a pilgrim on earth from the perspective of the consoling message of God's providence revealed in scripture.[68] He both imitates and transforms his model Boethius, especially in the way in which spiritual, even mystical, self-transcendence is crucial to the argument. Constructed as an interior dialogue between *Volucer* (discursive intellect) and *Monicus* (reflective intellect), the two sides of the mind of Gerson as pilgrim (*peregrinus/advena*), the four books of the work offer the consolations provided by hope, scripture, patience, and instruction. The pilgrim is pictured as someone struggling to move forward toward true peace with the aid of grace. As *Volucer* says, "Under the guidance of theology he rereads the writings of the devout doctors. . . . He struggles to recognize by experience (*experimento*) what the consolation of peace is. Soberly intoxicated with it the psalmist exclaims: 'How great is the multitude of your sweetness, Lord, which you have hidden for them that fear you' (Ps. 30:20). He explicitly says 'hidden,' because it cannot be handed over by one who possesses it." This, of course, is nothing else but mystical theology, as *Monicus* reminds him.[69] While the treatise is primarily a work of speculative theology, because speculative theology is meant to lead on to mystical theology, a number of the themes of Gerson's mysticism come up in the course of the exposition.[70]

During his final years of exile in Lyon, Gerson continued to write on mysticism. I noted above that *PMT* 5 held up the experience of psalmody and sacred song as a special access to the reception of the grace of divine sweetness. Between 1423 and 1426 the chancellor composed two works on the relation between music and mysticism, that is, how the song in the heart helps us reach out toward God.

These works, the Latin *Treatise on the Canticles* (*Tractatus de canticis*) and the French *Canticordum to the Pilgrim* (*Canticordum au pelerin*), have recently been edited and given detailed study by Isabelle Fabré.[71]

In the middle of the Lyon period, on October 1, 1425, Gerson sent off a letter-treatise (*Epistola* 55), titled *Some Notes on the Teaching of Ubertino's "The Life of Christ,"* an attack on the Spiritual Franciscan Ubertino of Casale (d. ca. 1330) and his work *The Tree of the Life of the Crucified Jesus*.[72] After commenting on Ubertino's possible involvement in the errors of Joachim of Fiore about the Eternal Gospel, on the Beghards on mystical union, and on some dangerous positions found in a number of doctors of theology, Gerson turns, once again, to different views of mystical theology, the affective and the intellective, and two main mystical authorities, Dionysius and Bonaventure. He admits that in dependence on Bonaventure and other commentators he had once followed the affective view that placed union "in love alone of the synderesis or acme of the mind" (*in sola dilectione synderesis vel apicis mentis*). Then he makes this remarkable statement:

> Now today for the first time I know not what mystical other [view] is revealed, which, if it is necessary to make it known in a scholastic manner, seems [to be] that a mystical theology of this kind, teaching union with God, does not consist in either the work of the intellect or in the operation of the affect, although these are required beforehand as necessary dispositions according to the common law. With the soul's essence simplified, purged, and stripped of every worry, concupiscence, and phantasm, while, as Dionysius says, " . . . with all accidental differences lost and desires and cares brought to an end," and with the intellectual soul brought back, "they [i.e., intellect and affect] are gathered together into the divine monad," while, as he says elsewhere, " . . . according to the better part of our mind and the power of reason, they are ineffably and unknowingly united to ineffable and unknown things."[73]

In the above passage Gerson seems to break with his earlier affective Dionysianism to propound a view of union more directly based on the Dionysian text and not unlike what we find in Meister Eckhart and other mystics who insist that ultimate union rests in an unknowing beyond *both* intellect and will. The chancellor also insists that union takes place in the soul's essence, not its powers, the way in which Thomas Aquinas's view of sanctifying grace (*gratia gratum faciens*) is rooted in the essence of the soul.[74] Combes argued that this shift resulted from a mystical experience Gerson had enjoyed shortly before writing these lines, but his evidence is unconvincing.[75] Rather, we may take it that this breakthrough was the result of a deepening engagement with the essential issues of mystical theology found in Gerson's major authorities, as the discussion of the implications of the new understanding in the remainder of the letter demonstrates.[76] The shift also seems to be confirmed by other late writings on mysticism, though here the evidence is more ambiguous.[77]

These late works include the *Scholastic Elucidation of Mystical Theology* (June 1424);[78] Gerson's longest work, the *Comprehensive Study (Collectorium) of the Magnificat*, composed between January 1427 and April 1428;[79] the *Anagogical Work about the Word and Hymn of Glory* (1428);[80] the *Commentary on the Song of Songs*, or *On the Bride's Love* (*De amore sponsae*) of 1429;[81] and the unfinished *Treatise of Master Gerson on the Mystical Theology.*[82] These works cannot be considered in full detail here, but a few points need to be addressed to give some sense of the chancellor's final views on mysticism.

The *Elucidation* reprises a major theme in Gerson's thought, that is, how academic (i.e., scholastic) theology relates to the *theologia mystica* based on experience. Gerson reviews the major *auctoritates* on mystical theology, primarily Dionysius but also Bonaventure and Hugh of Balma. The first eight sections attempt to show that Balma's interpretation of Dionysius as holding that mystical theology is received in love and not in knowledge can be scholastically defended, but in the final four sections (9–12) Gerson again distances himself from his previous views. Here he argues that loving union does not need preparatory knowledge, but it cannot exist without some form of concomitant knowing: "It is not possible that mystical theology can exist in the human mind without some kind of knowing."[83] But what kind of knowledge are we talking about? Gerson the scholastic had always admitted that the academic could have knowledge *about* mystical theology on the basis of his reflections on what mystical teachers had said and how this does or does not conform to correct doctrine. But now he speaks of a knowing attained *in* mystical theology, one which goes beyond pure negation (*nihil nos cognoscere de Deo nisi per abnegationem*) and which is best understood by appealing to the immediate knowledge the senses have through experience.[84] At the end he describes two modes of mystical theology, using the traditional pairing of Mary and Martha from Luke 10. Mary represents the "affective knowing of mystical theology" (*affectualis cognitio theologiae mysticae*), while Martha figures "the other mode of contemplation said to be purely and directly of divine truth" (*alter modus contemplationis qui dicitur pure et liquide veritatis divinae*). Both are recognized as true, although the latter form is more rarely achieved.[85] Gerson's appeal to the "spiritual senses" in this context deserves more study, but it is noteworthy that his view of knowledge in mystical theology has now abandoned any sense that we can have an intellectual *conceptus* of God, as suggested in the *PMT*.

The *Collectorium* is a detailed commentary on the "Magnificat" (Luke 1:47–56), a long and digressive exploration of Mary's wisdom (*sapientia*) as found in her hymn of praise to God. Divided into twelve treatises, the *Collectorium*'s most important reflections on mystical theology are found in Treatise 7 on the verse, "He has shown the power of his arm and has scattered the proud in the mind of their heart" (*dispersit superbos mente cordis sui*; Luke 1:51).[86] What is the *mens cordis*? What does it mean to "scatter the proud in the mind of the heart"? Gerson investigates the text using a wide range of mystical authors, especially Dionysius.[87] First of all, he defines *mens* as the highest power of the soul, that which is capable of attaining God. He then turns to the kinds of *dispersio mentis*.[88] What he is really interested in, however, is the way to "collect the mind," which is nothing other than devotion, "elevation of mind," union, or mystical theology.[89] The focus of this lengthy consideration of mystical theology is on "experimentive or tasting love" of God (*experimentativum vel gustativum amorem*; 8:302).

With the aid of *De mystica theologia* 1.1, Gerson analyzes the devotion of perfect souls in terms of *experientia* in two ways: first by way of what he calls *experimentalis intrinsecus*, that is, what it is in itself as presented by the mystics; and then by way of a *doctrinalis extrinsecus* analysis, that is, how scholastic theology investigates the testimony of the mystics. He defends his own right in the matter: "Someone may arise and say: 'What does the teaching of mystical wisdom have to do with you who have not participated in this experience?' I answer: 'I believe, because it has been said' (Ps. 115:1). I have believed the words of those who have had the experience, and therefore I have spoken in agreement with them, so that I may be led and I may lead [others], insofar as God gives me aid, towards the desire of so great an object."[90] On the basis of this scholastic investigation, Gerson then provides six definitions of *theologia mystica*, emphasizing its fundamental nature as "an experiential union of the mind with God [which] is a simple and actual perception of God in the gift of sanctifying grace."[91] The remainder of the treatise consists of a long analysis of the implications of defining mystical theology as *experimentalis perceptio Dei*, stressing the role of the darkness or cloud (*caligo*) and the negation (*abnegatio*) spoken of by Dionyius (8:309–16). Gerson closes with a consideration of the relation of mystical wisdom to union and the vision of God in heaven (8:316–22). It is clear that although ecstatic love still plays a central role in mystical theology, the union realized in *experimentalis perceptio* subsumes both knowing and loving. Dionysius had called mystical theology *sapientia amens* (DN 7.1), "not," says Gerson, "because the mind is lost or destroyed, but because at that time the mind does not think of itself, by understanding or loving itself in an actual way."[92]

Gerson's late *Commentary on the Song of Songs*, or *On the Bride's Love* (*De amore sponsae*), deserves more study in light of the long tradition of interpretation of the Song. In places it seems to reflect the accents of the affective Dionysian mysticism found in the writings of his early years, but this may be because Gerson is commenting on the Bible's great book of love. In treating the Song, there should be little surprise that the aged chancellor (always nervous about sexuality) was more ready to use the powerful erotic images of the Song of Songs to describe union with God than he had been previously.[93]

Two other works from his last year of life confirm the move away from his earlier views. The treatise known as the *Anagogical Work about the Word and Hymn of Glory*, written in late 1428, is an exposition of the meaning of the "Little Doxology" (*Gloria Patri, et Filio, et Spiritui Sancto . . .*), constructed as a Dionysian meditation on divine glory from the perspective of negative mystical theology leading to union with God.[94] Divided into four parts, the work compares the role of glory in the lives of both the *viatores* on earth and the *beati* in heaven. It reprises many of the main themes of Gerson's previous treatments of mysticism but now from the point of view summarized in the third part: "Highest in the word of glory, the rational spirit, while ascending to God in anagogy, leaves behind all operations as such, not only the intellectual, but even the affective or loving and delightful; indeed, absolutely every free and proper act we posit about God in the supreme degree objectively and positively."[95] This is the path of eminence to what Gerson now calls "the union of fading-away" (*unio defectiva*),[96] that is, the negative union found in divine darkness.[97] This seems to be in accord with the view first advanced in the *Epistle* 55 directed against Ubertino da Casale. Finally, the unfinished *Treatise of Master Gerson on the Mystical Theology* raises many questions about authenticity and interpretation, but it too suggests themes important to the late Gerson, especially the central role of grace in attaining union with God.[98]

Gerson's late works do not abandon the language of loving union, but they qualify his earlier preference for a purely affective reading of Dionysius. For Jean Gerson, as for all medieval students of mysticism, Dionysius remained the master of *theologia mystica*. The Dionysian writings, however, were notoriously difficult and capable of differing interpretations. Gerson pondered their meaning throughout his life, changing his mind dramatically, it seems. The aged Gerson seems to have adopted a more nuanced, if not always completely clear, perspective about the roles (and the limits) of both knowing and loving in the final union of *theologia mystica*. Also throughout his whole career, the chancellor insisted that mystical theology was not so much the purview of scholastic academics as it was the calling of all Christians, often most easily attained by the simple and unlettered (even women). But Gerson never overcame his suspicions about the dangers posed by unlearned lay mysticism, which for him always stood in need of guidance and control by academic theologians. In the Parisian chancellor the academic and the mystical stand in an uneasy tension—as has often been the case down through the centuries.

NOTES

This essay uses materials from an earlier work on Jean Gerson, "Appendix: Jean Gerson as Mystical Author," in my *The Varieties of Vernacular Mysticism, 1350–1550* (New York: Crossroad-Herder, 2012), 86–95. The essay expands on the late Gerson's views of *theologia mystica*.

I am happy to dedicate this essay to my colleague and friend Denys Turner, not only because the issues discussed reflect concerns that he has long made his own, but especially because he has provided his friends and students with an example of how the "mystical" and the "academic" need not always be in conflict.

1. For a biographical study, see Brian Patrick McGuire, *Jean Gerson and the Last Medieval Reformation* (University Park: Pennsylvania State University Press, 2005). Other works on Gerson that I have used include Louis Mourin, *Jean Gerson: Prédicateur français* (Bruges: De Tempel, 1952); John B. Morrall, *Gerson and the Great Schism* (Manchester: Manchester University Press, 1960); Louis B. Pascoe, *Jean Gerson: Principles of Church Reform* (Leiden: Brill, 1973); Christoph Berger, *Aedificatio, Fructus, Utilitas: Johannes Gerson als Professor der Theologie und Kanzler der Universität Paris* (Tübingen: J. C. B. Mohr, 1986); Catherine D. Brown, *Pastor and Laity in the Theology of Jean Gerson* (Cambridge: Cambridge University Press, 1987); Mark Burrows, *Jean Gerson and the "De Consolatione Theologiae"* (Tübingen: J. C. B. Mohr, 1991); G. H. M. Posthumus Meyjes, *Jean Gerson—Apostle of Unity: His Church Politics and Ecclesiology* (Leiden: Brill, 1999); Brian Patrick McGuire, ed., *A Companion to Jean Gerson* (Leiden: Brill, 2006); and Daniel Hobbins, *Authorship and Publicity before Print: Jean Gerson and the Transformation of Late Medieval Learning* (Philadelphia: University of Pennsylvania, 2009). Part of the modern interest in Gerson is due to his appear-

ance as a key figure in Johan Huizinga's *The Waning of the Middle Ages*, first published in Dutch in 1921 and translated into English in 1924.

2. On Gerson's public role, see Daniel Hobbins, "The Schoolman as Public Intellectual: Jean Gerson and the Late Medieval Tract," *American Historical Review* 108 (2003): 1308–37.

3. I use the edition of Palémon Glorieux, *Jean Gerson: Ouevres complètes*, 10 vols. (Paris: Desclée, 1960–73), unless otherwise noted, cited by volume and page (e.g., 8:322).

4. Gerson, of course, did not use the modern word *mysticism* or *mystic* to describe an individual (the term he would have used for the latter is *contemplativus*). *Mysticus* for Gerson and other medieval writers was an adjective qualifying most often a type of theology (*theologia mystica*) or the hidden meaning of scripture (*sensus mysticus*, etc.). Nevertheless, Gerson was concerned throughout his life with religious themes that are today generally treated under the category "mysticism."

5. For a brief sketch of Gerson's life and writings, see Brian Patrick McGuire, "In Search of Jean Gerson," in McGuire, *A Companion to Jean Gerson*, 1–39.

6. For a summary of Gerson's conciliarism, see Francis Oakley, "Gerson as Conciliarist," in McGuire, *A Companion to Gerson*, 179–204.

7. On Gerson as biblical scholar, see D. Zach Flanagin, "Making Sense of It All: Gerson's Biblical Theology," in McGuire, *A Companion to Gerson*, 133–77.

8. On Gerson's mysticism, see the older works of James L. Connolly, *John Gerson: Reformer and Mystic* (Louvain: Librairie Universitaire, 1928); Johan Stenzenberger, *Die Mystik des Johannes Gerson* (Breslau: Müller and Seiffert, 1928); Walter Dress, *Die Theologie Gersons* (Gütersloh: Bertelsmann, 1931); and the many books of André Combes. Besides Combes's four-volume *Essai sur la critique de Ruysbroeck par Gerson* (1945–72), see his *Jean Gerson: Commentateur dionysien* (Paris: Vrin, 1940), esp. 421–72; and *La théologie mystique de Gerson: Profil de son évolution*, 2 vols. (Rome: Desclée et Socii, 1963–64). More recent treatments include Brown, *Pastor and Laity*, chap. 6; Brian Patrick McGuire, "Jean Gerson, the Carthusians, and the Experience of Mysticism," in *The Mystical Tradition and the Carthusians*, vol. 3, ed. James Hogg (Salzburg: Universität Salzburg, 1995), 61–86; Jeffrey Fisher, "Gerson's Mystical Theology: A New Profile of Its Evolution," in McGuire, *A Companion to Gerson*, 205–48; and Marc Vial, *Jean Gerson théoricien de la théologie mystique* (Paris: Vrin, 2006). For an anthology of Gerson's spiritual writings in English, see Brian Patrick McGuire, *Jean Gerson: Early Works* (New York: Paulist Press, 1998).

9. Daniel Hobbins, "Gerson on Lay Devotion," in McGuire, *A Companion to Gerson*, 55. McGuire, Introduction to *Jean Gerson: Early Works*,

3–4, makes a similar point: "In his writings on the mystical life, Gerson offers instructions in reaching the very threshold of God's presence, and yet the closer he comes, the more reservations he has."

10. The "affective" reading of the Dionysian corpus has roots in the Victorine masters of the twelfth century and reached its full expression in the commentaries of the last Victorine, Thomas Gallus (d. 1246). For an introduction to Gallus, see Bernard McGinn, *The Flowering of Mysticism: Men and Women in the New Mysticism, 1200–1350* (New York: Crossroad, 1998), 77–87. Gerson would also have known this approach through the writings of the Franciscan master Bonaventura (d. 1274) and the Carthusian Hugh of Balma (ca. 1300), whose *Viae Syon Lugent* was often ascribed to Bonaventure.

11. See especially the detailed treatment by Vial in *Jean Gerson théoricien de la théologie mystique*, who agrees with Combes about a decisive shift around 1425, though he gives it a rather different reading.

12. Fisher, "Gerson's Mystical Theology," 214–15, argues for three periods in the evolution of Gerson's view of mysticism: (1) early Gerson (1400–1415), in which affect clearly predominates in attaining union; (2) transitional middle period (1415–25), in which the concern for finding peace and consolation become strong; and (3) late Gerson (1425–29), which sees an original rethinking of Dionysian apophaticism.

13. *La montaigne de contemplation* (7.1:16–55). I use the translation of McGuire, *Jean Gerson: Early Works*, 75–127. For a discussion, see Brown, *Pastor and Laity*, 183–94.

14. This is an important theme often repeated by Gerson; e.g., *De elucidatione scholastica mysticae theologiae* 9–11 (8:158–60). On this treatise of 1424, see Combes, *La théologie mystique de Gerson*, 2:395–465.

15. *La montagne*, Section 10 (trans. 83). The authority cited is actually Gregory the Great: *amor ipse notitia est* (*Homilia in Evangelia* 27.4, in PL 76:1207A). Gerson repeats the motto elsewhere, sometimes correctly ascribing it to Gregory (e.g., *De elucidatione* 11 [8:159]).

16. Section 39 introduces the "prayer of begging," which seems to be a practice of Gerson himself. Later in 1400 he wrote a whole treatise on this, *La mendicité spirituelle* (7.1: 220–80). See Brown, *Pastor and Laity*, 184–85, for a sketch.

17. Section 31 (trans. 104–6). Section 32 recommends Richard of St. Victor's *De arca mystica* for a detailed treatment of the kinds of contemplation.

18. Section 44 (trans. 123). At the beginning of this section Gerson notes the evidence of "a person" who was once so lifted up into contemplation, which could be a reference to himself (see also Sec. 39).

19. Gerson's mystical sermons from this period include "Videns autem Jesu" of Nov. 1, 1400 (5:604–10); the Good Friday Sermon of 1403, "Ad deum vadit" (7.2:449–519); and especially the sermon for the Feast of St. Bernard, Aug. 20, 1402, "Fulcite me floribus" (5:325–39; trans. McGuire, *Jean Gerson: Early Writings*, 128–48).

20. André Combes, *Essai sur la critique de Ruysbroeck par Gerson*, 4 vols. (Paris: Vrin, 1945–72). The titles and length of the volumes give an idea of the work's exhaustive nature: *I. Introduction critique et dossier documentaire* (1945; 900 pp.); *II. Le première critique gersonienne du De ornatu spiritualium nuptiarum* (1948; 461 pp.); *III. L'evolution spontanée de la critique gersonienne (Première partie)* (1959; 327 pp.); *L'evolution spontanée de la critique gersonienne (Deuxième partie)* (1972; 329 pp.). Whatever one thinks of Combes's interpretations, he has left later investigators in his debt by providing improved editions of the texts of the dispute, both those of Gerson and those of his opponents.

21. Helpful for the chronology, "The Ruusbroec-Gerson-Schoonhoven Controversy," in *Introduction to Iohannis Rusbrochii: De Ornatu Spiritualium Nuptiarum Wilhelmo Iordani interprete*, CCCM 207, ed. Kees Schepers (Turnhout: Brepols, 2004), 64–85.

22. The *Epistola prima ad fratrem Bartholomaeum* is edited in Combes, *Essai* 1:615–35, and also by Glorieux, *Jean Gerson: Oeuvres complètes* 2:56–62. I will cite the edition of Combes and the translation of McGuire, *Jean Gerson: Early Works*, 202–10.

23. Gerson praises the teaching of Books 1 and 2 of the *Brulocht* (Combes, 616.18–617.4). See also 620.2–3.

24. *Epistola* (Combes, 618.8–10). Combes (*Essai* 2:317–20, 428–30) argued that the decretal that Gerson had in mind was article 4 from the decree *Ad Nostrum* (1312), condemning the Free Spirit view that a person can attain full heavenly beatitude in this life. Gerson does seem to refer to this decretal later in the letter when he says that Ruusbroec's view is close to this error (Combes, 626.11–628.10). However, *Ad Nostrum* says nothing about *beatitudo* consisting in *visio et fruitio*. This, however, is the core of Benedict XII's decree on the beatific vision, *Benedictus Deus*, of 1336, so it seems that Gerson has conflated or confused the two texts.

25. A long text from Jordaens's Latin version of *Brulocht* is summarized in Combes, 618.15–619.9, and six passages are quoted verbatim at 620.10–621.13. Gerson generally seems to have followed the text pretty accurately, but the fourth passage (mistakenly or not) changes Ruusbroec's meaning. The translation of Jordaens says *"cum eo quo vident, et quod vident lumine unum fient"* (ed. Schepers, Bk. 3.210–11), but Gerson changes the last two words to *"idem fiunt."*

26. Bernard McGinn, *The Harvest of Mysticism in Medieval Germany* (New York: Crossroad, 2005), 104.

27. For example, Diego de Jesús's 1618 edition of the writings of John of the Cross contains an extensive hermeneutical introduction on how to read mystical texts, as studied by Michel de Certeau, *The Mystic Fable*, vol. 1: *The Sixteenth and Seventeenth Centuries* (Chicago: University of Chicago Press, 1992), 129–50. Later in the century François Fénelon's *Maximes des saints* (1697) is really a treatise about interpreting mystical speech. For a translation, see *Fénelon: Selected Writings*, trans. Chad Helms (New York: Paulist Press, 2006), 209–97.

28. *Epistola* (Combes, 621.15–16). See the whole passage 621.14–622.6, as well as 626.5–10.

29. Gerson's rejection of union conceived of as a return to the precreated state in God, strong in German and Dutch mysticism, remained constant during his life; see, e.g., *Collectorium super Magnificat*, Tr. VII (8:321).

30. *Epistola* (Combes, 624.14–626.4).

31. Even in his own time Ruusbroec's distinction of the three levels of union in the *Brulocht* and elsewhere provoked misunderstandings, as we can see from the canon's explanation of his position in *The Book of Clarification*. For a translation, see James A. Wiseman, trans., *John Ruusbroec: The Spiritual Espousals and Other Works* (New York: Paulist Press, 1985), 251–69.

32. This teaching on two ways to God and the superiority of the affective way is also found in Gerson's *Collectorium super Magnificat*, Tr. VII, which discusses the relation of the way of *simplex devotio* and that of *theologica intelligentiae depuratio* (8:315–16).

33. These texts were edited by Combes and include the Holy Thursday Sermon "A deo exivit et ad deum vadit" preached before the University of Paris (*Essai* 1:635–50); the *Notulae super quaedam verba Dionysii de caelesti hierarchia* (*Essai* 1:651–52); and especially the *De theologia mystica speculativa*, Consideratio 41, where he notes that Ruusbroec is said to have corrected the errors found in the third book of his *Brulocht* in his other works (*Essai* 1:666–70). I agree with Schepers ("Introduction," 75) that this does not represent a change in Gerson's view of the heretical nature of the work but only an attempt, as also seen in the first letter, to be fair to what is good in Ruusbroec.

34. On Jan van Schoonhoven (1356–1432), see Albert Guijs, "Jean de Schoonhoven," in *Dictionnaire de spiritualité*, 8:724–35.

35. Both works were edited by Combes: *Commendatio seu defensio* (*Essai* 1:684–716) and the *Epistola responsialis* (*Essai* 1:717–72). On the relation of the two texts, see Albert Ampe, "Les redactions successives de l'apo-

logie schoonhovienne pour Ruusbroec et contre Gerson," *Revue d'Histoire Ecclésiastique* 55 (1960): 402–52, 797–818.

36. The letter is in Combes, *Essai* 1:790–804; and Glorieux (2:97–103). I use the translation in McGuire, *Jean Gerson: Early Works*, 249–56.

37. *Epistola II* (Combes, 794.13–15).

38. *Epistola II* (Combes, 796.1–4).

39. Bernard qualified his use of three noted metaphors for mystical union in *De diligendo deo* 10.28 (*Sancti Bernardi Opera* 3:143) by insisting that they do not signify the loss of the creature's substance. Gerson surely knew this text, but he still disapproves of such metaphors. Gerson's longest discussion of incorrect metaphors and language about union is found in Consid. 41 of the *De mystica theologia speculativa* (A. Combes, *Ioannis Carlerii de Gerson: De mystica theologia* [Lugano: Thesaurus Mundi, 1958], 105–12), where Bernard is taken to task on 107–9, and Ruusbroec is condemned on 106. Gerson refers to this treatise at the end of the sixth consideration of *Epistola II* (Combes, 800.9–17).

40. To illustrate the kinds of "dreams" that enthusiasts can create, Gerson cites his encounter with "a certain woman considered by many to be a prophetess," who claimed that she had been annihilated and then re-created in contemplation. When Gerson asked her how she knew this, she said she had experienced it (*respondebat se expertam*: Combes, 802.1–6). The woman has not been identified.

41. The later texts directed against Ruusbroec can be found in Combes, *Essai* 1:808–78.

42. The best edition is Combes, *Ioannis Carlerii de Gerson: De mystica theologia*. There is a partial translation, *Tractatus speculativus* (hereafter SMT), in McGuire, *Jean Gerson: Early Writings*, 262–87, which also gives a full translation of the *Tractatus practicus* (hereafter PMT) on 288–333. I use my own translations. Combes has a detailed treatment of both treatises in *La théologie mystique de Gerson* 1:15–179. The most recent consideration is Vial, *Jean Gerson théoricien de la théologie mystique*.

43. Most of the fifteenth-century handbooks on mystical theology, like Gerson's, were written in Latin: John of Kastl (d. 1430), *De fine religiosae perfectionis*; Jacob of Paradise (d. 1465), *De mystica theologia*; Denys the Carthusian (d. 1471), *De contemplatione*; and Nicholas Kempf (d. 1497), *Tractatus de mystica theologia*. These are briefly treated in McGinn, *Harvest*, 404–6. For Denys the Carthusian's view of mysticism, see the essays in Kent Emery Jr., ed., *Monastic, Scholastic, and Mystical Theologies from the Later Middle Ages* (Aldershot: Ashgate, 1996). The major vernacular example of a mystical handbook was the Franciscan Hendrik Herp's *Spieghel der volcomenheit*.

44. *SMT*, Prol. (Combes, 2).

45. In good Dionysian fashion, Gerson distinguishes mystical theology based on internal experience from the *duplex theologia* (rational and symbolic) depending on extrinsic experience of things in the world.

46. *SMT* Consid. 2 (Combes, 10) provides a long list of the *cognitiones experimentales de Deo* used by the saints.

47. On Gerson's psychology, see Steven E. Ozment, *Homo Spiritualis* (Leiden: Brill, 1969), pt. 2.

48. *Simplex intelligentia* is the cognitive power by which the soul knows first principles in a light received directly from God (Consid. 10; Combes, 26–29).

49. Among the most important differences (numbers 5 and 7) is that while speculative theology demands much study and mastery of sciences, "mystical theology, even though it is the highest and most perfect knowledge, can be possessed by any of the faithful, even a weak woman or an uneducated person" (Consid. 30; Combes, 78).

50. *SMT*, Consid. 28 (Combes, 72): "Theologia mistica est cognitio experimentalis habita de Deo per amoris unitivi complexum." The other definitions are "Theologia mistica est extensio animi in Deum per amoris desiderium"; "Theologia mistica est motio anagogica, hoc est sursum ductiva in Deum, per amorem fervidum et purum"; "Theologia mistica est sapientia, id est sapida notitia habita de Deo, dum ei supremus apex affective potentie rationalis per amorem coniungitur et unitur"; and finally, citing Dionysius (*De divinis nominibus* 7.1), "Theologia mistica est irrationalis et amens, et stulta sapientia, excedens laudantes." Another set of definitions of theologia mystica is found in the *Collectorium super Magnificat*, Tr. VII (8:308).

51. *SMT*, Consid. 36 (Combes, 96). The source of Gerson's distinction between *raptus* and *ecstasis* has not been determined. Both Aquinas (*ST* IIaIIae, q. 175, a. 2, ad. 1) and Bonaventure (*Collationes in Hexaemeron* 3.30) distinguish the two but place *raptus* higher.

52. Gerson goes on to describe the kinds of rapture in Consid. 36–39 (Combes, 97–102). There is also an earlier discussion of rapture in Consid. 29 (Combes, 74–76).

53. *SMT*, Consid. 41 (Combes, 105): "Amorosa unio mentis cum Deo, que fit per theologiam misticam, congrue transformatio nominator, sicut divinus Dyonisius et sancti patres locuti sunt, sed in explicationis modo varietas." The Latin text and an English translation of Consid. 40–44 can be found in Steven E. Ozment, *Jean Gerson: Selections from "A Deo exivit"* (Leiden: Brill, 1969), 46–73.

54. At the end of the *PMT* Gerson provides a list of authors and books on mystical theology that he probably compiled about 1402 (Combes, 219–20; trans. McGuire, 332–33).

55. Gerson insists that human effort by itself cannot suffice (e.g., Prol. 4; Consid. 5.7; 6.4, 16, and 23), but he also discusses the need for our own exertions in Consid. 7.2–6 (Combes, 166–68; trans. McGuire, 307–9).

56. *PMT* Consid. 3.3 says that it is possible for some people to combine both action and contemplation, while Consid. 4.5–6 presents the traditional doctrine that the contemplative life is superior to the active life.

57. *PMT* Consid. 12.4 (Combes, 210): "ferat se spiritus per amorem in divinam caliginem, ubi ineffabiliter ac supermentaliter Deus cognoscitur."

58. *PMT* Consid. 12.6 (Combes, 211): "vel si possit dici intellectualis, non quidem intuitiva sed abstractiva seu cognitione vespertina, nec solum connotativa cognitione sed absoluta." *Cognitio vespertina* is the knowledge gained through created natures themselves, as contrasted to the *cognitio matutina*, by which the angels and blessed souls know natures in the Word. The distinction goes back to Augustine, *De genesi ad litteram* 4.23–25 (PL 34:312–13). Gerson goes on to give examples of what he means by *cognitio absoluta*, namely, the kind of *conceptus proprius et absolutus* the mind attains when all particularities and conditions are removed by abstraction to produce, for example: (1) *conceptus specificus hominis et absolutus*; (2) *conceptus Dei proprius et absolutus* (God as a concept, citing Exod. 3:14!); and (3) *conceptus boni absoluti* as God, citing Augustine and Bonaventure. On the innovative character of Consid. 12, see Combes, *La théologie mystique de Gerson* 1:169–79.

59. In the *De elucidatione* (8:154–61) Gerson also distinguishes between "affectualis cognitio theologiae mysticae" and the "alter modus contemplativus . . . pure et liquide veritatis divinae" (160).

60. For an introduction to late medieval treatment of the discernment of spirits, see McGinn, *Harvest*, 73–78. A more detailed treatment is Wendy Love Anderson, *The Discernment of Spirits: Assessing Visions and Visionaries in the Late Middle Ages* (Tübingen: Mohr Siebeck, 2011).

61. "De distinctione verarum revelationum a falsis" (3:36–56). There is a translation in McGuire, *Jean Gerson: Early Writings*, 334–64. An earlier study and translation can be found in Paschal Boland, *The Concept of "Discretio Spirituum," in John Gerson's "De Probatione Spirituum" and "De distinctione Verarum Visionum a Falsis"* (Washington, DC: Catholic University of America Press, 1959).

62. The *De probatione spirituum* (9:177–85) of 1415 is translated in Boland, *The Concept of "Discretio Spirituum,"* 25–38.

63. *De examinatione doctrinarum* (9:458–75).

64. Earlier questions about the authenticity of this work have been answered by the new edition and study of Daniel Hobbins, "Jean Gerson's Authentic Tract on Joan of Arc: *Super facto puellae et credulitate sibi praestanda* (14 May 1429)," *Mediaeval Studies* 67 (2005): 99–156.

65. See Anderson, *The Discernment of Spirits*, chap. 6; also her article "Gerson's Stance on Women," in McGuire, *A Companion to Gerson*, 293–315.

66. "Spiritus Domini" is found in *Oeuvres* 5:520–38, and partially in Combes, *La critique de Ruysbroeck* 1:811–22. For studies, see Combes, *La théologie mystique de Gerson* 1:315–86 and 2:3–228; and Louis B. Pascoe, "Jean Gerson: Mysticism, Conciliarism, and Reform," *Annuarium Historiae Conciliorum* 6 (1974): 135–53.

67. "Spiritus Domini" (5:535): "Hanc stabilitatem contemplationis in actione et actione in contemplatione fuisse crediderim in beatis Gregorio, Benedicto, et similibus plurimis."

68. The *De consolatione theologiae* (9:185–245) is translated by Clyde Lee Miller, *Jean Gerson: The Consolation of Theology: De consolatione theologiae* (n.p.: Abaris Books, 1998), which also reprints the 1471 *incunable* edition. See Burrows, *Jean Gerson and "De Consolatione Theologiae."*

69. *De consolatione theologiae*, Book I, Prose 2–3 (Miller, 68–71).

70. For example, in Book II, Prose 4 (Miller, 148–51), a discussion of concept formation by means of abstraction touches on how through contemplation "the mind comes to a pure and simple understanding which in a single intuition grasps at once present, past and future." In this state "the free will does not desert the place where it clings to God." In Book IV, Prose 3 (Miller, 244–47), there is a treatment of the false sweetness experienced by mystical heretics as contrasted with the true experience of God proved by charity toward others.

71. Isabelle Fabré, *La doctrine du chant de Coeur de Jean Gerson* (Geneva: Droz, 2005).

72. *Aliqua notanda super doctrina Hubertini "De vita Christi"* is edited in both *Oeuvres* 2:259–63; and Combes, *Essai sur la critique de Ruysbroeck*, 1:835–43. The letter is discussed by Combes, *La théologie mystique de Gerson*, 2:465–568; as well as by Vial, *Jean Gerson théoricien de la théologie mystique*, 152–60; and Fisher, "Gerson's Mystical Theology," 239–42.

73. Given the importance of this passage, I cite the full Latin (Combes, 841): "Nunc autem hodie primo mysticum nescio quid aliud aperitur quod, si scolastico more debeat reserari, videtur quod hujusmodi theologia mystica docens unionem cum Deo neque consistit in opere intellectus nec in operatione affectus, quamvis praeexigantur tamquam necessariae dispositiones de communi lege. Consistit autem, essentia animae simplificata, purgata et denudata ab omni sollicitudine, concupiscentia et fantasmate, dum *perditis alteritatibus*, ut Dionysius loquitur, *et concupiscentiis curisque conclusis*, revoluto animo autem, *in divinum monadem congregantur*, dum praeterea, ut alibi loquitur, *secundum meliorem nostrae* mentis *et rationis virtutem, ineffabilibus et ignotis ineffabiliter et ignote conjunguntur*." The italicized passages

are free citations from the Dionysian *De divinis nominibus* 1.4 and 1.1 in a version close to Eriugena (PL 122:1115A, 1113A).

74. *Epistola* 55 (Combes, 841): "Sicut ergo gratia non conjungit immediate Deo intellectum vel voluntatem et ceteras vires, sed principaliter et immediate ipsam essentiam animae, sive sit distincta formaliter vel essentialiter a potentiis sive non, sic theologia mystica non respicit operationem intellectus vel affectus, sed tantummodo unitatem vel unitionem essentiae spiritus vel mentis cum Deo."

75. Combes, *La théologie mystique de Gerson*, 2:535–39.

76. These issues (Combes, 1:841–43) involve (1) the role of sanctifying grace in uniting the soul's essence to God in an experiential way (*experimentabili*); (2) formal causality and the fruits of the spirit; (3) the gradual character of the deiform transformation; and (4) the difference between good (e.g., Bonaventure) vs. bad (i.e., carnal and proud) authorities on mysticism.

77. Jeffrey Fisher, "Jean Gerson's Meditation on Glory: A Study of the Semiotics of Medieval Negative Theology" (PhD diss., Yale University, 1997), 246–48, explains the different approaches found in Gerson's late works by arguing that they were written from a new "meta-theoretical" perspective allowing for different approaches to mystical theology.

78. The *De elucidatione scholastica mysticae theologiae* is found in *Oeuvres* 8:154–61. There is a treatment in Vial, *Jean Gerson théoricien de la théologie mystique*, 168–82.

79. The *Collectorium super Magnificat* appears in *Oeuvres* 8:163–534. For a study, see Combes, *La théologie mystique de Gerson*, 2:572–613.

80. There is a defective edition of the *Anagogicum* in *Oeuvres* 8:540–65. *Collectorium* VII and the *Anagogicum* are treated in Vial, *Jean Gerson théoricien de la théologie mystique*, 182–213.

81. The *Tractatus super Cantica Canticorum*, written in May–July 1429, is edited in *Oeuvres* 8:565–639; see Combes, *La théologie mystique*, 2:650–68; and McGuire, "Jean Gerson, the Carthusians, and the Experience of Mysticism," 78–84.

82. For an edition and comments on this unfinished commentary, see Edmund Colledge, O.S.A., and J. C. Marler, "*Tractatus Magistri Johannis Gerson De Mistica Theologia*: St. Pölten, Diöesanarchiv Ms. 25," *Mediaeval Studies* 41 (1979): 354–86 (362–71 for the edition).

83. *De elucidatione* 11 (8:159): "Stare nequit ut theologia mystica sit in hominis mente sine qualicumque Dei cognitione."

84. *De elucidatione* 11 (8:159–60).

85. *De elucidatione* 12 (8:160–61).

86. *Collectorium* VII (8:289–322).

87. Gerson comments in detail on the Dionysian *De mystica theologia* 1.1 in *Collectorium* VII (8:305–11), and *De divinis nominibus* 7.1 (8:317–19).

He also cites Gregory the Great, Hugh and Richard of St. Victor, Boethius, Bonaventure, Bernard, John Damascene, Anselm, the *De spiritu et anima*, and especially Augustine (ten times).

88. *Collectorium* VII (8:290–95) contains another analysis of the structure of the soul, showing how the *spiritus rationalis* presides over the three-fold *triclinium cordis*, consisting of a lower power (*anima*, the seat of *theologia activa*), a middle power (*ratio*, the seat of *theologia speculativa*), and the higher power (*mens*, the seat of *theologia mystica*).

89. The consideration of *collectio mentis et devotio* basically takes up the remainder of *Collectorium* VII (8:301–22).

90. *Collectorium* VII (8:307).

91. *Collectorium* VII (8:308).

92. *Collectorium* VII (8:319): "Propterea dicitur haec sapientia amens, non quod mens perdita sit vel destructa, sed quia pro tunc de se nihil cogitat, intelligendo seipsam actualiter vel amando."

93. See McGuire, "Jean Gerson, the Carthusians, and the Experience of Mysticism," 79–86.

94. I use the edition and translation found in Jeffrey Fisher's "Jean Gerson's Meditation on Glory," 4–110. My thanks to the author for providing me with a copy of this work. Dionysius is cited twenty-eight times, and it is noteworthy that *Anagogicum* III.4.d (Fisher, 30) cites the same two texts from *De divinis nominibus* 1.1 and 4 used in the passage from the *Aliqua notanda super doctrina Hubertini* quoted above. For an analysis, see Fisher, 241–45.

95. *Anagogicum* III.9.a (Fisher, 36; trans. 89). In what follows (III.9.b–g), Gerson notes his departure from his earlier works and defends this by citing Bonaventure (*In III Sent.* d. 14, q. 2, in fine). For more on abandoning intellect and affect, see II.4.d.

96. On *unio defectiva*, see *Anagogicum* I.3.b and I.8.a; III.9.f–g and III.10.b.

97. On Gerson's view of divine darkness, see *Anagogicum* II.4.b–d (Fisher, 17–18; trans. 70–71).

98. See Colledge and Marler, "Tractatus Magistri Johannis Gerson," 365–66, on *De mystica theologia* 1.

EIGHT

How Wrong Could Dante Be?

Authority and Error in *Paradiso* Cantos 26 to 29

ROBIN KIRKPATRICK

One of the most stimulating experiences in Cambridge—when Cambridge was lucky enough to number Denys Turner among its professors—was to speak about Dante in Turner's company and later see some passage or other that one might have mentioned brilliantly refreshed by his interpretation of it. That memory inspires the present essay. The cantos I want to discuss are drawn from an altitude of the *Commedia* so remote that readers and scholars, too, can often seem breathless while tackling them.[1] Yet the issues raised in this sequence are of exceptional importance. In Canto 26 Dante meets Adam; and the conversation that follows is primarily concerned with questions of language and in particular with the status of vernacular speech. Canto 28 includes Dante's first vision of God in the Empyrean, seen as an utterly simple point of light surrounded by the angelic hierarchies. Cantos 27 and 29—on which I shall mainly concentrate— focus on the workings of human, as contrasted with angelic, intelligence and include a violent polemic against the institutional church, as well as the idiocies of academic life (about which the present essay has a good deal to say). And Canto 29 also includes a thumbnail sketch of the creation of the universe.

My concern (being a teacher of literature) is primarily to concentrate on the details of Dante's text—which the reader of this essay may usefully want to keep open and to hand. Yet this analysis will also be shadowed by a number of more general questions—suggesting ample occasion for dispute and collaboration—as to the interconnection of theological and poetic discourse.[2] So, while making certain claims here for the validity of the contribution that poetry can make to theological understanding, I also write in the conviction that Dante scholars are not always best qualified to define the complexities of Dante's Christian thinking, or even of his linguistic theory. My title, speaking of authority and error, in part admits the obvious possibility that Dante's professional adherents can get things wrong. But it also raises the question of whether Dante himself could get things wrong. And my conclusion will be yes, he could—and risks doing so throughout his writing career. To this, however, I would add that Dante seems to know the risks he is taking and, in the later *Paradiso*, he develops a position which suggests, more generally, that there can be no authority at all which does not admit its own propensity to error.

Now the locus classicus on which any such argument will be based appears in the conclusion of *Paradiso* Canto 28, lines 130–35.

> And Dionysius with such desire
> set out to contemplate these nine-fold ranks
> that he defined and named as I do here.
> But Gregory departed from his view.
> And so, the moment that he reached this sphere,
> opening his eyes, he laughed, self-mockingly.

For a full discussion of these lines I refer to the work of Vittorio Montemaggi.[3] Let it be said only that, following the implications here to a conclusion, we may well discover that, for Dante, there are connections to be drawn not only between theology and poetry but also between theology and comedy. Quite legitimately, in reading this passage, Dante scholars, sober academicians, and, perhaps, even popes might well derive from it a certain hilarity that liberates them alike from overconfidence and self-importance. What is happening here?

Pope Gregory the Great arrives, on Dante's account, in Heaven. He instantaneously discovers that the ordering of the angelic hierarchy is significantly different from that which he had declared it to be in writing his *Moralia*—and bursts out in laughter over his earthbound mistake. The joke in fact is twofold in that Dante, in an earlier work, had himself adopted the erroneous scheme that Gregory once favored. Could it be that Dante's *Commedia* is truly comic in showing theology itself to be, at its best, a comedy of errors?

I mentioned a moment ago Dante's "position" in regard to authority and error. And I should now say, anticipating my conclusion, that I do not in the end want to attribute to Dante a "position" at all. I am more concerned with a process, articulated in his poem as much through narrative and linguistic experiment as through argumentation. This is close to saying that Dante is a poet and therefore affirms nothing and denies nothing. But this won't quite do. Dante plainly relishes polemic, far more than any other poet I know. At an early stage in his career, he is capable of maintaining in—significantly, perhaps—philosophical prose that faulty arguments are to be answered not in the decencies of debate but rather with "the knife."[4] And Dante the street fighter is still displaying his moves in the scathing diatribes that appear in *Paradiso* 27 and 29. Even so, when taken as a sequence, the cantos I am considering exemplify an aspect of Dante's intellectual and poetic (or narrative) procedure that has far more to do with process, or "unfolding," than with "positions," either authoritative or gladiatorial. Here, as indeed throughout the *Commedia*, Dante's poem registers an ability to shift constantly from one mode of thinking or discourse to another, approaching issues from a variety of different angles and adopting a range of different lenses. Some of these lenses are soft focus, some are telescopic, some incorporate night-vision technology. And while this analogy might seem to make Dante into a sort of visionary paparazzo, there is, I hope, justification for it in the cantos under discussion. Notably—in a passage to which I shall return—it is our first father, Adam, who in *Paradiso*

Canto 26 declares that all language is changeable, and changeable precisely because language is an effect of reason; and all effects of reason (as Adam has reason to know) are subject to change. In any case, as Dante stresses throughout these cantos, human intelligence, working sequentially through the senses and argumentation, differs from angelic intelligence, which is directly intuitive in nature.[5]

On that account human intelligence may be superior—at least to the intelligence of the rebel angels—in acknowledging the ultimately ungraspable reality of the divine. There is perhaps a lesson here for us all—Dantists, philosophical theologians, even popes. Except that this need not be seen as a finger-wagging prohibition but rather as an invitation such as Pope Gregory accepts to enter a process of correction or continual unfolding.[6]

Such a proposition requires, of course, not so much a logical defense as an entry, directly, into the details of the text itself—its twists and turns, its dislocations, its moments of unexpected, or God-given, coherence—and, not least, its pleasures. But before inviting that entry, there is a controversy that needs to be addressed in directly theological debate. For in regard to authority, have we not so far overlooked the peculiar authority of Holy Church, which might be said either to rest upon infallible final truths or to be, infallibly, the custodian of the processive truth? And does not Dante himself encourage this omission, forgetting about the church—or rather, angrily, consigning its officers to damnation? There are those who think he does. As will appear, I cannot in the end agree with that suggestion. And in developing an alternative, I want to bring into play an essay on ecclesiology by John Milbank. There are further reasons for this reference. In purely theological terms, there are certain respects in which Milbank might, with characteristic vigor, indeed contend that Dante was wrong. Yet on closer inspection, Milbank's concerns may well prove consistent with Dante's own. Consider, for instance, the following:

[Around the year 1300] there started to be a far greater gap between specialists and non-specialists in all fields: administration became more technical and distant; clerical control over the laity increased; sharper differentiations were made between academic disciplines; theology assumed a far more technical and difficult character; the traditional centrality in theology of participation, deification, apophaticism, allegory and the vision of the Church, as something engendered by the Eucharist all were abruptly challenged, in a fashion that proved epochally successful.[7]

Here the year 1300 is identified as that in which, on Milbank's understanding, a catastrophic error inserted itself into theological and ecclesial thinking. But 1300 is Dante's year—the year in which he chooses to set his journey through the other world. And it is by no means apparent that Dante can escape from Milbank's strictures on this annus horribilis. Milbank is concerned here with a movement in ecclesiology dating from that year away from a conception of the church as founded on the Eucharist toward the promotion of an administrative hegemony involving academic as well as legal institutions.

Now, I shall eventually suggest that Dante would have understood and favored Milbank's analysis. But to demonstrate this one will need to dig deep into the imaginative action of his poem, moving beyond the "positions" of parti pris argumentation. And for those who are content with Dante's explicit pronouncements on such matters, there are implications in Milbank's argument that certainly strike home. For on Milbank's account the year 1300 is also seen to anticipate the woes of the Counter-Reformation—and beyond— insofar as "a duality" began at that time to be encouraged in which there emerged the possibility of a "purely natural beatitude, accessible by philosophy."[8] Yet surely one of the central tenets of Dante's philosophy, as expressed in his prose works, the Convivio and De Monarchia, is that we can indeed come to enjoy a natural beatitude, distinct from the heavenly beatitude, and rightly should pursue this prospect in our secular lives.

When Dante scholars paraphrase Dante's philosophical position nothing is more familiar than their insistence on the separation of powers of church and empire. Both church and empire draw their authority directly from God, and each has the responsibility in its own sphere to lead humanity to a particular form of happiness. Hence Dante's famous insistence, at least in his prose writings, on the two beatitudes available to us: the empire has absolute authority over our moral lives and will bring us, under the dominion of perfect Justice, to beatitude in the natural sphere of our existence. The church, properly, should recognize that its function is to lead us, through the grace of poverty, to beatitude in the life-to-come. But of course the institutional church—I am speaking, of course, of the church in 1300—does nothing of the kind. Poverty in the perspective of eternity is no part of its existence. And worse still the involvement of the church in affairs that are the proper domain of the emperor leads to utter confusion in the secular realm. Dante indeed seems to have thought that his own exile resulted in part from papal involvement in Florentine politics. Conversely, Dante's enthusiasm for the empire as the divinely appointed agent of rational justice is carried to a point that verges, to some eyes, on the heretical. Paradise is possible in this life; and proper respect for the authority of the emperor will lead us to enjoy it.

From all of this there follow those unremitting, even paranoid, attacks on the church that punctuate Dante's poem, and are exemplified at their most vicious in *Paradiso* Cantos 27 and 29. Such thinking was enough to recommend Dante's political writings to the advisers of Henry VIII and must surely invite a bracing counterthrust from any in the Milbankian camp. I might add that if we are speaking of Dante being wrong, it is Kenelm Foster—the most scrupulous critic of Dante's thinking and a Dominican friar—who concludes that "even in the *Comedy* [Dante] reduce[s] to a minimum the conceivable contacts between human nature and divine grace. . . . And [this] perhaps reveals an important defect, from a Christian point of view . . . : an over-readiness to conceive of moral virtue in isolation from Charity."[9]

There is more to be said than space here allows about the two beatitudes, even taking *De Monarchia* as one's starting point. But I want now to move toward the text of the *Paradiso*, which offers at least a very different kind of evidence from that which can be excavated from Dante's prose works—evidence which points less to proof than to imaginative participation, through vision, liturgy, and poetry. And the suggestion must now be that Dante displays in these cantos an understanding (ultimately consistent with a Milbankian analysis) of the value of the true church which has long been obscured by his notorious attacks on popes such as Boniface VIII, who was pope in 1300, and the whole sorry crew that was tragically seduced by the Donation of Constantine.

In the larger perspective of the *Paradiso*, the process to which I want to draw particular attention in Cantos 26 to 29 begins with a single word in *Paradiso* Canto 23. And that word is *Mary*. It is surprising that Milbank's ecclesiology makes no mention of this name. Nor indeed has the name frequently been central when Dante scholars are discussing the poet's conception of the church.[10] Yet in *Paradiso* 23.88–90, Dante speaks movingly of how "at dawn and evening" he invokes the name of Mary. There can be little doubt here that Dante's conception of the true church is defined at this point by his confessed devotion to the Blessed Virgin. The narrative of Canto 23 describes the procession of Christ as he leads the Church Triumphant through the sphere of the constellations—the Heaven of Fixed Stars. Neither here nor anywhere else in the *Commedia* does Dante venture to describe the person of Christ: Christ's presence is invariably registered in appropriately apophatic mode. But once that presence here has risen out of sight, the community of the saints, described now as a true court, assembles around the figure of the Queen of Heaven. And two features, both profoundly characteristic of Dante's imagination, now come into special prominence. First, there is detailed attention in this canto (as at lines 79–84) to the phenomena of the natural world: thunderbolts, flowers, sunlight breaking through cloud to illuminate a garden. And second, there is an emphasis on the condition of "waiting." Thus the canto opens with the famous simile that compares Beatrice, awaiting Christ's coming, to a mother bird, out before dawn has yet broken, eager to forage for the food her nestlings require.

> Compare: a bird, among her well-loved boughs,
> has rested all night long while things lie hid,
> poised where her dear brood sleeps within their nest;
>   and then, to glimpse the looks she's longed to see,
> and find the food her fledglings feed upon
> (these efforts weigh with her as pure delight)
>   before dawn comes she mounts an open sprig,
> and there, her heart ablaze, awaits the sun,
> eyes sharpening, fixed, till day is truly born.
>   So too, head raised, tall, straight my donna stood . . .
>   (*Paradiso* 23.1–10)

Taken together, the twin concerns with natural phenomena and "waiting" point to certain evident implications. The church, for Dante, is the custodian of the natural world. In its liturgy, the images of that world are dedicated anew to worship. And worship is reverential waiting. Here, as throughout his poem, Dante's very use of the simile trope is profoundly significant: we speak of the natural world—even in the greatest detail—on the full understanding that such detail, along with the words that define it, are used legitimately when they are understood to be analogies—across the gap between our mind and the infinite—of the absolute truth on which they are all founded. Thus the initial simile of the canto, focused on a mother bird, anticipates its last in which the saints are compared to babies reaching out in satisfaction toward the mother who has suckled them.

> A baby suckling, once it's full of milk
> will hold its arms out wide towards its mum
> to make known outwardly its inner flame.
>   So at their incandescent peaks, these gleams
> stretched up. And this to me, made clear what depths
> of heartfelt love they bore towards Maria.
>   (*Paradiso* 23.121–26)

Now, in the overall narrative of the *Paradiso*, Canto 23 marks the beginning of a distinctly new phase. And a further indication that this is an ecclesial phase is that in Cantos 24, 25, and 26, Dante shows himself submitting to examination in the virtues of Faith, Hope, and Charity. Hitherto his theme has been the cardinal virtues and his interlocutors have been such muscular figures as Thomas Aquinas, one of Dante's own crusading ancestors, thousands of righteous kings, and the austere Saint Peter Damian. In the Heaven of the Fixed Stars, Dante's examiners are Saints Peter, James, and John. But the examination takes place under the aegis of Mary, the *stella maris*; and Dante is assisted here by Mary's surrogate—and Dante's particular "star"—Beatrice, who will have an especially complex role to play in the final third of the *Paradiso*. It is indeed Beatrice who delivers the account of the creation of the world, in Canto 29. And all of this points forward to the final cantos where the saints are once again assembled, now visible in human form, ranked as they might be in the shape of a rose. The significant factor, as Canto 32 makes clear, is that Mary, *in propria persona*, is the point of reference, at the summit of the rose, along with Beatrice, Rachel, Leah, and, of course, Eve, arranged in significant relationship to that point.

Let us, however, focus attention here on Adam in Canto 26. As I have suggested, this canto, surprisingly perhaps, concludes with a discussion of the nature of language. The burning question in Dante's mind as he encounters Adam is not what color Eve's eyes were, or how long in meters the serpent might have been. Rather, Dante is concerned to know (at line 114) what language Adam "formed and used" or spoke in the Garden and beyond it. And notably, not least because the utterance is so casual and untroubled, Adam (at lines 127–32) brushes aside all thoughts of Babel and insists that, even before that linguistic fall, language was subject to alteration— alteration being, he says here, the natural condition of all rational effects.

Yet for Dante to write in these terms—almost with a shrug— marks a highly significant turnaround. For questions of language— and above all, linguistic stability—have occupied Dante's philosophical and even political thinking from the moment he first set polemical pen to paper. Thus, the first book of the *Convivio* is wholly devoted to a consideration of the relationship between Latin and the vernacular, involving an all but truculent defense of his own determination to write this piece of philosophical prose in the vernacular rather than scholastic Latin. This determination is confirmed by the *De vulgari eloquentia*, which, though written in Latin, celebrates, from its opening chapters on, the vernacular, which is there emphatically defined as the language we learn as suckling infants at the breast of our nurse or mother. Latin remains in Dante's mind a "stable" language, and he continues to use it to the end of his life in political or scientific treatises. But the vernacular is indeed the mother tongue. And in *Paradiso* 26 Dante appears conclusively to dismiss the one worry on this score that hitherto has bothered him: the apparent instability of the vernacular when compared with Latin. Should we not, then, think of Adam's words as—appropriately enough—a new beginning where, in the realm of Maria, Dante can admit his former errors and see even in the instability of the vernacular the source of a greater authority?

That, of course, is the conclusion to which I am tending. But there is here, I think, a dawning realization on Dante's part, against his own previous intransigencies, of the obvious fact that Latin itself is a vernacular. And if "process" is at issue here, then there is ample evidence for its liberating importance in the text of Canto 26, which, first to last, is characterized by effects of generative mutability.

As the canto begins, Dante is blind and remains so as, in its first half, he is examined in the virtue of charity by Saint John. This is not the first time that Dante has associated discourse with blindness: in the central cantos of the *Purgatorio*, where love is defined as the ultimate goal of all acts of truly free will, darkness also surrounds his discussion with Virgil. One implication of this is evident: discourse, in whatever form, latinate or vernacular, must surely count as secondary to vision, a necessary but only provisional resource in our approach to God. So, as in previous stages of his theology exam, Dante now does make a soundly based propositional reply (in "*filosofici argomenti*") and is praised for his "well tuned" citation of appropriate authorities. But at line 64, the text shifts into a vibrantly metaphorical passage, which, in its arboreal references, anticipates the encounter with Adam: Dante loves all the leaves in God's orchard.

And it is at this point too that sight returns, wavering, shimmering, shifting in search of its proper focus.

> As fresh-leaved branches, when a breeze goes by,
> bend at their tip, and then—through inner strength
> which points them high—will straighten once again,
>   So I did, swaying, wavering at her words,
> to be re-made, complete in confidence
> that flowed from my own burning urge to speak.
>   "You are the single apple," I began,
> "produced as full and ripe. . . "
>
> (Paradiso 26.85–92)

So now—within the spiraling embrace of the Marian church that began in *Paradiso* 23—Dante sees Adam and reenters that primal unity which humanity was always intended to enjoy—a community rediscovered in reconciliation and charity. And, leaving aside theoretical questions, one notes the sheerly vernacular vigor (of imagination as well as phrase) that speaks of Adam, coruscating in superinfulgent light as, not "superinfulgent" at all, but rather (at lines 97–99) as comparable to some farmyard animal wriggling in a bag. We witness here in the extreme that ability on Dante's part to move with unexpected rapidity from one level of language to another. And this "polylingualism"—which directly results from Dante's happy acceptance of linguistic changefulness—will be further exemplified in Cantos 27 and 29.

For the moment consider a further example. "*O pomo maturo*" (translated as "Oh single apple produced as full and ripe") are the first words that Dante addresses to Adam. Now, there is a touch surely of comic indiscretion in any mention of apples in Adam's hearing. But apples are certainly something you can get your teeth into. And here I am not being facetious. From the very title of the *Convivio*—the Banquet—on, Dante at every point assimilates language, and in particular vernacular language, to nourishing substances—above all to bread and milk. And in doing so also he speaks, unabashedly, of the processes of digestion. So in *Paradiso* Canto 17 he speaks of the polemical words in which his own *Commedia* is so often written as "bitter" on first tasting but "vital nutriment" when once they are "digested."

At this point—were there space—one might argue at some length how when Dante speaks of the vernacular in nutritional terms—and so in terms of generative mutability—he is not really being metaphorical at all. But there is one sense in which no one whose concern is with the true church could suppose that the connection between word and essential life could ever be merely metaphorical. And that is when one is speaking of the Eucharist. In fact, at the conclusion of *Convivio*, Book 1, Dante does not hesitate to represent his choice of the vernacular in eucharistic terms: his vernacular words—so unexpected in a philosophical context—are comparable to the miraculous division of bread that feeds the five thousand. But with this in mind, along with the progressive establishment, since Canto 23, of a Dantean church, the "*Santo, santo, santo,*" which at *Paradiso* 26, line 69, announces the return of Dante's sight and the advent of Adam takes on particular significance. In the liturgy of the Eucharist, it is, of course, the *Sanctus* that concludes the prefatory prayers and points toward communion in the body of Christ as the fullest realization of charity on earth. It is precisely such a communion—easy, intimate, and vernacular—that Dante envisages in his meeting with the glorified Adam. Returning to the "apple" of our original condition, Dante here registers the intersection of sign and human reality.

Henceforth, when I speak of the church I shall also be speaking of the liturgy—which is itself a mode of performing truth, akin in certain respects to the practices of poetry.[11] Dante's text here invites that reference. One should note as well that the *Sanctus* is also the hymn in which our words and minds resonate with the choirs of angelic intelligence. So Canto 28 of the *Paradiso* is, appropriately, Dante's own glorious celebration of the angelic hierarchy. And if I were to pause on that canto, Milbank's ecclesiology would undoubtedly prove relevant. So Milbank points to the interconnection that exists or should exist between priestly (or episcopal) action and that of the angels. Invoking Nicholas of Cusa's *De concordantia catholica*, he pursues a notion of how the first shall be last and the last shall be first from a recognition of how the mystery of the Trinity operates, in sustaining yet subverting any crudely pyramidal conception of ascending prestige.

> Cusanus sustains the thesis that the Eucharist gives the Church. For him what stands topmost in the Church hierarchy is not *de jure* legal power, but rather sacramental signs. . . . Within the ecclesial hierarchy, the priesthood is linked to the angelic in terms of teaching function[;] . . . the angels are guardians of ecclesial places. [Cusanus] offers in this treatise perhaps one of the fullest exhibitions ever of the multiple paradoxes of hierarchy.[12]

But mention the number 3, and Dante will certainly have something to contribute to the discussion. And, sure enough, in Canto 28, speaking of how the angels in their threefold ranks of three contemplate the utter simplicity of God's presence, Dante does envisage a logic—but a miraculous logic, a *"mirabil consequenza"*—whereby (at lines 73–78) numerical or quantitative factors are all, hilariously, overthrown in lines which register in ecstatic rhythms the "boiling over" of any merely mathematical conception of angelic order (lines 23–39 and 88–93). This is the process that underlies the whole of creation, sustained by the incalculable action of angelic intelligence.

This is not the place to dwell on this wonderful canto.[13] Rather, it is time to turn to the textual drama enacted in Cantos 27 and 29 where Dante traces, among other things, the negative consequences that flow when human beings—including even university lecturers— ignore the lessons implicit in the Adam episode and consequently distort the realities of liturgical communion.

It is consistent with the implications of *Paradiso* 26 and also with Dante's vision of the angels that the poet should insist in Canto 29 at lines 76 to 81 on a distinction between angelic and human intelligence. Angels understand by direct intuition. Their sight of God is not *"interciso"*—that is, "cut" or "divided." It also follows from this, as Dante emphasizes from the early chapters of the *De vulgari eloquentia*, that angels do not speak. They do not need to pursue their thoughts in sequential process employing the physical instruments of language and the apparatus of argument. Which is not to say that Dante wants us as human beings ever to become angels, at least in this life. The unique characteristic of the human animal is that it is discursively rational and above all linguistic. So until we become greater than the angels, better just get on with it and enter the Adamic sphere—which so far from being a sphere of magical nominatives is one in which our discourses are in constantly refreshing motion.

So, then, to Canto 27, lines 121–23:

> Crass, itching greed! You plunge our mortal sense
> so far within your depth that none can drag
> their eyes above the mounting turbulence!

Dante's target here is Greed; and nothing could be more predictable than that. Greed is the vice which Dante particularly discerns in the protocapitalist culture of his native Florence, whose bankers were often in cahoots with the papacy. But there are certain unusual features here. First, greed is usually taken by Dante to be the direct opposite of secular justice. And the empire is, for Dante, the agency appointed by God to eradicate the inequalities of distribution that greed engenders. But the present context is one in which Saint Peter himself has spoken vehemently about the corruption of the church. Greed has corrupted its hierarchies so that some of Christ's own race are supposed to sit higher than others; and the images of which the church should be the custodian have come to serve as battle standards in factional warfare. The Bride of Christ has become the Whore of Babylon. Which is to say that greed perverts not only justice but also that original desire on which a community of *caritas* could have been founded. But Dante's own authorial intervention echoes the prophetic vigor of the speech that he attributes to Saint Peter. Indeed, the remarkable thing about this passage is that greed is seen here (at lines 127–35) to erode the very foundations of language and turn the mother tongue against itself.

> Good faith and innocence are only found
> in infant-schools. And both will long have fled
> before the cheek is covered with a beard.
>
> There's one kid, burbling still, awaiting food,
> who when he's fluent in his speech will gorge
> on every dish, beneath whatever moon.
>
> There's one there (burbling, too) who loves his mum,
> and heeds her words, who, when his tongue grows whole,
> will long to see her buried in her grave.

These are arguably the most harrowingly visceral—and polylingual—lines that Dante ever wrote, and yet they go to the heart of his own poetic enterprise, which is to forge a language that is as nuanced and heartfelt as any mother tongue must be, yet, at need, will burn with prophetic zeal—with a fervor born out of charity. (Aquinas, one remembers, sees a connection between charity and anger, as does Dante himself in the central cantos of the *Purgatorio*.)[14]

But if language can be subject to greed, then so, too, can intellect—the very faculty on which imperial justice—or academic study—might seem to depend. And Dante touches on this consideration at line 83 of Canto 27 where he alludes to the myth of Ulysses who was condemned to Hell in *Inferno* 26 for an irrepressible—and cupidinous—desire for comprehensive knowledge of the world, which leads him to breach the limits that even the pagan gods had set on human activity. But Ulysses never really stays put in Hell. References to his story occur at every point in the *Commedia*, to the extent that he becomes something of an alter ego for Dante himself in his journey beyond the boundaries of natural experience. Indeed, for Dante as author, Ulysses is a kind of mirror in which he can inspect the errors and advantages that might be discerned in his own philosophical and poetic enterprise. As early as the *Convivio* Dante had tussled with the question of whether there was any difference between an appetite for material goods and an appetite for knowledge. The short answer is that true philosophers understand the reality of rational limits and, working within that reality, mark out for themselves a productive home ground in the midst of change. This lesson has just been reiterated by Adam in Canto 26, whose original sin (line 117) is not seen as an inordinate appetite for apples but rather the transgression of a divinely given limit: "a passing beyond the sign."

In fact, in Canto 27 Dante's own journey is about to take him beyond all boundaries and indeed beyond all signs, beyond the sequences of space and time and ultimately into the Empyrean. So well he might—with a smile comparable to Saint Gregory's—turn around (at lines 79–84) and recognize the madness of Ulysses' flight across the terrestrial globe. But the basis of that transcendence is his newly discovered footing in the church, which is also, paradoxically, a rediscovery of his true earthly home. When Saint Peter contemplates with agonized authority the errors of his successors, he does so to reclaim his place (*luogo*) on earth: "*il luogo mio, il luogo mio, il luogo mio.*" The vernacular "rootedness" of these lines is unmistakable. But so too is a subtextual tension which allows an interplay of the local and the transcendent. The repetition is threefold; and, tacitly, that is as much as to say that Peter here acknowledges the radical error of his own threefold denial of Christ. But 3 is also a liturgical number, invoking that trinitarian Three on which salvation and indeed creation itself depends. The church on earth is the very home of the liturgical celebrant, of that paradox.

There is not space enough to explore in full the opening phase of Canto 27. In lines 1–6 an intoxicating *Gloria* heralds, doxologically, the end of the Adam episode, and the whole Universe bursts into laughter. But then, anticipating Saint Peter's tormented, guilt-ridden diatribe, the universal smile immediately turns to a flush of shame. The whole hierarchical structure of the planetary heavens dissolves into a psychosomatic flinch, as though the cosmos were truly now the Body of the Logos. And significantly at lines 31–33 the flush is compared to a woman's innocent indignation. This reference recalls us to the realm of Beatrice—and of Mary. It also invokes a form of language even more radical than that of vernacular speech—the body language of a living being, shifting in time and nuanced beyond all possibility of definition. I will not attempt to argue here for the importance that Dante, throughout the *Commedia*, attaches to smiles, blushes, and even at times hairs-standing-on-end. But turning now, by due process, to Canto 29, one will, I think, find that there, too, in contrast to the spiritual circlings of angelic intelligence, body language continues to matter.

It is in this canto that university lecturers get their comeuppance. And one obvious reason why they should—in the perspective of Canto 28—is that university lecturers are no angels. They tend to speak in rather long sequences, knowing nothing of angelic instantaneity. Instantaneity is, from the first, an issue in Canto 29. Beatrice is the speaker throughout this canto, as she was in the previous one. There is a moment of silence, over the canto break, between these two discourses. But the measure of this moment when Beatrice stands at lines 4–9 with laughter brushed across her face is no moment at all. The first two terzine here employ all the machinery of astronomical calculation and of mythology to capture an uncapturable instant out of time. For an authoritative analysis of this passage, I refer to the brilliant analysis offered by Christian Moevs.[15] Here one may note only the emphasis given to Beatrice's "laughter," since, polemical as this canto becomes, we should be prepared to read it, overall, in a spirit of exhilarating comedy—of readerly body language psychosomatically spelled out in the rhythms to which we must respond.

The first half of the canto offers an account of creation. Much of this is familiar from accounts offered by Aquinas. It is, however, the manner in which this philosophy is delivered that calls for attention. The surprise of it all (creation is nothing if not surprising) is registered first in the surprise of Beatrice being the speaker—rather than, say, Aquinas. But this shock to the (male) system resonates also in the breathtaking concision and (let me say) generative energy that (at lines 22–27) Dante's terzine here as always brings to his contemplation of the Trinity, at least in Italian.

> *Forma e matera, congiunte e purette,*
> *usciro ad esser che non avía fallo,*
> *come d'arco tricordo tre saette.*

E come in vetro, in ambra o in cristallo
raggio resplende sì, che dal venire
a l'esser tutto non è intervallo . . .

    [Real form and matter (both conjoined and pure),
issued in being where there was no flaw,
as from a three-string bow three arrows fly.
    Light rays that enter amber, crystal, glass,
display such luminescence that, from when
they reach, then *are* there wholly, there's no pause . . .]

Process and poise here far outweigh any mere proposition—or so the literary critic might contend. Or could it be that doxological verve is always prior to, and the proper goal of, theology?

Leaving questions of verve aside, there are still, in the shifting focus of this canto, certain rights and wrongs, polemically, to be settled. After all (at lines 109–10): "Christ did not say, to his first holy band, / 'Go out and preach pure prattle to the world.'" And, alarmingly, prattle is found here to affect even the mighty Saint Jerome, who at line 37 is roundly reprimanded for two particular errors. But the same passage also envisages an antidote to error. Note, first, that in his account of creation Jerome failed to recognize the principle of instantaneity, supposing that centuries elapsed between the creation of the angels and that of the physical universe. Aquinas, also, disagreed with Jerome on this point. Then, second, Dante insists that the error occurs because Jerome had failed to read aright the scriptural account of creation. And the note struck here resounds throughout the second half of Canto 29.

I have referred to the Marian church as the custodian of signs and temporal images. I have mentioned the Eucharist, through which our original nature is recovered. Now, Gospel Truth takes its place in the liturgical triad. And this requires some comment. For it is only recently—thanks to the work of Peter Hawkins[16]—that we have come to recognize the absolute centrality of the scriptures in Dante's poetic and theological understanding. In this new perspective it is plain to see from the *Inferno* on to the present canto that whenever Dante speaks about creation and our participation in God's order, he refers to the scriptures as the authority that must always regulate our thoughts and words.

This is emphatically not to suggest that, for Dante, scripture can be independent of the other factors—the Eucharist and Marian prayer—which in the liturgy generate the body of the church. Indeed, the whole point of my speaking of "process" is to suggest that the triad only reveals itself in full interrelationship as the narrative of the *Paradiso* unfolds. And further support for that contention could be drawn from the literally "processive" cantos that conclude the *Purgatorio*. But a sharp emphasis on this same understanding occurs throughout *Paradiso* 27 and 29. So in Saint Peter's defense of his "*luogo*" there is also an urgent recognition that Gospel truth is always supported by martyrdom as the ultimate expression of our bodily, bloody engagement with the truth of the church. In martyrdom our dying, mutable bodies conclusively assent to and help to nurture the signs and practices by which the church participates in creation. And in Canto 29 this same connection is pointedly underscored at lines 89–93 in Beatrice's attack on those verbally intoxicated philosophizers who wholly ignore the blood that was shed in sowing the seed of scripture on the earth.

> God's Holy Writ
> is put aside or twisted out of true.
> No thought is given to what blood it cost
> to sow that seed on earth nor what delight
> is given when we humbly stick to that.

Instead, these false preachers are possessed by greed and self-importance—and, of course, will do anything at all to raise a cheap (and very unfunny) laugh at lines 115–17.

> Now preachers go with feeble jokes and gags
> and, just so long as they can raise a laugh,
> their hoods puff up. They ask for nothing more.

Against such attempts at academic stand-up, there is matched the scathingly comic energy which Dante musters here in his attack, and comedy is certainly part of the tonal complexity of this canto. But there is also a specific emphasis in these lines on that ultimate act of martyrdom which, on the cross, secures the foundations of the church. Why was there darkness over the earth at the moment of Christ's death? Experts and scholars offer their various opinions, invoking speculative theories of eclipse and retrograde movements of the moon. "All lies!" (line 100): the darkness was willed by the same God who willed his own death. That darkness was therefore instantaneous, and universal. And it is in contemplating rather than analyzing that darkness that the community of *caritas*—as though intent once again on seeing Adam—will reveal its true unity.

And so it does. For the greatest comedy in this canto is the exhilarating doxology with which it concludes at lines 136–45.

> *La prima luce, che tutta la raia,*
> *per tanti modi in essa si recepe,*
> *quanti son li splendori a chi s'appaia.*
> *Onde, però che a l'atto che concepe*
> *segue l'affetto, d'amar la dolcezza*
> *diversamente in essa ferve e tepe.*
> *Vedi l'eccelso omai e la larghezza*
> *de l'etterno valor, poscia che tanti*
> *speculi fatti s'ha in che si spezza,*
> *uno manendo in sé come davanti.*

> [The primal light, whose rays shine out on all,
> is taken up in ways as numerous
> as there are splendours that it couples with.
> Therefore, since depth of feeling follows act,
> in each of these the sweetness of their love
> seethes differently—and different, too, in warmth.
> See now the height and all the generous breadth
> of God's eternal worth. These mirrors all
> were made by him, where He himself now breaks,
> one in himself remaining as before.]

God's purpose was seen in the first half of the canto at lines 13–15 as endowing all things with the vital capacity to say "*Subsisto*": "I am." Now the canto speaks in Christological terms: "The primal light, whose rays shine out on all, / is taken up in ways as numerous/ as there are splendours that it couples with."[17] God's light is indeed broken ("*si spezza*") but broken to make creation possible and to allow, in the unity of creation, a voice to all its diversity. The mirrors of the created world—angels, saints, images, and signs—receive instantaneously the primal light "where He himself now breaks, / one in himself remaining as before."

Now, one conclusion might be that what we urgently need is a conference on martyrdom. But my own preferred conclusion is to point back (as an agenda for further discussion) to a number of passages in Milbank's "Ecclesiology," which would seem to resonate with the underlying implications of Dante's poetic narration.

Most tellingly, perhaps, if our concern is the "comedy" of theological writing, Milbank speaks of how "only those possessed of a true light-hearted folly will dare to abandon everything to pursue [redemption]."[18] Martyrdom and comedy, at any rate *hilaritas*, need not, it appears, be at odds.[19]

Or else consider the pithy suggestions that "theological truth first of all abides in the body of the faithful"[20] and that "doctrine is first of all a body and not words."[21] These considerations lead Milbank, as they might also lead Dante, to a eucharistic conception of ecclesial hierarchy: "The Bishop is the original President at the Eucharist; he is also the prime preacher of the Word,"[22] and in turn this understanding of the "primacy of the sacramental"—drawing on Cusanus[23]—produces the realization that "even erring clergy can be true ministers."[24] But this emphasis on error also leads finally to a consideration of our radical dependency on signs: "Since we cannot command the meaning of any sign, true signs will always outwit our worst intentions, and inhabit us promisingly despite ourselves."[25] Gregory the Great is now—astonishingly, comically—associated with Jorge Luis Borges: "Gregory the Great had said [in his commentary on Ezekiel] that when he read and commented on the Bible the text itself expanded. It was up to the commentator to go on trying to achieve the Bible as the infinite Borgesian library spoken of at the end of St. John's Gospel."[26]

But finally, with questions of authority and error still in mind, might one return to the year 1300? In that year—to Milbank a dreadful turning point in our spiritual history—Dante may indeed have been wedded to an overrationalistic understanding of empire. After all the pope in this year was Boniface VIII, a bureaucrat of the first water and Dante's papal bête noire throughout the *Commedia*. Yet this does not stop Dante from recognizing that 1300 is a Jubilee year and proclaimed truly as such by Boniface, who must be considered—in Milbankian, no less than in Dantean, terms—as the very worst of "the erring clergy." The sacraments allow us to have it both ways. They are true signs that "outwit" our most corrupt intentions. But could not the same be said of the poetic word? In their own small fashion, poets are caught up in the comic, ever generative play of language. And—as with philosophers, dare I say—cannot poets have it both ways, too—inviting their readers to relish the truth that no truth ever stands single or alone. A true author—and authority—is one perhaps who can turn error into an active demonstration of—and confessional involvement in—the act of creation itself.

NOTES

1. All quotations from Dante are my own translation. Readers may wish to refer to the following editions of the *Commedia*, which include the original Italian and my English translation: Dante Alighieri, *Inferno*, trans. Robin Kirkpatrick (London: Penguin Classics, 2006); Dante Alighieri, *Purgatorio*, trans. Robin Kirkpatrick (London: Penguin Classics, 2008); and Dante Alighieri, *Paradiso*, trans. Robin Kirkpatrick (London: Penguin Classics, 2008).

2. Such questions are raised directly by Anna Williams in her contribution to the present volume. Discussion at the conference centered on mention of Gerard Manley Hopkins's poetry in the opening pages of John Hare's paper concerning Duns Scotus, also published in the present volume. Here, too—since poetry is the active exercise of language—there are questions concerning the connection between theory and practice: Is theology, professionally understood, to be seen as an analytic reflection on liturgical practice or

as preparation for developments in such practice. See the discussion of this issue in Daniel W. Hardy and David F. Ford, *Jubilate: Theology in Praise* (London: Darton, Longman and Todd, 1984), esp. 53–55.

3. See Vittorio Montemaggi, "Dante and Gregory the Great," in *Reviewing Dante's Theology*, vol. 1, ed. Claire Honess and Matthew Treherne (Oxford: Peter Lang, 2013), 209–62. Also see R. Kirkpatrick, "Afterlives Now: A Study of *Paradiso* 28," in *Envisaging Heaven in the Middle Ages*, ed. Carolyn Muessig and Ad Putter (New York: Routledge, 2008), 166–84.

4. *Convivio* IV 14 9. The *Convivio* is Dante's first attempt to produce a sustained piece of philosophical argumentation, intended to share his philosophical learning with his fellow citizens.

5. See *Paradiso* 29.76–81.

6. Dante has already in *Purgatorio* 26 made a connection between purgatorial refining and the process of poetic craft in refining words.

7. John Milbank, "Ecclesiology: The Last of the Last," in *Being Reconciled: Ontology and Pardon* (London: Routledge, 2003), 111.

8. Ibid., 113.

9. Kenelm Foster, *The Two Dantes and Other Studies* (London: Darton, Longman and Todd, 1977), 253.

10. This failure is now being remedied by the excellent work of Brian Reynolds in his *Porta Paradisi: Marian Doctrine and Devotion, Image and Typology in the Patristic and Medieval Periods*, vol. 1: *Doctrine and Devotion* (Taipei: Fu Jen University Press, 2009).

11. See, as for any discussion of the liturgy, Catherine Pickstock's magisterial volume, *After Writing: The Liturgical Consummation of Philosophy* (Oxord: Blackwell, 1998). See also Matthew Treherne, "Liturgical Personhood: Creation, Penitence, and Praise in the *Commedia*," in *Dante's "Commedia": Theology as Poetry*, ed. Vittorio Montemaggi and Matthew Treherne (Notre Dame: University of Notre Dame Press, 2010), 131–60. The issue of "performance" frequently arose in the course of discussion at the conference from which this volume arose. It was also a central topic of importance in a conference at Cambridge in 2003, which owed a great deal to Denys Turner's contribution.

12. Milbank, "Ecclesiology," 126–27.

13. See Kirkpatrick, "Afterlives Now."

14. Aquinas writes, "The passion of anger is useful, just like all the other movements of sense appetite, in that it enables one to execute more promptly what reason dictates. Otherwise the sense appetites would exist to no purpose" (*Summa theologiae*, IIa–IIae, q. 158, a. 1, ad. 2; a. 8, ad. 2). Dante sees anger as a passion that may indeed stray from the target to which love would rationally be directed but which nonetheless can be redirected in all its vigor to a zealous pursuit of the good.

15. See Christian Moevs, *The Metaphysics of Dante's Comedy* (New York: Oxford University Press, 2005).

16. See, in particular, Peter Hawkins, *Dante's Testaments: Essays in Scriptural Imagination* (Stanford: Stanford University Press, 1999).

17. There are stimulating suggestions relating to the ultimate enactment of the Word to be found in Karl Hefty's essay in the present volume, particularly where reference is made to the writings of Michel Henry.

18. Milbank, "Ecclesiology," 105.

19. It is notable that a comic spirit, in the most serious sense, characterizes the exchanges between John Milbank and Slavoj Žižek—which often explicitly invoke the writings of G. K. Chesterton—contained in their jointly authored, *The Monstrosity of Christ: Paradox or Dialectic?*, ed. Creston Davis (Cambridge, MA: MIT Press, 2009). For an allied discussion of Milbank and Žižek, see Eric Bugyis's contibution to the present volume.

20. Milbank, "Ecclesiology," 122.

21. Ibid., 128.

22. Ibid., 122–23.

23. Reference may be made appropriately to Mary-Jane Rubinstein's essay in the present volume.

24. Milbank, "Ecclesiology," 130.

25. Ibid.

26. Ibid., 134.

MARXISM
AND
NEGATIVE THEOLOGY

NINE

The Turning of Discourse

Generous Grammar or Analogy in Ecstasy

CYRIL O'REGAN

Denys Turner would almost certainly acquiesce with the not uncom-
mon judgment that his work evinces a certain promiscuity. Indeed,
he would probably relish its aptness, and in a puckish moment might
go on to defend the episodic nature of his literary production by insisting on the nonsystematic nature of thought in general, even if he
would do so with more civility than most who have had significant
training in analytical philosophy. He also would be generous enough
to provide cover for those somewhat hapless creatures of different
persuasion by confessing that he does not understand system,
whether the venue is philosophy or theology, and that in any event
the Anglo-Saxon race of which he is a member in some definite respects fails to have any observable gifts for that kind of enterprise
which seems to belong to the past and to the Germans. Turner, then,
could be read to have installed a three-headed prophylaxis against
any quest to espy principles of unity and coherence in his work: (a)
confessional/autobiographical; (b) ethnic; and (c) argumentative.
However charming Turner is in his various modes of prevention, it
is far from obvious that any of these tactics really work. Turner is
as alive to authorial fallacy as the next person; since he refuses to

support essentialism in general, no case can be made for its support with regard to ethnicity in particular; and as for argument, the claim that the business of theology and philosophy is more or less the sorting out of a limited number of problems, metaphysical, epistemological, and ethical, is hardly confirmed by the practice of philosophers and theologians over the centuries who seem to think that thought was about vision, fundamental orientation, and form of life. Included among these would be Augustine and Aquinas, Aristotle and Marx, all of whom are thinkers Turner deeply admires. To have offered what amounts to little more than stipulation as to the way to combat Turner's protection from the question of unity might itself seem insufficient, but here I am interested less in a decisive argumentative victory than deflating the impossibility of providing something that might look like explanation or the provision of coherence. If the kind of strictures I identify with Turner fail, or at least do not obviously succeed, he does not have others in his arsenal. His is not the kind of work that would have recourse to such postmodern sophistications as *différance* (Derrida) or hetorology (Lyotard) to justify why his discourse appears to lack unity,[1] for the use of these kinds of postmodern concepts or jargon would themselves smack of being overly systematic, specifically, of having an invariant view of the behavior of discourse and concept formation and their relation.

That impossibility cannot be allowed to reign does not necessarily enhance the real possibility that one can find an equation that makes sense of all of Turner's work or even his main work, that is, the six books that he has written. Given the massive heterogeneity of the texts, the difficulties are enormous. There is no small challenge to bringing together the book on Marx, *Marxism and Christianity*,[2] and the book on mystical theology, *The Darkness of God*,[3] and either of these with the defense of Vatican I in *Faith, Reason and the Existence of God*.[4] The lore of Herbert McCabe functioning as a kind of covering cherub for the unlikely combinations of Aquinas and Marx, even if a refreshed Aquinas and a somewhat culled Marx, is as much evasion as clue. The difficulty now can be referred to McCabe, which is precisely not to speak to the difficulty of determining the relation between Turner and McCabe. For surely Turner and McCabe are not identical in every respect, and in any event to articulate this relation would presuppose that we have got clarity with regard to how Turner's own work goes together.[5] So we return to the question, can any unity or coherence be espied in Turner's texts? I answer in the positive, although I prefer the weaker view of "coherence" to the stronger view of "unity." I will make two passes at answering the question.

First, I would like to extract some of the more salient traits of Turner's philosophical and historical thinking from his actual textual performance. Specifically, I would like to concentrate on the priority he gives to questions over answers; his view that for certain kinds of questions, for instance, religious, philosophical, and ethical questions, neither determinate nor definitive answers are possible; that this fact does not lead to agnosticism, but through careful analysis of our claims we can come to an understanding that all questions point to a transcendent reality that both exceeds language and concept and provides their raison d'être; and finally that as questions arise from real people, that is, historically and socially situated embodied persons, the questions have as their subtext what kinds of relation and quality of relations are constitutive of human flourishing.

Second, and relatedly, I will argue that Turner's thinking enacts a particular view of the Christian tradition that is fundamentally "catholic." This means that however determinately voiced Turner's work is, in the final analysis what is truly important about it is that it enacts the movement and logic—I would prefer "grammar"—of tradition. Given the variety of meanings of *grammar* currently deployed in philosophy and theology, I will have to sort out those views that Turner actually rejects and would likely reject from those that he might plausibly support. In any event, I will underscore the generosity of Christian grammar, which allows for maximal plurality and even tension among instances. This is at least in part what I mean in the title by "analogy in ecstasy." At the same time, the "catholicity" is neither absolutely permissive nor slack: not all putative forms of Christianity can be vindicated as Christian. There are a number of aspects of the grammar that I would like in particular to explore. First, Christian grammar is not readily available for inspection and is more nearly discernible when it is challenged by theological discourses, practices, and forms of life that at first blush seem to be eccentric. Second, there may very well be tension between the real grammar of Christian faith and the sedimented tradition, or what we might call the received or accepted grammar, and thus part of the task of Christianity is self-critique. A viable Christian grammar of belief, but also practices and forms of life, demands sifting. In this sifting process, apparently well-formed grammatical species of Christian thought, practice, and forms of life are revealed to be in fact ungrammatical, and, conversely, apparently not-so-well-formed species of Christian thought, practice, and forms of life are revealed to be grammatical. It is a point with Turner to expose the tension but also the stretch of the Christian tradition by looking to liminal discourses and liminal figures who challenge the received grammar: the negative theology tradition and the philosophy of Marxism are pointed to as liminal discourses; in terms of figures Meister Eckhart, Julian of Norwich, and Marx seem to be some of the more conspicuous examples. Liminality makes sense only if the obverse of centrality also makes sense, and one comes to see that there are expressions that are so exquisitely and complexly balanced that it makes sense that they have achieved a kind of canonicity. Given Turner's catholicity, there are any number of such expressions of Christian grammar, but it should come as no surprise that Aquinas is held to be a plenary expression.

NOTES OF TURNER'S THINKING

The most obvious note of all of Turner's books is quite formal. In all cases questioning is in play. One can and should ask questions about everything and anything. The more important the object of inquiry, the more point there is to the question. Ethical, religious, and philosophical questions are rightly held to be important; resting on received assumptions is not something that Turner can affirm. In terms of Christianity he is persuaded that temptations abound with regard to closing off question; the atheist does not show herself immune from this pattern of subintellectual behavior any more than the theist. We are beset by stories, which provide incentives not to do that thing which defines the philosophical mind, that is, to inquire and to pursue the truth wherever it leads us. Although he is allergic to heroizing the enterprise, Turner is totally convinced that it is worthwhile. If inquiry is a game, then it is a serious one—serious, not portentous—and is conducted under the assumption that assumptions matter, those not provided as well as those provided, and with the presumption that there will be disagreement. And if an argument, then, one is required to yield to the better one, although it should be said that Turner has a much more substantively metaphysical view as to what that would look like than Habermas, whose locution I have just used.[6]

Questions enjoy, therefore, a privilege over any and all answers without prejudice to the probity of the answers. The available answers can be more or less adequate. But even if we sustain these answers in the end, it is our responsibility to vet and to judge. To stipulate that questions be serious in some way serves as a necessary but not sufficient condition for identifying the questioning of Turner. What we need in addition is some sense of the coherence or "analogy" between the kinds of questions Turner asks. Looked at aright, although Turner's work ranges over ethics, political theory, modern philosophy of religion, and the history of Christian thought, the set of questions he addresses is quite finite. For example, Turner deals with such obviously important questions as to whether Christian faith is rationally defensible in the modern world and, conversely, whether Christianity is or has been throughout its history sufficiently self-critical. Other questions which engage Turner include how factually and normatively belief and practice hold together without one necessarily being the foundation of the other, how also there is a tensional relation in Christianity between exuberant (even exorbitant) saying and unsaying, and how desire can be, and usually is, parsed in a variety of ways in the Christian tradition. If Turner is a philosopher of religion, then he is not one in an unrestricted sense. There are almost no references to non-Christian religions, and his theological canon is by and large a Catholic one. Correlatively, in his work the operation of reason is more craft—whether *technē* or *poeisis* or both at once is not absolutely clear—than method, which regulates all inquiry irrespective of the object of inquiry. Turner is irreducibly Aristotelian in this respect rather than Cartesian, and by dint of this fact irreducibly Thomist. Reason operates reasonably only if it is faithful to what is under consideration and is sufficiently apt and subtle to sort out what can be said and denied with certainty, what is probable or possible, what is impossible, and what is undecidable in fact or in principle.[7] What Turner states quite generally in *Faith, Reason and the Existence of God* about the "shape" of reason applies in the particular case of Turner.[8] In that text the term *shape* is used to assure of the incarnate, embodied nature of our reasoning, not only *not* excluding but also *especially* involving religious matters. It is a happy coincidence that the common noun *turner* refers to a craftsperson shaping wood on a lathe, possibly to turn this wood into barrels that hold ale and which thus serve as the condition of celebration. Hopefully what "shaping" is for will in due course get emphasized appropriately, for celebration is important throughout Turner's reflections on practices (prayer, Eucharist), as well as his reflections on the nature of the tradition of negative theology and even theological discourse considered more broadly. Thinking involves necessarily a skilled "shaping" of concept but also discourse. To practice thinking is to be entirely invested in such shaping. To use the more theological language that Turner sometimes resorts to, it is to have kenotically entered a process, which, however, is rule governed, even if only some of the more explicit rules (such are those of logic) are immediately available.

A number of Turner's books deal with the issue of the defensibility of faith in the modern world. *Faith, Reason and the Existence of God* and *The Darkness of God* are crucial texts in this regard. If in the first named text, the defense is straight up insofar as it is a defense of reason in the modern world which either assumes that reason is unnecessary or that what is required is a more instrumental or utilitarian understanding of its protocols,[9] in the case of the second, the argument is indirect and shows how the magisterial thinkers of the Christian tradition, Augustine and Pseudo-Dionysius (and not simply Aquinas), offer accounts of the shaping of reason that continue to be fertile and relevant even today.[10] In *Faith, Reason and the Existence of God*, Turner does not shy away from defending the notion of reason advanced by Vatican I that there is natural knowledge of God. Turner is not simply playing provocateur, for if, on the one hand, he sees Vatican I as advancing a very positive view of reason's reach against the backdrop of the surge of agnosticism and atheism, on the other, he also distinguishes the position being advanced by Vatican I from the hyperrationalistic position that God's existence and attributes can be demonstratively proven.[11] It seems evident that the account of how reason functions in Vatican I would, on Turner's grounds, provide a precedent for the position that gets articulated in the papal encyclical *Fides et Ratio* (1998), which affirms reason against the tidal wave of relativism, supported by modern and postmodern philosophies, and insists that with respect to God reason will encounter that which it cannot comprehend.[12] Reason and mystery, interestingly, turn out to be correlative. Moreover, mystery is not only an epistemological limit, where the concepts of the finite mind cease to lay hold of the reality, which in Platonic language is referred to as "the really real." Ingredient in the encounter with the reality that exceeds percept and concept is the intuition that this reality is superdeterminate rather than indeterminate.

Turning to the other book under consideration, it could be said that *The Darkness of God* is best read, not as a short history of mystical theology à la Andrew Louth,[13] but as an argument as to how central this two-tracked (Augustinian and Dionysian) tradition was in keeping open the critical potential of Christian discourse to temper its own claims vis-à-vis its object which resists being caught in any conceptual web. In some obvious sense the issue here is one of religious epistemology. But, of course, it is at the same time metaphysical in that God is what Derrida pejoratively refers to as "the transcendental signified."[14] Turner remains unembarrassed by this, and by no means thinks that it is a trick of grammar, even if he does grant that as the *intendum* of discourse, God underwrites discourse and most certainly its self-transcending character. Throughout this book, Turner is fond of speaking of the discourse of mystical theology as being self-subverting. Turner is not merely pointing to the historical fact that Christian thinkers such as Augustine, Pseudo-Dionysius, Meister Eckhart, Bonaventure, and Saint John of the Cross are aware of this, he is also making the point that mystical theology serves the general Christian good by reminding us of this fact.

Although there is nothing inconsistent about Turner's defense of the competence of reason with respect to access to God as the really real and his insistence on the inadequacy of language and concept with respect to God and thus his elective affinity to negative theology, there is an obvious sense in which championing either one rests on an interest in restoring balance in the economy of Christian discourse. When Christian discourse becomes complacent about its competence to render the truth, which is coincident with the really real, Turner recommends huge doses of negative theology. Conversely, when the Christian tradition becomes identified with apophasis or unsaying or when this is the only aspect of the Christian tradition of discourse in play, since only this aspect of Christian discourse finds modern or postmodern sanction, Turner recommends a medicinal dose of cataphasis and insists on the principal difference between apophatic theology and agnosticism and skepticism.[15] In his essays as in his books, Turner explains that apophasis is never free-standing but rather is parasitic on positive speech about God which is not untrue but which would fetter and fetishize God should it be allowed to stand without qualification.[16]

Similarly with a number of other binaries. For example, contemplation and action are equally important features of Christianity, historically but presumably also in terms of essential possibilities. As with positive and negative language about God, Turner supposes that the requisite balance of emphasis between the two is liable to being upset, either by an activism devoid of Christian vision and thus not Christian action or perhaps more usually by a disengaged theoretical stance that privatizes Christian existence. For example, forms of praxis (Marxist or otherwise), which are purely instrumental, have to be Christianly resisted. Thus, certain forms of liberation theology are logically open to criticism, even if in particular cases the criticism is not sustainable. Conversely, forms of Christianity which are resolutely antipolitical also have to be opposed. Importantly, the critiques do not necessarily have the same venue. While Turner could not respect Aquinas's theological achievement more than he does, he does not usually attempt positively to outline a *tertium quid* that would redress the exaggerations of both contemplation and action. Here, too, with the binary of contemplation and action, as with cataphasis and apophasis, we see the intuition of imbalance and the felt need to intervene in order to equalize and restore balance by critiquing a perceived dominant.

GRAMMAR OF CHRISTIAN DISCOURSE, PRACTICES, AND LIFE

Although on a number of occasions Turner has recourse to the notion of "grammar" to make a point about the general consistency in Christianity about the rules of theological speech,[17] which have a certain kind of oddness since they have as their object God who is not an object, which in turn means something like a schedule breakdown of speech,[18] his mode of deployment is decidedly ad hoc rather than systematic. Thus, "grammar" does not serve as a concept, not to mention a metaconcept. Nonetheless, I want to suggest that the coherence of Turner's work comes into focus if we see his individual texts as various soundings with regard to the scope, flexibility, and tensile strength of Christian grammar. Here God is in the details, but at the outset I want to make clear that I have no desire to baptize Turner into the Yale tradition of theology. Although, en passant, it should be noted that some common ground might be found between Yale school theologians and Turner on this point via Wittgenstein's notion of grammar, which at least by implication covers not only language, but practices and forms of life.[19] Importantly, this Christian grammar is generous and allows multiverse instances which are irreducible, is systemically self-correcting, is enlivened by the challenges both from within and without, and is open to whatever is reasonable in reason. I would like to say something to each of these points, although I will focus mainly on the second and third points.

However affirming of Aquinas Turner is, the Christian tradition is not exhausted by the Angelic Doctor, nor could it be. The tradition is necessarily pluriform in terms of its distinct aspects of belief, practice, and forms of life; in terms of its various charisms, institutional and noninstitutional; and in terms of its different reflective theological takes. The theological aptness and aptitude of Aquinas does not displace the achievement of Augustine, the dynamics of whose theology is quite different, nor does it render redundant the theologies of Bonaventure, on the one hand, and of Eckhart, on the other, which not only have a different tonality, but productively force issues that are not strongly encouraged by Aquinas—in the case of Bonaventure the issue of human desire for God and the insistence on love being the ultimate name for God,[20] in the case of Eckhart a sharper therapy of desire and greater vigilance regarding the prospect of idolatry even or especially in theological systems which are formally correct. This is not to mention medieval women mystics in general and Julian of Norwich in particular, nor to bring forward the name Pseudo-Dionysius and the tradition of negative theology that evolved from him, not excluding the author of *The Cloud of Unknowing* and the Cappadocean theological tradition on which Pseudo-Dionysius depends. Christianity is a many-name tradition and exceeds a single exemplar, no matter how plenary this exemplar is taken to be. Nor is Turner a party to a revanchist prejudice that the tradition comes to a conclusion in the medieval period. Turner has no natural affinity or sympathy with Chateaubriand. There are other major thinkers after Aquinas, and these include not only Eckhart and Julian, perhaps Marguerite Porete, but also even Duns Scotus, who does not fare particularly well in terms of theological adequacy when he is directly compared to Aquinas.[21] And Turner can and does praise Vatican I, any number of modern Catholic philosophers of religion, and even—albeit with significant caveats—the work of John Milbank and Catherine Pickstock.[22]

Although strictly speaking the notion of "grammar" is not necessary to affirm plurality, theological or otherwise, over the course of a two-thousand-year, still ongoing, tradition—one could after all simply be making an empirical observation—it certainly helps to support the pluralism obviously in operation in Turner's texts, and it could be thought simply to extrapolate on comments Turner makes on the grammar of negative theology in *Faith, Reason and the Existence of God*.[23] In quite formal terms, and not simply in support of the claims of reason and its dynamic openness to mystery, the position that Turner articulates throughout his oeuvre matches that articulated in *Fides et Ratio*, which insists on the plurality of discourses in the philosophical tradition—and by implication, the theological tradition—while still suggesting a special place for Aquinas. Nothing Turner writes suggests that he supports neo-scholasticism in general or makes common cause with antimodernists who insist on Thomism being the official ideology of the Catholic Church. Indeed, this would constitute, for Turner, an ecclesial and intellectual disaster, the one because the other. But ruling out this does not militate against regarding Aquinas as totally exemplary when it comes to understanding the questioning and questing embodied finite self in its dynamic movement toward a God who will not be contained and who is the very ground of desire. Nor can Aquinas's genius for allowing the kenotic potential of reason have full sway in a shaping of inquiry not be vouchsafed,[24] as well as his genius for introducing equilibrium into a philosophical and theological tradition which is argument as well as conversation. Very similar to *Fides et Ratio*, Aquinas is a figure who should count for more than one but who is ill served if he is substituted for the tradition as a whole. In the end, for Turner, this most replete of Catholic thinkers makes a contribution to a tradition that can never be closed, since even in its temporal entirety it is never adequate to its objective correlative. And, in any event, on Turner's view, the rigor of Aquinas's thought is not such that in fact or in principle it requires completeness.

This brings me to the second aspect of tradition which I judge Turner's work to endorse, namely, its self-correcting tendency. To read Turner carefully is to discover that there are different modes of correction in the Christian tradition that operate at different levels of explicitness. At one level, correction is built into Christianity by dint of the irreducible plurality of its discourses, practices, and forms of life. Unless the plurality is forcibly shut down and dominant discourses, practices, and forms of life insisted on as absolute—Turner does not deny that this has happened and can happen—then catholic Christianity will incline to correction, since one-sided positions will often enough tend to cancel each other out. This is Christian self-correction functioning at its most implicit, and is connected in the closest possible way with the wide space of option, which can also be regarded as the wide space of analogy in the Catholic tradition. But self-correction can also be self-conscious and relatively generic. I suppose Vatican II—one of whose catchphrases is *semper reformanda*—and the thought of Thomas Aquinas illustrate this in different ways. Explicit reflection on Vatican II is not to the fore in Turner's work, but it is not difficult to surmise that he shares a common vision with Herbert McCabe to the effect that Vatican II represents a process of introducing reflective equilibrium in the Catholic Church, which has come to be riven by such unsustainable dualities of faith and reason, church and world, liturgy and social action, religious and secular life, and authority and service. And, of course, one obvious way to read Aquinas and to account for his relative preeminence is to think—without prejudice to his adequacy or inadequacy on particular theological topics or even when it comes to choice of method—that his genius is that single-handedly he attempts a critical balance on all the fundamental methodological and substantive theological questions that have emerged in the Christian tradition while respecting that balance is there for truth, not truth for balance. More specific corrections of the theological tradition are illustrated by other figures. I would like to speak to two figures who make important corrections with regard to the sedimented tradition's take on desire as defining of human being and the nature and effects of sin. The first of these is Meister Eckhart, the second Julian of Norwich.

I begin with Meister Eckhart, who shares equal billing with Augustine in *The Darkness of God* by having two chapters devoted to him (6 and 7). In chapter 6 Turner speaks to the liminality of negative theology discourse as exhibited in Eckhart's sermons. Chapter 7, which is equally important, concerns the ineluctably positive side of

Eckhart's departure from the received theological tradition. Although Turner realizes that there exists only an analytic distinction between speculative theology and practice in Eckhart—indeed, the split is subsequent to him in the history of Christian thought and hardly nonmischievous—in chapter 7 he interprets Eckhart as elaborating an apophatic anthropology as a critical practice which liberates the theological tradition from binds that have bedeviled it throughout much of its history. For this purpose the two key features of Eckhart's discourse are his notion of detachment—"*Gelassenheit*," in the German sermons—and the interesting turn Eckhart gives to the Mary-Martha polarity as this gets played out explicitly in the "mystical" tradition before and after.

Turner sees in Eckhart's elaboration of detachment a subversion of two binaries in which the first represents what has to be overcome, the second the overcoming. The first of these is the binary desire and nondesire, with nondesire being regarded as the terminus ad quem of Christian life. For Turner, it is far from obvious that the elevation of apathy is Christian, and he is inclined to think that it represents more nearly a Platonic or Neoplatonic inflection or infection of the Christian tradition.[25] In *The Darkness of God* Turner provides no genealogy, and does not mention any particular figures, but he evidently thinks of "disinterestedness" or "desirelessness" as having become over time key components in the Christian imaginary—to evoke and modify the locution of Charles Taylor concerning the "social imaginary."[26] *Gelassenheit* is not identical to apathy and in a quite definite sense is not a state of mind.[27] It is in fact more like a way of holding truths and a disposition for engaging in practices that avoids apotheosis.

The second binary to be subverted is the primacy of contemplation over praxis that had come to be coded in the Mary-Martha contrast. On the standard account, one, indeed, which the author of *The Cloud of Unknowing* repeats, Mary chose the better part by contemplatively sitting at the feet of Jesus, whereas Martha chose the lesser by being very busy and merely useful. This evaluative distinction in the order of desire is harmful in that it suggests not only that there are particular spiritual practices and forms of life that are privileged but also that these effect a certain kind of control over God. Turner is fully persuaded that Eckhart sets himself against the fact or disposition toward "spiritual technologies," which have to be regarded as scenes of power. Turner is making more than a historical point. He suggests that Eckhart's subversion of long-established errors in the Christian tradition is a telling example of the exercise of critical Christian reason. In the language I am using one could say that what Eckhart enacts is a therapy with respect to a fundamental distortion of Christian grammar.

There is a revealing moment of comparison in *The Darkness of God* in which the negative theology of the Dominican is praised for dismantling a whole series of binaries such as body and soul, flesh and spirit, and, finally, God and creation.[28] Turner fairly nonchalantly labels these endemic binaries as forms of "false consciousness."[29] Of course, Turner suggests—but does not exactly argue—a connection between negative theology as it is practiced in Eckhart and Marx's notion of ideology as it achieves its classical rendition in *The German Ideology* (1845).[30] I think Turner here provides an important clue as to how and why Marxism can be assimilated by and into a Christianity faithful to its own grammar and its possibilities. There are three obvious questions to be asked. First, what is the extent of the analogy between the self-subverting discourse of negative theology and Marx's view of ideology, and how do the processes of critical subversion mutually illuminate? Second, does or can Eckhart enjoy any special privileges over other forms of negative theology in the Christian tradition, or does he function simply as a representative? Third, however we answer this second question, could it still be said that Eckhart is especially well positioned to intimate through criticism a positive state of affairs? I would like to comment briefly on all three questions, even if I do not aim strictly speaking at a resolution.

With regard to the first question, the homology between apophatic practice as it concerns Christian discourse and Marx's view of ideology is fairly transparent. Ideology depends on the generation of a binary between the material and the spiritual, which gets absolutized when the former becomes a function of the latter. In *The German Ideology* Marx speaks pejoratively of this as a mystification; in other texts he speaks of fetishization. In the case of Eckhart, and plausibly in the case of the negative theology tradition as a whole, theological language must fight against the down drag that seems as native to Christian concepts as mystification seems native in the arena of social life. The hypostatization of the spiritual conceals itself as natural,[31] but it also functions as symptom, which suggests that inversion is required. One might say then that what unites Eckhart and Marx is a distinction between operative and acquired grammar and the real grammar of Christian and social-political discourse: the former has to be broken in order to reveal the latter.

With respect to the second question, the evidence goes in different directions. On the one hand, since Eckhart is in significant respects inscribed in the negative theology tradition, it is the negative theology tradition as a whole that is really being connected with Marx. On the other hand, Turner notes that there is a self-consciousness and relentlessness in Eckhart's subversion that make him excessive vis-à-vis the received negative theology tradition.[32] It is not clear whether the difference in degree should or should not be regarded as a difference in kind. In a way unlike his twin sources, in a way unlike Bonaventure and Aquinas, in ways beyond John of the Cross and the author of *The Cloud of Unknowing*, Eckhart might be considered something of a "revolutionary."[33] One way of taking Turner is to suggest the possibility that the negative theology discourse of Eckhart either breaks with or comes near to breaking with not only the received or sedimented tradition of Christian speech that tends toward highlighting doctrinal grasp and clarity of prescription but also the tradition of negative theology itself which systemically challenges both the ultimacy of propositional speech and the tendency toward reducing Christian grammar, with its manifold possibilities, to a limited set of actual instances. To make the point in another way: in Eckhart there is a riskiness that comes close to breaking Christian grammar itself which the negative theology tradition deploys and lubricates. Just to think this possibility of "rupture" differentiates Turner from a number of influential commentators on Eckhart.[34]

The answer to the third question trades on Eckhart's liminality, the indecision or nondecision to say definitively whether Eckhart validates or breaks with general Christian grammar and more specifically the regional grammar of negative theology, which is at once a kind of tool kit to prevent excessive claims and an opening up to a transcendent reality which exceeds all theological discourse. For very few thinkers in the mystical theology tradition, who as a group tend to be speculatively brave, really challenge standard operational theological procedure. For Turner, only Julian of Norwich and Marguerite Porete approach Eckhart in this respect,[35] and we are not given real reason to think that they match him. For any number of reasons Turner does not put forward Joachim de Fiore as does de Lubac, who famously traces the line from Joachim to Marx.[36] But to explore whether Eckhart still remains special, and whether a closer relation between him and Marx can be maintained than between Marx and any other negative theologian, depends in significant part on the level of challenge Eckhart represents with respect to another binary in the Christian tradition, that is, contemplation and action. One of the hallmarks of Reiner Schürmann's interpretation of Eckhart,[37] for example, is that he focuses on the subversion of this endemic Christian binary—one inscribed also in the negative theology tradition. This encourages the dialogue he conducts between Eckhart and Heidegger, in which Eckhart turns out to be as anti-Platonic as Heidegger is anti-Cartesian and in which both are taken to affirm modes of activity which are not regulated by the will to control.[38] It would not be difficult here to substitute Marx for Heidegger, even if it is Heidegger rather than Marx who explicitly engages the negative theology tradition. This would certainly be possible with the pre-1845 Marx. This Marx affirmed the primacy of praxis but ultimately the praxis that had finally escaped particular class interest and the prevailing historical structures of power and injustice.[39]

The other liminal figure in Turner's oeuvre is Julian of Norwich, to whom Turner's *Julian of Norwich, Theologian*, is devoted. The most obvious thing about Turner's book on Julian is the concerted effort he makes to rescue her from misrepresentations that would limit what is truly interesting about her, for one, charting her uncritically in the mystical tradition concerned as John of the Cross and Bernard of Clairvaux are with stages of spiritual progress and specific kinds of experience,[40] for another, determining that she provides a good—happily successful—example of personal experience and vision gaining critical leverage over doctrine and institutional authority. For Turner, the former is thoughtless in that there is not only a manifest failure to take account of genre, but also to understand that properly understood Christian mysticism is neither uniquely nor even importantly tied up with special experiences but rather by practices and forms of life that facilitate an openness to mystery which cannot be fully grasped. In contrast, Julian's *Showings* are of considerable theological substance, disclosing in particular who the God of Jesus Christ is and who we are in relation to this God. When Turner underscores the aporetic character of Julian's theology,[41] the issue is that of "formal consistency" between the received doctrine of the church and what her interpretations as well as visions seem to be intimating. This means that the tension experienced is fundamentally internal to the church, especially given that the status of visions and interpretation resides in their character as gifts of the Spirit whose ultimate recipient is the church rather than the individual who displays charismatic traits. In exposing the problem of formal consistency, Julian does not attempt anything like a dialectical resolution, which would have the character of completeness.[42] Indeed, she thoroughly forswears it as being essential to the Christian tradition.

As with Meister Eckhart, Turner addresses the question of Julian's possible heterodoxy straight on.[43] Even if he concludes that Julian necessarily should be acquitted of the charge,[44] Turner acknowledges that Julian is something of a liminal figure in that she corrects, stretches, and even challenges the tradition. All of this is the subject of praise, since it appears that devoid of these interpretive strategies the tradition stagnates and fails precisely as tradition. Two fairly obvious examples of correction are Julian's depiction of Jesus as mother and her granting of parity to action and contemplation. In the case of the former Julian corrects the conventional gender typing in the tradition by an explicitly oxymoronic conjunction, thereby suggesting that all gender typing of the divine is mere human construction.[45]

In the case of the latter, Julian is one more distinguished medieval thinker who reads the Mary-Martha story of Luke 10:28–32 in such a way as to undermine the priority of Mary and thus contemplation.[46] Of course, the most famous example is supplied by Eckhart, and Turner takes note. In *Julian of Norwich, Theologian*, there are hints that Eckhart might be the more radical of the two. First, and most important, whereas Julian equalizes, Eckhart inverts the order of priority, and whereas Julian may very well have a pastoral motive in equalizing action and contemplation, Eckhart's subversion is the more theologically pointed in that contemplation may very well tend toward a self-congratulation expressive of self-will (*Eigenwille*).

All corrections of customary Christian imagination and interpretation involve a healthy stretching of the Christianity that shows repeated signs of tending toward inertia. But Julian also challenges a number of established theological positions, and an even more fundamental theological optic. In the case of the former, she does so by apparently radicalizing the dualism of the standard Christian anthropology by means of an anthropology that on the surface looks more Manichaean and ontological than that encouraged by the Augustinian tradition; in the case of the latter, she does so by inflecting the Christian metanarrative of creation-fall-redemption otherwise or on a slant to the received tradition. The first radicalization of the standard Christian dualism of spirit and flesh, or in Julian's language substance and sensuality,[47] is to think that the substance of humans is immutable and impervious to sin and its effects. This seems to reinscribe the Manichaeism that Augustine putatively overcame. The anthropology bears obvious resemblance to Eckhart's reflections on the ground or spark of the soul that remains outside the order of temporality and mutability.[48] Without prejudice to Eckhart, Turner argues that Julian's real meaning is less ontological than it might appear. Julian wishes, on the one hand, to think of the self from the point of view of God's intent, which, accordingly, relativizes sin and its effects, and, on the other, to offer a hyperbole of a long-standing tradition of Christian participatory metaphysics.[49]

The second radicalization of the received tradition that functions as a default is the distinction between a "godly will" and a "bestly will." Once again, we seem to be dealing with a regression behind Augustine to a doctrine of two wills held by a Manichaean such as Faustus, who is the object of a famous rebuttal by Augustine. What is actually happening, however, is that this hyperbolization in which a "godly will" is envisaged as being intact plays a critical and/or dialectical role vis-à-vis the sedimented tradition which tends to think of desire or love in static terms as being defined by two different kinds of object, one up, one down, one that is God, the other that is the self. In this case, Julian's support of the "godly will" not only represents a denial of absolute corruption, but functions critically by posing the question of what one desires when one desires, including problematizing what one desires when one desires God. Contrary to received Christian opinion, "godly will" is not immediately recognizable. Excavation is required in order that one's true desire or love can come to the light, which means reformatting one's desires, especially but not only those desires that have as their object what is other than God.[50] Implicitly, however, one's desire for God also comes under inspection for the self-love that infects our most innocent constructions. While Turner does not exactly describe it in this way, Julian's strategy is to correct a Christian anthropology that is functionally Manichaean by means of an anthropology that at first appears to be more substantively Manichaean, with the view, however, to putting before the Christian subject the dynamics of a self-critical desire which, as it opens up the self, permits God to be free of the limitations desire imposes on him.

The third challenge presented by Julian is entirely different in scope. At issue is the way in which the Christian metanarrative of creation-fall-redemption is held.[51] The standard way is punctiliar and episodic: God creates a good and perfect world; in the fall human beings reject God's world, are alienated from God, and are subject to divine punishment; and God redeems human beings by sending his only Son to bring humans back to God in and through his vicarious sacrifice on the cross. The issue here is neither local nor formal—not local in that how the cross is understood relates to how the elements of the metanarrative are understood together, not formal in that the issue is hardly one of justification, epistemic or otherwise. What

Julian is doing ought not to be confused with what Hegel is doing in the *Encyclopaedia*,[52] that is, demonstrating that the real value of the Christian narrative is revealed if and only if we extract from it the pure logical code (which in turn guarantees consistency and completeness). Julian's correction is thoroughgoingly substantive and theological. For, according to Turner, Julian's point is that the standard inflection of the narrative encourages theological positions that are not Christianly intuitive, a view of human beings as absolutely fallen, a view of a juridical and possibly sadistic God, and a very parsimonious view with respect to the scope of salvation. Thinking of the Christian narrative in a nonepisodic way, and especially from the point of view of divine intent as manifest in the cross which appears to show a trinitarian God of love rather than the righteous God, allows for very different takes on creation, sin, and redemption. Creation is participation in the triune God which can never be totally obviated; the fall disrupts the order of creation but is not sufficiently potent to rupture the relation between God and human beings—so, at worse, sin is a *felix culpa*;[53] and redemption cannot be defined solely by being a response to sin but in significant part must be understood to continue the divine self-communication that began at creation and as creation. The Christian narrative is neither reductively contingent, as the popular imagination suggests (also in theology), nor logically or metaphysically necessary, as suggested later by Hegel who in *Lectures on the Philosophy of Religion* points to Anselm as a precursor.[54] The Christian narrative is "behovely"; that is, the Christian narrative belongs to the order of convenience (*convenientia*) or what we might now call verisimilitude.[55] It does not involve much by way of extrapolation to imagine that Balthasar could and would include Julian under the banner of theological aesthetics.[56] After all, he is capacious enough to imagine Anselm himself making it by construing Anselm's demonstrative reasons as just another form of reasons of convenience.[57] Crucially, however, for Turner, Julian is more interested in correcting and balancing than in a theological victory. For example, in the standard version of the Christian narrative sin is taken to be real and damnation of more than a few taken for granted. Julian does not want this view to disappear but, along with its opposite, to remain probative. For the eschatological state is a mystery too important not to extrapolate but too risky not to be circumspect.

Turner is an ascetic as well as a synthetic thinker. There is much in *Julian of Norwich, Theologian* about Julian's uncovering of the deep-seated tendency in the Christian tradition to invent and perpetuate damaging dualities. To a considerable extent Turner simply offers a wonderfully accurate description of an eccentric mode of thought that amounts to an intervention in the theological field in which a properly functioning theological grammar exceeds popular constructions and traditional theological arguments. Nonetheless, as in the case of Eckhart in an earlier book, there is some hint of a subtext that involves Marx. In writing of the generation of dualisms, Turner very suggestively demurs that it "is not in any simple way a false consciousness."[58] By so doing, he once again evokes Marx of *The German Ideology*. The connection between Marx and Julian is easy to dismiss: to which denial one could add that in the twenty-first century the construct of ideology and its false consciousness label have essentially detached themselves from Marx and Marxism to become general intellectual property. Nonetheless, the analogy seems to be strong. If we leave aside for the moment Marx's diagnosis of the power interests served by ideology, we can note a number of parallel features between popular and theological constructions of binaries and Marx's view of ideology: (i) the dualisms function as self-evident and universal; (ii) nonetheless, their construction has a history; (iii) in their constructed form they function as absolute; (iv) the dualisms need to be deconstructed in order for truth and healing to occur.

CHRISTIANITY AND MARXISM: NEW PROTOCOL

I have concentrated on two liminal figures because it is here that one best sees Christian discourse in its self-correction but also in its reaching out toward other discourses of critique and praxis, and especially that of Marxism. Almost thirty years ago Denys Turner wrote an important book arguing for the compatibility of Marxism and

Christianity. There was nothing jejune in an analysis that attempted to remove deep-seated prejudices concerning incompatibility from both sides and at the same time represented an intervention in Marxist historiography inclined to accept Louis Althusser's influential reading of Marx as a thinker who simply outgrew the moral humanism of his early years. There is no reason to suppose that Turner would take back his view that Christianity logically embraces Marxism to the extent to which it embraces—as it must—social justice. Indeed, one could further update what he wrote in 1983 by considering the more self-conscious Catholic reflection on social justice elaborated differently in papal encyclicals and in liberation theologies, and by readings of Marxism that refuse to bleed it of its messianic impulse. Echoes of affinity with Marxism are fairly thinly scattered in his subsequent writings,[59] and it might seem as if I have made much of them, indeed, far too much of them. Not only do I wish to deny this; I want to suggest that the kinds of couplings to which I have spoken in and through my presentation of the liminal figures of the theological tradition indicate an entirely new protocol for conjugation. What compatibility would now consist of is a profound affinity of grammar rather than some freestanding morality which both Christianity and Marxism might be thought to share. What would necessarily have been suspended is any third-party point of view that would critically assess the relative ratios of hospitality between these regimes of discourse, practice, and forms of life and present a critical judgment. The only way in which the issue of Christianity and Marxism would matter is if it could be shown that Marxism can be assimilated to and by the depth grammar of Christian discourses, practices, and forms of life as these are richly and thickly registered throughout history.

More clearly than in *Marxism and Christianity*, the specifically Christian interests of the question of relation have to be brought out. From the Christian perspective Marxism functions as a form of anamnesis whereby Christianity comes to reappropriate its grammar which proscribes idolatry; prescribes questioning that has truth as its object; encourages critical vetting of the matrix of desires for the desire that is ultimate because its object is as unattainable as it is

regulative of all else; and telescopes the bodily nature and vulnerability of all selves in themselves, in their relations, in their hopes and
fears, and also in their practices, not only the practices of justice
or what in the Christian tradition have been referred to as corporal
works of mercy, but also in the Eucharist. Turner's recent turn to
the Eucharist suggests that far from being the site of alien authority
and mechanical repetition,[60] which it is often taken to be and sometimes in fact degenerates into, the Eucharist is the practice in which
redemption is made effective, and in and through which we are reminded that redemption takes a bodily form as we experience the
presence (sacramental) of the risen bodily Christ in bread and wine
in the company of others. In being the primary form of anamnesis
in and for the Christian community, the Eucharist is a language and
praxis in which saving presence is present and absent, here and now
and deferred. It is also a language and praxis of critique, for while
redemption—contra scholastic Marxism—reaches beyond any envisaging of a merely temporal kingdom, it is through and through bodily.
The bodily nature of the redeemed state, and also its communitarian
or social nature, testifies against the tendency of the Christian tradition to articulate an individualist and spiritualistic eschatology as
it also testifies against the tendency to individualize and spiritualize
this side of the eschaton.

In reading the Eucharist in the way he does, Turner seems to
have a number of different but related aims. He wishes to underscore
the central role the Eucharist plays in putting the entire Christian
grammar of the love of the created and embodied and questioning
subjects have for God who answers in love by disclosing himself paradoxically as a question. Here the formal similarity to negative theology is obvious. Turner wishes to indicate its continuing vitality by
suggesting that the Eucharist is not the stuff of magic or mystification but a memory of the past that represents a critique of the past
and its assurances as it bears a hope for the future of the dead. In its
repetition the Eucharist enacts at once a kind of ideology critique
while unveiling as prejudice the presumption that the only future
permitted is the one vouched for by a science that is substantively
and not simply procedurally atheistic. Here it is not difficult to see

how reflection on the Eucharist can reach out to embrace critical aspects of Marxism only to reject elements of its immanentist axiomatics. Turner wishes to suggest that the Eucharist is a kind of politics because it carries with it the prescription to bring the worlds its says into being—a world in which the dignity and fragility of embodied selves is granted, a world of mutual recognition and assistance, a world which is convivial and in which gratitude has the last word. The eucharistic center is found throughout the broad Catholic tradition. Turner recognizes it in Pseudo-Dionysius, remarks on it in Julian, and comments on it at length in Aquinas.[61] Yet the testimony exceeds these few and is general throughout the "catholic" tradition. And in any event, the Eucharist and what it enacts has for two millennia bound together Christians and formed them into communities that take on eschatological shape.

CONCLUSION

It is fitting that as I hurry toward conclusion I have returned to Aquinas, who perhaps shows more than any other theologian the ability to divest himself of personality in order to channel the flow of the Christian tradition, founded on faith in the biblical God who gives himself and demands a total response of intellect, practice, and forms of life, none of which, or even the sum of which, will be adequate to what is given. Since the Christian tradition is interpretation, conversation, and also argument, it is an ongoing task to achieve equilibrium. The claim that Aquinas is one of the foremost "turners" or "shapers" of reflective equilibrium is relatively uncontroversial. And, for Turner himself, no greater "shaper" can be thought. But the crafting and shaping is not only plural. There are different kinds of shaping: not only the measured and epic shaping of Aquinas, but the nervous analytic shaping of Scotus; the erotic shaping of Saint Bernard; the agonistic shaping of Augustine; the hieratic shaping of Pseudo-Dionysius; the disruptive shaping of Eckhart; the ecstatic shaping of Bonaventure; the visionary shaping of Julian. And much more, although it hardly needs to be said that in every case I have simplified and that in a sense every qualifying adjective has relative value with regard to each.

Various shapings and inflections are needed to enliven and refresh by stretching, correcting, and challenging the tradition. If Aquinas enacts a center, he unveils not so much a theological synthesis but a Christian grammar that can be expressed and completed in a variety of ways. Other thinkers have less theological range and operate on the margins but do so precisely to equilibrate the grammar that continually displays signs of falling lower than its capacity, or becoming frozen in its more revered instances of thought, practice, and forms of life. Aquinas finds the measure of grammar through an untoward theological measure. Figures like Julian and Eckhart gain it by recourse to the nonmeasure of hyperbole and upsetting the received tradition. Turner negotiates between the two poles, forever admiring Aquinas but not shy about supporting those thinkers who more nearly scourge and scour the tradition of Christian discourse, practice, and forms of life. The aim is not destruction but rather allowing the Christian grammar to function in all its intellectual and practical richness. This grammar does not admit of formalization, and it cannot be reduced to code. Nor does it exist for its own sake: it exists in order that desire and its many languages will be appropriate to its ultimate object; it exists in order that it will commence to babble at the right time and in the right way. It exists so that the silence to which it gives way is the right kind of silence, a healing silence far more eloquent than the most precious and poised form of speech.

In his own complex way, Turner is a shaper who attempts to effect equilibrium by stretching the tradition, by correcting one-sided emphasis when it comes to theological language, Christian practice, and Christian forms of life and their intricate, interdependent relations. Not cataphatic or apophatic theology alone, not Christian discourse or practice alone, not Eucharist or social justice alone. His work is not in the slightest promiscuous but rather gives itself as a series of interventions to allow the grammar of Christianity to declare itself. He too is a shaper or corrector who knows the value of shaping and correcting by having a compendious grasp of the tradition's history. And this grammar of Christianity, the grammar of its faith, practice, and form of life, what can that be? The answer can only be theological, and theological in the strict sense. There are at least two options: the first, the grammar of Spirit, the second, the grammar of love. And this leaves us with one more question: how can we decide the difference?

NOTES

1. Jacques Derrida, "Différance," in *Margins of Philosophy*, trans. Alan Bass (Chicago: University of Chicago Press, 1982), 1–27. This essay argues against efforts in philosophy to exclude (Parmenides, Plato) and contain (Hegel, Heidegger) difference by arriving at truth or definitive meaning and argues for radical semiosis. This famous essay depends on Derrida's prior articulation of the nature of language prosecuted against the philosophical (Plato, Rousseau), linguistic (Saussure), and theological (Augustine) traditions in *De la grammatologie* (1967). See *Of Grammatology*, trans. Gayatri Chakravorty Spivak (Baltimore: Johns Hopkins University Press, 1974). Heterology as a logic of the other, and a logic other than binary or Hegelian logic, has been a French experiment which includes Derrida as well as Baudrillard and Bataille. It also includes Jean-François Lyotard. With respect to the latter, while perhaps it is invidious to choose one particular text, arguably, if one had to choose, the best representative would be *The Differend: Phases in Dispute*, trans. Georges Van Den Abbeele (Minneapolis: University of Minnesota Press, 1988).

2. Denys Turner, *Marxism and Christianity* (Oxford: Blackwell, 1983). This book constitutes an argument for the compatibility between Christianity and Marxism against Christians but also Marxists who either assume or argue for incompatibility. This is not Turner's only book on Marxism. Fifteen years earlier he wrote an introductory book titled *On the Philosophy of Karl Marx* (Dublin: Sceptre, 1968).

3. Denys Turner, *The Darkness of God: Negativity in Christian Mysticism* (Cambridge: Cambridge University Press, 1995). See also its companion volume focused on interpretation of the Song of Songs, *Eros and Allegory* (Kalamazoo, MI: Cistercian Publications, 1995).

4. Denys Turner, *Faith, Reason and the Existence of God* (Cambridge: Cambridge University Press, 2004).

5. For more on McCabe, particularly concerning his influence on Turner and Terry Eagleton, see Eric Bugyis's essay in the present volume.

6. Yielding to the better argument is an important feature of Habermas's "discourse ethic." For Habermas, see especially his *Moral Consciousness and Communicative Action*, trans. Christian Lenhardt and Shierry Weber Nicholsen (Cambridge, MA: MIT Press, 1990), 43–115.

7. Here it is difficult not to think of another concept of Aristotle not playing something of a regulative role with respect to the shaping of reason, that is, his view of *phonesis*, or practical reason. Here an interesting conversation between Turner and Newman's *A Grammar of Assent* is possible. A splendid modern philosophical text which promotes *phronesis* as a general epistemological principle is Joseph Dunne's *Back to the Rough Ground: Practical Judgment and the Lure of Technique*, 2nd ed. (Notre Dame: University of Notre Dame Press, 1997).

8. Turner, *Faith, Reason and the Existence of God*, chap. 6, "The 'Shape' of Reason," 108–22. See also chap. 5, "Reason and Rhetoric."

9. Turner, *Faith, Reason and the Existence of God*, chap. 1, "Clarifications and Issues," 3–25.

10. See Turner, *Darkness of God*, chaps. 2–4, 19–101, where Turner makes the case that Pseudo-Dionysius and Augustine represent the twin foundations of the Christian mystical tradition. Obviously both have their close followers and genuine synthesizers. For Turner, Bonaventure provides a good example (chap. 5). But Augustine and Pseudo-Dionysius also set the table for more experimental conjugations that exceed them. This is the case with Meister Eckhart (chaps. 6 and 7). A number of the essays in the present volume explore particular figures in the Christian mystical tradition. Philip McCosker concentrates largely—although not exclusively—on Maximus the Confessor, who depends largely on Pseudo-Dionysius even if he emends him in some ways. Bernard McGinn illustrates beautifully how Jean Gerson tries to remain within the conventional Augustinian-Dionysian parameters of Christian mysticism, which he interprets to have been interrupted and challenged by Jan Ruysbroeck and his school. In her contribution, Mary-Jane Rubenstein shows well how the fifteenth-century Christian Neoplatonist Nicholas of Cusa develops rather than repeats the Augustinian-Dionysian tradition and in this respect is very much more like Eckhart than Gerson.

11. See Turner, *Faith, Reason and the Existence of God*, chap. 11 (226–47).

12. See John Paul II, *Fides et Ratio: On the Relationship between Faith and Reason* (Boston: Pauline Books, 1998).

13. Andrew Louth, *The Origins of the Christian Mystical Tradition: From Plato to Denys*, 2nd ed. (Oxford: Oxford University Press, 2007).

14. This is a term popularized by *Of Grammatology*. Put simply, Derrida inveighs against attempts in the philosophical and theological tradition to secure meaning and truth by having recourse to some immovable nonlinguistic content that stabilizes the play of meaning. In modernity it can be the monological self or stable system of linguistic meaning (Saussure). In the ancient world it can be dialogue (Plato). Crucially and extraordinarily effectively in Western discourse, it can be God. Derrida points to Augustine's *De doctrina christiana* as an exemplum. In *Faith, Reason and the Existence of God*, Turner is offering a defense of the alethic potential of reason against relativist attack. It is obvious that one modality of relativism is provided by Derrida. See also Turner's fine essay, "Apophaticism, Idolatry, and the Claims of Reason," in *Silence and the Word: Negative Theology and the Incarnation*, ed. Oliver Davies and Denys Turner (Cambridge: Cambridge University Press, 2002); and my review in *Religion and Literature* 37 (Autumn 2005): 103–8.

15. Certainly it is there in the two figures whom Turner regards as the twin foundations of the Christian mystical tradition. But the distinction between apophasis and skepticism is, arguably, just as clear in Gregory of Nyssa. In *Against Eunomius*, which is against the rationalist reduction of the Trinity, Nyssa continually has recourse to apophasis. Sensing the danger of confusion, however, he insists that apophasis involves neither a denial of the reality of the triune God nor a lack of connection with him. By contrast, agnosticism involves both.

16. The following statement is a fairly typical one in *Darkness of God*: "Negative language about God is no more apophatic in itself than is affirmative language. The apophatic is the linguistic strategy of somehow showing by means of language that which lies beyond language" (34). Here Turner is writing about Pseudo-Dionysius. Turner makes similar points speaking about *The Cloud of Unknowing* (48, 204, 208). For similar statements, see *Darkness of God*, 39, 50, 150–51, 188.

17. See Turner, *Faith, Reason and the Existence of God*, chap. 8, "God, Grammar, and Difference," 149–68, esp. 155–62.

18. See Turner, *Faith, Reason and the Existence of God*, 50; and *Darkness of God*, 48, 204, 208.

19. The notion of grammar is especially important for George Lindbeck. See his *The Nature of Doctrine* (Philadelphia: Westminister Press, 1984).

20. Turner, *Darkness of God*, 131–34. Nonetheless, Turner differs from the early Jean-Luc Marion in not preferring Bonaventure's *bonum* to Aquinas's *esse*. See his *God without Being*, trans. Thomas A. Carlson (Chicago: University of Chicago Press, 1991). Of course, in a 1995 essay Marion retracted the contrast and argued that the work that the good or love does in the Christian Neoplatonic tradition is capable of being performed by Aqui-

nas's *esse*. See "Saint Thomas d'Aquin et l'onto-théo-logie," *Revue Thomiste* 95 (1995): 31–66.

21. If Turner avoids parodying Scotus, as is too often the wont of those who prefer Aquinas, nonetheless, he does poorly by way of contrast. See Turner's comparison in *Faith, Reason and the Existence of God*, chap. 7, "Univocity and Inference," 125–48; and its companion, chap. 10, "Analogy and Inference," 193–225.

22. Unsurprisingly, the Catholic philosophers of religion who tend to exercise most influence all deal in significant ways with Aquinas. In *Faith, Reason and the Existence of God*, the thinkers who, arguably, are most important are Herbert McCabe (172, 173, 178) and Fergus Kerr (15–16, 17–20, 196–97). David Burrell and Peter Geach are also cited. For Milbank, see 94–97, 193–202; for Pickstock, see 94–97, 119, 126, 203. For the purposes of this particular work, the important texts of these authors are Herbert McCabe, *God Matters* (London: Geoffrey Chapman, 1987); Herbert McCabe, *God Still Matters* (London: Continuum, 2002); Fergus Kerr, *After Aquinas: Versions of Thomism* (Oxford: Blackwell, 2001); Fergus Kerr, *Theology after Wittgenstein* (Oxford: Blackwell, 1986). While Pickstock's book on liturgy, *After Writing: On the Liturgical Consummation of Philosophy* (Oxford: Blackwell, 1998), is generally important to Turner, in *Faith, Reason and the Existence of God* the important text is Milbank's and Pickstock's joint work, *Truth in Aquinas* (London: Routledge, 2001).

23. See Turner, *Faith, Reason and the Existence of God*, 151, 162–63, 186.

24. Ibid., 186–88.

25. Two passages are especially important in *Darkness of God*. The first reads: "To be detached is to live without a why. It is to love God with an uncreated, undifferentiated love. It is not to be without desire" (182). The second reads: "The practice of detachment is that of opposing oppositions between one desire and another, between the desire for God and the desire for created things, as if the desire for God was just another created desire for another created object" (184).

26. See, e.g., Charles Taylor, *Modern Social Imaginaries* (Durham, NC: Duke University Press, 2003).

27. For this point, see Turner, *Darkness of God*, 179, 209–10.

28. Ibid., 147.

29. Ibid.

30. See Karl Marx with Friedrich Engels, *The German Ideology* (Amherst, MA: Prometheus Books, 1998), esp. 33–102. Cf. Turner, *Marxism and Christianity*, pt. 1, 1–81. In his contribution to the present volume, Oliver Davies also suggests a connection between Marx's account of ideology and Eckhart's negative theology.

31. Turner, *Darkness of God*, 179.

32. Ibid., 151.

33. Ibid., 166.

34. See, e.g., Bernard McGinn, *The Mystical Thought of Meister Eckhart* (New York: Crossroad, 2001); and Oliver Davies, *Meister Eckhart: Mystical Theologian* (London: SPCK, 1991).

35. Turner links Porete and Eckhart in *Darkness of God*, 139. There are a number of other mentions of Porete (137–49, 180, 183). Turner's original intention was to have a separate chapter on Porete. In the unpublished chapter, however, Turner essentially defends Porete's orthodoxy. Julian of Norwich also does not have a chapter devoted to her, but again there are more than a few mentions (159–62). Of course, Julian eventually is the subject of an entire book.

36. Henri de Lubac, *La postérité spirituelle de Joachim de Fiore*, 2 vols. (Paris: Lethielleux, 1979).

37. Reiner Schürmann, *Mystic and Philosopher: Translations with Commentary* (Bloomington: Indiana University Press, 1978).

38. Reiner Schürmann, *Heidegger on Being and Acting: From Principles to Anarchy*, trans. Christine-Marie Gros in collaboration with the author (Bloomington: Indiana University Press, 1990).

39. I am being minimalistic here. Based on Turner's rejection of Louis Althusser's suggestion of a decisive "break" between the earlier (pre-1845) and the later Marx in *Marxism and Christianity*, there are good reasons to suggest that Turner thinks this position is supported by the later Marx exemplified by *Capital*.

40. Denys Turner, *Julian of Norwich, Theologian* (New Haven: Yale University Press, 2011), 27–31.

41. Ibid., 137; also 16.

42. Ibid., 17–21. One of the more interesting things in Turner's very interesting book is that he pairs Julian with Dante on this point. Needless to say, the case with respect to Dante is much more difficult, given the epic style and the knowing that attends the eschaton, which in the Christian tradition is decidedly limited. In his piece in the present volume Robin Kirkpatrick broaches the issue of completeness in Dante by focusing on the issue of authority.

43. Ibid., 169.

44. Ibid., 180.

45. Ibid., 198–99.

46. Ibid., 145–47.

47. Ibid., 167–204.

48. Ibid., 178–79.

49. Ibid., 179.

50. Ibid., 203–4.

51. Ibid., chap. 3, "Two Stories of Sin," 68–99.

52. See G. W. F. Hegel, *Philosophy of Mind, Part 3 of the Encyclopaedia of the Philosophical Sciences*, trans. William Wallace (Oxford: Clarendon Press, 1971), #564–77. See also my discussion of this aspect of Hegel's thought in *The Heterodox Hegel* (New York: State University of New York Press, 1994), 331–70.

53. Turner, *Julian of Norwich*, 214.

54. See G. W. F. Hegel, *Lectures on the Philosophy of Religion*, vol. 3: *The Consummate Religion*, ed. Peter Hodgson, trans. R. F. Brown, P. C. Hodgson, and J. M. Steward (Berkeley: University of California Press, 1985), 69–73, 179–84, 352–54.

55. Turner, *Julian of Norwich*, 119–20; also 201.

56. This is not to say that the Balthasar-Julian connection cannot be made on other grounds. The incentives to bring them together are significant given Balthasar's tendency toward universal salvation and his interest in not evacuating the traditional narrative in which perdition is a possibility. An interpreter of Julian who explores the connection between Julian and Balthasar under the rubric "drama" or "theo-drama" is Frederick Christian Bauerschmidt, *Julian of Norwich and the Mystical Body of Christ* (Notre Dame: Notre Dame University Press, 1995), 164–73. Interestingly, the interest in connecting Julian and Balthasar is to secure a relationship between God and the world that is neither necessary nor accidental.

57. See Hans Urs von Balthasar, *The Glory of the Lord: A Theological Aesthetics*, 11: *Studies in Theological Style: Clerical Styles*, ed. John Riches, trans. Andrew Louth, Francis McDonagh, and Brian McNeil, C.R.V. (San Francisco: Ignatius Press, 1984), 211–59. Of course, if it is legitimate to apply the concept of theological aesthetics to the reason or reasoning of Julian, then it is possible that it might apply elsewhere, for example, to Aquinas. Without the assistance of Balthasar, this is what Anna Williams does in her article on Aquinas. See A. N. Williams, "Mystical Theology Redux: The Pattern of Aquinas' *Summa theologiae*," *Modern Theology* 13 (1997): 53–74.

58. Turner, *Julian of Norwich*, 193.

59. Ludger H. Viefhues-Bailey in his contribution to the present volume helpfully draws our attention to Turner's article, "Decentering Theology," *Modern Theology* 2 (1986): 125–43. He rightly interprets the article as constructing negative theology as a form of ideology-critique.

60. Turner, *Faith, Reason and the Existence of God*, 62–74.

61. While Turner's reflections on the Eucharist in Aquinas in his most recent book have to do with the unfinished state of the *Summa*, it also signifies the interest that the topic has for Turner both historically and as a principle of explanation for Catholic Christianity. See Denys Turner, *Thomas Aquinas: A Portrait* (New Haven: Yale University Press, 2013), esp. 230–66.

TEN

"Love was his meaning"

On Learning from Medieval Texts

OLIVER DAVIES

Wit it wele, love was his meaning
—Julian of Norwich

We are, without doubt, creatures in time. The ideas that shape us come to us from different historical layers. We read ancient texts and are inspired by these. We read contemporary texts and are inspired by these too. Nor are we unaffected by the significant changes which occur in our own day, whether these be geopolitical, technological, scientific, or cultural changes that shape our everyday reality. And the world has indeed changed in the time that Denys Turner has been thinking and writing. Born in 1942, Turner may have as his very earliest memories a world at war. Certainly the complexities of the Cold War are everywhere present in his first book, *On the Philosophy of Karl Marx* (1968), to which he came as a scholar taught in the analytical tradition at Oxford under R. M. Hare. In its directness, the later *Marxism and Christianity* (1983) seems also to belong to the late modern period of intense reflection on the limits of capitalism, which

242

inspired Catholic Marxist thinkers such as Terry Eagleton and Herbert McCabe.[1] Twelve years later, Turner published his first books on mysticism (*Eros and Allegory* and the influential *The Darkness of God*, both in 1995). From 2002 (*Faith Seeking* and *Faith, Reason and the Existence of God* through to *Julian of Norwich, Theologian*, and the most recent *Thomas Aquinas: A Portrait*), his focus turned to the nature of reason itself, especially in its religious extensions and expressions. Here, at least in the later work, it may be possible to see parallels with the cultural turn to "nonreductive physicalism" arising from the biological sciences, with their "embodied cognition." These potentially offer a strong orientation to the same embodied account of reason found in Turner's classical philosophical and theological sources.[2]

In sum, what we can see in Turner's work is an interplay of different historical "moments," extending from thirteenth- and fourteenth-century scholastics and mystics through to the nineteenth-century Marx and down to the present day and our contemporary concerns with the ever-changing, ever-shifting meanings of reason and, above all, with the kind of reasoning which we do in faith. We can perhaps understand this to be first and foremost a concern with the rational nature of personal and social change. If Thomas was a teacher and Eckhart a transformative preacher, if Julian was a visionary who was herself caught up in a transformational spiral of meaning and counter-meaning, leading to a deeply expressive engagement with the nature of transformative Christian love as rational, then Marx too, in his own way, was a man concerned with effecting social change through the use of language in a way that stripped away false understandings which cloud judgment and obscure reality, leading to the apprehension of the truth of our social and political relations. In other words, what we may be able to see here is a concern, worked out in different historical registers, with the potential of human speech and writing to correct far-reaching false alignments: to heal misshapen reason and to make whole our human capacity to *see things as they are*. This is a very Christian, very Marxian optimism in our social powers of human social transformation through forms of self-correction. By speaking with one another, we can get it right.

But we have to set the range of Denys Turner's oeuvre against the broader cultural landscapes of modernity, in which technology and the general expansion of education have led to a collapse of the linearity of history as presented in texts, whereby one period supplants another. The increasing accessibility of texts from different historical periods has often led also to the uncritical assimilation of ancient texts into contemporary forms of understanding, whereby these texts are shorn of their distinctiveness in the process. It has been Turner's case that we need not and should not do that. We can also allow these texts to subvert our expectations and to be a recalcitrant other. If we can attune our ear to their otherness, then we can also learn from them.

But learning, of course, is a dynamic and multilayered exercise. We need to put into practice what we have learned. This raises the further question of how we can use this otherness today, since we cannot all become Thomists. In other words, how can we read these texts responsibly but also constructively? Bound up with our enthusiasm for Thomas, Dante, Eckhart, and Julian will be the wish to integrate them into our society and even, perhaps, to apply what we can learn from them in ways that will allow us better to address the many challenges we face today. And so we are left with the further question: how can we realistically build—with modern materials—on what we can learn from texts which are classically the product of such different times but which might nevertheless contain important new insights for us today, not only of a religious kind, but also concerning possibilities within the human as such? The very process of learning obliges us to ask these kinds of constructive questions.

This essay has three points of departure therefore. In the first place, language is simply too fundamental to us as communicating, reflecting beings not to be intrinsically part of our own history. All human beings have linguistic competence (although of course this will be actualized in varying degrees and ways according to capacity). But the question of what language *is* has been addressed and answered differently across historical periods. In the light of this historicity of language, which is intimately bound up with our own historicity (or evolving self-understanding over the centuries), it becomes important that we should have a properly historical understanding of language. If language is our theme, then this kind of critical, historical perspective on language will allow us also to be properly self-critical. The failure to think critically about language in historical terms will mean that we are more likely to fall victim to our own pretensions as these are bound up with our tacit, assumed positions on the nature of language, not just as a topic to be discussed, but as the very medium of that discussion.

We can be more explicit here. If material words can be considered our first and most fundamental "technology" (and so the first interface between our minds and the material world around us), then it may be that what we think language is, which is mediated to us consciously and unconsciously through the diverse explicit and implicit conduits of the society and culture of our day, will in part condition our own possibilities of its use.[3] And that, in turn, might mean that how we understand and use language may also determine, again in ways that are mediated by culture, the possibilities of who we can be.

Ironically, in certain key respects our contemporary understanding of language seems much closer to that of the premodern rather than the modern or Enlightenment/post-Enlightenment period, from which we are emerging. The varied and subtle dualisms of modernity have given way to a broadly integrated way of understanding the relation between body and mind. In particular, language is seen today as being much more closely associated with the human body, both in terms of the development of language within human evolution and in terms of the neurology of language use and the proximity between the ways in which we use words and the ways in which we use tools. Our second point of departure here is then that certain kinds of medieval texts may be becoming legible in new ways, on account of the contemporary turn (or return) to an "integrated," nondualist understanding of language and of the self.[4] Theory of language in our own times may be beginning to open up new points of access into medieval texts, for instance, precisely where they performatively embody, or are embedded in, premodern understandings of what language is. The texts from Dante, Thomas, Eckhart, and Julian on which Denys Turner has worked all sit within performative genres (literary, pedagogical, kerygmatic, and visionary, respectively). These are all texts that set themselves the task of communicating revelation dynamically to society. They are in effect socially transformative texts, all of which have a certain performativity and are expressive of human possibilities, which arguably are bound up with premodern presuppositions about what language is.

We can understand our second point of departure in another way therefore. If our contemporary scientific theory of language offers a fuller and more complete (or more accurate) account of what language is than the modern or Enlightenment/post-Enlightenment accounts and if it is closer to premodern understandings of what language is, then it follows that certain "performative" texts which have been preserved within religious traditions throughout the modern period may in fact disclose the possibilities of language to attentive recipients of these texts, in ways which have defied their modern thematization. It may be that deeply "nondualist" texts, which are themselves the performative product of integrated cosmologies and cultures of the premodern period, cannot be thematically understood in the modern period, or understood according to modern theories of language, but can nevertheless be inchoately recognized as communicating something "impossible," beyond modernity's reach. Indeed, it could be argued that in a dualistic age we will inevitably fail thematically to recognize the functionality of nondualistic, performative texts from the premodern period, except perhaps by explication in their own terms. In this way we will enjoy them as something very valuable and distinctive, but we will be strictly limited in what we can learn from them or indeed put into practice through this learning.

The third point of departure then is the following. Our contemporary understanding of language as material form does not of itself commit to an understanding of language as transformational. Although contemporary science may inform language theory today in ways that emphasize the material properties of words (which are like tools), this does not of itself deliver new ways of theorizing the transformational properties of words as we find them in the dynamically performative texts of the medieval authors. In the face of these texts, as their modern readers, we need to learn to think of our human language in new cultural or phenomenological ways but now informed by the new scientific knowledge concerning the materiality of language and the nondualistic nature of the self, which also belongs to our contemporaneity. That this may be a task worth doing is supported by the fact that the very occasional explicit advocacy of the material nature of language during the modern period can be associated with Karl Marx and Julia Kristeva. Both of these authors are strongly linked with a linguistic performativity of a social transformative kind. Moreover, the context here is not one of the medieval genres but rather the very distinctively modern one of *political* writing. If at least a tacit advocacy of, and manifest performativity within, the material nature of the sign is something principally confined to religious culture and to the arts in the modern period, both of which are arguably marginal to the more secularized primary places of public debate and controversy, then Marx and Kristeva both witness to the continuing relevance of this explicit advocacy in modern public and political life. To this extent, we can see perhaps a continuity between premodern ecclesial genres of social transformation through a dynamically performative use of language and certain modern political genres, aimed also at renewing society.

THE LINGUISTIC SIGN AS MATTER AND CONCEPT

If indeed language is so intimately part of us that it shares our history, then a survey in broad outline of that history shows two quite contrasting schools of thought about the nature of language, divided by the Enlightenment/post-Enlightenment and the advent of modernity. We can begin with the medieval approach, with its intrinsically transformative account of language.

The Middle Ages

The medieval approach characteristically emphasized the materiality of the sign, looking back to the Origenist-Augustinian inheritance, with its account of scripture as standing in parallel with the incarnate body of Christ and the material signs of history.[5] It was classically defined by Dante, for whom words are both *sensuale* and *rationale*: "This signal, then, is the noble foundation that I am discussing; for it is sensible, in that it is a sound, and yet also rational, in that this sound, according to convention, is taken to mean something."[6] This means that language, as a system of visible or oral signs, reproduces that peculiarly human mix that we ourselves are, of matter and mind, materiality and conceptuality. This is our "rational animality," in Thomist terms.[7] As Denys Turner has written, "A human being is not a body plus meaning: for Thomas a human being is matter plus meaning, *that is*, a body, just as language is not words plus their meanings, but bits of matter organised into meanings, *that is*, words."[8] But for an age deeply influenced by strong Christian accounts of the Word becoming flesh, such an account is also intrinsically one that is open to the transformational effects of the revelation of the creator God.

And it is arguably in Dante himself that we find the most extended performative representation of language as both matter and mind. Dante's *Divine Comedy* shows a very close connection between the environment of his characters, whether in Hell, Purgatory, or Heaven, and the way that their language is imaged. The sounds of Hell that meet Dante's ears include "Sighings and complaints and howlings."[9] Here there is "a jumble of languages, deformities of speech, / Words which were pain, with intonations of anger / Voices which were deep and hoarse, hands clapped together /. . . ."[10] In Hell, the natural properties of communication are debased and destroyed, stripped of the clarity of human communicative reason. Materiality destroys communication and, with it, the sociality of language (language has become like "sand," deadening, homogeneous in the sense of admitting of no distinctions, and dry).[11] In Purgatory, however, language returns to its sociality, becoming the shared resource of the "work song" and of psalms which express penance and thanksgiving for divine mercy: "But while we were turning our bodies there / Voices were singing: '*Beati pauperes spiritu*' / And no words can tell how sweetly they sang. / Ah, how different these approaches are / From those of hell! For here we have songs / As we go in, and there ferocious laments."[12] And in Heaven, human communication increasingly takes on the qualities of angelic communication while remaining nevertheless human. Following Thomas, Dante maintains in *De vulgari eloquentia* that angels do not need language to communicate; they do so immediately.[13] In the heavenly realms, communication increasingly takes place directly, through the light of flashing glance and radiant smile. But for all the angelic luminosity of Heaven, Dante (again following Thomas) maintains the difference between angelic and purified human communication and importantly evokes the human body even at the place of the Trinity, where Dante glimpses Christ's presence as "our image," in the "smile."[14] In our ultimate corporeal state, then, we will communicate as the angels do, though of course we will do so through the transparency of the now-glorified human body (glorified, that is, through the glorification of Christ's own body).[15]

A strongly transformational hermeneutic can be found likewise in the world of Meister Eckhart, though in this case it is in a quite different genre. Eckhart is a preacher, whose preaching of the divine Word had such effects upon those of his day that his sermons were preserved. Reconstructing Eckhart's sources has been one of the major tasks of his reception in the modern period. We are aware today, however, of the influence on him of Thomas of Erfurt's Modist semiotics, which emphasized that the word mediates to the mind the real properties of the thing to which it refers.[16] This is a realist semiotics that allows a place to mind, word, and thing. This tying of words communicatively to existent objects in the world offered a potentially transformational semiotic to Eckhart, who was concerned precisely to engage with how the mind needs to pass from its anchoring in concrete objects, or "denominated being," to the divine source and ground of knowledge in God. In modern terms, we can state that Eckhart's preaching is aimed at shifting the center of consciousness away from the multiplicity of the material world in which we find ourselves as creature (as "flowing out") to the unicity of the divine reality which is the source of that material world as this exists within ourselves at the source of our consciousness (as "centering within").

For Eckhart as for Dante, words span the space between the angelic "above" or "within" and the animal "below" or "without." Our communicative capacities can bring either reality to expression. Within the order of things, language is thus the dynamically transformational center of human life since it can itself embody either the pleroma of the divine reality or the contingency and multiplicity of the created one. For Eckhart, by their nature, "words" reach up and back into the very center of the trinitarian life, on the one hand, and yet flow out and down into the composite, denominated reality of our everyday existence, on the other. The latter is forever marked by creaturely nothingness. This is fundamentally an Augustinian vision, but with his strong, contrastive account of unicity and multiplicity and, doubtlessly, with the communicative mission of the *ordo praedicatorum* which Eckhart shares with Thomas Aquinas, this Augustinianism is communicatively intensified. Also, we sense in Eckhart the same fourteenth-century élan and optimism that we find in other fourteenth-century figures who, like him, newly embrace the vernacular language (from Dante to Julian).

"All words have their power from the first Word," Eckhart tells us.[17] And indeed Eckhart's are texts of "power" since we are confronted everywhere with linguistic performativity rather than language theory. But in Sermon 18, taken together with his commentary on the Prologue of John, we can begin to see the more formal shape of Eckhart's theory of language.[18] It includes trinitarian structures around the notion of the eternal generation of the Word, leading to an account of creation also as the Word "spoken" by God and of the intellect as arising from our ground as the divine word in us. Within such a structure, the words preached are themselves the communication of the divine outflow as creative Word. Against the background of such a "trinitarian" theory of language, Eckhart tells us in a crucial passage that he knows that he needs to purify the words used, freeing them from their material and sensual connotations or references in order that the capacity of speech to change other human beings can be realized.[19] If we speak of earthly things, he says, then our minds will engage with those, while if we speak of angelic or spiritual things, then our minds will engage with spiritual realities.

Here lies the rationale for his many abstract neologisms and, indeed, his insistent capacity to break down or de-essentialize his *way* of speaking in terms of the signs used.[20] In Eckhart's words, the materiality of the sign is exploited, as much as it is stressed and transformed, in order to convey what are for him spiritual or "intellectual" truths. These are truths, however, which *can only be conveyed in language*. They are material or fundamental truths about who we are as embodied creatures, in space and time, as creatures who are both materiality and *intellectus*. Language, for Eckhart, is the creative word that speaks materially-culturally to human beings for whom meaning itself bears a Christological form and is closely bound up with our creatureliness as unity of both body and mind, as it is with our spatiotemporal contexts and community.

The Modern School

The kind of linguistic theory that we find in the modern period, however, in thinkers such as Hegel, Husserl, and Frege, is of a quite different kind. Arguably, the modern tradition begins in the work of J. G. Herder, who reflects extensively on the nature of language. His work can be seen to complement Kant's transcendental philosophy to the extent that Herder identifies the human capacity for language as that which grounds the possibility for reflection in the first place. He links the "sign" character of language with "consciousness" or "self-awareness" and argues that forms of reasoning or rationalizing the world are therefore bound up with the particular language that we speak.[21] Herder stands between the Enlightenment emphasis on words as the achievement of human consciousness and intellect, extending our powers of signifying, and the Romantic sense that words are given (or divinely ordained) and, as such, are also the traditions that already ground the possibilities of our reasoning before consciousness itself comes into play.

Together with Herder, we need also to consider another transitional figure, the Hebraist Johann Georg Hamann, who offered an unusually material understanding of human language as "an act of translation—from a language of angels into a human language, which is to say, thoughts into words—things into names—images into signs."[22] Words themselves have a double nature, part "aesthetic" and part "logical": "as visible and audible objects they belong with their elements to the senses and to perception, but, according to the spirit of their application and signification, they belong to reason and concepts."[23] In his anti-Kantian text *Metacritique of the Purism of Reason*, Hamann also argues that reason itself is bound up with language and thus with the senses in a way that determines it as tradition-centered, on the one hand, and as dependent on experience, on the other. He passionately disputes the legitimacy of reason in abstraction from the senses and the world, and he embraces the skeptical philosophy of David Hume as showing the fragility of autonomous reason.

In a scientific age, it was inevitable, however, that linguistic "transparency" would predominate over Romantic "opaqueness." Hegel strongly accented the universal and abstract properties of language, annulling its particularity through analyzing its relation to the here and now. For Hegel, the speaking or writing by which we refer to what seems to belong to a particular here and now effectively always dissolves it into a universality: speaking annuls spatiotemporal actuality by showing that it is effectively already held in the flow of consciousness and only properly exists here.[24] In the deterministic, materialist age of early modern science it was inevitable that philosophers would be very wary of allowing meaning to be fixed or constrained by the materiality of words in their respective material contexts. Only in a Romantic opposition to science and Enlightenment could that be allowed as a counterculture. Hegel, in contrast, effectively defines and accomplishes the Idealist option of "thinking away" materiality and so of grounding a "scientific," "universalistic," and dualist account of the human self in a material world, and again it is language and decisions about what language is which are the decisive, transformational moment.

With the thought of Husserl on language and reference, however, we come closer to our own times. The same kind of abstractive rationalism pervades Husserl's approach as we find it in the *Logische Untersuchungen*, where he argues that it is only language (and not physical signs in the world) that can truly mean, since language alone is sufficiently abstract and convertible with consciousness to be free of the vagaries of contextual change.[25] Thus, as in the case of Hegel, Husserl assimilates the material properties of the sign into the consciousness of its conceptual contents. The "heroic" spirit of this rationalism is echoed in Frege's contemporary advocacy of the *Begriffschrift*, which is likewise the attempt to fulfill the "task of philosophy." This is to "break the power of words over the human mind."[26] The new logical code establishes the "conceptual content" of things, freeing thought "from the taint of ordinary linguistic means of expression" and from its dependence on "particulars."[27] Again, we see here the link between linguistic transparency (supported by an "immaterial" account of language) and authoritative knowledge in our public spaces.

But there are also some few counterproposals. Consider these words of Karl Marx (himself from a Orthodox Jewish background on his mother's side), from *The German Ideology*:

> From the start the "spirit" is afflicted with the curse of being "burdened" with matter, which here makes its appearance in the form of agitated layers of air, sounds, in short, of language. Language is as old as consciousness, language is practical consciousness that exists also for others, and for that reason alone it really exists for me personally as well; language, like consciousness, only arises from the need, the necessity, of intercourse with others. Language is as old as consciousness, language is practical, real consciousness that exists for others as well, and only therefore exists also for me; language, like consciousness, only arises from the need, the necessity, of intercourse with others.[28]

Here Marx is pointing to the fundamental communicability of consciousness and so also, by implication, the capacity of the embodied truth of one individual to be communicated to another. In the background here is the further Marxian principle that language as the medium of interpersonal relation can also disclose error and illusion between people, which we associate with false consciousness or the internalized perspectives of others as ideology. Language can in a certain sense liberate. That Marx should have such a "thick" account of language at the outset of his political work suggests at least one modern parallel to our medieval transformational texts. In Marx's case, he is laying the foundation for a potential linguistic, communicative dynamic which is distinctively liberationist and political, pointing toward freedom and bondage in the potential generativity of human productivity not as language but as labor.[29] This is not quite the same kind of transformation as envisaged in the personal socioethics of Thomas's pedagogy, Eckhart's preaching, Dante's poetry, or Julian's visionary contemplation, but it is nevertheless not wholly dissimilar.

Kristeva offers a related, thick account of language as "text" in her *Revolution in Poetic Language*. She makes the distinction between the "genotext" and the "phenotext," the former embodying the hidden, as process or desire, and the latter making its content conceptually explicit in the transfer of ideas.[30] "Poetic language," for Kristeva, is the communicative expressivity of language as material form, as process and rhythm, which needs to be affirmed as opening up not "a semiology of products" but rather "a semiology of production" (in Roland Barthes's words).[31] For Kristeva, "text" functions most distinctly as "practice," which in its openness or shedding of "narcissistic fixations" and in its display of "process" can also be defined as "ethical practice."[32] She states, "The ethical cannot be stated, instead it is practiced to the point of loss, and the text is one of the most accomplished examples of such a practice."[33] In Kristeva we can see a revolutionary moment in texts, as openly showing and sharing human language as production in ways that break down abstract universals and constitute a new space of the "affirmation of freedom."[34]

Language Today

We shall in effect only be able to situate both a premodern theory of language as uniting materiality and conceptuality and a modern theory as privileging conceptuality in the sign in such a way as to be able to learn important things about the human self who is both premodern materialist and modern/postmodern dualist if we can find a theory of language which will account for both of these contrasting views.[35] It is precisely this hope today that motivates the present essay. It is a hope grounded to no small degree in the fact that our contemporary scientific account of language combines the authoritative scientific perspective we inherit from the modern period, in contrast to the medieval one, with understandings of what language is which appear in fact far closer to medieval than to modern understandings. This is not yet the contemporary cultural and philosophical understanding we are seeking of what this *means* for us today, but it is an important step on the way. The knowledge that comes to us from science is at the end of the day constituted as measurement, description, and explanation, while what we are seeking here is a cultural-philosophical work of meaning. Such a cultural-philosophical framework needs to be informed by our scientific self-understanding, however, if it is to transcend the limitations of our own time and so become a possible hermeneutic for understanding human communicability as such, across historical and also, potentially, global cultural divides.

We need to view language, scientifically, from two perspectives, both of which pivot around the materiality of words. Evolutionary biology suggests that the development of tool use and language use in our past are linked, and, neurologically, words seem to be like "tools."[36] Andy Clark describes words as "material objects" which are "amodal" to the extent that they can be "carried" (like tools) between different contexts.[37] An important article on the theme of the relation between "action," "gesture," and meaning as "representation" bears the title "A Word in the Hand."[38] Comparative work with other higher primates suggests that human language may have developed from facial expressions or rhythms.[39] Language is a performative product of the body and extends the body's rhythms and gestures into new modes of expressivity. In the intimate interrelation of neural coupling and what one research group in social cognition refers to as the "dark matter" of face-to-face communication, conversation is a constructive exercise which we undertake with another human being in order to explore whether we can "build" a conversation together, thus signaling the likelihood that we can work together constructively in other ways too, such as harvesting crops, building temporary dwellings, fighting off foes, or hunting antelope (or any of their modern analogues).[40]

Contemporary science supports the premodern sense of the materiality of words but goes further in describing the effects of this. Andy Clark suggests that words are "potent real-world structures" which ground the "neural wet-ware" of the fluid processes of our consciousness and cognition, helping us to consolidate and objectify through material form what it is that we think.[41] Clark, an artificial intelligence specialist, associates the materiality of words with the capacity of the human mind to recruit elements in the environment that will allow the generation of higher levels of awareness, through forms of objectification. Arguably, it is these processes that led to the extension of human subjectivity in time, with memory and projection beyond the immediacy of the present and with a capacity to tell stories about different places and different times.[42] In Clark's phrase, words "press minds like ours from the biological flux" in our own immediate environment.[43]

This means that we can in fact identify a two-way movement in language here: one of the mind, away from immediacy and into temporal distension, involving memory and futurity, and another which is a movement back into the complex here and now by a subject-self who is also embodied, communicative, social, and real. The former implies the instrumentalization of matter by mind (as a kind of primary or proto-technology or robotics), while the latter implies the "becoming material" of mind through word use or conversation. The polarity in play here is that the materiality of words is borrowed from our environment (as sound or shape), while their content is constituted within our mental world. Words then are most dynamically the place of our interaction with, or belonging in, a material world as intelligent creatures. But since language is also shared, they are also the place where "what I think" comes closest to "what you think" through communicative process. Words, which are grounded in common, communitarian, material patterns of meaning, also constitute the primary environment of my social being. In a sense, words *are* my social being which, at the same time, to paraphrase Marx, is my *real* being.

But science offers us a second, thought-provoking perspective on language as a form of primary or proto-technology. If the acquisition of advanced language skills which we associate with *Homo sapiens* is one which can be associated with the development of stable, medium-sized communities (or early town dwellings), then it might be right to think of human language in its advanced forms as having developed fairly recently in our history, perhaps within a period of only a few tens of thousands of years.[44] This in turn would mean that there is a case for the view that language is a technology of which we have as yet only an uncertain grasp. It may be that we are better at controlling this "new" technology the closer we are to the face-to-face as the point of its origination, and so communications at a greater distance, through contemporary extended media, are less under our social and personal control.

A DIALOGUE BETWEEN SCIENCE AND RELIGION

In sum, there is a case for the view that our contemporary scientific understanding approximates, in a different register, to Denys Turner's principle that language is the form of our body's meaning.[45] But we have to ask whether we need to make such a move in the first place. Is there not a case for the view that fine expositions of medieval authors do not stand in need of a contribution from contemporary science? These are skilled, freestanding introductions to the work of major writers and thinkers who have something important to tell us. I think the answer to this is both yes and no. It is yes because many of us will find this sufficient (especially perhaps if we share with our texts the same Catholic tradition). But it is also no because to learn from these highly successful, socially transformative texts also implies that we should be able to apply what we have learned. This would mean that we should be able to apply insights gained to other potential or active socially transformative situations, in which, for instance, "deep" or "radical" communication between individuals or communities is called for. If—with the help of contemporary science—we can grasp the structure of human social communication in its transformational mode, across the boundary that separates the modern from the premodern in the West, then this surely ought to have implications too in all kinds of other cultural contexts, including the global encounters, often between Western societies and the more traditional cultures of the emerging economic powers, which are influential in our geopolitical landscapes today. Traditional forms of cultural reasoning in China and India will have much in common with the medieval West. It should likewise have implications in principle for dialogue between religions, which are often at different stages in the movement from "premodern" to "modern." It would seem that only contemporary science could provide such a "species-wide" account of how we use language in order to effect change together: moving beyond the kerygmatic, literary, pedagogical, and visionary genres of our exceptionally communicative medieval texts to contemporary social and political language use where change may be powerfully contested.

But science alone cannot achieve this. After all, science alone is not properly "meaning" (and reductionism or scientism is the all too frequent failure to understand this). What we are seeking here is a cultural-philosophical account that has internalized our new scientific self-understanding. One of the key tasks for such an account would be the imperative of learning in depth from its own history. There is much to be gathered from Kant, for instance, who produced a philosophy of meaning, having internalized the limit imposed on mind by the newly discovered properties of matter as these exist outside or beyond us. We can learn from him that the scientific discovery of the material properties of the world casts new light on the causal effects of matter and specifically on these causal effects as they impinge on our minds as limit. Kant's project was the recognition within critical philosophy of the effective limiting of mind, through the material world, which had always been the case but which was now, for the first time, properly understood reflexively and philosophically. And importantly, Kant alerts us to where the effects of such a limit are to be found. They have an impact within us, on the nature and power of our reasoning, as our minds turn out and engage with the world around us. Kant lays out the different ways we reason and shows critically the varying material parameters within which these different kinds of reasoning work: transcendental, practical, and aesthetic. In this way, Kant was able to articulate a meaningful account of the human self, having internalized the new knowledge about the nature of the material world around us, which came to us from early modern science.

There will be a Kantian inheritance here. But what we are seeking today is not an account of how the *external* causal effects of materiality can have an impact on us as limit internally but rather, with the new discoveries of genetics and neuroscience, how the causal presence of materiality *within us* might also present limits to mind internally and invisibly. This is a different kind of proposition. It presupposes, for instance, a far more intimate order in which mind and matter combine than that merely of external causal effects. It suggests also a concern with the point at which mind and matter inflect one onto the other most comprehensively and dynamically. This suggests language itself, and so we shall have to include also in our inheritance of learning some of Kant's critics, such as Hamann and the Romantic philosophers, who saw even then that Kant had not in fact taken due account of how reason and language are intertwined.[46] This criticism seems even more forceful today when we consider the emphasis neuroscience places on the central place of language in human social cognition. It is here, in our "face-to-face conversations," that physicality and mind intensively compress in a dynamic processional combination of intimate and subtle neural, mimetic responses together with intensively reflexive processes of monitoring both the other and oneself (and others who may be overhearing our conversation). This is the most fundamental area in which we seek to gauge the subjectivity or personality of the other through interactive, mutually responsive material communications which attain such a rapidity and density that, as we have seen, a leading research team in social cognition has metaphorically dubbed this interactivity "dark matter."[47] The need to arrive at high-level judgments about our

compatibility with others, from the perspective of our potential capacity to work closely together in pursuit of shared goals (hunting,
harvesting, building, warfare), has probably been fundamental to our
species survival, from an evolutionary biological perspective, so we
should not be surprised at how versatile and central a tool language
is in "inter-face" communications for building an effective and reflexively aware social solidarity.[48]

But language is vital with respect to our integration as both body
and mind in another way too. We cannot use words without assuming a certain responsibility for what we say. We can and should *choose*
our words. Indeed, if we cannot be responsible for what we say, or
write, then the very nature of human discourse breaks down (and
with it the possibility of science as a field of reasoned and responsible
human knowledge). This means that human language use already
presupposes a certain kind of freedom which allows us to be asked,
"Why did you say that?" or "Why did you say it that way?" This is consistent with Clark's case that it is through the material form of words
that our consciousness is raised to higher levels of self-awareness,
and so also of self-possession.

But still we are left with the question, where in language use
might we be able to find the new limits of matter and materiality, as
identified in its causal effects through science? What kind of limit
are we talking about here, and how can it be internal to us: a constitutive part of our own subjectivity? We cannot identify such a limit
straightforwardly here, for instance, with the mere fact that we know
that mind or consciousness is dependent on a certain material configuration in the brain such that a massive stroke or blow to the head
rapidly leads to the cessation of consciousness. In this case the material effects may be "within us," but they are decisively "outside"
consciousness in the sense that this kind of limit is not constitutively
present in our subjectivity (our death marks the cessation of our phenomenal consciousness and is not a fluctuation within it). But can
the limit we are seeking then be like the fact that a lack of zinc in the
brain can contribute to schizophrenia, for instance?[49] (Schizophrenia
is something we can experience and survive after all.) Probably not.
While the effects of a lack of zinc in the brain are experienced within

consciousness as abnormal, unwelcome states which call for treatment, they are anomalous and not a natural part of our consciousness. We can only be aware of the *effects* of zinc in the brain where it is insufficiently present, and remedying this removes this effect on us. This too therefore is properly "outside" consciousness.

A much stronger candidate for an "internal" effect of matter on mind are our habits, whereby we know today that material pathways are forged in the brain which we experience as a preconditioned or habitual response. To change or lose a bad habit can take two weeks or so as we effectively apply our willpower to reshaping the structure of the brain in specific ways. This would seem then to be a place at which we encounter our own limit, as consciousness, and have to make *conscious* efforts to overcome the material causation that does indeed press on us *internally*. We cannot, however, rightly interpret this as being a limit that is experienced or is operational within or with respect to *reason*, at the very core of our humanity. Bad habits constrain our behavior, and perhaps our will, but they are not internally constitutive of who we are as consciousness, possessed of powers of reasoning and self-determination. Habits, which we know today to be grounded in the material formations of the brain, are powerful indicators of the extent to which we can understand our consciousness to be "within materiality": material but not reducible to materiality. But they do not tell us about how matter and material causation may in fact be internal to the way we reason, in ways that have constantly conditioned our reasoning as subjects but which we have nevertheless not hitherto objectively understood.

Perhaps then we should return to what we can now describe as the third or earliest and most unfamiliar part of our learning inheritance, namely, our medieval, transformational texts. We can ask the question whether it is here, in these exuberantly pre-Kantian language texts, that we might possibly be able to discern what contemporary neuroscience with its integrated paradigm of body and mind seemingly implies that there should be: namely, the *internal* operation of a material limit on the expansiveness of mind. The very question seems strange, however, since these are not texts that suggest limit. Rather they suggest inclusivity and expansion and spreading transformational horizons that include creativity, spirituality, and growth. No modern reader can journey with Dante, Julian, Eckhart, or Thomas for very long without feeling that there is in fact at the heart of this encounter the sense of an *absence* of limit: precisely the thing that we do not find in the same way (or do not generally find) in modern texts.

And that perhaps is the key. Why do we not discern here, in our magically creative, transformational medieval texts, the effect and perhaps performance precisely of mind integrated with matter? Why do we not see here the embodied functioning of mind beyond the "limit" of matter, *in the act of communication itself*? Maybe what we experience in reading these texts from another age is the absence and overcoming of the limits of matter internally that are, arguably, such a condition of the modern world. In other words, their alien performativity may be precisely a kind of creativity that itself "embodies" and communicates the impossibility for us of a different kind of public discourse which is itself dynamically transformational precisely on the grounds of its personal and existential wholeness.

And indeed the link between ways of reasoning and ways of inhabiting our own body has been clearly set out by Hannah Arendt. She argues, for instance, that we reason as an observer when we should reason as a participant when she complains that we live on earth "as if we viewed it from another planet."[50] Indeed, there is much in the critical reasoning of the Frankfurt school which points to this "limit," where reason is falsified in its functioning by the context in which it is performed (as when we use "theoretical" and individualistic reasoning to decide practical goals which should be determined from within "ethical" or "communitarian" reasoning). And so we come to the question, can our study of these transformational premodern texts show us something about ourselves that the Frankfurt school authors do not know? Can they add a further critical dimension which is obscured by the Frankfurt school commitment solely to present forms of discourse? And what would that dimension be?

The study of our premodern and modern texts together in the light of what we now know, scientifically and objectively, about the nature of human language as such strips from us a naïveté which both premodern and modern authors share. This is the historical naïveté that the possibilities of our language use, in any one period, is a given and cannot be otherwise. We know today that this givenness of language is in fact an effect of culture and is therefore one that is itself subject to change. Language shares our history. It can, therefore, and indeed needs to share in our own critical historicality: our capacity to exercise a Gadamerian reflection on our own points of departure especially when confronted by ancient texts. In fact, the transformational historical hermeneutic which is in play here may itself be the radicalization through an internalized neuroscientific optic of these same Gadamerian principles of understanding as the convergence of different "horizons." If this is the case, then it is their radicalization through accessing new depths of our capacity to learn from these ancient texts. This is not a moment within "*nouvelle théologie*" then, which would be more the translation of integral texts from one historical context to another. This would be a different kind of historical engagement with ancient texts, one concerned with understanding—through texts—how other people from past times have been in space and time in ways subtly different from our own habituated modes of being in space and time (in which the implicit and explicit understandings of mind and matter, which differ across historical periods, are themselves constitutively part of our being in space and time). After all, to be "historical" is fundamentally to be in "space and time" as a creature who both acts and is acted upon.[51]

But where might such a new "historical sensibility" or form of "historical self-awareness" take us? Here we are firmly in the realm of speculation, but we can wonder what robust contemporary cultural-philosophical paradigms might deliver which have internalized the principle that words are "material objects" which not only connect us with the world and with one another but which are also the means, part air and part mind, by which we make our home in this world in the first place, as persons who are first of all within community: the community of speech. Could we gain real insights into how we can create human solidarity by breaking down cultural differences through new forms of our public, political, and diplomatic speaking,

which is to say, precisely where we speak across differences and historical boundaries? After all, we generally speak communally with our
own, whereas our public communicative spaces are generally places
where community or traditional discourses coexist, in a depersonal-
ized space of "bureaucratized" coexistence rather than where they
converge and interrelate. Might such an organic, humanly inclusive,
transcommunitarian, and above all *informed* speech allow a different
order of discourse to arise in those public spaces: one with a properly scientific and so also public understanding of the fundamental
rules of human transformational discourse? These would include its
affectivity, generativity, spontaneity, hospitality, open rationality, and
giftedness as simultaneous self-offering and speech, as reasoning
body made present for the other, productively, communicatively and
rhetorically, to be imaginatively conceived and responsibly thought
about; to be this: love received as human meaning.

NOTES

1. For a discussion of the connections between McCabe, Eagleton, and
Turner, the continuity of influence they shared, and the contemporary relevance of their Christian Marxism, see Eric Bugyis's essay in the present
volume.

2. For introductions to embodied cognition, see, e.g., Alva Noë, *Action
in Perception* (Cambridge, MA: MIT Press, 2004); and Mark Johnson, *The
Meaning of the Body: Aesthetics of Human Understanding* (Chicago: University of Chicago Press, 2007).

3. See notes 16–38 below.

4. By "nondualistic" here, I mean a way of thinking that recognizes that
matter poses a real limit to mind, laying the basis for some form of critical
philosophy. "Dualism" presupposes a separation between mind and matter in
such a way that mind is no longer obliged to recognize its own limit in the
material and proceeds without that sense of encounter. Many forms of "narrativism" therefore may fall within this category, for all their thematization of
materiality, since the real question is to what extent narrativism avoids the
sometimes abyssal separation between how we construct the world mentally
and how we intelligently and responsibly act in the world, as human material
cause, encountering resistance.

5. See Morwenna Ludlow, "Spirit and Letter in Origen and Augustine," in *The Spirit and the Letter: A Tradition and a Reversal*, ed. Paul S. Fiddes with Günter Bader (London: Bloomsbury T & T Clark, 2013), 87–104.

6. Dante Alighieri, *De vulgarii eloquentia*, trans. Steven Botterill (Cambridge: Cambridge University Press, 1996), 1.3, 7. Botterill's translation of *sensuale* here as "perceptible" could be judged to pull the word back to cognition rather than participative belonging in the world.

7. Denys Turner, *Faith, Reason and the Existence of God* (Cambridge: Cambridge University Press, 2004), 89–93.

8. Ibid., 93; original emphasis.

9. *Inferno* 3, 1.22. See Dante Alighieri, *The Divine Comedy*, trans. C. H. Sisson (Oxford: Oxford University Press, 1993), 56. For a fuller discussion of this theme, see Oliver Davies, "Dante's *Commedia* and the Body of Christ," in *Dante's "Commedia": Theology as Poetry*, ed. Vittorio Montemaggi and Matthew Treherne (Notre Dame: University of Notre Dame Press, 2010), 161–79.

10. *Inferno* 3, 11.25–27; Sisson, *The Divine Comedy*, 56.

11. *Inferno* 3, 1.30.

12. *Purgatorio* 12, 11.109–14; Sisson, *The Divine Comedy*, 250.

13. Thomas maintains that angels don't need to speak at all but choose to speak when either teaching or praising God (*ST*, Ia, q. 107).

14. *Paradiso* 33, 11.124–26.

15. Thomas draws an analogy between the communicative luminosity of the angelic mind and our own resurrected bodies of the future, stating of the latter that "the brightness of the risen body will correspond to the grace and glory in the mind; and so will serve as a medium for one mind to know another" (*ST*, I, q. 57).

16. Thomas of Erfurt's *Grammatica speculativa* was the most widely copied manuscript on semiotics of the medieval period. See G. L. Bursill-Hall, ed. and trans., *Tractatus de modis significandi seu Grammatica speculative* (London: Longmans, 1972). It was later falsely attributed to Duns Scotus in which form Martin Heidegger studied it in his doctoral thesis and Charles Sanders Peirce lectured on it. The influence of Thomas of Erfurt on Meister Eckhart was the topic of a recent colloquium, "Thomas von Erfurt und Meister Eckhart," Max-Weber-Kolleg, Erfurt, November 14–15, 2013.

17. "Adolescens, tibi dico: surge." See Meister Eckhart, *Meister Eckhart: Die deutschen und die lateinischen Werke*, ed. J. Quint and G. Steer (Stuttgart: Kohlhammer, 1936–), DW I, Sermon 18, 306.

18. Ibid., DW I, 297–307.

19. Oliver Davies, "zu Predigt 18: Adolescens, tibi dico: surge," in *Lectura Eckhardi: Predigten Meister Eckharts von Fachgelehrten gelesen und gedeutet*, ed. Georg Steer and Loris Sturlese (Stuttgart: Kohlhammer, 1998), 110.

20. Quint refers to this as the "deconcretization" of language. See Joseph Quint, "Die Sprache Meister Eckeharts als Ausdruck seiner mystischen Geisteswelt," *Deutsche Vierteljahrsschrift für Literaturwissenschaft und Geistesgeschichte* 6 (1928): 671–701, esp. 684–85.

21. Herder's writings on language can be found in Erich Heintel, ed., *Joh. Gottfr. Herder's Sprachphilosophie: Ausgewählte Schriften* (Hamburg: Felix Meiner Verlag, 1960).

22. Johann Georg Hamann, *Sokratische Denkwürdigkeiten: Aesthetica in Nuce* (Stuttgart: Philipp Reklam, 1968), 88.

23. *Metakritik über den Purismum der Vernunft*, in *Johann Georg Hamann: Sämtliche Werke*, ed. Josef Nadler (Vienna: Herder, 1949–57), 3:281–89, at 288.

24. See, e.g., G. W. F. Hegel, *Phenomenology of Spirit*, trans. A. V. Miller (Oxford: Oxford University Press, 1977), §90–110, 58–66.

25. Edmund Husserl, *Logical Investigations*, vol. 1, trans. J. N. Findlay (London: Routledge and Kegan Paul, 1970), Investigation 1, §5, 187.

26. Gottlob Frege, *Conceptual Notation and Related Articles* (Oxford: Clarendon Press, 1972), 104–6.

27. Ibid.

28. Karl Marx and Friedrich Engels, *The German Ideology*, ed. C. J. Arthur (London: Lawrence and Wishart, 1970), 51 (translation slightly adapted).

29. On the transformational effects of language in Marxism, see also Louis Althusser, "Interview on Philosophy," in *Lenin and Philosophy and Other Essays* (Delhi: Aakar Books, 2006), 8–9.

30. Julia Kristeva, *Revolution in Poetic Language*, trans. Margaret Waller (New York: Columbia University Press, 1984), 86–89.

31. Ibid., 10.

32. Ibid., 233.

33. Ibid., 234.

34. Ibid., 3.

35. On modern/postmodern dualism, see note 4 above.

36. James Steele, Pier Francesco Ferrari, and Leonardo Fogassi, "From Action to Language: Comparative Perspectives on Primate Tool Use, Gesture and the Evolution of Human Language," *Philosophical Transactions of the Royal Society B* 367 (2012): 4–9.

37. Andy Clark, *Supersizing the Mind: Embodiment, Action and Cognitive Extension* (Oxford: Oxford University Press, 2011), 44–60.

38. Erica A. Cartmill, Sian Beilock, and Susan Goldin-Meadow, "A Word in the Hand: Action, Gesture and Representation in Humans and Non-Human Primates," *Philosophical Transactions of the Royal Society B* 367 (2012): 129–43.

39. Asif A. Ghazanfar, Daniel Y. Takahashi, Neil Mathur, and W. Tecumseh Fitch, "Cineradiography of Monkey Lip-Smacking Reveals Putative Precursors of Speech Dynamics," *Current Biology* 22 (July 10, 2012): 1176–82.

40. Leonhard Schilbach, Bert Timmermans, Vasudevi Reddy, Alan Costell, Gary Bente, Tobias Schlicht, and Kai Vogeley, "Towards a Second Person Neuroscience," *Behavioural and Brain Sciences* 36 (2013): 393–414. For a more linguistic approach to the constructive role of language in social cognition, see Herbert H. Clark, *Using Language* (Cambridge: Cambridge University Press, 1996).

41. Clark, *Using Language*, 56.

42. Clark, *Supersizing the Mind*, 44–60.

43. Ibid., 60.

44. For an overview of Kazuo Okanoya's work on Bengalese finches, language development, and domestication, see Kate Douglas, "Talk Is Cheep: Do Caged Birds Sing a Key to Language?," *New Scientist* 2955 (2014): 36–40. For the theory of human self-domestication, see Peter J. Wilson, *The Domestication of the Human Species* (New Haven: Yale University Press, 1994); and, more recently, Richard Wrangham, *Catching Fire: How Cooking Made Us Human* (New York: Basic Books, 2009).

45. See note 7 above; and Denys Turner, *Marxism and Christianity* (Oxford: Blackwell, 1983), 9–23.

46. On this question, see, e.g., Michael N. Forster, "Kant's Philosophy of Language?," *Tijdschrift voor Filosofie* 74 (2012): 485–511.

47. Schilbach et al., "Second Person Neuroscience."

48. Michael Tomasello, *Why We Cooperate* (Cambridge, MA: MIT Press, 2009).

49. C. C. Pfeiffer and E. R. Brevermann, "Zinc, the Brain and Behavior," *Biological Psychiatry* 17 (1982): 513–32.

50. See Hannah Arendt, *The Human Condition* (Chicago: University of Chicago Press, 1958), 10.

51. See Dante, *De vulgarii eloquentia*, 1.5, 11: "it is more truly human for a human being to be perceived than to perceive."

ELEVEN

Ideology and Religion, Yet Again

LUDGER VIEFHUES-BAILEY

Denys Turner has critiqued the ideological nature of theological desires. I wish to apply this critique to the debate over the question of whether the modern concept or discourse of religion itself is ideological, a position advanced by, among others, Timothy Fitzgerald and Russell McCutcheon.[1] This inquiry into the ideological nature of religion is motivated by a conversation that Turner and I began at Yale University about the category of religion. "Do you think that people really have 'religion'?" he asked over a cup of coffee and a cigarette. "I don't think they do!" In this essay I wish to continue this conversation by arguing critically that an expanded version of Denys Turner's use of ideology critique reveals two important weaknesses in the charge that modern religion (MR) is an ideological formation. Both the epistemology and the concept of religion operative in this charge fall victim to a Turner-inspired ideology critique. Thus the question arises concerning what concepts of ideology and religion enable us to analyze MR as ideological. Constructively, I present a reworking of both notions and demonstrate how they allow me to develop a full account of the political nature of MR.

At the outset allow me to clarify my use of the term *ideology* as well as the function of *ideology critique*. As an umbrella term, ideology

268

can denote the "mental frameworks—the language, the concepts, categories, imagery of thought, and the systems of representations—which different classes and social groups deploy in order to make sense of, define, figure out, and render intelligible the way society works."[2] Through these epistemologies hegemonic social classes or groups exert power.[3] This baseline definition of *ideology* leaves open, however, multiple venues for how to decide whether a concept or an epistemic frame is ideological and how to critique it. Since differentiating between these venues is central for my project, let me spend some time describing them.

First, one could claim that concepts are ideological in the following sense: in contrast to what we may call innocent concepts that describe reality, ideological[One] concepts distort this description for hegemonic purposes. Instead of doing their advertised epistemic work these concepts surreptitiously do the work of politics. Thus an ideological[One] concept is "false" because due to its epistemic distortion, it cannot refer to reality as it is. Here ideology critique would mean to show the undistorted epistemic relation of an undistorted concept or to show that the "false" concept has no universal referent.

Second, one could claim that *all* of our concepts are embedded in cultural and social politics. Consequently there are no "innocent concepts" that could provide the contrast necessary to identify some concepts as ideological[One]. In fact, underlying the very idea of innocent concepts is a vision of epistemic "objectivity" devoid of human and thus political entanglement. The idea is that we could successfully refer with our concepts from a position outside of our entanglement with the world and with each other. However, by presenting some concepts as capable of producing "objective" knowledge, this metaepistemic vision itself is ideological[Two] because it makes invisible its own hegemonic entanglement. In this case, ideology critique involves the labor of demonstrating in which sense the desire for disentangled "objectivity" itself involves a fantasy. Interpreting this point in Turnerian terms, I suggest that at stake here is a desire for a central source of meaning that secures by itself and without human interaction that our words succeed in referring and thus describing the world as it is. The center that the defender of theism desires to fill with God or that the atheist wishes to occupy is conceived of as the one place from which to objectively describe the world.

What then can the charge that MR is ideological amount to if we cannot claim that MR is ideological[One], because doing so would require an epistemic frame that is ideological[Two]? Discussing the concept of the free market, Stuart Hall suggests that a concept is ideological if—by emphasizing only one element of the relevant political relation (here the economic relation)—the concept hides the other important parts where hegemonic power is produced. Thus, by fetishizing only a part the working of the entire conceptual and political machine remains unintelligible. In other words a concept is ideological[Three] if it makes invisible the production processes by which it is embedded in and advances struggles for cultural hegemony. Here the task of ideology critique is to expand the conceptual frame such that we can see the political urgency to which the concept reacts and thus how it achieves its hegemonic goals.

Given the Turnerian undercurrents of ideology[Two], I will begin the critical section of this chapter by arguing with the help of Grace Jantzen and Stanley Cavell that the distorted desire operative in ideology[Two] reflects an epistemic vision where the knower imagines inhabiting a God's-eye point of view. Thus, the knower imagines being disentangled from the world he describes and the people to whom he describes it. Following Cavell, I characterize this particular desire as reflecting a skeptical epistemology (SE). We will see that SE motivates what constitutes an ideological[Two] distortion, that is, the wrongheaded desire for a center or in Jantzen's words a desire for "objectivity" instead of objectivity.[4]

In the second step of the critical section I will argue with reference to Timothy Fitzgerald's and Russell McCutcheon's work that the claim that MR is ideological[One] is itself ideological[Two], if the charge is that MR is a false universal because it produces political hegemonies. This charge requires us to assume that it could be possible for us to have concepts that are not embedded in and entangled with human and political interests.

If these two points of critique are apt, the question is, how can we do ideology critique of MR? A constructive approach capable of accepting that and how religion is entangled with political power requires acknowledging that "religion" has productive effects. Thus in the first section of this chapter's constructive segment I will follow Hilary Putnam in presenting an epistemology that allows for the entanglement of descriptive and evaluative concerns. This epistemological option is the antidote for SE in that we can conjoin the productive and descriptive effects of our concepts. Mistakenly thinking that language only has productive effects and thus fails to refer at all introduces again a longing for SE. Based on a more complete picture of reference, we can account for the fact that our linguistic practices are political and material. If all of our concepts do things (in addition to doing the job of referring) and thus reflect normative practices, then an analysis of MR can lead us into particular modern webs of contestations. Instead of asking whether "religion" has a true referent or not, we can ask how contestations over religion reflect particular struggles over political hegemony and whether our epistemic practices allow us to develop a more complete picture of these struggles. At stake here is whether our concepts ("agency," "tradition," "the West," "religion as private," etc.) fetishize elements of these struggles by standing in for the more complex realities of these contestations. Thus, in the second part of this section, I will outline ideology[Three] as fetishization, followed in the third part by a non-fetishized concept of religion, namely, MR as *dispositif*, which avoids fetishizing the quietist protestant history of MR. Instead of only focusing on this Weberian strand of MR, I bring to the fore the connection between both this heritage of conceptualizing religion as private and the Durkheimian one that conceptualizes religion as an inherently cultural-political phenomenon. This segment on MR as *dispositif* allows us to see not only the global production circuits but also the embodied effects of the discourses of religion involved in this *dispositif*. Given the global and bodily nature of MR, I demonstrate, from the perspective of political theory, the precise political urgency to which respond the entangled Weberian and Durkheimian elements in the *dispositif* MR.

CRITICAL EXPOSITION: CRITIQUE OF IDEOLOGY CRITIQUE

Denys Turner began his multifaceted career with a subtle defense of Marxism and with a lashing of those who saw a Marxian use of ideology critique as detrimental to the project of proper theologizing. On the contrary, Turner argues that we need to reflect on how capitalist conditions of production distort our language in general and our theological discourse in particular. The desire operative in such distorted language, to link this early phase of Turner with the title of this volume, produces a particularly modern fantasy that subjectivity be grounded in a transparent relationship to a central source of meaning and value.

In his works on ideology, Turner calls for theology to embrace the "wholesale decentering of theology, the abandonment of its commitment to a universe centered upon the competing autonomies of God or man."[5] Man and God should not be conceived as competing for the same center. Characteristic for this ideological and idolatrous epistemic configuration in late capitalism is the assumption that there is within our grasp a center of value and meaning that stabilizes our human self and our engagement with the world.

What if, however, there is no such central place? What if the desire for it is itself the product of an ideological malformation? From the works of Sarah Coakley and others we know that knowledge of the divine results not from just any desire but that such knowledge requires a *schola affectus*, a schooling of affectivity or desire. Thus, I take Turner's intervention to be that the debate should not be over whether or not such a central source of meaning is divine or human but whether it makes sense to desire it. If the desire for such a center is malformed, then it seems that the resulting epistemology is as well. Instead of providing us with an objective description of the world, it provides us with a version of "objectivity," which projects our infelicitous desires onto the world and the divine. In sum, critiquing the distortion of our language about the divine and ourselves implies critiquing a specific epistemic desire.

Indeed, in *Becoming Divine*, another British theologian, Grace Jantzen, connects this desire for a central source of unmediated knowledge with Thomas Nagel's idea of a "view from nowhere." Under the grips of this desire we imagine a position that can observe the world without being entangled in it. For both Jantzen and Turner the claim that objective knowledge is only possible if the knower could inhabit such a position is theologically problematic. Embedded in this epistemological fantasy is a theological one: a divinity that is disentangled from the world and human beings.[6]

Who, however, desires this kind of divinity? Where do we find it? In the biblical record we encounter a vision of God who seems rather entangled in human affairs; in a sacramental worldview divine and human power are notoriously enmeshed; and the great chain of being (while ontologizing a stratified and thus hierarchical worldview) connects—not through a unified concept of being, but through a modulation of it—the highest and the lowest ranks of the cosmos. In other words, it is not self-evident that Christians did, do, or should desire a divinity that can occupy the epistemic position that could enable the "view from nowhere." Whence then this desire?

The American philosopher Stanley Cavell provides a helpful answer to the question of who desires a God from nowhere or, alternatively, to occupy this God's place. In short, his answer is, the modern skeptic. In Cavell's analysis, modern Anglo-European philosophy is haunted by a form of skepticism that is characterized by a deep dissatisfaction with our ordinary claims to knowledge, and he raises the question of whence this particular dissatisfaction. According to Cavell, the skeptical quest for knowledge begins when we remove ourselves from the concrete circumstances of our practices of knowing or doubting whether something is the case. The skeptic desires epistemic certainty in-and-of-itself. Thus the skeptic transfers a question ("How do you know?") out of contexts in which it can make sense into one where nothing is claimed and thus nothing can be doubted. Instead of asking, "How do you know this or that?," the question becomes, "How do you know in principle?" A consequence of this radical doubt is that the phenomenal world of concrete interactions itself, the lifeworld of the skeptic, becomes condensed into an abstract *x*, and is imagined to be situated in opposition to the skeptic. Thus, Cavell thinks that the skeptic deals with the world as if it were like a giant "tomato" or the dark side of the moon. The world in its totality becomes objectified. As Cavell writes:

> The experience is one I might now describe as one of looking at the world as though it were another *object* on a par with particular envelopes, tomatoes, pieces of wax, bells, tables, etc. If this is craven [*sic*], it is a craving not for generality (if that means for *generalization*) but for *totality*. It is an expression of what I mean when I said that we want to know the world as we imagine God knows it. (I do not necessarily deny that *earth* is an object and has objects on it. The world does not have objects on it.)[7]

By now we should be wary of Cavell's claim that this is how "we" imagine God's knowledge of the world. In fact, if this is how we imagine God's epistemic standpoint, then we imagine God as a skeptic would. For the skeptic, in Cavell's technical use of the term, *this* epistemic position alone can guarantee knowledge so he either despairs and rejects any claim to objectivity or aims to defend it. Thus, both denial of the objectivity allegedly gained from this view from nowhere and the defense of its possibility reflect a skeptical desire, according to Cavell. To imagine God's knowledge of the world as being predicated on the view from nowhere model is, however, not a felicitous move.

The skeptic in Cavell's analysis expresses simultaneously a vision of penetrating potency and of isolated impotence. The skeptic seems to imagine the world as a suitable object of intellectual desire, something readily available for his epistemic grasp, all the while envisioning the knowing subject as one who is (ideally) mastering its object. In this master vision of the subject, the epistemic ideal is total epistemic access and access to totality. I have to know all-of-the-object, under all circumstances. Yet, at the same time, the epistemic subject is construed as being impotent vis-à-vis the world, because the knowing subject's position is eternally fixed as one of separation. I am isolated from the world. The same distance that makes possible the vision of mastering the totality of the world engenders the fearful suspicion that the object of intellectual desire is perpetually removed from my grasp. The skeptic gazes longingly at the world with a desire for total epistemic control, and he experiences himself as being "sealed off from the world." To place God in this skeptical position would make for a divinity that is torn between epistemic omnipotence and impotence—a rather melancholic God. Thus, we should not follow Cavell in claiming that "we" imagine God to know the world in the manner that the skeptic imagines knowledge of the world to be possible. Rather, we should further inquire into the sources that fuel this epistemic imaginary.

While Cavell's analysis points to a specific moment in European intellectual history—the emergence of modern skepticism—other sources can enlarge our analytic scope. For example, the anthropologist Stanley Tambiah distinguishes two possible orientations toward the world, which we can find, to varying degrees, in all cultures. Tambiah calls them "causality" and "participation." By "causality," he means to designate an attitude toward the world characterized by a logic of opposition. "Causality," Tambiah writes, "is quintessentially represented by the categories, rules and methodology of positive sciences and discursive mathematico-logical reason. The scientific focus involves a particular kind of distancing, affective neutrality and abstraction to events in the world."[8] Individuals in all cultures are capable of relating to the world in this manner, yet modern Western science has made this the dominant orientation in Western contexts. Tambiah contrasts this way of relating oneself to the world and others with the one he labels "participation." Here we find language of "solidarity, unity, holism, and continuity in space and time."[9] On this view, the Ego is not positioned in opposition to the world but seen as deeply intertwined with it.

I mention these anthropological observations to strengthen the claim that the specific epistemic position that the skeptic imagines is not simply the result of linguistic or metaphysical structures. It is not language or theology that seduces us to be engaged in the skeptical problem but rather our attitudes toward the world and each other. Thus, the skeptical desire for context-independent certainty reflects a specific attitude toward the world and society—one of distantiation writ large. Here the world in its totality is ideally completely exposed to the skeptic's desire to know. In the skeptical imagination the causal attitude toward the world becomes free floating, disconnected from the concrete practices of knowledge production and exchange. The skeptic's pose is reminiscent of "a modern scene of existence as controlled by a spectator at once impossible and divine who organizes everything without ever acting or participating," to use Stefanos Geroulanos's reading of Foucault.[10] Again, we should be wary of taking these claims to divinity at face value. Instead, this is an imagined divine position shaped under the influences of skepticism. Thus, this theological vision itself reflects a particular epistemology, namely, a fearful rejection of what Tambiah called "the participatory orientation toward world and society." The skeptic fears an epistemic position where relationships, not abstract rules, secure the meaning of our words.

Where does this leave us for Turner's project of ideology critique? At the heart of the ideological[Two] malformation that creates a desire for a center as precondition for objective knowledge of the world lies a refusal of entanglement. The skeptic fears being entangled with the objects we describe and being entangled with each other as we describe the world and live in it with others.

Consequently, the skeptic desires an epistemic position from which we can observe the world without being entangled in it. If we can describe the objects in the world from this position, then our descriptions are "objective." If we cannot describe the objects in the world from this position, then our descriptions are not "objective." In Cavell's—and Jantzen's—analysis, this type of "objectivity" cannot be had because it would require a position that is purely imaginary, that is, the view from nowhere. Thus, it would be futile to endeavor to prove that we have any knowledge that is "objective."

Next I will discuss the main points of the literatures that claim that MR is an ideological term that fails to refer to something universal. Given what I have said so far, the question is whether or not the claim that religion is ideological[One] can be made without itself repeating SE, and thus being ideological^{Two}. In other words, does a Turner inspired critique of ideology^{Two} prevent the claim that MR is an ideological^{One} formation?

RELIGION AS IDEOLOGICAL^{One} FORMATION

For the past two or three decades, scholars like Talal Asad, Timothy Fitzgerald, and Russell McCutcheon have argued that the twin discourses of "the secular" and "the religious" are ideological formations produced by Western modernity for the benefits of North Atlantic hegemonic nation-states.[11]

Let me focus on two main claims in these literatures. One claim is that religion itself is an ideological formation and therefore does not reflect a true universal. While "religion" may have a referent in the history of European or American hegemonic cultures, this category fails to describe anything outside the scope of these cultures. This epistemic failure of the category of religion is linked, second, to its hegemonic function in the exercise of North Atlantic colonial and postcolonial power.

Both claims taken together characterize the position that the category "religion" is ideological in nature. Consequently, it seems that in order to disable the ideological formation of religion we would need to replace it with a concept that has universal reach and one that is not embedded in hegemonic power struggles. Thus, the charge that MR is ideological is in fact the charge that MR is ideological^{One}.

However, a conceptual framework for describing reality that is not entangled in cultural politics is hard to come by. As Martin Riesebrodt noted critically in a discussion of Talal Asad's work, allegedly "more 'neutral' concepts like 'ideology,' 'culture,' 'knowledge,' or 'discourse' fail to capture differences and complexities the concept of 'religion' is able to address. This may also explain why some critics who maintain that the concept of religion should be given up still use it in their book titles. Asad even compares Medieval Christianity and Islam, obviously assuming that the two have something in common, but unwilling or unable to define what it is."[12]

I would hasten to add to Riesebrodt's critique the observation that the allegedly more neutral concepts he enumerates seem to be embedded as well in the history of Western political struggles. If—as Turner shows—the concept of subjectivity is profoundly ideologically inflected, then those of ideology, culture, knowledge, or discourse are as well. Thus it is worthwhile to recall what Graham Ward writes in reaction to Fitzgerald:

> The employment of the term [religion] is fraught with certain cultural politics; enmeshed in ideologies, if you will. In his book *The Ideology of Religious Studies*, Timothy Fitzgerald proceeds as if the term has been used naively, as an objective, scientific label, and he now is exposing the politics of such usage. But anyone with any insight into the history of the term, any knowledge of its embedded employment in a given culture, recognizes that never is religion or the labeling of what is religious non-ideological.[13]

Ward's critique brings me to the claim that SE is operative in the claim that religion is ideological[One]. The argument that our epistemic concepts, like "religion," are distorted *because* they are enmeshed in cultural politics implies that there are or could be concepts that are undistorted by such politics. Otherwise, the charge that some concepts are ideological whereas others are not would not stick. Gail Hamner put this point succinctly: "What Fitzgerald and McCutcheon must know but do not emphasize is the fact that the ideological force of *all* concepts generates visible, bodily, and practical consequences. . . . Concepts are real because they are asserted and used, and through this assertion and use, concepts become embedded in physical, linguistic, and social habits, and thus have real, material effects."[14] In this view, "religion" is no better or worse off than any other concept. As Ward and Hamner point out, all of our concepts are shot through with politics. The question then is whether we can find a mode of doing ideology critique that neither involves platitudes (concepts are enmeshed in cultural politics) nor assumes, like SE, that our concepts can do their job by being disentangled from each other in our lives and in the world.

One option would be to give up the idea of reference altogether and to focus on the political effects of our conceptual framework. Here the claim would be that the problem with "religion" is not that it fails to refer; the problem is that wherever it holds sway "religion" creates specific real effects in the world. Thus, Gail Hamner argues that "religion" is real because it has "real, material effects"—not as an isolated concept that picks out an isolated object, but as part of a web of practices. In this sense "religion" refers to what "religion" produces. Neither that religion is productive in this way nor that religion is enmeshed in cultural politics is unique to this particular concept. Thus one could argue that the work of concepts is not to refer but to produce.

On the basis of this productive epistemology, however, it is difficult to see what difference it would make to claim that "religion" or any other concept is ideological, if by that marker we wish to point out an epistemic distortion. We could say that MR has certain effects because it implies a universal reach that it does not possess. Yet note that this counterargument relies on our ability to adjudicate what are false universals—and that ability requires us to think that concepts can refer. Thus without some form of referential epistemology the term *ideology* becomes very broad. In the words of Stuart Hall, "We *now* use it [ideology] to refer to *all* organized forms of social thinking. This leaves open the degree and nature of its 'distortions.'"[15]

In order to do the work of distortion, however—taken literally and not in scare quotes as Hall uses it—we need to assume an epistemological model according to which the reference relation allows us to pick out a specific object in the world. This is what Hamner calls referential epistemology. She assumes that McCutcheon rejects this model, yet it seems clear that he would need to endorse some version of it for his project of "ideology critique of religion" to work, at least if he has more in mind than the trivial claim that all of our concepts are enmeshed in politics.

When saying "some version" of it, I want to flag that not all "referential epistemologies" are friendly to the project of differentiating between concepts that are humanly distorted and those that are transparent to reality. For an example of those that could be friendly to such a project, the work of William Alston comes to mind. In *Perceiving God*, Alston writes:

> I am interested in whether th[e] practice [of forming religious beliefs] yields beliefs that are (often) true in this robustly realist sense—not, or not just, in whether it yields beliefs that conform to the rules of the relevant language-game, or beliefs that carry out some useful social function. . . . [Rather I am interested in] whether the practice succeeds in accurately depicting a reality that is what it is however we think of it.[16]

Alston would not deny that concepts could have social effects (useful or otherwise), yet he would nevertheless argue that this function alone does not secure reference. For a concept to truly refer it would need to succeed in depicting a reality that is "what it is however we think of it." This standard guarantees what he calls a robustly realist epistemology. It is clear that this kind of referential epistemology (a) expresses a desire for a relationship to reality in which it anchors meaning independently of what we think of it; and (b) allows for the contrast of distorting concepts that fail to refer and those that succeed because they depict reality as it is independently of how we think of it. It is also clear that this kind of referential epistemology is in fact a version of SE.

Thus we seem caught between a rock and a hard place. If we endorse SE and with it referential epistemology's distinction between distorted and undistorted concepts, then we can substantively charge that "religion" is epistemically problematic and thus ideological[One]. However, by endorsing SE our framework is ideological[Two]. If, in contrast, we do not endorse SE and avoid succumbing to ideological[Two], then we seem to be unable to claim that "religion" is ideological[One], because we have no tools to substantiate the charge that this concept is epistemologically distorted.

Note that a way out of this dilemma would be to find a form of referential epistemology (i) that is not under the sway of SE and (ii) that does allow us to distinguish somehow between ideologically distorted and undistorted concepts in a manner that is not ideological[One].

In the following I wish to begin the constructive segments of this chapter by presenting such an epistemological option. To do so, I now turn to the register of analytic philosophizing and particularly to the work of Hilary Putnam whose late writings contain this desired nonskeptical referential epistemology.

CONSTRUCTING A VIABLE CONCEPT OF "IDEOLOGY" AND "RELIGION"

Hilary Putnam's idea of "conceptual relativity" allows me to outline an alternative referential epistemology, one in which reference is entangled with our evaluative and thus political projects. In this sense, Putnam can be read as rejecting SE. However, his version of a referential epistemology will allow us to rethink the charge that MR is a distorted and thus ideological concept. If my argument succeeds we can therefore leave SE behind and at the same time identify the precise nature of the claim that MR is an ideological formation.

For a quick introduction to Putnam's views it helps to remember Eberhard Herrmann's description of his work: "Putnam's goal is to find a way which enables one to keep truth objective, while rejecting the idea that truth is a correspondence between sentences and unconceptualised mind-independent facts."[17]

But why would a critique of the idea that truth is a correspondence between sentences and unconceptualized mind-independent facts be beneficial for our project here? In this idea we find again the skeptical desire that the world can settle for us what is or is not the case. Thus by imagining truth as correspondence we also imagine the world being separated from our activity of describing it. Mind and world are disentangled. What then is the problem with such a type of correspondence theory of truth?

According to Putnam, the problem is that too many correspondences are possible between our sentences and the world, conceived of as mind-independent reality. In *Reason, Truth and History*, Putnam reminds us, for example, that in the context of Newtonian physics any physical event could be described in the following two ways: as particles acting at a distance over empty space or as particles acting on fields, which act on other fields (or particles therein), which in turn act on particles. Metaphysically these alternate descriptions are incompatible, since one assumes that there are and the other assumes that there are not causal agencies that mediate action between separate particles, that is, fields. He writes, "The Maxwell field theory and the retarded potential theory are incompatible from a metaphysical point of view . . . but the two theories are mathematically intertranslatable. So if there is a 'correspondence' to the noumenal things which make one of them true, then one can define another correspondence which makes the other one true."[18]

How do we decide which one of these possible relationships is the right one, if the only criterion admitted is an abstract relationship of correspondence? For Putnam, the decision between different models of description depends on context-sensitive and pragmatic considerations. The world itself does not force on us one or the other of these incompatible models, since either one seems to "fit our experiential beliefs equally well." Rather, understanding truth as a *single* correspondence implies a desire for a situation in which the facts speak for themselves. We are back under the sway of SE. The problem with this desire is that finding the one single correspondence relationship between the domain of the world (understood as a set of not conceptualized facts) and that of our descriptions would require "some independent access to both domains."[19]

In his discussions of skepticism, Cavell notes that making a claim is an activity that we do as speakers (and not something that the world does for us or that sentences or parts of sentences do simply by themselves). And Putnam's example was meant to show that our ability to assert what is the case depends on how we chose to describe things: "Our empirical knowledge, or any piece of it, is conventional relative to certain alternatives and factual relative to certain others." However, according to Puntam, "it does not follow that the truth or falsity of everything we say is simply 'decided'" by our descriptive choices.[20] In other words, it is not true that just any description of the world can be true; nor is a true answer true just because the framework makes it so, within which we describe the state of affairs in question, to paraphrase Alston.

If Putnam is correct, then we have here an account of a referential epistemology that acknowledges that our practices of describing the world are entangled with our descriptive choices. These in turn are entangled with our frames of evaluating a situation. How we describe an object depends on what we want to do with our descriptions, which in turn depends on our goals and values, and on what we consider an issue at hand that demands a specific description. In other words, it would be a fantasy to expect our concepts to be disconnected from evaluative and thus political practices. The fact that concepts such as religion or culture are thus entangled does not make them ideological[One] in the sense that they distort an otherwise transparent epistemic lens. Like all concepts they reflect descriptive, evaluative, and thus political interests. Attentiveness to what we do with our concepts or to how our language enables specific forms of political power and claims to hegemony can therefore go hand in hand with at least one form of representational epistemology.

Consequently, we can ask whether MR, as it is embedded in specific local and global, descriptive and evaluative contexts, manages to refer to things in the world. It may not be always felicitous to describe something as religion, and consequently we may disagree over the value and implications of the descriptive choice. But these are disagreements over success or failure of reference and not over epistemic distortion.

Here we should recall Hamner's claim that "religion," like any concept, also produces material effects. Once in circulation globally as a hegemonic concept, "religion" produces global effects and will therefore find referents globally. Thus Hamner encourages us to inquire into how our concepts allow us to describe networks of contestations over hegemonic and counterhegemonic exercises of power. In particular, if we return to the Marxian concern of how our concepts "naturalize" and "eternalize" bourgeois knowledge, we may see that "religion" is a particularly effective category.[21]

As Ward pointed out, the history of the academic study of religion (like that of "civilization" or "culture" or "modernity") is full of examples demonstrating the disciplining nature of bourgeois knowledge. Thus contestation is built into the discursive field of religion. Far from claiming to identify a clear set of objects, MR opens up conflicts over who has it, who should have it, and what would constitute it. It is precisely this contested nature of MR that prevents it from being distortive in the sense of both ideological[One] and ideological[Two]. Because religion is clearly a concept of bourgeois aspirations and exclusions, it wears its normative and disciplining qualities on its sleeves.

If a Putnam-inspired epistemology can escape the sway of SE and can allow for the entanglement of descriptive and evaluative practices, in which sense, however, can we then analyze the ideological nature of MR? To answer this question we need to shift from a notion of ideology critique predicated on SE to one that is interested in avoiding what Hall calls "fetishization."

CONSTRUCTING IDEOLOGY[Three] AS FETISHIZATION

Let us recall what Hall wrote with reference to the ideological construction of the market relationship. It is certainly incorrect to assume that the market does not exist, as Hall writes. To phrase this for the context of our discussion: it is not felicitous to argue that the concept "market" has no referent. Indeed Hall writes that the market "is *all too real*. It is the very life-blood of capitalism."[22] Yet how can we account its reality? "If, in our explanation, we privilege one moment only, and do not take account of the differentiated whole or 'ensemble' of which it is a part; or if we use categories of thought, appropriate to one such moment alone to explain the whole process; then we are in danger of giving what Marx would have called . . . a 'one-sided' account."[23] The problem, then, with using the terminology of the market is not that it has no referent but that in using market terminology *alone* we are "creating an explanation which is only *partially* adequate—and in this sense, 'false.'"[24] These categories "mystify our understanding of the capitalist process: that is they do not enable us to see or formulate other aspects invisible."[25] The ideological nature of the market terminology rests, therefore, not on a failure of reference but on a failure to provide a fuller account of the capitalist process by substituting "one part of the process for the whole—a procedure which, in linguistics, is known as 'metonymy' and in anthropology, psychoanalysis and (with special meaning) in Marx's work, as *fetishism*. The other 'lost' moments of the circuit are . . . unconscious . . . in the sense of being invisible, given the concepts and categories we are using."[26] Thus what we need is "a more complete grasp of all the different relations of which that [market] relation is composed, and of the many determinations which form its conditions of existence."[27]

Now let us apply this insight to the debate over the ideological nature of religion. The task for the ideology critique of religion is not to show that religion is "false" because it lacks a referent but to show how the category involves a distorting focus, one that prevents us from seeing a more complete picture in the exercise of cultural and political hegemony of which religion is a part. Such critical work requires us to examine in very fine-grained detail MR as a process.

Here we can turn to, for example, the works of Robert Sharf or Donald Lopez in the discipline of Buddhist studies[28] or to anthropological studies, such as Jean DeBernardi's book on spirit possession and media in Penang, Malaysia, who writes:

> Although I prefer not to see the individualism of their practices solely as the product of the influence of modern capitalist structures, I do regard Penang's spirit mediums as interpreters of the postmodern condition. They practice in Penang, an urbanized, multiethnic, religiously diverse setting, and they express respect for differences of race and religion. They analyze the differences, but also claim that all gods are true, all religions are the same, and all peoples share a single humanity. Indeed, they draw the same conclusion as scholar Max Müller did when he argued that the comparative study of historical religions would lead us to see that the gods of different religions were "nothing but names for what is beyond names."[29]

DeBernardi's case highlights clearly that the ascription of the term *religion* leads to contested territory. Many proponents of the more institutionalized religions in Malaysia (Islam, Buddhism, and Christianity) reject the idea that spirit possession is a religious practice at all since the mediums lack a formal structure of institutional formation. As a counterclaim, some mediums insist that they are the only ones actually teaching "Chinese religion." Indeed, in order to increase their social standing "some spirit mediums now emphasize teaching and exegesis as a complement to ritual performances," and they take inspiration from late-nineteenth-century Theravadin reformers for their own religious revival.[30]

Cases like these abound in religious studies scholarship and in the history of religious modernity. We see in them not that MR is an empty concept but rather that it is a concept related to a particular set of hegemonic discourses linked to the production of a modern, urbanized bourgeoisie with political aspirations in a postcolonial nation-state.

At the same time we should take note as well that MR is not simply the property of this or any particular class. As Hall reminds us, "Laclau has dismantled the proposition that particular ideas and concepts 'belong' exclusively to one particular class."[31] Likewise, contrary to Fitzgerald and McCutcheon, MR does not simply belong exclusively to the Western hegemonic project. MR is not solely a Western product, but one that is produced globally by various actors who are placed at different gradients of postcolonial power and who have various local strategic or tactical concerns. Now it is important to note that this global production and reproduction of religion does not result from the linguistic interactions of an ideal speech community. Rather, as part of multiple contestations over hegemony, MR operates to silence as well as to provide the standing for socially honored speech.

As a global process MR's production does not follow a pattern of simple assimilation but rather one of "intercultural mimesis," to quote the Buddhist studies scholar Charles Hallisey.[32] Mimesis involves a double movement of appropriating power by imitating its exercise, and it reveals both an adoption and a rejection of its normative production. Yet, as Hallisey points out in his discussion of changed reading practices in Theravadin Buddhism, the move of appropriation involves also a retrieval of precolonial practices.

MODERN RELIGION AS *DISPOSITIF*

If what I have argued thus far is convincing, then it will be incorrect to say that MR is simply the continuation of Protestant Christianity by other means. Pace Jean-Luc Nancy and perhaps even Talal Asad, the deconstruction of modern religion does not simply yield a belief-centered faith, disconnected from practices and ready for commoditization. Rather this vision of religion as a particular form of "quietism" is itself a fetishization, that is, a move to see the part for the whole.

Let us briefly consider what Asad states as a central claim in his *Genealogies of Religion*:

> The point is that, in contemporary Protestant Christianity (and other religions now modeled on it), it is more important to have the right belief than to carry out specific prescribed practices. It is not that belief in every sense of the word was irrelevant in the Christian past, or irrelevant to Islamic tradition. It is that belief has now become a purely inner, private state of mind, a particular state of mind detached from everyday practices.[33]

My question here is not whether there is some truth to this description. Surely, belief as a state of mind is important to the story that some Protestants sometimes tell themselves and others about themselves. And this story has made it sensible for many philosophers of religion to focus with particular gusto on mystical experiences—only to realize, like Alston, that such experiences do require socially grounded practices. Yet is it an adequate description in Hall's sense to claim that, for Protestant Christianity (note the singular), belief is a "purely, inner, private state of mind . . . detached from everyday practice?"

First, the idea that beliefs could be disjointed from practices requires again a peculiar understanding of reference. Even William Alston makes room in his work for the particular Christian mystical practices that produce the beliefs he deems to be properly Christian. As Gail Hamner reminds us, "Deployed as categories that seem natural, . . . general concepts constitute discursive and practical support, such that what a concept means depends on where the user stands (i.e., her subject position and set of social practices); but general concepts also constitute what Badiou calls the 'movement of thought,' what Foucault describes as the 'force field of power,' and what Giroux terms the subject's 'relations of power.' In other words, general concepts become the vehicle for a pedagogy of self."[34] Thus it would make little sense to see Protestant Christianities as reflective of an allegedly complete distinction between belief and practice. Doing so would prevent us from seeing a fuller picture of Protestantisms as shot through with bodily practices.

In my own work, I have demonstrated, for example, how for Evangelical Christians in the United States sex practices are importantly connected to their understanding of Christ's headship of the church. In other words their doctrinal understanding has a direct bearing on embodied practices, practices that need to be learned and gradually perfected.[35] This type of Christian doctrine can exert power only because it manages through the commoditized sex manuals to move bodies in particular ways. Finally, as we know from studies like DeBernardi's or from Partha Chatterjee's work on the reorganization of Hinduism, modern religious revivals built in response to and on the template of colonial Protestantisms indeed involve embodied practices.

This connection to bodily practices becomes visible most clearly if we consider the link between the rising of urban middle classes and the global production of religion, as DeBernardi's study intimated. In order to account for this link we need to slightly change our categories of analysis. Instead of talking about religion as a conceptual reality (one that favors inner states of belief over practices) or even as a discursive reality (if we understand a discourse as a web of linguistic practices alone), we should consider religion as a Foucaultian *dis-*

positif. The value in using this somewhat unwieldy frame lies in the fact that *dispositif* allows us to highlight the interplay of discursive and nondiscursive elements in the production of modern religion, thus linking closely together varied practices of speaking and living. As Foucault writes:

> What I try to pick out with this term is, firstly, a thoroughly heterogeneous ensemble consisting of discourses, institutions, architectural forms, regulatory decisions, laws, administrative measures, scientific statements, philosophical, moral and phil-anthropic propositions—in short, the said as much as the unsaid. Such are the elements of the apparatus [or *dispositif*]. The appa-ratus itself is the system of relations that can be established be-tween these elements. Secondly, what I am trying to identify in this apparatus is precisely the nature of the connection that can exist between these heterogeneous elements. . . . [B]etween these elements, whether discursive or non-discursive, there is a sort of interplay of shifts of position and modifications of func-tion which can also vary very widely. Thirdly, I understand by the term "apparatus" a sort of—shall we say—formation which has as its major function at a given historical moment that of re-sponding to an urgent need. The apparatus thus has a dominant strategic function.[36]

Given the third characteristic of *dispositif,* we can ask the following question: What is the "urgent need" to which the *dispositif* religion answers? To answer it we need to pay attention to a fuller picture of the meaning and function of religion, one that goes beyond the claim that religion is built on interiorized faith. Thus an advantage of the framework of religion as *dispositif* is that it allows us to inquire into the interconnection of multiple discourses of modern religion and their materiality.

In particular, we see a peculiar tension in how modern religion is imagined and produced. On the one hand, we have an emphasis on religion as an individual and private practice. For example, medi-tation practices in modern forms of Buddhism are emphasized over public rituals; and the discipline of philosophy of religion focuses on inner experience and discovers the category of mysticism, as I have already mentioned. On the other hand, however, religion is seen as a marker of cultural identity defining a particular nation. In short, *modern religion interiorizes and territorializes*. Religion is both a matter of inner personal experience and one of cultural and national identity.

THE URGENCY OF MR

As I have discussed in more detail elsewhere, in this peculiar tension between the discourses that denote and produce religion as a matter that can be privatized and one that serves as the cultural foundation preceding the nation, the *dispositif* religion answers to a particular question: If sovereignty is located in and exercised by the people, who are the people?[37] Given that the paradigm of liberal secular nation-states is that all of its citizens are equal authors and recipients of the law, how can we demarcate the scope of citizenship? This is the question of how to define "peoplehood," to use Jonathan Lie's term.[38] The need to define *peoplehood* is urgent *ad extram* (with a view of consolidating national outer boundaries) and *ad intram* (with a view of regulating the internal flows of power such that middle-class citizens are privileged over others). In sum, in a liberal secular state the *dispositif* of religion and not theological or buddhalogical institutions and practices are involved in the shaping of middle-class national identity.

Indeed, in this form modern religion legitimizes state action, both legislative and judicial, not only in postcolonial states but also in secular North Atlantic states. Thus it makes sense that modern religion is in fact implicated in both the current legislative and judicative processes in the United States and Germany. As an example of legislative processes, I want to simply flag the debates about same-sex marriage in the United States. Here let me mention a second example, from Germany, that will highlight the role of religion in judicative processes.

In 2007 the highest court in the German state of Bavaria had to adjudicate the following question: Does it constitute an undue discrimination of Muslim public school teachers that the Bavarian state bars them, but not Roman Catholic nuns, from wearing an item of religious garb, namely, a headscarf, while on duty? The court ruled first that the scarf was indeed a religious symbol, one representing a particular kind of political Islam. It furthermore ruled that the Bavarian state was within its right to disallow Muslim teachers from wearing a headscarf, all the while allowing Roman Catholic nuns to teach in their religious habits.

The court reasoned that the message implied in the Roman Catholic garb was in line with the Christian humanist foundations of the Bavarian state and that the state had an obligation to protect these foundations. While the government could not give preferential treatment to specific Christian denominations, the state nevertheless had a legitimate interest in incorporating into public school education the Christian "religious form of life and tradition of the Bavarian people."[39] The court hastened to define the term *Christian* in this context as follows: *Christian* does not refer to the content of beliefs held by "individual Christian denominations but to the values and norms, which, formed primarily by Christianity, became the shared cultural basis of occidental culture."[40]

The court makes, therefore, a distinction between the beliefs of a specific denomination, on the one hand, and the Occidental Christian cultural tradition, on the other. This means that the property of "sharing the occidental Christian cultural tradition" seems independent from the property of "holding specific Christian beliefs." Thus we could conceive of a religious group that shares the cultural Christian foundation of the Bavarian state without being a Christian denomination itself. According to the logic of the Bavarian Supreme Court, the wearing of religious garb of certain Jewish religious groups, for example, could be considered to be permissible in the public school system, if these items of clothing pass the following test: they express attitudes that are in line with the Christian Occidental tradition that founds Bavarian values and norms. At the same time, we could imagine a religious group that, while denomination-ally Christian, is not to be considered part of the Occidental Christian culture on which the Bavarian state is based. For example, the former National Socialist German Christians come to mind.

Needless to say, the question arises, who decides what constitutes the scope of the Christian-Occidental tradition on which the Bavarian state is based? In short, we should ask who has the competence to delineate the scope of this alleged consensus of values and norms of the Occidental Christian culture. Since denominational adherence is not the defining character of what constitutes the kind of Christianity in question, it seems clear that this power does not simply lie with the various Christian denominations and their institutions.

This example shows a peculiar conception of religion, one in which religion is both supposedly private and public. Certain religious symbols have to be kept private for political reasons, yet others are part of the fabric of the state. The justices made clear that the state has a responsibility not only to follow the strictures of due process and equal protection but moreover to preserve the cultural foundation of the nation. Thus a religious symbol representing the values of the alleged Christian humanist tradition on which is founded the Bavarian state need not be fully privatized. Hence Roman Catholic nuns are allowed to veil in the classroom. Moreover, a symbol is acceptable for public consumption only if it is deemed to represent a value system in line with said Christian humanist tradition, like a yarmulke, as we may presume, or a veil that does not represent so-called Islamism.

The *dispositif* religion can address a particular conundrum of legitimacy that liberal nation-states face. Political justice in these states, that is, the demand that we treat fellow citizens as equals, involves a problem of scope: how do we delineate who counts as fellow citizens?

The problem of scope points to two competing, yet interacting, strands in liberal political theory: the Enlightenment ideal of civic equality, on the one hand, and the romantic idealization of cultural homogeneity, which is expressed as national identity, on the other. In terms of the history of religious theory, both strands are echoed in Weberian and Durkheimian approaches to religion. This entanglement of ideas leads to a peculiar syllogism aimed at establishing the scope of civil equality: because we are all citizens of the same state, we can expect legitimately equal treatment before the law; and we are all citizens of the same state because we share the same cultural and national traits.

Jacques Derrida analyzes this tension as a founding aporia at the heart of liberal democracies in *Politics of Friendship*: among all who are equally befriendable I have to choose this one or these ones.[41] But since friendship, according to Derrida, is based on the idea of equality, the choice itself is capricious. If all could be my friends, why do I choose these friends and not others? Derrida argues that talk of brotherhood masks the capricious quality implied in the necessary selectivity of friendship. The friends I have selected are—after the fact—declared to be my brothers. Since this language of fraternization naturalizes the bond of friendship, such rhetoric undercuts the problem of choice and thus of responsibility. A familial relationship and imagination of shared bloodlines and origins justifies ex post facto my decision to befriend these and not other friendlies.

Besides evading responsibility by naturalizing the bonds of friendship, the rhetoric of fraternization raises, therefore, the issue of exclusion and particularity. As Alex Thomson writes in *Deconstruction and Democracy*:

> Democracy contains both a universal appeal—equality for all— and necessary limits which condition and govern that appeal. These mostly form around the question, again, of fraternization: of the naturalization of the decision which would limit democracy and equality to the members of one state, to one set of boundaries or one people, grounded in a spiritual or ideal identification which need not, but always potentially could, be expressed in a violent particularism or an ideology of nation, blood or soil.[42]

Historically and systematically, the ideal of civic equality presupposes that citizens recognize each other as belonging to the same polis. References to a shared culture or identity aim to secure such mutual recognition and the particular scope of the citizenry. Thus, for example, the legislations that regulate citizenship are notoriously connected to idealizations of the particular national character in question.[43] Moreover, cultural and class identity has an impact on whether and how residents of a given state can participate in its civic and therefore political life.[44] And, as the Bavarian case demonstrated, "religion" plays an important role in defining the contours of the imagined community of the nation.

In short, here we can see a theoretical account of how the actions of liberal democratic nation-states require, for their intelligibility and legitimacy, a specifically constituted civil society, namely, civil-society-as-forming-the-nation. Echoing these discourses within the *dispositif* religion, we find two movements of secularization: first a Weberian privatization and the decline of traditional institutions; second, a Durkheimian creation of religion as cultural phenomenon in support of national identity. In both modes, MR therefore supports the creation and functioning of a liberal secular nation-state.

This dual movement leads to two lines of tension. On the one hand, under the pressure of the Weberian side, we will see traditional "ecclesial" institutions combating their diminishing political and cultural influence by emphasizing their claim to political authority as sui generis. These institutions have to contend both with the development of a political and economic sphere beyond their control and with the emergence of modern cultural religion. On the other hand, we will find, on the Durkheimian side, the emergence of cultural religion in support of national identity, supported by middle-class actors and media. Importantly, modern religion in this sense is not dependent on direct influences of state institutions. Rather they—like the Bavarian Supreme Court—have to posit it as foundational for their own actions. Instead institutions of civil society, from the mediated public sphere to the commodity market of spiritual products, create a network of forces negotiating the contours and limits of acceptable religion.[45] Given this analysis it makes sense that the European public is less and less religiously bound by traditional institutions and simultaneously profoundly engaged in debates about the Christian character of the Continent. Consequently we will find MR involved in situations where the contours of the nation (or federation of nations) are unclear or under threat—be it through immigration or foreign, economic, or military threats, and so on. It is not the case, however, that religion is mobilized in these threat scenarios as if it was originally a bystander to the game of national politics. Rather, being part and parcel of the forces bringing the modern nation into existence, modern religion is inherently part of the violence that the state (or state-to-be) marshals for its defense.

Do people have religion then, to go back to the conversation I had with Denys Turner? They do in the same way that people under the sway of modern Western governmentality have sexuality, another modern *dispositif*. For many human practices of erotic desire and pleasure are now organized along the lines (or in contrast to) the *dispositif* of sexuality; likewise, for many, practices of devotion, reading, fervent hope, and believing are now being organized along the exigencies of MR. This insight poses a stark challenge for our theologizing: if our practices are shaped by MR, how can we learn to desire the divine in ways that are not dependent on and supportive of the project of the modern nation?

NOTES

1. Timothy Fitzgerald, *The Ideology of Religious Studies* (New York: Oxford University Press, 2000); Russell T. McCutcheon, *Manufacturing Religion: The Discourse on Sui Generis Religion and the Politics of Nostalgia* (New York: Oxford University Press, 1997); Russell T. McCutcheon, *Critics Not Caretakers: Redescribing the Public Study of Religion* (Albany: State University of New York Press, 2001).

2. Stuart Hall, "The Problem of Ideology: Marxism without Guarantees," in *Critical Dialogues in Cultural Studies*, ed. Stuart Hall, David Morely, and Kuan-Hsing Chen (London: Routledge, 1996), 26 ff.

3. See Antonio Gramsci et al., *Selections from the Prison Notebooks of Antonio Gramsci* (New York: International Publishers, 1971).

4. The pronoun *he* is used here intentionally, since skepticism, according to Cavell, is a particular masculine temptation.

5. Denys Turner, "De-Centring Theology," *Modern Theology* 2 (1986): 138.

6. Grace Jantzen, *Becoming Divine: Towards a Feminist Philosophy of Religion* (Bloomington: Indiana University Press, 1999).

7. Stanley Cavell, *The Claim of Reason: Wittgenstein, Skepticism, Morality and Tragedy* (Oxford: Clarendon Press, 1979), 236 ff.; original emphasis.

8. Stanley Jeyaraja Tambiah, *Magic, Science, Religion, and the Scope of Rationality* (Cambridge: Cambridge University Press, 1990), 109.

9. Ibid.

10. Stefanos Geroulanos, "Theoscopy: Transparency, Omnipotence, and Modernity," in *Political Theologies: Public Religions in a Post-Secular World*, ed. Hent de Vries and Lawrence Eugene Sullivan (New York: Fordham University Press, 2006), 649.

11. Talal Asad, "Anthropological Conceptions of Religion: Reflections on Geertz," in *Man*, n.s., 18 (1983): 237–59; Talal Asad, *Formations of the Secular: Christianity, Islam, Modernity* (Stanford: Stanford University Press, 2003).

12. Martin Riesebrodt, "'Religion': Just Another Modern Western Construction?," Martin Marty Center, http://marty-center.uchicago.edu/web forum/122003/riesebrodtessay.pdf.

13. Graham Ward, "The Future of Religion," *Journal of the American Academy of Religion* 74 (2006): 180.

14. M. Gail Hamner, *Imaging Religion in Film: The Politics of Nostalgia* (New York: Palgrave Macmillan, 2011), 134.

15. Hall, "Problem of Ideology," 26; original emphasis.

16. William P. Alston, *Perceiving God: The Epistemology of Religious Experience* (Ithaca: Cornell University Press, 1991), 4.

17. Eberhard Herrmann, "A Pragmatist Realist Philosophy of Religion," *Ars Disputandi* 3 (2003): 65–75.

18. Hilary Putnam, *Reason, Truth and History* (Cambridge: Cambridge University Press, 1981), 73.

19. Ibid.

20. Hilary Putnam, *Ethics without Ontology* (Cambridge, MA: Harvard University Press, 2004), 45 ff.

21. Hall, "Problem of Ideology," 32.

22. Ibid., 36; original emphasis.

23. Ibid.

24. Ibid.

25. Ibid.

26. Ibid.

27. Ibid., 38.

28. Donald S. Lopez, ed., *Curators of the Buddha: The Study of Buddhism under Colonialism* (Chicago: University of Chicago Press, 1995); Donald S. Lopez, *Prisoners of Shangri-La: Tibetan Buddhism and the West* (Chicago: University of Chicago Press, 1998); Robert H. Sharf, "The Zen of Japanese Nationalism," in Lopez, *Curators of the Buddha*, 107–60.

29. Jean Elizabeth DeBernardi, *The Way That Lives in the Heart: Chinese Popular Religion and Spirit Mediums in Penang, Malaysia* (Stanford: Stanford University Press, 2006), 171.

30. Ibid., 172.

31. Hall, "Problem of Ideology," 39.

32. Charles Hallisey, "Roads Taken and Not Taken in the Study of Theravada Buddhism," in Lopez, *Curators of the Buddha*, 31–62.

33. Saba Mahmood, "Interview with Talal Asad: Modern Power and the Reconfiguration of Religious Traditions," *SEHR: Contested Polities* 5, no. 1 (1996), http://web.stanford.edu/group/SHR/5-1/text/asad.html.

34. Hamner, *Imaging Religion in Film*, 135.

35. Ludger Viefhues-Bailey, "Holiness Sex: Conservative Christian Sex Practices as Acts of Sanctification," *Journal of Men, Masculinities and Spirituality* 6 (2012): 4–19. See also Laurie F. Maffly-Kipp, Leigh Eric Schmidt, and Mark R. Valeri, *Practicing Protestants: Histories of Christian Life in America, 1630–1965* (Baltimore: Johns Hopkins University Press, 2006).

36. Michel Foucault and Colin Gordon, *Power/Knowledge: Selected Interviews and Other Writings, 1972–1977* (Brighton: Harvester Press, 1980), 194–95.

37. See Ludger Viefhues-Bailey, "Religious Violence in the Secular State," in *Religionspolitik-Öffentlichkeit-Wissenschaft: Studien zur Neuformierung von Religion in der Gegenwart*, ed. Martin Baumann and Frank Neubert (Zurich: Pano, 2010), 81–102.

38. John Lie, *Modern Peoplehood* (Cambridge, MA: Harvard University Press, 2004).

39. Bayerischer Verfassungsgerichtshof, "Entscheidung des Bayerischen Verfassungsgerichtshofs vom 15. Januar 2007 über die Popularklage der Islamischen Religionsgemeinschaft E. V. in B." (2007), www.bayern.verfassungsgerichtshof.de/11-VII-05-Entscheidung.htm.

40. Ibid.

41. Jacques Derrida, *Politics of Friendship* (London: Verso, 1997), 13.

42. Alex J. P. Thomson, *Deconstruction and Democracy: Derrida's "Politics of Friendship"* (London: Continuum, 2007), 19, http://site.ebrary.com/lib/yale/Doc?id=10224804.

43. Silvia Brandi, "Unveiling the Ideological Construction of the 2004 Irish Citizenship Referendum: A Critical Discourse Analytical Approach," *Translocations* 2, no. 1 (2007), http://www.translocations.ie/docs/v02i01/translocations-v02i01-03.html; Nancy F. Cott, *Public Vows: A History of Marriage and the Nation* (Cambridge, MA: Harvard University Press, 2000).

44. Jens Schneider, *Deutsch Sein: Das Eigene, das Fremde und die Vergangenheit im Selbstbild des Vereinten Deutschland* (Frankfurt am Main: Campus, 2001); Diana Forsythe, "German Identity and the Problem of History," in *History and Ethnicity*, ed. Elizabeth Tonkin, Malcolm Chapman, and Maryon McDonald (London: Routledge, 1989); Peter van der Veer, "The Moral State: Religion, Nation, and Empire in Victorian Britain and British India," in *Nation and Religion: Perspectives on Europe and Asia*, ed. Peter van der Veer and Hartmut Lehmann (Princeton: Princeton University Press, 1999), 15–43; Veena Das, "The Figure of the Abducted Woman: The Citizen as Sexed," in de Vries and Sullivan, *Political Theologies*, 427–43.

45. Jeremy R. Carrette and Richard King, *Selling Spirituality: The Silent Takeover of Religion* (London: Routledge, 2005).

TWELVE

Is Marxism a Theodicy?

TERRY EAGLETON

I should begin by declaring a personal interest. I was once married to a woman who is the sister of Denys Turner's brother's wife. It is hard to imagine a more intimate relationship, or one more likely to distort one's feeble efforts at scholarly objectivity. In what follows, however, I shall struggle to put these intense emotional entanglements to one side and approach the theologian as he really is. My title employs a word that a great many nonspecialists will find bafflingly esoteric. Even so, it is my belief that the term *Marxism*, a topic on which the early Turner has written with impressive insight and originality, should not be avoided on that account. A biography of Denys Turner might be titled "From Marxism to Mysticism." Yet it is part of the meaning of his work that the implied opposition is a false one.

As with many thinkers of genius, there is less that is original in Marx than some of his acolytes imagine. The idea of communism is of ancient pedigree, as is the notion of revolution. The concept of history as a succession of modes of production was a commonplace of the Scottish Enlightenment. Marx himself denied that the notion of social class was his own invention, and the same might be said for class struggle and exploitation, ideas that were by no means unknown to (among many others) Jean-Jacques Rousseau. The notion of alienation Marx took from Hegel and the great Irish socialist and feminist William Thompson. The idea that the state exists to defend private property was being touted as early as Cicero. The so-called economic theory of history has ranked among its supporters the egregiously un-Marxist Sigmund Freud, who held that without the coercion of labor we would simply lie around the place all day in various interesting postures of *jouissance*. My own mentor, the late Raymond Williams, was one of many to champion the idea of socialist revolution and a workers' state without being a Marxist. And so on.

There is at least one strikingly original doctrine in Marx, one which lies at the very core of his thought. This is his theory of the mechanisms by which one mode of production changes into another, which is not to be found elsewhere. It involves both class struggle and the concept of a mode of production, neither of which, as I have just pointed out, are ideas peculiar to Marx; but it combines them in a way that is indeed peculiar to his thought. Taken overall, this is known as the doctrine of historical materialism. It is also, ironically, one of the features of his thought most vulnerable to criticism.

Historical materialism is not to be confused with materialism as such. In Marx's work, the contention that being determines consciousness is an ontological position, not a historical one. The doctrine of materialism is of course by no means peculiar to Marx; yet his own interpretation of it is strikingly original, as indeed he himself was well aware. Marx has no interest in the kind of philosophical materialism that traditionally asks what the world is made of. Whether it is made of matter, atoms, *Geist*, green cheese, or rat droppings seems not to be a question over which he lost much sleep. Materialism for Marx, as is clear enough from the early *Economic and Philosophical Manuscripts*, meant beginning from the fact that we are practical, material, corporeal beings. He is very conscious of the radical philosophical advance involved in rooting his reflections in the concept of the human subject as agent. As Alfred Schmidt remarks in his great work *Marxism and Nature*, the understanding of man as a needy, sensuous, physiological being is the precondition of any theory of subjectivity. Thomas Aquinas, as Denys Turner has reminded us, believed in his materialist way that we think the way we do because of the kind of bodies we have. If our thought is discursive, that is because of the way our senses and practices are too. Marx certainly stands in this tradition of thought. Ludwig Wittgenstein famously remarks that if you want an image of the soul, you should look at the human body. Human practices for Marx dismantle the distinction between mind and body, spirit and matter, subjective and objective, because they are material phenomena incarnate with signification.

All theory, then, must begin for Marx from the premise that men and women are in the first place practical agents—a view that runs clean contrary to certain older strains of philosopher materialism. In fact, as far as this point goes, Etienne Balibar is surely right to call Marx one of the greatest *anti*-philosophers of all time—"anti-philosopher" meaning not just someone who has no time for philosophy, which I suppose would include Mel Gibson and Lady Gaga, but those who are opposed to the philosophical project for philosophically interesting reasons. Marx writes in a Heideggerian vein in his *Comments on Wagner* that human beings do not in any sense begin by finding themselves in a theoretical relationship to the things of the external world. This is the authentic note of the anti-philosopher.

I am not of course out to claim that this exhausts the meaning of materialism in Marx's work. I am simply trying to light up the topic from what I believe is a relatively unfamiliar angle. My concern here, however, is neither with Marx's materialism as a whole nor even with historical materialism as such but with a specific aspect of the latter. I want to ask whether historical materialism is a theodicy or justification of evil—whether it imagines that certain historical evils are necessary, however rebarbative, because good will eventually flow from them. Because if Marxism does hold something like this, then no amount of talk about the creative body or the subject as agent is going to make a good many sensitive-minded people sign up for it.

There is surely no doubt that, one or two qualifications aside, Marx held that to go socialist you had to be well-heeled. Or at least if *you* weren't well-heeled, some well-disposed neighbor had to be. Socialism is possible only on the basis of a massive material surplus.

And capitalism has kindly ensured that such a massive surplus is indeed to hand. It is just that we cannot lay our hands on it. Without these resources at our disposal, class struggle, which is essentially a struggle over an insufficient surplus, will start up all over again. Having to accumulate such resources from scratch is a backbreaking, soul-destroying business to which men and women are unlikely to submit themselves freely; and if they do not, then a despotic state is likely to step in and accomplish this task on their behalf. The consequence of this, as with Stalinism, is that the political superstructure of socialism will be undermined by the very attempt to lay down its economic basis. Besides, socialism requires shortening the working day so that people may have time to engage in political self-government, and this is not possible if they have no bread or shoes. To go socialist, you need the proper material preconditions. Marxian materialism must apply to its own political project.

Just as Marx sees social practice as a deconstruction of the material and (what we can broadly call) the moral, the same is true of his conception of history. In one sense, material development is also moral development, as the advance of the productive forces involves the unfolding of creative human powers and capacities. In Marx's view, capitalism makes us finer, subtler, all-around, complex, communicative, and diverse people, whatever those comrades selling socialist newspapers on the high street might tell you. But for Marx the moral and material are at loggerheads as well as being sides of the same coin, which is where the comrades on the high street are right. Under class society, every advance in civilization is also one in barbarism. If such progress brings in its wake new possibilities of emancipation, it also arrives coated from head to foot in blood. We pay for our freer, finer, more intricate existence, our keener sense of individual selfhood, our enhanced and enriched powers, in a currency of blood, wretchedness, and fruitless toil, which is why Marxism is essentially a tragic creed. Tragedy is not, of course, the same as pessimism. It doesn't necessarily mean that things end badly. The *Oresteia*, *Oedipus at Colonus*, and *Macbeth* do not end badly, or not entirely so. Tragedy is not necessarily without hope. It is rather that when it affirms, it does so in fear and trembling, aware of the alarming fragility of all such gestures. To call Marxism tragic means that you have to be hauled through hell to arrive at a felicitous ending. Much the same can be said of Christianity, which is a tragic creed in just the same sense, whatever future glory it anticipates. And whether the kicks are worth the ha'pence, as the British say—whether being hauled through hell is justified by the comic conclusion—is then always an open question. It is a question that Marx might have pondered rather more than he seems to have done.

In one sense, history for historical materialism is not at all a tale of progress. This is where Marxists differ from the likes of old-fashioned, backward-looking, nineteenth-century liberal rationalists like Richard Dawkins, for whom we are all getting nicer and nicer, give or take the odd imperial war or spot of genocide, and only barbarous mythologies like religion prevent us from sailing triumphantly ahead into a kind of North Oxford utopia. Christopher Hitchens, who was once that man selling socialist newspapers on the high street along with myself, held some similar retrograde view of the world.

For Marx, by contrast, history lurches from one form of exploitation to another. Yet this process, viewed from another angle, is also in his eyes a movement onwards and upwards, as the forces of production develop *in general*, whatever setbacks they suffer here and there, and men and women thereby amass through blood and fire the material resources that may eventually form the basis of socialism and communism. It is testimony to both our indolence and our ingenuity that advances in the productive forces are rarely lost. Having stumbled upon toothbrushes, we are unlikely to revert to twigs. Marx writes in *Theories of Surplus Value* that the development of the capacities of the human species takes place at the cost of the majority of individuals and even classes, meaning that the good of the species of the whole will finally flourish in the shape of communism but that the process of attaining this goal involves suffering and injustice for most members of the human race. The end and the means are notably askew to one another. The material prosperity that will in the end fund freedom is the fruit of unfreedom. History, as he famously remarks, progresses by its bad side. It is, as he remarks in his writings on India, a hideous god who drinks nectar from the skulls of the slain. Is history for Marx, then, an uplifting tale of progress or one long nightmare? The only unequivocal answer is surely yes and no.

So the advent of socialism would seem inseparable from violence and exploitation, in the sense that the accumulation of resources, which only class society can secure, is one of its enabling conditions. It looks as though injustice now is necessary for justice later. The same goes for oppression and freedom, or inequality and equality. Of course, it may be that there is no inevitable link in practice between class society and communism, for the simple reason that the latter is not itself inevitable. History may simply culminate in barbarism, a plausible enough prospect for those of us who have been reading the newspapers. Even Marx himself, in one of his glummer moments, speculates in *The Communist Manifesto* that the class struggle might end in what he calls the common ruination of all classes. Even so, he did not have the pleasure of living on a planet rattling with nuclear weapons and rapidly running out of ecological steam, not to speak of a world that has proved able to deploy social democracy to buy off socialism. So barbarism was less of a global prospect for him than it is for us.

In general, Marx seems to have thought that socialism was inevitable, and says so in *The Communist Manifesto*, volume 1 of *Capital*, and at various scattered places in his work. This is not because he was an iron determinist, though he sometimes speaks like one. It is because he thought that capitalism would grow a lot worse as its contradictions sharpened, and since there would then be no reason why the working class should not rise up and overturn it, it would inevitably do so. It would do so not because it was the puppet of historical forces but because it would have absolutely nothing to lose. Paradoxically, then, the inevitability of capitalist decline would itself lay the basis for free political agency. For us, the inevitable is usually pretty unpleasant, and unless you resist it you will never know how inevitable the inevitable actually was. For Marx, as for some other nineteenth-century thinkers, this seems not to be the case.

Marx is speaking, then, about what he thinks relatively free individuals are bound to do in specific circumstances. But this is surely a contradiction, since "free" means that there is nothing that they are bound to do in specific circumstances. If there is only one course of action I can take, and if it is impossible for me not to take it, then I am not free. We know that if you try to build socialism in backward, isolated, wretchedly impoverished conditions, a project Marx himself never remotely anticipated, the result is very likely to be some species of Stalinism. But Stalinism is not inevitable even then: the common people might rise up against the bureaucracy, or you might discover that you are sitting on the largest oil field in the world, or a more affluent nation may fly to your aid. Anyway, it is hard to see how class struggle, as opposed to some broader historical trend, can be predetermined. Marx may have thought that socialism was inevitable, but he surely did not think that the Factory Acts or the Paris Commune were. He clearly believed in freedom, and talks all the time in a way that implies that people could have acted differently.

Even so, there is a strong case to be made that he thought socialism could only follow from capitalism. He believed at one point that Germany would have to pass through a period of bourgeois rule before the working class could triumph, though it is true that he later held that a telescoping of historical stages might here be possible. In a lecture of 1847, he defended free trade as hastening the advent of socialism. He also at one point considered that the unification of Germany would promote German capitalism—a development he cheers on at several places in his work as throwing open the path to socialism. It is well known that he thought Russia might be able to achieve a form of socialism based on the peasant commune, thus bypassing capitalist development; what is less commonly stressed is that he did not imagine that this could be accomplished without the help of capitalist resources parachuted in from elsewhere.

There is, then, a good deal in Marx to justify the charge of theodicy. It would appear that the evils of capitalism play their part in the emergence of socialism. But there is also quite a lot to be said on the other side. For one thing, the fact that there is an internal link between capitalism and socialism does not mean that such links exist between the historical modes of production as a whole. By and large, Marx doesn't seem to have thought so. He registered his distaste for so-called universal laws of history more than once, insisting, for example, that his views on the transition from feudalism to capitalism in the West were not to be universalized. Nor does he seem to imagine that feudalism or capitalism *had* to emerge. There are, within limits, various possible routes out of any particular mode of production, even if you would not shift straight from consumer capitalism to hunter-gathering (unless perhaps a nuclear war had intervened). Stages can be leaped and compressed, as with the Bolsheviks; different modes of production can be synchronous rather than sequential; and no stage in the historical process exists for the sake of any other. In this sense at least, historical materialism is not a teleology. To say that capitalism can and must be drawn upon for socialism is not to suggest in teleological or functionalist spirit that capitalism exists for that reason, or that its existence is anything but contingent. Most Marxists these days do not accept that socialism will follow ineluctably on capitalism's heels, apart from those who have been sitting in darkened rooms with paper bags over their heads. And even those who do embrace the inevitability of socialism are scarcely likely to hold that the whole of history has been secretly laboring away to this end. The problem is simply that on Marx's own theory, if capitalism happens not to arise, it is hard to see how socialism can either.

There is a difference between doing evil in the hope that good may come out of it and seeking to turn someone else's evil to a constructive end. Socialists did not perpetrate capitalism, and are innocent of its crimes; but given that it exists, it is rational to make the best of the resources it has evolved. Even then, it does not follow that the crimes of capitalism can be retrospectively justified by the advent of socialism. In any case, capitalism is by no means simply criminal. Some of its inventions are precious human goods.

Despite this, we can still ask, given Marx's theory, whether history has been worthwhile. It is surely possible to argue that even if class society happens in the end to lead to socialism, the price countless generations of men and women have been forced to pay for this felicitous outcome has simply been too high. How long would social-ism have to endure, and how vigorously would it have to flourish, to justify the misery which went into its making? Could it ever? How could we possibly make recompense to these humiliated, dispos-sessed billions? Might someone not, like Alexi Karamazov handing in his ticket to heaven in protest at the atrocious sufferings of small children, simply choose to return his or her entry ticket to the New Jerusalem?

Marx himself presumably believed that it would have been far preferable if human emancipation could be achieved with rather less blood, sweat, and tears. But he could not see how you could hold this and still be a materialist. His followers do not have to believe that capitalism is essential for socialism, though the point is simply academic, since capitalism is with us anyway. If they do not, how-ever, they have to show that one could develop the forces of pro-duction from a very low level in ways compatible with socialist and democratic values. This was argued by some, notably Trotsky and the Left Opposition, in Bolshevik Russia. But it is a fearfully dif-ficult project to carry through. All the same, we can surely specu-late on what might have happened had capitalism never emerged. Could not humanity have hit upon some less atrocious way of evolv-ing what Marx regards as its major goods—democracy, liberalism, material prosperity, and a consequent freedom from labor, collective self-determination, the flourishing of richly self-realizing individuals, and so on? The question may prove more than academic. Suppose a handful of us were to crawl out on the other side of a nuclear or ecological catastrophe and set about the dispiriting task of building civilization again from scratch. Given what we would know of the causes of the catastrophe, would we not be well advised to try it this time the socialist way?

I SHALL end on a more personal note. One has become gloomily accustomed to encountering self-centered, power-hungry theolo-gians, soi-disant socialists who will buy their shoes only from certain, very special, New York establishments, and Western postcolonial theorists who would blanch at the very idea of spending a night in a hotel in downtown Lagos. It is thus all the more heartening to observe that Denys Turner's brilliance as a theologian is all of a piece with his personal holiness—that the courage, devotion, generosity of spirit, and resplendent honesty so marked in him as a man also shine constantly through his work. He will, of course, be embarrassed to hear it said; but he might draw consolation from the thought that it is not half so embarrassing as having one's prose style rigorously dissected, which was one of the things I was intending to do until I thought better of it.

NOTE

Editors' note: This is the text of a public lecture delivered by Terry Eagleton at the conference, "The Trials of Desire and the Possibility of Faith," held at Yale University on March 22–24, 2012. The chapter immediately following this one in the present volume is the transcript of the conversation that took place at the conference after Eagleton's remarks.

THIRTEEN

"If you do love, you'll certainly be killed"

A *Conversation*

DENYS TURNER AND TERRY EAGLETON

DENYS TURNER: It is so refreshing, isn't it, to hear this kind of irony at the end of Terry's paper. I am not at all sure how to respond to this, Terry. When, in that first incarnation, I wrote that book on Marxism and Christianity, one of the issues that preoccupied me was precisely the issue that you have taken up here. That is: What strategies can we commit ourselves to, to the end of bringing about what the possibilities of capitalism have made available to us? I agree with Terry that there is nothing inevitable about the emergence of socialism out of capitalism, but I also agree that there is also something necessary about capitalism if socialism is going to emerge. And that raises the question of the relationship between means and ends from the point of view of practices. I think the question of whether Marxism is a theodicy comes down, in the terms in which you related the issue to us, to that question of whether Marxism necessarily involves a misrelating of means to ends, allowing by virtue of the justification of its outcome atrocious means to be employed so as to bring it about.

It seems to me that there is an important distinction that needs to be made in order to just simply get one's mind clear about what these issues are that Terry was raising in his paper, and it is a distinction between two ways of understanding the relationship between means and ends. The first of them is simply causal. If it is the case that by doing *x*, you can bring about *y*, where there is no necessary connection between *x* and *y* other than that causal relationship, then it looks to me as if (if that is the only way in which you can construct an account of the relationship between agency and the ends which one wants to achieve) one is vulnerable to the possibility that the means that one might employ are in themselves thoroughly evil and can only be justified (if they can be justified) in terms of the outcomes which they bring about. Now, Terry resists this because that would be a theodicy. That would be an account which would say, "The evil employed in bringing this outcome about is justified by the outcome it brings about." And that, I take it, is what Terry is attempting to resist as being the whole story of Marxism. Although there are versions of Marx which seem to entail that that is all that is involved, that that is all that could be involved, that when one says that capitalism is necessary to the emergence of socialism, one is somehow or other licensing the evils of capitalism so that socialism may come.

The alternative picture is a picture according to which the relationship between means and ends is a participative rather than a merely causal one. That is to say that the means are appropriate for bringing about an end, if, in some way or other, the end is present in the means which achieve it. In other words, the morality of socialism has to be somehow or other present within the agency of bringing it about. The values of socialism have to be present in the actions from which socialism emerges, and that is why a purely mechanistic account of the relationship between capitalism and socialism simply won't do, and I don't think it does for Marx either.

When I wrote about Marxism and Christianity, in fact, the publisher said to me, "Why not just call it 'Marxism and Morality'?" because that is essentially what it was about. What Marxism offers one is the possibility of a truly moral existence coming about. But it could not possibly be, in that way, the agency bringing about moral possibility, if it itself frustrated the very morals that it was the agency of bringing about. Therefore, the means by which the outcome of socialism is to be brought about must in some way or other participate in the values of socialism itself, otherwise, it seems to me, you are left with a purely mechanistic, mechanical, causalistic account of the relationship between means and ends.

Now, what Terry is saying is, it seems to me, a little bit unclear. Well, sorry, what Terry is saying is that Marxism, as we find it, is itself a little bit unclear about whether Marxism entails the construction of violent means, the organization of violent means, that good may come. And I don't know what I want to say about that anymore. I used to know what I thought about this, that there were possibilities of radical revolutionary action, which themselves did not destroy the very values that one engaged in that revolutionary action to bring about. I don't know whether that is possible or not, and I'm not quite sure how far you would go down the line of saying, "It is a possibility. I can show it is a possibility." Or whether, "It is an open question, which we are not in a position to determine. We do not know what the answer to that is." My own view is, I don't think we do.

I think that is where I leave it: in a certain position of skepticism about whether one can construe a strategy of means, socialism as means, revolutionary action as means, which is not itself a betrayal of the ends which it aims to bring about. I simply do not know.

TERRY EAGLETON: I'll just try to briefly take this up. On the last point, Denys, about violence, it's not generally known that Marx and Engels did hope for a nonviolent revolution despite the caricatures of their right-wing critics. Indeed, they thought that in certain societies, it was quite a possibility. Of course, one of the reasons for that was the majority presence, in those days at least, of the industrial working class. In a certain sense, for them, a revolution was not in any sense a coup d'etat. It wasn't a palace revolution in that way, because it consisted of the actions of millions of people. And that, they thought, could proceed peacefully. It is also, of course, well worth remembering that there is no direct correlation whatsoever between revolution and violence or reform and nonviolence. Many processes of reform, not least in this country, have been very violent ones. Reforms that we now take for granted as enlightened and natural were fiercely and bloodily resisted by ruling classes so often in their time, and conversely, if there are violent revolutions, there are velvet ones as well. In fact, the Bolshevik Revolution involved very little bloodshed until the civil war which followed in its wake, when imperial nations invaded the country.

DAVID NEWHEISER: Does this prospect of nonviolent revolution provide an answer to Denys?

T.E.: Yes, absolutely. Processes of social change involve both—of course, it's banal enough to say—continuities and discontinuities. One of the precious continuities is the fact that certain values that can flourish to some extent in the present should also be the values that carry through, that underpin a process of social change. That is actually quite difficult, and this is part of Denys's skepticism, I think, quite rightly. Bertolt Brecht says that "we who laid the grounds of friendship could not ourselves be friendly," speaking of revolution-aries.[1] They had to be hard and bitter and commonsensical and prag-matic, but, as it were, values that were to a certain extent to be self-negating, because they were intended to bring into existence a state of affairs where those would not be the dominant values. So there is a certain askewness there, Denys.

One of the ways in which there is a connection between where we are now, in terms of value and the future, is the fact that capi-talism, as Marx sees, has done things like organizing people coop-eratively, called factories. For its own selfish ends, capitalism puts in train various forms of social organization, which can then form the basis of solidarity among people. So there's a kind of continuing thread through there.

D.T.: I want to shift the thing a little bit. Just speaking personally, I fell into Marxism largely as a result of—well, it's almost entirely your fault, Terry. I mean, there I was just sort of laboring away in Univer-sity College Dublin, and two guys, one called Terry Eagleton and one called Herbert McCabe, come over, and they start telling us, in 1965, about why Catholics should be Marxists. They published a journal called *Slant*. One edition of which, I seem to remember, Terry, was the *Slant* line on sex.

T.E.: Oh, yes. "Sex: The *Slant* Position."

D.T.: "Sex: The *Slant* Position." Exactly! Anyway, my model tends to come not so much *from* Marx, but applied *to* Marx, or it interrogates Marx, from within a Christian theological position. And it is this: the idea that the ends should somehow or other be present, very problematically, in the means is just fundamentally the idea of a sacrament. Because a sacrament is the future insofar as it can be present here and now, but that is problematic. The reason why it is called a sacrament, *sanctum secretum*, is that there is a tension involved between the way in which the future can be present in the present and the present's being a present. And that tension means that the present is also an absence. So that that real presence within the Catholic tradition, to which I subscribe, is also a real absence. And that play between presence and absence is precisely, I think, a well-tuned account, just in theory, of the problematic which we are facing here, of how the future of socialism can be present within the means of achieving it without their being betrayed simply by, it seems to me, the inherent amoralism of capitalism. One is left, as it were, with instruments which are provided by capitalism, which are themselves achieved by highly immoral means and are essentially amoral in character, and yet, somehow or other, in that context, one has to identify the means to achieve socialism, which are not themselves a betrayal of socialism by virtue of the means adopted to achieve it. It seems to me that a sort of sacramental model is telling you, "Well, somehow or other, you have got to resolve this problem in terms of a contemporary politics," and translating it into contemporary politics is where I remain, as yet, unconvinced. I'm not sure how one does this.

What one does have to say is that we can only work immanently within the processes which are available to us. This is Marx's materialism—that we cannot haul a solution out of the sky. We've simply got to work within what's available, with the possibilities which capitalism makes available to us, which are not themselves a

betrayal of the end which we are attempting. That is the difficulty—
the moral difficulty—it seems to me you are raising. It's a theodicy if
there is no answer to that. If there is an answer to that, then we have
got a way out of Marxism as a theodicy. That is where we are left.

D.N.: I want to put a question to you, Terry. To rephrase what Denys
just said, reframing your title, is Marxism sacramental? I mean, is
there a sacramentality there, that lies behind it?

T.E.: Well, in the sense that Denys has outlined, I think that the
same tension between the present and the future is there. You can't
predetermine the eschaton for Marx any more than you can for
Christianity, and you must be aware, in a sense, perhaps to rephrase
what Denys is saying, of the irony of signs, sacraments, which partly
negate themselves because they are not real things. Yes, I think there
are parallels to that in socialist practice. Marx himself pointed to
meetings of prescient workingmen such that when they came together in their warm demeanor after labor, they were engaging in a
community for the sake of it. Then one knows one is in the presence
of the sacramental, because, of course, the whole point of socialism,
which I take to be one of its profoundest affinities with Christianity,
is that it thinks that human beings have absolutely no point. And that
is the doctrine of creation, in the case of Christianity, but it is also,
in Marx's case, the doctrine (he's a good old romantic in this respect)
that the realization of human powers is purely and simply an end in
itself. There's no reason to lie around all day in various postures of
juissance sipping absinthe and swapping crimson garments. You do
it, to use the technical theological term, for the *hell* of it.

D.T.: It reminds me of something Herbert [McCabe], since I mentioned Herbert already, once said about prayer, and that is, the thing
about prayer is that it is entirely pointless, and there is no justification of it otherwise than in terms of its pointlessness.[2] There's nothing it is for. In that sense, when one engages in prayer, one is engaging in a practice here and now, which is at once a means to an end
but is so only insofar as it is already the end somehow or other

present within the means. It's that correlation like at the end of the working day, knackered, they just simply get together in the pub and enjoy the conversation, and that is a sort of model of what it is about. That is where we have to be, and what do we have to do in order to get there? Well, that's where the blood comes in, the price comes in. The question is, Are you requiring that price to be paid as part of the instrument of getting there, or is it just simply that, as you put it in your paper, you are turning this price, which capitalism is already requiring to be paid, to an end, which capitalism itself cannot realize?

T.E.: Or, to put it another way, Denys, Marx is saying, you can only get beyond an instrumental rationality, instrumentally. Yet there must be, as you are stressing, something more than just the instrumentality. There must be some prefiguring, quasi-sacramentally, of where you are going, but there is a sense in which, for Marx, instrumental rationality, political rationality, fitting the means to ends, is not an image of the end.

D.T.: Yes, that's right.

T.E.: But, in that sense, as in many others, socialism, like Christian faith, is a self-canceling enterprise. As I sometimes enjoy shocking innocent, young students, when I'm busy professionally corrupting the youth, by saying that if there are still feminists around in twenty years' time, it will be a shocking state of affairs. Of course, it will be. The only point of being a feminist, or a socialist, or a radical, is to get to the point where you can stop being one, where you will have helped to bring into existence the conditions which, as it were, allow you to go and do something more interesting, like think about color imagery in Joseph Conrad. Similarly, Christian faith has a built-in self-negation device.

D.T.: Well, that's right. In the New Jerusalem, in the Book of Revelation, there is no temple, because the point about a sacrament is that it is self-canceling. It is sacramental only insofar as it is not yet achieved, and yet it is also the presence of what is to be achieved within the means of getting there. I think it is this relationship that one has to play with, and whether Marxism can meet the conditions required is, for me, the question. Can you construe Marxism as morality? It would be construable as morality only on the condition that it met this possibility of, as it were, already being the end insofar as it is the instrument of achieving it.

D.N.: Is that why we haven't heard much about Marx since your essay in the *Cambridge Companion* [*to Liberation Theology*]?[3] I mean, why the turn to medieval mystical theology? What does it offer . . . ?

D.T.: No, I mean, look: I don't know how many times I've applied for jobs and rewritten my CV in which I say somewhere down the line I am going to pull the two halves of my career together, and that is the Marxism stuff with this mysticism stuff. I mean, I'm going to die before I do it, but I'm still going to write CVs. I managed to persuade Harry [Attridge] over there that I was an impressive candidate for the job I am in by telling him of this ambition in the CV that I gave him.[4] But I do think it is possible. I mean, that's not the reason that I gave up writing about Marxism. I just think that, well, it's probably better to leave it to Terry, because he's a whole lot better at it. But what I did think was necessary was to rethink the whole business of the Christian tradition in terms which ultimately, I felt, would have to meet certain conditions laid down by Marxism, because I think there are conditions of authenticity of action, which Marxism encapsulates. So let's turn the thing back again: instead of raising questions about the capacity of Marxism to be a morality, let's ask about Marxism as the condition of the possibility of there being a morality. Do you see what I mean? That's what I was arguing in *Marxism and Christianity*. That the necessary material conditions for a properly moral society were somehow or other contained in what Marxism required of capitalism.

D.N.: That is a striking claim. Let's open it up for questions.

AUDIENCE QUESTION: What about the role of primitive communism as showing what a future of a more developed communism would be?

T.E.: Well, one situation for Marx where there isn't class struggle is when you don't really have a surplus to struggle over, and that's basically, I suppose, primitive communism. Then there's a sort of interim period when you do have a surplus, but it is not enough to go around. And then there's, for Marx, a situation where you would have a surplus to fund what you needed to do all-around, as it were. Marx, of course, was certainly interested in primitive communism. He was wary of rather retrograde, possibly nostalgic, forms of politics. Not least, of course, because he really began his career in contention with utopianism. I mean, he learned something from utopians, although not from the utopian belief that in an ideal society the ocean would turn into lemonade. There was a utopian thinker at the time of Marx who believed that.[5] Marx would have preferred a rather fine Riesling. He did learn from them. But, of course, this connects in a way with what Denys was saying, because Marx didn't believe that socialism could, as it were, exist in the subjunctive mood, that it could just be a matter of, "Wouldn't it be nice if . . . " "If we were all peaceful." You know, full of Bob Geldof stuff. As Denys was saying, all of that has to be rooted somehow in the present. There has to be a way of reading the present, perhaps against the grain of the present, which gives you the dim outline of the future, or, indeed, reading the past, in the case of primitive communism.

D.N.: Would you like to speak to that, Denys?

D.T.: I'm sort of toying with a thought, and I'm not quite sure that I want to say it, because it will probably come out wrong if I do. It's something or other about this sort of practice. If here and now, within a world in which the material conditions do not exist for a mature communism, one could, as it were, playact it. Just to see what it's like, if you see what I mean. And that sounds like a very trivial way of talking about the Christian church, but I actually think that there's a certain sense in which the community which is the church is kind of playacting for something which is actually unrealizable until such time as the material conditions exist for its realization and therefore is a sort of primitive communism acted as drama in order simply to remind us of where we are going. Although it's not realizable otherwise than in this playacted fashion. In that sense, I think that primitive communism is still a live option, because it's a live option only insofar as it represents a possibility, not insofar as it actually is one. So it's pretending. It's like children playing.

T.E.: Fiction. Make-believe.

D.T.: Yeah, make-believe.

ERIC BUGYIS: I wanted to ask about Julian [of Norwich] in this context. Your book on Julian, in particular, Denys, because it seemed like one of the things that you are trying to get beyond, and Terry was sort of trying to negotiate, is the relationship between necessity and contingency, mechanism, and a mechanistic relationship between means and ends. Of course, the category that you develop so beautifully in that book is the "*behovely*," the "fitting," which is an aesthetic category. But yet it seems to be the condition of the possibility for a truly moral engagement with the question of theodicy, and maybe the beginnings of coming up with an antitheodicy. So I was wondering if you could reflect on the relationship between the aesthetic and the moral and the theological. Is Julian a Marxist? Does Marx need a liturgy?

D.T.: No, but I can see why you would ask that question. It's a classical trope within medieval theology that the incarnation is "*behovely*." For instance, Thomas Aquinas's question at the beginning of the third part of the *Summa*: "Was God's becoming man *conveniens*?"[6] Now, not necessary, but not just fun and games, but somehow or other fitting within a narrative which made sense of it and, in fact, even more than that. Although clearly you could not predict the outcome that God becomes man, a human being, when it happens you can then retrodict the whole of history in terms of it. It begins, then, to offer you a rereading of history. Now, when Julian moves this whole category of the *conveniens*, or, in Middle English, the *be-hovable*, or *behovely*, however you find it in the two different texts, to sin, you are faced with the same problem that Terry is facing. Is this to say, "Sin is okay because look at the outcome, look at what one brings about"? In that sense, I think that the problem that Terry raises about Marxism is equally problematic for what Julian is saying. Is Julian saying, "Sin is *behovely*," like Marx saying, "Well, it's okay that there's all this bloody bloodshed of capitalism, because look at what it's going to bring about"? Now, really, is that what you mean to say? Well, the answer is no, it isn't. But it is very, very mysterious as to what she is saying. Perhaps what she is saying is that there is a narrative, which is not available, which we are not in possession of, within which the unpredictability of sin is retrodictably intelligible, and is not so much justified by that narrative as, well, "now we can see how it had to be that way." So there's a kind of analogy between the two, and there's a reading of Julian according to which she would be as atrocious as the reading of Marxism according to which, well, "let's have some bloody capitalism, because the more blood there is, the more likely we're going to get socialism." There are versions of Marxism which are pretty close to that.

DAVID BURRELL: With regard to your last point, Denys, if you think of the complacent power relationships in Western Europe at the end of the nineteenth century, including the Treaty of Berlin, which carved up Africa so they could have slaves, it's highly unlikely that an encyclical like *Rerum Novarum*, which triggered a whole archive of social teaching, would have happened without Marxism. It would be almost unthinkable that that could have emerged without Marxism. That's my own *feeling*, anyway.

T.E.: Yes, well, I suppose that's a theodicy of a kind. All of this awful Marx at least gives birth to this *Rerum Novarum*. I never thought of that, actually. It may be, quite possibly.

D.T.: I think that what one has to say is that the events to which Marx is responding are the same events to which *Rerum Novarum* is responding. So they are very very clearly responses to those events.

D.B.: But also that *The Communist Manifesto* triggered a kind of consciousness of those events which had to be responded to at all.

T.E.: But I think another key there, David, is the Paris Commune, isn't it? That's what Marx himself takes as the model of socialist democracy, however short lived and partial, and so on, and that's what sends utter shockwaves of fear and revulsion through the ruling classes of Europe. And, yes, in the fullness of time, results in a certain vein of Catholic social thinking that knows that something, no matter how averse it is to socialism, something has to be done about unbridled capitalism.

DAVID MAHAN: I once heard a fast and ready distinction between Marxism and Christianity as the one saying, "What you have is mine," and the other saying, "What I have is yours." So I wonder if you could elaborate on that.

D.T.: Which is which?

T.E.: Yes, quite.

D.M.: I don't know how you want to qualify that. But if we were to draw a distinction between mandated or forced redistribution and generosity, how might the latter be a way of constructing or beginning to construct a positive Christian political theology?

T.E.: I'm not sure that I would want to describe socialism in terms of "*mandated* redistribution." Socialism is democratic or nothing, as I said. The trouble with both of those phrases, it seems to me, is that they still hinge on the notion of property. However you carve it up, however you exchange it, whatever mutuality is involved, you still are essentially depending on the bourgeois notion of ownership, which, of course, is most virulent not in terms of owning garages and factories and corner stores, but owning yourself. That's where that ethic surely bites deepest. So I do think that although Marx—again, an example of Denys's point that you have to trade in the corrupt present—has a decent socialist concept of common ownership, which you have to have, he has it only so that eventually you can get beyond the concept of ownership altogether. Not only did Marx think that "ownership" was a bourgeois concept, by which, of course, he didn't mean "bad, don't use it," but somehow enter into it, use it differently; he also thought that about "equality." He thought that "equality" was a bourgeois notion, because, in its abstract form, rarely are people more abstractly and equally interchangeable than on the market. So one has to (in the true spirit of deconstruction) not simply throw out those concepts and say, "Oh, they're contaminated with the present," but, as Denys is saying, you have to work your way through them and come out somewhere on the other side.

D.T.: Yes, I think if you read chapter 5 of Locke's *Second Treatise of Civil Government*, you get a classic account of the association of personal identity with the ownership of property, and it's a kind of play that he goes into on the word *mine*.[7] The "I" or the "mine" of identity gets tied up in a sort of wonderful equivocation with the "mine" of ownership in such a way that you can't really be a self except in your relationship to property. And, I think, ever after this, the tie-up between ownership and identity becomes inseparable to the point where people even begin to think of socialism itself as a form of it, just a different form of it, a reconstruction of it. The point about socialism is that it actually breaks apart that relationship between ownership and personal identity. That means it is revolutionary. It isn't just a series of smooth changes which one could envisage by just redistributing property this way, that way, or the other way. It means the abolition of property, and the point about the abolition of property is that what you are abolishing is the sense of identity, personal identity, in terms of a relationship of ownership.

D.N.: Can I ask a follow-up? How does this differ from the Eckhartian dispossession of desire? Meister Eckhart's "detachment"? Is there a relevant difference, or is it the same? Because formally it sounds quite similar.

D.T.: Well, Eckhart is talking about an ascetical dispossession, I think, of which he offers no politics. And I'm not sure about how to construct a relationship between Eckhart and this discussion.

D.N.: That seems significant.

MARY-JANE RUBENSTEIN: Denys, to go back to your response to Eric earlier, is the only thing keeping Julian from a theodicy, or Marx from a theodicy, not having access to the way the story goes? Not knowing the end of the story? Because if you think about Hegel's *Lectures on the Philosophy of History*, he gets into the bit about the logic of history and the "cunning of reason" is that it uses the passions of the individual and tosses them away like empty—which sounds a lot like the passage that Professor Eagleton was referring to as the bad possibility in Marx, and Hegel then says this makes his story a theodicy, this then vindicates history, vindicates reason, and he uses the term *theodicy*.[8] So where does Marx depart from Hegel that allows him not to be offering a theodicy? Or where does Julian? Is it just because Hegel says, "I know how this story goes," that makes his thought a theodicy as opposed to Julian or Marx?

D.T.: No, that's not the only reason. I think it's back to this point: How can one live the Kingdom now, given that the conditions of its being realized have not yet been obtained? It's not the unknowability of it; it's just the impossibility of realizing it that prevents it from becoming a theodicy. I better not say more, though, because I'll just be babbling.

T.E.: This may not meet your point, but surely one difference between Hegel and Marx is that Marx is trying to get history off the ground and Hegel thinks that it has just culminated inside his own head. Hegel is an "end of history" thinker in that sense. There are, of course, many other differences, but they are radically opposed surely as far as that goes. But, for Marx, things haven't started.

STEPHEN OGDEN: Denys, you mentioned this movement to try to get Catholics to become Marxists, but I am wondering about the other way around, particularly in the thought of Peter Geach. So Geach thinks that you could have quite a lot of moral knowledge without mentioning God whatsoever, but he, in his essay "The Moral Law and the Law of God," thinks you have to have divine commands come in, in order to know that you shouldn't do bad in order that good may come.[9] So if Geach is right about that and if you are right about Marxism being true to its moral principles, does Marxism need Christianity? Does it need something like a divine revelation to help it stay true to its moral principles and to help it resist a kind of utilitarianism?

D.T.: You see, that is what I actually argue in *Marxism and Christianity*. It is precisely that. The way I put it was that Marxism is the condition of the possibility of an authentic Christianity but that authentic Christianity rescues Marxism from the danger it is in of becoming a theodicy. So it's a kind of reciprocity going on between the two. But one of the ways, it seemed to me, that Marxism kind of played into something very, very important for Christians was Marx's rejection of atheism. I think this is hugely important from the very earliest of the writings, which actually didn't become available until well into the last century, the *Economic and Philosophical Manuscripts*, where he says, look, concerning Feuerbach and his opponents, a plague on both their houses. Atheism and theism are playing on the same tennis court, and they are opponents on the same mistaken territory. Let's get off this territory on which atheism and theism are playing. So it's a kind of post-atheism. Now, it seems to me, therein lie the possibilities of a relationship between Marxism as a critique of capitalism and negative theology. That's the connection that I would still want to explore, in some way or other, and that is where I left it the last time I wrote about this. That is what still needs

to be done, so far as I'm concerned, but that's my business, it's nobody else's business. Nobody else is really interested in this.

CHRISTOPHER BEELEY: Would you say then that Marxism ever
could be a theodicy, if it is, in fact, fundamentally, purely materialist?
That is, could Marxism be a theodicy without God? And, second, if
that is the case, to borrow Terry's line, is Marxism tragic enough, or
do we need something darker?

D.T.: There's something you wrote, Terry, in the seventies, about
the silence of Jesus before Pilate and the refusal of Jesus to be hijacked into a conversation of the kind that Pilate wanted to engage
in. That made me think about the relationship between Marxism
and Christianity, because I think that it was in that context that you
were writing. I think it was some article you wrote in *New Blackfriars*, or something.[10] Anyway, it made me think about the need for
Christians to just simply shut up until they were in a position to talk
about the conditions under which they could speak authentically,
and that Marxism had something to do with the realization of those
conditions under which Christian talk would cease to be ideological,
cease to be a betrayal, and that this lay somewhere in the silence of
Jesus before Pilate, the refusal to allow Christian talk to be hijacked
by the people in power. I think that's why it seemed to me that Christianity needed Marxism as its own philosophical theology, but in the
course of doing that, it rescued Marxism from the possibility of its
own betrayals. So that there was a sort of reciprocity going on between them of that kind.

This connects with a theme that we got into this afternoon. We
got into a really interesting discussion about only talking when you
need to and about the overproduction of talk, which is like the surplus under capitalism.[11] It's got to go somewhere. So you have institutions like universities, so that it can go there. Yet there is a need to
give answers only when there are real problems. I think that silence
of Jesus before Pilate was a refusal to engage in conversation with a
person who clearly had no sense of what he was asking about. So you
could not answer Pilate's question, because as Bacon writes in one

of his essays, "'What is truth?,' said jesting Pilate, and would not wait for an answer."[12]

T.E.: Or, as the character says in P. G. Wodehouse, in one of the novels, when he realizes to his alarm that the person he is speaking to doesn't understand the word *pig*—"A lot of tedious spade work *there*."[13]

Can I just come back on both of the points you made, Christopher, the first point about materialism and the second point about tragedy? I think Marxism and Christianity are much more united on the first topic than they are on the second. Part of what I was trying to say about Marx's notion of materialism, you know, the active, communicative, laboring, relating body, seems to me thoroughly spiritual. Marx is a deeply spiritual thinker, in any useful meaning of the term. He is not a religious thinker, to be sure, but he is a deeply spiritual thinker and wouldn't accept, as I was trying to argue, this sort of material/spiritual distinction.

On the concept of tragedy, however, though I think that both Marxism and Christianity can be seen as tragic creeds, I do think that you are right in suggesting that Marxism isn't tragic enough. It sounds like a rather sadistic thing to say, "We need a little more tragedy." When I sat the tragedy paper in my finals at Cambridge, one of my fellow students said she thought the trouble was that the examiners seemed to think that tragedy was a good thing. Arthur Miller is a fine playwright, but he doesn't quite rise to the level of tragedy, or something. There's no real equivalent in Marxism, is there, of the kind of tragedy involved in the descent into hell, which is confronting not only suffering and wretchedness and dispossession, which is common to both doctrines, but also, for example, utter futility and absurdity. That notion of hell, which is a kind of farcical, cynical cackle at the whole idea that anything human could be meaningful or valuable. You've got to confront that Medusa's head as well, and hope it doesn't turn you to stone in the process. So I do think that you are right. Christianity is at once greatly more pessimistic than a great many views and, of course, greatly more hopeful at the same time.

D.T.: The price is higher. I mean, the price is death. That is just so central to Christianity, that the price of whatever it takes has got to be death. Martyrdom is the one thing that marks Christianity out, that martyrdom is inevitable, necessary, bound to happen. As Herbert McCabe once put it, "If you do not love, you are scarcely alive, but if you do love, you'll certainly be killed."[14] That is the radicalness of Christianity. It is about death.

T.E.: That's your pie in the sky.

BERNARD McGINN: I am thinking of the silence of Marguerite Porete before the Inquisition. It is perhaps the most powerful example of mystical silence that we have in the tradition, and it fits exactly with what you were just saying, Denys.

D.T.: Yes, that's right. She refuses to take the oath and refuses to respond to her inquisitors, knowing that to respond is to be complicit in . . .

B.M.: . . . her execution.

D.T.: Exactly.

NOTES

Editors' note: This is the transcript of a conversation that took place at the conference, "The Trials of Desire and the Possibility of Faith," held at Yale University on March 22–24, 2012. It immediately followed a public lecture by Terry Eagleton, titled "Is Marxism a Theodicy?" The text of this lecture is presented in the preceding chapter of the present volume.

1. Bertolt Brecht, "To Posterity," in *Selected Poems*, trans. H. R. Hays (New York: Grove Press, 1959), 175.

2. Herbert McCabe, *God Matters* (New York: Continuum, 2005), 224.

3. Denys Turner, "Marxism, Liberation Theology and the Way of Negation," in *The Cambridge Companion to Liberation Theology*, ed. Christopher Rowland (Cambridge: Cambridge University Press, 1999), 199–217.

4. Harry Attridge was dean of Yale Divinity School when Turner was hired and at the time this conference was held.

5. This was Charles Fourier. See Terry Eagleton, *Why Marx Was Right* (New Haven: Yale University Press, 2011), 67–68.

6. Thomas Aquinas, *Summa theologiae*, vol. 48, *The Incarnate Word*, IIIa, qq. 1–6, ed. R. J. Hennessey (Cambridge: Cambridge University Press, 2006), 5.

7. See John Locke, *Two Treatises of Government*, ed. Peter Laslett (Cambridge: Cambridge University Press, 1988), 285–302.

8. See G. W. F. Hegel, *Lectures on the Philosophy of World History: Introduction*, trans. H. B. Nisbet (Cambridge: Cambridge University Press, 1975), 42, 89.

9. P. T. Geach, "The Moral Law and the Law of God," in *God and the Soul* (London: Routledge & Kegan Paul, 1969), 117 ff.

10. See Terry Eagleton, "Marxists and Christians: Answers for Brian Wicker," *New Blackfriars* 56 (October 1975): 470. Cited in Denys Turner, *Marxism and Christianity* (Oxford: Basil Blackwell, 1983), xii.

11. See especially the essays by Ludger Viefhues-Bailey and Vittorio Montemaggi in the present volume.

12. See Francis Bacon, "Of Truth," in *The Major Works*, ed. Brian Vickers (Oxford: Oxford University Press, 2002), 341.

13. P. G. Wodehouse, *Summer Lightning* (New York: W. W. Norton, 2012), 93.

14. See McCabe, *God Matters*, 90–100.

FOURTEEN

As We Were Saying

Marxism and Christianity Revisited

ERIC BUGYIS

In 1967 Herbert McCabe, Dominican priest, philosopher, and theologian, was swiftly relieved of his editorship of the journal *New Blackfriars* for arguing that, "with all their decadence, their corruption, and their silliness," one should still support the "hierarchical institutions of the Roman Catholic Church."[1] McCabe's comments were in response to the decision of the "known and loved" theologian Charles Davis to leave the Catholic Church because of what he perceived to be its many moral failings. Given that the "Church is quite plainly corrupt," McCabe claimed, it is actually the more radical and theologically serious course of action to remain in it with a solidarity born of equal parts realism and hope.[2] As Terry Eagleton has more recently pointed out, "Radicals are those who believe that things are extremely bad with us, but that they could be feasibly much improved."[3] This is in distinction to those dour conservatives who seem to think that things could only get worse and to those cheery liberals who rather implausibly believe that "we are all getting nicer and nicer all the time."[4]

It is hard to know where to place the ecclesiastical authorities that sought to discipline McCabe, but it is safe to say that they basically agreed with Davis: "If you think that the Church is corrupt, it's probably best to get out and try your luck in the secular world." Were McCabe still alive today, he might have found it curious that this line of reasoning is now running in the opposite direction, with many Western secularists looking to the Christian churches to provide a refuge from the creeping corruption of their late capitalist societies. For McCabe and his comrades, it was Marxism that held out the promise of returning a church that had grown smug with neo-scholastic, metaphysical certainties to its more worldly, if considerably more fraught, mission to proclaim a particular "interpretation of history" and to persuade Christians that "being in the church involves commitment to imaginative culture and the political left" if one is to witness to a life that "goes deeper than mere possession."[5] However, as Eagleton jokes in his contribution to the present volume, it now seems as if it is Marxism that deals in the esoteric and, as he claims elsewhere, it is religion that has become the most effective spokesperson for the life historical in the face of contemporary claims that "History" as such has been superseded by the timeless truths of global capital.[6]

The collapse of the Soviet Union and the end of the Cold War seemed for some to have dealt a deathblow to the plausibility of any serious Marxist political program. Yet the rise of various forms of fundamentalist protest, typically fueled by a potent blend of nationalism and religion, aimed at the newly victorious triumvirate of Western capitalism, democracy, and mass culture, which symbolically culminated just months after McCabe's death in the September 11, 2001, terrorist attacks, has shown the hope of some kind of Pax Americana to be the fantasy that it probably always was. The seeming lack of alternatives to this short-lived dream of a global order united under the banner of commerce has led a number of political theorists on the secular left to look to the Christian tradition for intellectual resources to construct a new political vision.[7] Thus one finds Jürgen Habermas talking with then-Cardinal Joseph Ratzinger about whether religion might be able to foster the kind of solidarity necessary to provide the prepolitical foundations of the secular, democratic state, which has been destabilized by the alienating conditions of late capitalist technocratic administration.[8] Giorgio Agamben and Alain Badiou are looking to the writings of Saint Paul to inspire a universal consciousness comparable to Marx's proletariat.[9] Slavoj Žižek, in conversation with the Radical Orthodox theologian John Milbank, and Antonio Negri are discovering potent images in the suffering of Job and Christ that might offer insights into the nature of revolutionary, class struggle.[10]

On the other side of the secular/religious divide, this newfound political relevance has emboldened many Christian theologians and philosophers to suggest, as Milbank has, that "the universalist project of the West" is and has always been a "Christian project" and that its current failures might be traced to certain heterodox lapses in its own historical evolution.[11] In his highly influential *After Virtue*, Alasdair MacIntyre made a similar if less genetically overdetermined and more philosophically rigorous argument, which has been taken up by a number of contemporary Roman Catholic thinkers with an enthusiasm bordering on triumphalism.[12] Perhaps to the chagrin of these would-be disciples, however, it is the insights of his former comrades, McCabe and Eagleton, that MacIntyre says should be developed in a "more systematic way" if we are to better characterize "the predicaments generated by the ethics, politics, and economics of advanced modernity."[13] Among other things, this means that, for MacIntyre, the problems of late capitalism are not going to be solved by isolating some congenital defect in the *intellectual* history of its founding ideas. Rather, it is the *material* conditions that led to the emergence of these ideas and the deformations of life that they continue to support that must be our primary concern.

With this, then, we seem to have come full circle. Now that the dust has settled on the kind of Cold War polemics that had hagiographers casting the recently sainted Pope John Paul II as rending the Iron Curtain with one hand and wagging a disapproving finger at dissident, liberation theologians with the other, the time is ripe for asking whether Christianity and Marxism might have anything left to say to one another.[14] Indeed, the present Pope Francis seems keen to continue the conversation that McCabe was engaged in some sixty years ago, writing in his apostolic exhortation, *Evangelii Gaudium*,

"As long as the problems of the poor are not radically resolved . . . by attacking the structural causes of inequality, no solution will be found for the world's problems or, for that matter, to any problems."[15] If one makes the safe assumption that these problems include the "quite plain" corruption both within and outside the church, which McCabe was so bold as to point out, then it might not be too much to expect him to respond to this recent rapprochement as he did in his first "Comment" on being restored to the editorship of *New Blackfriars* three years after his dismissal: "As I was saying before I was so oddly interrupted . . . "[16]

In what follows, I consider what McCabe and his friends, the most significant of whom for the present volume is of course Denys Turner, might have to contribute to both the present resurgence of interest in the revolutionary, political potential of Christian theology by those on the secular left and the renewed attempt by theologians to offer and encourage prophetic critiques of global capitalism on behalf of those least among us. I argue that for these thinkers, any conversation between Marxism and Christianity will have to confront three interrelated sets of questions: (1) What kind of revolution is necessary to overthrow the present, capitalist order, and how continuous or discontinuous with this order will this event be? (2) How are we to make sense of the suffering and violence that is both the motivation and the means for this revolution? And (3) Whence the confidence that anything "new" could ever emerge from this corrupt history?

SAINT PAUL, REVOLUTIONARY

When it comes to the question of revolution, the writings attributed to Saint Paul have proven to be a fruitful resource for secular leftists looking to overthrow the present order.[17] Badiou claims that Paul was the "Lenin" to Christ's "Marx."[18] For Paul, according to Badiou and others, the present order that is to be overcome is the one governed by ancient Jewish and Roman Law, which is translated by modern legal theorists, like Carl Schmitt, as having concealed the arbitrary, death-dealing violence of its grounding authority behind the facade of natural necessity.[19] Milbank calls this his "Schmittian addition to Marxist political economy," because it borrows from Marx's basic insight into the dynamic process by which money, like law, is first used merely as a tool for facilitating certain kinds of relationships, for example, exchanging goods, and then is reified into the normative measure for society as such.[20] Thus the mystifying logic by which pragmatic law takes on the mantle of normative necessity is the same as that which turns mere economic exchange into a system that seems as unbending as the laws of nature themselves.

It is just this kind of ideology—which Turner has helpfully defined as a discourse that bridges "the gap between 'is' and 'ought' without having to acknowledge that there is any gap to be bridged"— that Paul's interpretation of what Badiou calls the "truth-Event" of Christ's resurrection allows him to overcome.[21] It is fidelity to this "truth-Event," which bears the necessity of its injunction within the contingency of its happening, and not obedience to legal precepts, which are based on the arbitrary assignation of necessity to the contingent exercise of power, that makes Paul a "subject."[22] Žižek compares this to the truth-Event of falling in love, which "subjectivizes" me by shaping the form of my subsequent life such that everything I do is determined by it.[23] Falling in love, for Žižek, is historically contingent insofar as it did not *have to* happen while being necessary insofar as it is absolutely essential for making sense of the life to follow. Žižek opposes the "historicity" of love in this sense to the "historicism" that would give an account of love relations in terms of the "complex interaction" of "economic, political, cultural, and other circumstances" that make them possible.[24] On this account, Paul's faith in Christ, like falling in love, is therefore strictly speaking inexplicable in terms of anything that came before it.[25]

The consequence of this for Badiou's reading of Paul is that Christian faith is radically discontinuous with the Judaism out of which it has traditionally been thought to emerge. Though he is careful to distinguish, if just barely, this position from the "ultra-Pauline" doctrine of Marcion in the second century, which claimed that the

New Testament revealed a completely different God and a new "absolute beginning," Badiou's understanding of the Christ event as "heterogeneous to the law, pure excess over every prescription, grace without concept or appropriate rite," threatens to leave us without any means of perceiving the Event as an event *in history*, which would seem to entail some minimal continuity with what came before it.[26] Moreover, apart from his blatant supersessionism, Badiou appears to share Marcion's Manichaean belief that the flesh is infected with the "sin" of death, which is not simply a "biological fact," but a normative state, and for this reason the resurrection of Christ is not an "overcoming of death" but a "distinct function" that takes place at the site of incarnation without requiring it. It is for these reasons that Milbank argues that Badiou leaves us with merely a kind of Platonic idea of the "truth-Event as such" rather than a fully incarnate revolutionary politics.[27]

For his part, however, Milbank does not fare much better. He sides with Badiou by giving priority to the resurrection over the incarnation as the key to understanding the new life in Christ that Paul proclaims. In this, Milbank preserves Badiou's view of death as belonging to a life of flesh that is "literally" left behind in the resurrection such that we are relieved of those "defensive passions that rage against mortality" and "can no longer sin."[28] Because we can no longer sin, Milbank claims, Paul's "politics of resurrection" stands as "a critique of law as such—Roman, Greek, Jewish, whatever—and not just of Jewish law," and in the place of law, he recommends "an overcoming practice of psychic medicine rather than a disciplinary police procedure."[29] This therapeutic politics is supposed to enable us to see ourselves differently. We are no longer those insecure Hobbesian subjects, for whom life is "nasty, brutish, and short" and politics is the cynical means by which we simply forestall the inevitable.[30] Rather, the resurrection is supposed to reveal that the body is "immortal," and, as such, it is "the site of a perfect harmony and goodness," which can be restored by us if we only trust in God.[31]

At this point, Milbank begins to look like the inverted mirror image of Badiou. If the latter denies the reality of death in favor of some ideal revolutionary promise, the former seems to suggest that death is only an idea and revolutionary love the only reality. Following Eagleton's typology, we might say that Badiou offers a conservative account of revolution, which must radically break with a history that only seems to be getting worse, and Milbank gives us a classic liberal vision, whereby we only need to be brought to see that in our heart of hearts we all have a little goodness in us.[32]

Of course, if corruptions of the flesh, including sin and death, happen not to be merely fictive aspects of our creaturely life, then Milbank's dream of a world without the "damage-limitation exercise of legality" would, in fact, be hell.[33] The problem with his "Schmittian addition" to Marx's critique of ideology is that it assumes that law is simply the arbitrary exercise of power all the way down, as opposed to the means necessary for making relationships possible between finite persons who are otherwise confined to their individual, bodily experience. As McCabe argues, law and language make it possible for us to transcend an initial experience of the world that is, as with most other animals, specific to the individual, bodily interactions made possible by our senses.[34] Without the means to extend our bodies through law and language, we would lack the species consciousness that is necessary to take us beyond the Hobbesian state of nature into which we were born. Of course, what Hobbes failed to recognize was that we were born with the capacity to transcend this state of nature by our own nature, because it belongs to our nature to be linguistic beings and, therefore, lawful beings. Thus, while laws do have a tendency to divide and enslave rather than unite human persons, a world without law would be one in which there were no humans at all.[35]

This is why, as Agamben notes, "the lawless one" of Paul's second letter to the Thessalonians has been traditionally associated with the "antichrist" of the Johannine correspondence.[36] As Eagleton has argued, the demonic posture is one of "derisive laughter" at all those middle-class mores that do no more than mask petit bourgeois resentment, and while, as Milbank knows, this cynicism has "a seductive smack of radicalism about it," it remains purposively indistinguishable from the nihilistic violence of the reactionary suicide bomber or the aristocratic hedonist.[37] For Agamben, however, this ambiguity prevents the "juridicizing of all human relations in their entirety" by disconnecting the normative force of law from the certainty of action and rendering the exercise of power as such "weak" insofar as it cannot know *in principle* whether it is to be used for good or ill.[38] In every attempt to incarnate the necessity of law within our contingent history, the space between the prescribed act and the failed one speaks with a silence that "extinguishes" language because it only can remember what *could not* have been done and *cannot* be said.[39]

On this account, revolution is the mere failure of the present order rather than an overcoming. It does not have any "specific content," nor does it "found a new identity," but it seeks to "create a space that escapes the grasp of power and its laws, without entering into conflict with them yet rendering them inoperative."[40] From McCabe's perspective this is "a mere riot rather than a revolution—not transcending the law but merely failing to keep it."[41] And, for Eagleton, Agamben's celebration of failure as the truest form of "weak power" would come close to the "obscene enjoyment" traditionally afforded to those damned souls "who are bound fast to the Law because they are in love with the act of violating it."[42] These are the souls that Turner describes as inhabiting Dante's *Inferno*, who would rather rehearse the story of their own failure to enter into those relationships that the law seems to require than risk their freedom by admitting that things could have been otherwise.[43] Similarly, Agamben's exigent silence echoes the "pyrrhic victory" of Dante's Satan, who would rather remain "impotent and inarticulate, . . . frozen into immobility in the deepest pit of hell" than risk living life governed by a law and a language that is not his alone.[44]

Badiou, Milbank, and Agamben have each given us an account of Paul's revolutionary insight into the ideological nature of law as obscuring the contingency of its use with the natural necessity of its being. For all of them, the fact that the law often represents the way things are as the way they ought to be is reason enough to reject it altogether and take the chance that any normative interpretation of history as having been otherwise is either futile (Badiou and Agamben) or redundant (Milbank). Either way, on this reading, the Pauline revolution is going to require a complete break with the present order of things. However, for McCabe and his friends, authentic revolution requires that there be "at least a 'revolutionary continuity'" between this world and the one to come.[45] What this means for the present discussion is that however arbitrary the law may seem, however much it may just be an accident of this mortal life that is destined for death and decay, this law and the sin that it trails must be redeemable as a part of the world that is to come. This is to say that the contingency of its present excesses must come to be seen as a necessary part of the history of our redemption when it is told *as a whole*. For Paul, the law must still have a place in the "new creation" brought about by Christ, just as both Jew and Greek now "fit" within the one people of God. Turner has helpfully articulated the "fittingness" by which the law might be understood as both presently contingent and yet a necessary part of all that is to come by using the medieval Latin notion of "*conveniens*," specifically as it seems to have been translated into Middle English by Julian of Norwich as "*behovely*."[46]

The "*conveniens*" and the "*behovely*" pick out a modality that is neither necessary nor contingent while not merely being privative.[47] The present order that is governed by legal and economic values is clearly not the only *logically* necessary way that things could be, since if it were, normativity would simply be absorbed by description and the very question of what *should* be the case would never arise. On the other hand, this order cannot be *logically* contingent, or arbitrary, because it clearly has a certain intuitive appeal to those looking to make sense of their relationships to the world and other persons. This is to say that the sorts of relationships prescribed by the laws governing our political, social, and economic lives cannot be necessary, because they do often fail to obtain; but they also seem to succeed just as often, and when they do, we tend to find these laws helpful at least insofar as they let us know where we stand. Turner argues that when this happens, both the failures and the successes of the present order need not be seen as *logically* necessary, since they could have been otherwise, but the simple fact that things happened the way that they did means that they are at least *historically* necessary.[48] As Eagleton suggests in his contribution to the present volume, this is how Marx understood the relationship between capitalism and socialism. It is not that the former is logically necessary for the emergence of the latter, nor is it the case that the latter has absolutely nothing to do with the former. Rather, capitalism is *historically* necessary insofar as it happens to be the only economic order that we know of that can create the material conditions for the emergence of socialism, but of course things could always have been otherwise.

This understanding of the relationship between revolution and the order that precedes it as "*conveniens*" or "*behovely*" makes it possible for us to see both the law and its overcoming as belonging to the same narrative, which, as Turner argues, is simply to say that both are events in history.[49] This is important for both the Marxist and the Christian, if they are to avoid the flights of utopian fancy of which they are often accused. As McCabe claims, if the Christian and the Marxist are to be seen as more than riotous upstarts seeking to undermine the present order for the *hell* of it, they will have to show how the "new creation," once it emerges, can be contained within a single interpretation of human history. Just as a mature person must find a way of integrating all that has happened to her into an autobiography that makes sense of who she is now, "after a revolution a society *must* re-write its history; it must, that is to say, re-create its identity."[50] This means that the law and the corruption that it so often occasions must still have a place in the story of humanity when viewed from the perspective of the new revolutionary reality. It cannot be forgotten or denied, but it must be affirmed as necessary for "the plot—or, if you like, that the plot needs [it] in the way that plots do—contingently indeed, but all the same just so."[51]

It is at this point that this account of "revolutionary continuity" runs up against the question of suffering, or theodicy. For Badiou, Milbank, and Agamben, suffering is no more valuable than the failed law that administers it, but for McCabe and his friends, death and its law are given, at the very least, a kind of aesthetic validity within the narrative of revolution, also known as salvation history. For the Christian, this poses an even deeper problem insofar as she is going to insist that a benevolent God was the author of every grim twist on the way to our final redemption. From a Marxist perspective, as McCabe argues, all of this is going to seem like a "diversion from the real demands of history," which would do well to affirm its dark past as something of a necessary evil, even if contingently so, and avoid the rather monstrous thought that, as Julian affirms, *"alle maner of thinge shalle be wel."*[52] This is to say that for the Marxist we seek a "new creation" in spite of our awareness of death, not because of it. Yet, for the Christian, given the *fact* that death remains an inextricable part of our existence as necessarily embodied creatures, a true materialist cannot ignore the question of its meaning, which is the only hope for bringing about what Paul calls the "new mind" of revolution.[53]

SUFFERING FROM CHRIST TO JOB

In his *Philosophical Investigations*, Ludwig Wittgenstein famously remarks, "The human body is the best picture of the human soul."[54] For McCabe, Eagleton, and Turner, this is a frequently cited idea not only because it has an auspicious philosophical pedigree extending from Aristotle to Thomas Aquinas to Marx but also because it is an important corrective to both the idealist excesses of Christianity and the reductive materialism of Marxism. The former arise, according to McCabe, when certain Christians speak of the "soul" as if it were an immaterial substance that exists apart from the body, is immune from decay and death, and belongs only to the private and interior life of human beings.[55] It is this view that gives us the kind of "wishful thinking about death" that, as I suggested above, can be found in Milbank, who claims that our political lives would be much improved if we only realized the new immortal and sinless postresurrection self within. It was to avoid such fantastic nonsense that McCabe once wrote a brief introduction to Christianity that assiduously avoided the use of the word *soul*.[56] For, from the point of view of McCabe's

Aristotelian Thomism, as Turner has explained, to say that a body "has a soul" is "no more than a synonym for 'is alive.'"[57]

Like many Marxists today, Thomas was criticized by his contemporaries for being a reductive materialist, because his view of the body-soul relation "would seem to have no basis for an account of what is 'spiritual' about human beings."[58] But this is only true, Eagleton argues, if one "tends to see spiritual questions as a realm loftily remote from everyday life," as those "prosperous bourgeois" of our day do, or as those "economically self-sustaining monastic communities" in Thomas's time did.[59] By contrast, "for the Judaic tradition of which," as Eagleton reminds us, Marx "was an unbelieving offspring" and of which Thomas of course was a believing descendant, "the 'spiritual' is a question of feeding the hungry, welcoming the immigrants and protecting the poor from the violence of the rich. It is not the opposite of mundane, everyday existence."[60] This is because, contrary to what cultured despisers of the "merely ordinary," like Milbank, would seem to suggest, there is no such thing as existence without meaning, or "bare life."[61] If Eagleton and Turner are right, for both Marx and Thomas, the common mistake made by both the "atheistic materialism of the twenty-first century and the theological immaterialism of the thirteenth" is "the conviction that matter is meaninglessly dumb."[62] It is this presupposition that lies behind Milbank's fear that the obviously corrupt conditions of late capitalist life could actually deprive human being of all meaning and dignity.[63]

For Turner's Thomas, however, the "misty conceit" that some spiritual *thing* is needed to supplement our ordinary experience to give it meaning is simply the inverted mirror image of the zombie-scape imagined by those reductive materialists who would have us believe that we might actually be, like the walking dead, bodies without souls.[64] Between "the mainstream Augustinians" of his day, who believed "there must be something more than matter," and the materialists of ours, who believe "that matter is all there is," Thomas argues that matter simply "could not exist if it were not alive with meaning, or as he called it, 'form.'"[65] This means that there is nothing that must be added to existence to render it meaningful, and, more important, nothing can harm existence so thoroughly that it is left without meaning, since meaning is not separable from the "bare" stuff of existence. It is here that we come to the question of suffering, which, as Wittgenstein points out, is only perceptible if our attitude toward the one who suffers "is an attitude towards a soul."[66] This is to say that we must see suffering as a true de-formation—an absence of form in an entity that requires its presence in order to be. Thus suffering takes on a positive ontological weight as having a meaning that is present insofar as it appears to be absent from that which nevertheless clearly still exists.

Among Christ-curious secular leftists, Žižek is the most concerned with preserving the painful everydayness of theological materialism. To this end, he argues that it is only in the "suffering God" of Christianity that one finds "the failure of any *Aufhebung* of the raw fact of suffering."[67] By becoming incarnate, this God identified "himself with his own shit" and, thereby, made it possible for "the properly Christian notion of divine love" to be apprehended "as the love for the miserable excremental entity called 'man.'"[68] It is his faithfulness to this "event," in spite of his own atheism, that Žižek claims makes him "more Christian than Milbank," because he neither turns away from the bleeding, crucified God in defeat nor looks past this cross to the resurrected God, who appears in his restored glory as if nothing had happened.[69] Thus Žižek boasts that he has the courage, which G. K. Chesterton said was lacking in many of his fellow Christians, to speak the "four words: He was made Man."[70]

The problem that most Christians have with this statement, according to Žižek, is that they tend to privilege the subject over the predicate either by casting God the Father as the one who "continues to pull the strings" in heaven while his "son" suffers on earth or by stressing the "pure" divinity of Christ as if it were the sacred soul that preserves itself in a kind of mystical detachment ("*Gelassenheit*") from the corruptions of the profane body.[71] Both of these readings avoid "the *monstrosity* of Christ's Incarnation," which Žižek defines as the revolutionary insight that the almighty, universal "God" must become a part of our weak, particular history if it is to have any meaning for us, confined as we are to this finite, spatiotemporal existence.[72] This "incarnation" is "monstrous," or "singular," because in order for the universal to be made available to us completely, it cannot simply be given as another experience of judging some contingent entity as an instantiation of some necessary law, which would thereby remain remote from the experience itself as that by which we are able to judge it and, in the case of suffering, find it wanting. Just as Badiou's Paul sought to overcome the slavery of the law by realizing a love that bears the necessity of obligation within the contingency of its happening, Žižek's Christ makes it possible for us to see suffering as bearing within itself the hoped-for wholeness that is the condition of its mournful brokenness.

This is why Žižek, following Hegel, calls Christ the "vanishing mediator" that makes it possible for one to see our "community of outcasts" gathered amidst the rubble of history as the only true "spiritual community."[73] For Žižek, the monstrous suggestion that "He was made Man" frees us from the torturous thought that there is something more than "Man" and "his" suffering existence. We are freed from our futile hope for a new creation and given license to embrace this less than perfect one in which "every normal thing is a monstrosity" and "there is nothing but bodies and languages" that are destined to fail and falter.[74] At this point, however, Žižek's "shift from subject to predicate," that is, from the divine "He" to human "Man," begins to sound too much like a perverse celebration of suffering itself.[75] Here, Žižek would seem to share with Badiou a surprisingly old-fashioned belief in the "intrinsically redemptive function" of "suffering and martyrdom," which leads one to look upon the suffering masses with the gaze of a kind of sadistic patron.[76]

Žižek's Hegelian reading of Christianity has traded the sovereign subject-God, who is able to neutralize the threat of self-annihilation with "his" power to create ex nihilo, for a narcissistic predicate-God, who sees the suffering of the world as an opportunity to more fully understand "himself" as an object of "his" own perception. "The crucial point," Žižek writes, is that "for Hegel the Incarnation is . . . a move by means of which *God looks at himself from the (disorienting) human perspective*," and this means that "God dies *for himself*."[77] Žižek's God, then, is like those wealthy communities of Christians who take trips to serve and live among the poor in order to learn about the human condition so that they might better understand themselves and return home beating their breasts with self-serving clichés about the inherent unfairness of life or, what Žižek might call, its "ontological incompleteness."[78] It is in this sense that he reads Chesterton's claim that only the Christian God "has himself been in revolt" as expressing the idea that God is revolting against *himself* rather than considering whether it might not be a revolt against the suffering *of the world* that puts God in solidarity with the rest of us.[79]

For Eagleton, Žižek's self-proclaimed "love for the miserable ex-cremental entity called 'man'" might sound a bit too close to the self-satisfied attitude of the tragic hero, "who bows to the inevitable in a spirit of *amor fati*" with a "combination of nihilism and trium-phalism" that allows him to preserve his "infinite freedom" in "the noble-hearted gesture of giving it away."[80] On this account, suffering is inevitable, and therefore the only rational response is to embrace it as an opportunity to prove one's mettle. With this, one joins "Job's comforters" in advising "the ill and infirm to reconcile themselves to their suffering" as an opportunity to gain in virtue, even if the virtue to be gained is one of "egoistic rebellion."[81] According to Žižek, the seemingly meaningless and divinely inflicted suffering of the righteous Job is perhaps the purest expression of the logic of Christianity, which "refuses any 'deeper meaning' that obfuscates the brutal reality of historical catastrophes."[82] It is in the figure of Job, Žižek suggests, that we finally get "all those perverse twists of redemption through suffering, dying of God, and so on, but without God."[83] What we get in the Book of Job is the truly forsaken one, who has been relieved of "the temptation of *meaning* itself" by a God who answers his des-perate questions by simply affirming their status as questions, as if to say, "Yes, that's it. . . . I leave it to you."[84]

Of course, Žižek thinks that he is avoiding the grotesque ra-tionalizations of Job's friends, who speak as if they could discern meaning in his suffering. But does Žižek not shrink from the conver-sation with Job in another direction by giving up on the very idea of meaning altogether? If there is no meaning, then its absence cannot really be suffered. As Eagleton points out, Žižek is right to see that "if Jesus had submitted to his death with one canny eye on his immanent resurrection," he would not have really experienced the horror of mortality, but Žižek fails to understand that Jesus would also not have been troubled by death "if he had given way on his desire—a desire which in his case consisted of that particular species of love known as faith."[85] This is a desire for life in the face of death that is not simply the wish that one might not have to die, but rather it is the conviction that life can, in fact, be brought out of the nothingness of death itself. This is why, for McCabe, it is absolutely essential to read the incarnation and crucifixion through the lens of the Hebrew tradition, to which the Book of Job belongs, and not the other way around, as Žižek explicitly claims to be doing.[86]

The Hebrew "God," according to McCabe, is simply the name for whatever it is that answers the "creation question," namely, "Why *anything* anyway?"[87] It is this radical, ontological challenge (not Žižek's banal, epistemological query, "Why is *this* happening?") that Job presses against God, when he asks, "Why did I not die at birth, come forth from the womb and expire?"[88] And it is in light of this uniquely "Jewish question" that we should understand the Lord's rhetorical response to Job when he finally makes an appearance out of the whirlwind and asks, "Where were you when I laid the foundation of the earth?"[89] Of course, the unspoken answer is, "Nowhere, because I was nothing, that is, I was *not* before the moment of creation." For McCabe, it is this idea that before there was anything, there was quite literally nothing, including all potentiality and actuality, that separates the materialism of Thomas and the Judeo-Christian tradition of which he is a faithful disciple from the Greek cosmology of Aristotle. The latter, McCabe writes, "does not, as Aquinas does, ask the question of *esse*, of the existence of things not over against potentiality but over against nothing."[90] What this means is that one cannot stop at a description of the universe as what Žižek has called "a kind of positively charged void" inhabited by both God and humanity in which both exist to the extent that they are brought from the potentiality of this void into actuality and wherein "suffering" is the name for a kind of unrealized potential that nevertheless speaks the presence of a positively absent universe.[91] For McCabe, such an account would allow us to "lose sight of the Jewish creation question," forcing us "to settle for worshipping an inhabitant of the world, to betray the biblical inheritance and to regress to a worship of the gods; it is a form of idolatry."[92]

Despite his claims to the contrary, then, Žižek's suffering deity is nothing more than another person in the world who must "create a space for creation," as a parent might make space for a nursery in his or her house.[93] This is what Eagleton, following McCabe, has called "the idea of God as Big Daddy," suffering with his creation in the same way that a parent suffers from lack of sleep due to the late-night screams of a sick child.[94] Because the parent and child occupy the same spatiotemporal universe, the latter's language of pain, which McCabe understands to be an extension of the body as "intrinsically communicative," physically competes with the material integrity of the one who must be present to it and, thus, suffer a diminishment of potential at its hands.[95] Once again, in spite of his stated intentions, Žižek's understanding of Christ as revealing a "weak God" leaves creatures locked in an Oedipal struggle with the "big Other" who made them and whom they therefore must kill.[96] McCabe's creator God, by contrast, cannot be "other" to creatures in any competitive way, because this God is not just the cause of a particular creature coming to be such-and-such an entity and not another, in the way that my parents may be responsible for me being the person that I am as wholly distinct from them and all others. Rather, the God of creation "is the reason for everything that is," and therefore "there can be no actual being which does not have the creator as its centre holding it in being."[97]

At this point, however, I have already begun to consider the final question of relevance for any conversation between Marxism and Christianity, which concerns the nature of whatever "new creation" is supposed to follow the painful revolutionary struggle for liberation from our corrupt, contemporary order. In order to bring the present consideration of suffering to a close, though, it is perhaps enough to point out that, on McCabe's account, to ask after the meaning of suffering *as such* is already to have gotten things wrong, even if one is ultimately going to follow Žižek in denying it meaning altogether. The problem is that such questions always assume that the failures of the world, which lay at the root of all suffering, have some status independent of the world itself. As if one could have the world as it is without the failures that so obviously belong to it, such that after asking, "Why failure?," one could stop short of asking, "Why *anything*?" If we truly want to avoid the tendency to explain away "the raw fact of suffering," then we have to take the entire universe, including all its failed potentials and realized actualities, as our starting point and ask, "Why *this*?" Just as every individual must take the finite number of things he or she is along with the infinity of things he or she therefore fails to be and ask not, "Why am I this and not that?," but "Why am I at all?" Or, as Job laments, "Why is light given to one who cannot see the way, whom God has fenced in?"[98]

A NEW CREATION

Before it became fashionable for secular leftists like Agamben, Badiou, and Žižek to turn to Judeo-Christian sources for answers to the challenges of revolutionary politics, Antonio Negri was working on his own reading of the Book of Job and the question of suffering. In the early 1980s Negri was near the end of serving a prison sentence in Italy for being convicted on trumped-up charges of "kidnapping, murder, subversive association, and armed insurrection against the powers of the state," after which he would be released into exile.[99] From behind the bars of his cell, Negri says, the question of suffering was, for him, not one of "merely understanding" but "a practical problem."[100] Like Job, Negri was not interested in explanations of his pain, whether justified by the order of God's relationship to creation or hidden in the radical transcendence of the divine. Rather, he found it necessary "*to go beyond the justification of pain and comprehend the practical transfiguration of pain.*"[101] In spite of the potentially mystifying language of "transfiguration," Negri is actually concerned here with the very straightforward question of how one is to move past the confinement of suffering toward liberation.

I argued above that Žižek's intramundane concern with suffering is actually drowned out by his metaphysical bluster to the point that he no longer engages with it as a "raw fact." What Negri realized in prison is that suffering as such is not that philosophically interesting. As McCabe says, we are *all* "born into a revolutionary situation," which Augustine knew is why "we begin this life not with laughter but with tears."[102] The tears of our infancy are not the metaphysical tears of the well-endowed philosopher writing at his or her desk on a full stomach; they are the more humble cries of one who suddenly feels the pain of embodiment without the language to transcend it. It is this insight that Negri says his experience of imprisonment gave him by bringing his "brain into contact with [his] body," and, like Mc-Cabe, Turner, and Eagleton, he found support for this embodied understanding of liberation in Wittgenstein, for whom the solution to suffering only comes through a "dialogue between bodies."[103] The implication of this is that liberation is not going to come through abstract argument but the through laborious creation of a newly embodied form of existence. Or, as Negri claims, borrowing from the Christian tradition, we must find a way to move "*from exploited labor to the resurrection of the flesh.*"[104]

Once again, in spite of the seemingly abstract talk of "resurrection," Negri is advocating for something that is more banal than Žižek's piety for the Theo-drama by which the universal enters into the profane particularity of history. For Negri, Job's desire for the "resurrection" of bodies "from pain, unhappiness, and death" is as basic as the cries of a newborn child. There is nothing monstrous, or "singular," about it. It does not evince the mysterious "weak power" separating thought from action, as Agamben or Badiou would have it. Rather, it refuses all such dialectics "and understands being only as creation"—that is, "ontology becomes ethics."[105]

From the perspective of Negri's Job, the Messianic promise of resurrection does not serve merely as a critique of all temporal constructions as inherently ideological, but it stands as that which might "help man in his work of justice" by displacing the "fetish" of redemptive suffering as a dialectical phenomenon with the bodily experience of pain as nothing more than a present impediment to life.[106] As Eagleton points out, in the New Testament Jesus spends "much of his time curing the sick," which suggests that suffering is something to be relieved, not dialectically sublimated.[107] And while Badiou may dismiss such miracles as an "extravagant waste of energy," Negri understands that they are the only basis of charity.[108] True charity is miraculous, according to Negri, because it aims at relieving suffering through the restoration of the body, which means that in order to be successful, it must allow "us to participate in the power of creation" by which our bodies were first made.[109] This means that the only true healing emerges from the same source as creation itself, and for McCabe, as we have seen, the traditional name for this source is "God." In a similar way, Negri affirms that when Job confronts God, what Job "sees" is that *creation is the content of the vision of God.*"[110]

The Book of Job succeeds in avoiding an account of suffering that places it within the bounds of calculating rationality, either adding up to or falling short of what might count as a proper explanation, by showing us that the only humane response to the pain of another is the miraculous, creative activity of healing. However, for Negri, when God reveals this truth to Job, "God *is* torn from the absolute transcendence that constitutes the idea of him. God justifies himself, thus God is dead."[111] The idea here seems to be that once we understand that the power of God to which Job has been appealing simply consists in our own capacity to heal one another, God is no longer needed and, as Nietzsche instructed, should therefore be let go.[112] For the moment we can leave aside the fact that, from the point of view of a proper Judeo-Christian doctrine of God, this conclusion is predicated on the false idea that the divine and the human could enter into a relationship of mutual exclusion, as if they shared some common ground over which to compete. From an atheistic perspective, Negri's enthusiasm for the creative power of human beings would seem to leave him with, what Roland Boer calls, "the old revolutionary problem: how do you prevent the revolution from running into the mud."[113]

For this reason, Boer concludes that Negri provides us with "a well-worn Marxist story" based on "Feuerbach's 'discovery' that the gods and all that they entailed were projections by human beings."[114] While this might indeed be a well-worn Marxist story, it is not the entire story that Marx himself tells. As Turner has argued, Marx came to reject this Feuerbachian atheism, which "is a negation of God, through which negation it asserts the existence of man," because "socialism as such no longer needs such mediation. . . . It is the positive self-consciousness of man, no longer mediated through the abolition of religion."[115] For Marx, the atheism of Feuerbach still traded in the same abstractions as the Christianity that it rejected by positing the essence of humanity as an earthly incarnation of the perfections represented in the divine. A true and radical atheism, for Marx, is one in which the very question of God does not arise, because the "sigh of the oppressed creature," which speaks the presence of the absence of divine fullness, has been silenced by the "*real* happiness" and, indeed, "*real life*" made possible by a communism that is no longer predicated on a dialectic of scarcity and surplus, whereby the happiness and, indeed, life of the few is supported by the deprivation of the many.[116] The challenge that Marx places at the feet of both Christian theists and Feuerbachian humanists is to give an account of "God" and "Man" that is not just an abstract projection, predicated on the perpetuation of a state of concrete abjection.

As Marx understood, for the humanist, this challenge will only be met once the critical project of communism is abolished as the goal of revolutionary politics, because the capitalist oppression on which it depends has been overcome. In this way, as Eagleton has argued, to be a Marxist "is more like being a medic. Medics are perverse, self-thwarting creatures who do themselves out of a job curing patients who then no longer need them."[117] And, for Turner, the situation is surprisingly similar for Christian theists. If "God" is not simply going to name that which is lacking in the human, it cannot be the case that there is something "in particular which God's existence explains, as if there were some things it did not explain: just everything whatsoever."[118] "Consequently," Turner continues, "theism stands together with a radical atheism" in rejecting the "fundamentalist God who would be a knowable 'something-in-particular'" along with "the hegemony of a promethean human."[119]

Marxist humanism and Christian theism, then, are united in the provisional relationship they must have to their respective discourses.[120] Just as the former must be prepared to stop speaking of the "dictatorship of the proletariat" when and if the alienating class relations that make the "proletariat" a meaningful category are abolished, the latter reach out for a "God" who is responsible for all that is insofar as it *is* or it *is not*, including the language by which we are able to speak of those things that "are" and those that "are not."[121] It is for this reason that if and when we come to stand in the presence of this "God," we will be in a place that is not simply beyond all language, as if it were the negation of every affirmation, but, as Turner says with reference to Pseudo-Dionysius, we will be in the presence of the one who is "beyond every possibility of affirmation and negation and so beyond the possibility of being in a relation of 'either/or' with anything whatsoever."[122] However, this also means that, although they share the same grammar, Marxism and Christianity ultimately belong "to incommensurable, if not exactly inconsistent kinds of discourse."[123] For Marxism, liberation concerns the possibility of human being as it is within the world, whether happy or unhappy, enslaved or free, healthy or sick. If Christianity is right, however, these oppositions cannot be overcome unless one asks after the reason for the world as such.

As Negri already seems to understand, any movement from sickness to health is going to require not simply an act of negation, which would recognize the latter only in opposition to the former, therefore requiring the continued presence of its absence—that is, the perpetuation of sickness. Rather, true healing requires that one be restored to the fullness of being ex nihilo. This is an act of *creation*, not simply a kind of *causation*. It is not the world as it is brought about out of the potential of its not being, but insofar as it is "over against nothing at all."[124] This means that true liberation would seem to require not just a new order but also a new way of bringing about that order. For Turner, Marxism is doomed to a stance of parasitic irony vis-à-vis the present order insofar as "it can justify its criticism of bourgeois morality only in terms of that morality's incapacity to realize its own truth."[125] This is why the best that Eagleton is able to offer in defense of Marx's supposed determinism is to say that in the event that the present, capitalist order implodes and we are able to build a new political regime, "given what we knew of the causes of the catastrophe, would we not be well-advised to try it this time the socialist way?"[126]

The problem with Marxism is that it "knows but the absence of God. It does not know how that absence is the characteristic form of divine presence."[127] This means that it is only ever able to be silent with respect to the question of *how* it is actually possible to act freely in history. Of course, if one is going to break the deterministic chain of inner-worldly causes that proceed from one order to the next by the logic of alternating takeover attempts, such freedom must be possible. The question is: What reason do we have to hope that it actually is? For McCabe, what differentiates human action from that of other animals is that it participates directly in the power of the divine, which is the only power that is able to bring things about completely independent of all preexistent material—that is, to *create*. "In human freedom," McCabe writes, "we have the nearest thing to a direct look at the creative act of God (apart, says the Christian, from Christ himself, who *is* the act of God)."[128] This last parenthetical statement is important insofar as in most of our activity there is an admixture of a number of material influences that constrain us and keep us from experiencing ourselves as spontaneous creatures. In Christ, on the other hand, we get a look at a completely free person, whose action is motivated by nothing other than the same gratuitous love by which the world was created ex nihilo.

It is for this reason, McCabe argues, that there was nothing necessary in the crucifixion. Jesus did not die for any *cause*, revolutionary or metaphysical. He was not a *means* for the unification of the human and the divine. And, much to the chagrin of some of his followers, he was not the scapegoat sacrificed *in order to* inaugurate and legitimate a new political order.[129] It could even be argued that Jesus was crucified precisely because he refused to serve any function at all. If it was because he refused to contribute anything to the struggle of the Jewish people against their colonial oppressors that they did not greet Jesus as much of a Messiah, it is for the same reason, as Eagleton points out, that Lenin or Trotsky would not have recognized Jesus as much of a revolutionary.[130] For while he certainly did not *oppose* the project of overthrowing the present order, he refused to *identify* his mission with participation in it. In a way, by moving freely and indiscriminately among opposing social groups, he seemed to act as if the revolution had already occurred; at the same time, by continually speaking of a kingdom that is not of this world, Jesus seemed to suggest that the revolution might never come.

For Christians, this "more *and* less" revolutionary mission of Jesus is preserved in the sacramental life of the church.[131] In the ritualization of our everyday, embodied life together, McCabe argues, Christianity offers a "creative interpretation" of our present life in light of the "revolutionary future of the world" revealed in Jesus Christ.[132] These rituals, like the life of Jesus himself, do not give "us the extra will-power needed to keep in line with a moral code," nor do they provide "a pattern of life from which such a code might be theoretically deduced."[133] Rather, as McCabe continues, "they function more as does the experience of literature or drama: providing us with an insight, (but a uniquely authentic insight) into the nature and destiny of man."[134] For example, in the meal of the Eucharist, we participate in "a creative interpretation of all man's attempts to form a community of love symbolized in the common table."[135] This means that the "real presence" in the Eucharist is not primarily about the "transubstantiation" of bread and wine into Christ's body and blood by way of some sort of metaphysical "hocus pocus," but it is about the way in which we all come to share in the same *physical* substance, through sharing the food that makes all animal life possible. Thus, McCabe says, "when a man gives you dinner he is responsible for the existence of a part of you."[136]

When we eat together, then, we should be acutely aware of the way in which we are all "transubstantiating" into one another by means of the food, the substance, and the *"real life"* that we will soon share. In the Eucharist, Christians simply take this one step further by symbolizing a food that is not responsible for only *part* of their existence but for *all* of it. As Turner writes, following Thomas Aquinas, "The only defensible account of eucharistic change is that the whole substance of bread is changed into the whole substance of the body of Christ: what was bread has now become the body of Christ, even though what remains the same in either case is that both are *food*, the one sustaining life for a time, the other sustaining life eternal."[137] It is in the eucharistic meal, then, that Christianity continues to speak of the reality of creation out of nothing, which it claims is visible in the most politically pointless of tasks: eating together.

CONCLUSION

It has been my task in this essay to consider the attempts of contemporary secular leftists and Christian theologians to work together to confront the corruption in our late capitalist societies and to advocate for the needs of its victims as well as to articulate some of the ways that the work of an earlier generation of Christian Marxists, including McCabe, Eagleton, and Turner, might contribute to this conversation. In light of the urgency of the present situation, however, it may seem rather glib to both Christians and Marxists to end with the suggestion that the best way to fight the structural injustices of globalization and to quell the violence of those driven to take drastic measures by the resulting deprivation is to simply sit down for a communal meal. For Marxists, this would seem to lack all of the heroism and righteous anger of those ostensibly successful revolutions of the past. Even if they were to admit that the October Revolution or the Arab Spring did not actually bring about a political paradise on earth, surely breaking a loaf of bread or, for that matter, the birth of a baby to a poor, working couple is not the kind of explosive, world historical event sufficient to loose the economic chains that keep us everywhere bound in relationships of mutual exploitation.

In a similar vein, many Christians would consider McCabe's suggestion that the sacramental life of the church is primarily about our everyday life together to be a radical reduction of its revolutionary firepower. For example, Catherine Pickstock has argued that liturgical rituals are supposed to lead us out of our "fallen, secular reality" and into an alternate "time and space" in which we put on the roles that we live "more intensely than we inhabit our everyday characters."[138] This is to say that the revolutionary potential of Christianity lies not in the degree to which it leads us into a deeper experience of our "secular" lives, but rather that it contributes to the project of revolution to the extent that it promises to free us from this fallen world by radically breaking with the present order. Thus Francesca Murphy worries that McCabe and his fellow "grammatical Thomists" trivialize the divine by locating the meaning of "God" in the contingency and questionability of the created order rather than by proving the classical transcendence of the divine in its sovereign self-subsistence.[139]

For those of us in the relatively affluent parts of the world, it may indeed seem rather "melodramatic" to insist on the radical contingency of creation and to look for God in something as simple as a meal shared among friends.[140] Just as *intellectual* complacency might lead us to conclude with Bertrand Russell that "the universe is just there," it would seem to be our *material* complacency that would lead us to believe that loaves of bread or babies are "just there"—or, what is more likely, that for the right price all of this can "just be there."[141] As I have already pointed out, Marx suspected that the question of God would tend not to occur to those who do not want for their subsistence, and presumably, this is why we are told that "it is easier for a camel to go through the eye of a needle than for someone who is rich to enter the kingdom of God."[142] For those, however, who are less assured of whence and when their next meal will be coming, there is nothing exaggerated about finding cosmic significance in eating. What is more, how much faith would it take to *share* food under such conditions of deprivation? Far from leaving the question of God and the Love that is responsible for creation "unresolved," those who share the substance of that creation, that is, food, in the midst of its lack would seem to evince a conviction more "real" than anything that could be given by means of philosophical proof.[143]

It is for this reason, then, that sharing a meal or welcoming a newborn child, despite the shadows of scarcity cast by the present capitalist order, can be a more flamboyant witness than the most polyphonic doxology—and the longer the shadows, the louder the witness. This is also why many liberation theologians have argued that the Christian faith shows a "preferential option for the poor," and this is not simply because the poor are meant to be the primary recipients of the church's charity but because the poor are the most perfect practitioners of that charity, which is rooted in "belief in God and God's gratuitous love."[144] And this "preferential option for the poor" should not only be at the core of Christianity, but it should also be a defining feature of Marxism, for which the most authentic form of revolutionary solidarity obtains among those who are most aware of their mutual dependence. This is the awareness that Job finds in the last two lines of his response to God, which Negri could not find space for in his romantic celebration of human creativity. As Gustavo Gutiérrez has argued, when Job sees God and says, "Therefore I despise myself, and repent in dust and ashes," he is not declaring his worthlessness in comparison to the majesty of God but apologizing for the very act of lamentation. Reading the original Hebrew text, Gutiérrez says that Job should be translated as saying, "I repudiate and abandon (change my mind about) dust and ashes," which means that "Job is rejecting the attitude of lamentation that has been his until now."[145]

This idea is significant for those secular leftists who are interested in combating the corruption of the present order. To the extent that corruption would seem to be motivated by the belief that one is owed more than he or she has, thereby lamenting the unfairness of his or her state of dependency and longing for the kind of material autonomy that would be immune from such indignities, the realization of the gratuitousness of existence might serve to guard against the sense of entitlement that seeks isolation from one's fellows. If the life of each person is radically and singularly contingent—that is, *created* and not *caused*—then the deprivation of one and the prosperity of another need not be locked into the either/or logic of economic exchange. What the Book of Job shows us, according to Gutiérrez, is that it is despair, not greed, that is the root of our present corruption. It is despair over our losses, which we are tempted to see as the logical consequence of the success of another, that leads us to "the envy that paralyzes reality and tries to put limits to the divine goodness, that leaves no room for generosity and, even worse, tries to take

God's place."[146] For McCabe, when we pass bread around a common table, we break free from the paralysis of envy, which would fix the loaf in a single pair of hands. We, then, give and receive the gift of existence as this food is passed from one to another but possessed by none. And as the bread moves among us we might just speak those words that could serve as a common motto for theists and atheists alike in this revolution: "Thank you."[147]

NOTES

I would like to thank Cyril O'Regan and Katie Ann-Marie Bugyis for their helpful comments on an earlier draft of this essay.

1. Herbert McCabe, "Comment," *New Blackfriars* 48 (1967): 229. McCabe's dismissal caused quite a stir in England and was widely protested. See Simon Clements and Monica Lawlor, *The McCabe Affair* (London: Sheed and Ward, 1967).

2. McCabe, "Comment," 227.

3. Terry Eagleton, *Reason, Faith, and Revolution: Reflections on the God Debate* (New Haven: Yale University Press, 2009), 70.

4. Ibid., 87.

5. Herbert McCabe, *The New Creation: Studies on Living in the Church* (London: Sheed and Ward, 1964), 39; and Terry Eagleton, *The New Left Church* (Baltimore: Helicon Press, 1966), vii–x.

6. Terry Eagleton, *Culture and the Death of God* (New Haven: Yale University Press, 2014), 196–200.

7. See Creston Davis, Introduction to *Paul's New Moment: Continental Philosophy and the Future of Christian Theology*, by John Milbank et al. (Grand Rapids, MI: Brazos Press, 2010), 1–19.

8. Jürgen Habermas and Joseph Ratzinger, *The Dialectics of Secularization* (San Francisco: Ignatius Press, 2006).

9. Giorgio Agamben, *The Time That Remains: A Commentary on the Letter to the Romans*, trans. Patricia Dailey (Stanford: Stanford University Press, 2005); and Alain Badiou, *Saint Paul: The Foundation of Universalism*, trans. Ray Brassier (Stanford: Stanford University Press, 2003).

10. Slavoj Žižek and John Milbank, *The Monstrosity of Christ: Paradox or Dialectic?* (Cambridge, MA: MIT Press, 2009); Milbank et al., *Paul's New Moment*; and Antonio Negri, *The Labor of Job: The Biblical Text as a Parable of Human Labor*, trans. Matteo Mandarini (Durham, NC: Duke University Press, 2009).

11. Žižek and Milbank, *Monstrosity of Christ*, 11. See also John Milbank, *Theology and Social Theory: Beyond Secular Reason* (Cambridge: Blackwell, 1991). Similar Christian genealogies of the West have been offered by the philosopher Charles Taylor, *A Secular Age* (Cambridge, MA: Belknap Press, 2007); the historian Brad S. Gregory, *The Unintended Reformation: How a Religious Revolution Secularized Society* (Cambridge, MA: Belknap Press, 2012); and the literary theorist Thomas Pfau, *Minding the Modern: Human Agency, Intellectual Traditions, and Responsible Knowledge* (Notre Dame: University of Notre Dame Press, 2013).

12. Alasdair MacIntyre, *After Virtue: A Study in Moral Theory*, 2nd ed. (Notre Dame: University of Notre Dame Press, 1984). Here, I am particularly thinking of Gregory and Pfau.

13. Alasdair MacIntyre, "Epilogue: What Next?," in *What Happened in and to Moral Philosophy in the Twentieth Century? Philosophical Essays in Honor of Alasdair MacIntyre*, ed. Fran O'Rourke (Notre Dame: University of Notre Dame Press, 2013), 479–80.

14. For an example of such a hagiography, see George Weigel, *Witness to Hope: The Biography of Pope John Paul II* (New York: Harper Perennial, 2005).

15. Pope Francis, *The Joy of the Gospel: Evangelii Gaudium* (Washington, DC: USCCB Publishing, 2013), §202. Francis responded to claims, mostly made by commentators on the Christian right in America, that he was "a Marxist," by saying, "I have met many Marxists in my life who are good people, so I don't feel offended." See Andrea Tornielli, "Never Be Afraid of Tenderness," *Vatican Insider*, December 14, 2013, www.lastampa.it/2013/12 /14/esteri/vatican-insider/en/never-be-afraid-of-tenderness-5BqUfVs9r7W1 CJIMuHqNeI/pagina.html (accessed June 12, 2014).

16. Herbert McCabe, "Comment," *New Blackfriars* 51 (1970): 451. This assumption is supported by the fact that Pope Francis has not only spoken against the corruptions of secular capitalism but has also taken steps to reform the Vatican Bank as well as the Roman Curia. See David Gibson, "Pope Francis Overhauls Vatican Finances, Names Australian Cardinal as Comptroller," *Religion News Service*, February 24, 2014, www.religionnews.com /2014/02/24/pope-francis-overhauls-vatican-finances-names-australian -cardinal-comptroller/ (accessed June 23, 2014); and Desmond O'Grady, "Can Francis Cure the Curia?," *Commonweal Magazine*, August 31, 2013, www.commonwealmagazine.org/can-francis-cure-curia (accessed June 23, 2014).

17. I do not have space in this essay to engage with the historical-critical accuracy of these interpretations of the Pauline corpus, which, to be sure, stray quite far at times from the concerns of the original author. For com-

mentary of this kind, see John D. Caputo and Linda Martín Alcoff, eds., *St. Paul among the Philosophers* (Bloomington: Indiana University Press, 2009).

18. Badiou, *Saint Paul*, 2. See also Davis, "Introduction."

19. The key texts here are Carl Schmitt, *Political Theology: Four Chapters on the Concept of Sovereignty*, trans. George Schwab (Chicago: University of Chicago Press, 2006); Walter Benjamin, "Critique of Violence," in *Reflections: Essays, Aphorisms, and Autobiographical Writings*, ed. Peter Demetz (New York: Schocken Books, 1978), 277–300; and Jacques Derrida, "Force of Law: The 'Mystical Foundation of Authority,'" in *Acts of Religion*, ed. Gil Anidjar (New York: Routledge, 2002), 228–98. In his contribution to the present volume, David Newheiser takes up this theme indirectly with his discussion of the fragility of love and the threat of violence in Derrida and Meister Eckhart.

20. John Milbank, "Paul against Biopolitics," in Milbank et al., *Paul's New Moment*, 27. Cf. Karl Marx, "Economic and Philosophical Manuscripts," in *Early Writings*, trans. Rodney Livingstone and Gregor Benton (London: Penguin Books, 1992), 375.

21. Denys Turner, *Marxism and Christianity* (Oxford: Basil Blackwell, 1983), 46. Here, Turner should not be understood as endorsing the popular thesis among contemporary moral philosophers that a normative "ought" conclusion can *never* be argued from a set of descriptive "is" premises. Rather, Turner is merely claiming that the process of deducing the normative from the descriptive involves some difficulty, and it is the function of ideology to suppress this difficulty by making it appear that the way things are simply *is* the way that they *ought* to be *without argument*. Cf. MacIntyre, *After Virtue*, 51–61.

22. Badiou, *Saint Paul*, 30.

23. Slavoj Žižek, "Paul and the Truth Event," in Milbank et al., *Paul's New Moment*, 76.

24. Ibid., 79.

25. Ibid., 82. Cf. Agamben, *Time That Remains*, 128.

26. Badiou, *Saint Paul*, 35, 57.

27. John Milbank, "The Return of Mediation," in Milbank et al., *Paul's New Moment*, 225, 215.

28. Ibid., 43. Cf. Agamben, *Time That Remains*, 124–29.

29. Ibid., 48 n. 54, 49.

30. Thomas Hobbes, *Leviathan*, ed. Richard Tuck (Cambridge: Cambridge University Press, 1991), 89.

31. Milbank, "Paul against Biopolitics," 47 ff.

32. Ibid., 64–65. This is in spite of his well-known animus for the radically autonomous subject of political liberalism. Cf. John Milbank, "What

Lacks Is Feeling: Hume versus Kant and Habermas," in *Habermas and Religion*, ed. Craig Calhoun, Eduardo Mendieta, and Jonathan VanAntwerpen (Cambridge: Polity Press, 2013), 322–46.

33. Milbank, "Paul against Biopolitics," 73.

34. Herbert McCabe, *Law, Love and Language* (London: Continuum, 1968), 35–67, 104–25; and Herbert McCabe, *God Still Matters*, ed. Brian Davies (London: Continuum, 2002), 139–51.

35. Here, following the argument of Ludger Viefhues-Bailey's contribution to the present volume on the category "modern religion," one might advocate a shift from an ideology critique of the law as such to one that merely seeks to avoid turning the law into a fetish, perhaps, as Viefhues-Bailey argues, by recognizing its function as a *"dispositif."*

36. Agamben, *Time That Remains*, 108–12. Cf. 2 Thess. 2:8 and 1 John 2:18–22.

37. Terry Eagleton, *On Evil* (New Haven: Yale University Press, 2010), 74, 119–21.

38. Agamben, *Time That Remains*, 135, 95–99.

39. Ibid., 137.

40. Ibid., 23, 26–27.

41. McCabe, *Law, Love and Language*, 30.

42. Eagleton, *On Evil*, 111.

43. Denys Turner, *Julian of Norwich, Theologian* (New Haven: Yale University Press, 2011), 88–99.

44. Ibid., 134.

45. McCabe, *Law, Love and Language*, 30. See also Terry Eagleton, *Trouble with Strangers: A Study of Ethics* (Oxford: Wiley-Blackwell, 2009), 276.

46. Turner, *Julian of Norwich*, 35–38.

47. Cf. Agamben's notion of the "exigent" in *Time That Remains*, 39–43.

48. Turner, *Julian of Norwich*, 41.

49. Ibid., 47.

50. McCabe, *Law, Love and Language*, 26–27.

51. Turner, *Julian of Norwich*, 51. In his contribution to the present volume, Cyril O'Regan more explicitly connects Turner's reading of Julian with Marxist ideology critique.

52. McCabe, *Law, Love and Language*, 135; Julian of Norwich, *The Writings of Julian of Norwich: "A Vision Showed to a Devout Woman" and "A Revelation of Love,"* ed. Nicholas Watson and Jacqueline Jenkins (University Park: Pennsylvania State University Press, 2006), 209. Cf. Turner, *Julian of Norwich*, 35.

53. McCabe, *Law, Love and Language*, 173; Rom. 12:2.

54. Ludwig Wittgenstein, *Philosophical Investigations*, 3rd ed., trans. G. E. M. Anscombe (Oxford: Blackwell, 2001), 152^e.

55. Herbert McCabe, *Faith within Reason* (London: Continuum, 2007), 123–25.

56. Ibid., 123; Herbert McCabe, *The Teaching of the Catholic Church: A New Catechism of Christian Doctrine* (London: Darton, Longman, Todd, 2000).

57. Denys Turner, *Thomas Aquinas: A Portrait* (New Haven: Yale University Press, 2013), 57.

58. Ibid.

59. Terry Eagleton, *Why Marx Was Right* (New Haven: Yale University Press, 2011), 139; Turner, *Thomas Aquinas*, 11.

60. Eagleton, *Why Marx Was Right*, 140–41.

61. Žižek and Milbank, *Monstrosity of Christ*, 176; Milbank, "Paul against Biopolitics," 35. Cf. Giorgio Agamben, *Homo Sacer: Sovereign Power and Bare Life*, trans. Daniel Heller-Roazen (Stanford: Stanford University Press, 1998).

62. Turner, *Thomas Aquinas*, 97.

63. Milbank, "Paul against Biopolitics," 66; Žižek and Milbank, *Monstrosity of Christ*, 122.

64. Žižek and Milbank, *Monstrosity of Christ*, 160–76.

65. Turner, *Thomas Aquinas*, 97.

66. Wittgenstein, *Philosophical Investigations*, 152^e.

67. Slavoj Žižek and Boris Gunjević, *God in Pain: Inversions of Apocalypse*, trans. Ellen Elias-Bursać (New York: Seven Stories Press, 2012), 158.

68. Ibid., 163.

69. Žižek and Milbank, *Monstrosity of Christ*, 248.

70. Ibid., 25. Cf. G. K. Chesterton, *The Complete Father Brown Stories* (Ware: Wordsworth Editions, 2006), 394–95.

71. Žižek and Milbank, *Monstrosity of Christ*, 29, 39–40. Žižek associates the first misunderstanding with Eastern Orthodoxy as it is represented in the theology of Vladimir Lossky, and he locates the second in the Roman Catholic Christology of Meister Eckhart. Needless to say, Žižek is taking a relatively small sample of these two diverse and complex strains of Christian thought, and even then, he his offering a pretty selective reading of these sources. O'Regan makes this point in his review of *The Monstrosity of Christ* with particular attention to Žižek's use of Eckhart. In his contribution to the present volume, O'Regan offers a reading of Turner's interpretation of Eckhart, which suggests that Turner is perhaps more successful than Žižek in both confronting Eckhart's heterodox tendencies and leveraging his liminal status in the Catholic tradition as an example of a self-critique of tradition

that can be simultaneously orthodox and revolutionary. See Cyril O'Regan, "Žižek and Milbank and the Hegelian Death of God," *Modern Theology* 26 (2010): 285.

72. Žižek and Milbank, *Monstrosity of Christ*, 40, 73–82; original emphasis.

73. Ibid., 29; Slavoj Žižek, "A Meditation on Michelangelo's *Christ on the Cross*," in Milbank et al., *Paul's New Moment*, 179–81.

74. Žižek and Milbank, *Monstrosity of Christ*, 88, 92. Žižek borrows the latter phrase from Alain Badiou, *Logiques des mondes* (Paris: Editions du Seuil, 2006), 9.

75. Žižek and Milbank, *Monstrosity of Christ*, 29.

76. Badiou, *Saint Paul*, 65–66.

77. Žižek and Milbank, *Monstrosity of Christ*, 80–81, 237; original emphasis.

78. Ibid., 100.

79. Ibid., 48. Cf. G. K. Chesterton, *Orthodoxy* (San Francisco: Ignatius, 1995), 145.

80. Eagleton, *Trouble with Strangers*, 285–87. In this connection, see Žižek's approving comments about Antigone and Rosa Parks, both of whom he reads as tragic heroes for confronting the inevitability of suffering by choosing to endure it for the most seemingly insignificant and idiosyncratic causes—the funeral of a brother, a seat on the bus (Žižek, "Meditation," 173).

81. Eagleton, *On Evil*, 134; Žižek, "Meditation," 173.

82. Žižek and Milbank, *Monstrosity of Christ*, 55.

83. Slavoj Žižek, "Thinking Backward: Predestination and Apocalypse," in Milbank et al., *Paul's New Moment*, 200.

84. Ibid., 178–79; original emphasis.

85. Eagleton, *Trouble with Strangers*, 287.

86. This is a point that McCabe originally pressed against the so-called God-is-dead theologians, the most prominent among whom is probably Thomas Altizer. In this connection, then, it is significant that Žižek seeks to rehabilitate Altizer's theology in his final response to Milbank. In his review of *The Monstrosity of Christ*, O'Regan claims, "Indeed, it could be argued that Altizer's theology represents the prototype for Žižek's synthesis of genealogy and kenotic Christology." See McCabe, *God Matters* (London: Continuum, 1987), 10–24, 39–51; Žižek and Milbank, *Monstrosity of Christ*, 254–68; and O'Regan, "Žižek and Milbank," 281. For a sustained critique of Altizer, which, it seems to me, could also be applied to Žižek, see Cyril O'Regan, *Gnostic Return in Modernity* (Albany: State University of New York Press, 2001).

87. McCabe, *God Matters*, 42.

88. Žižek, "Meditation," 178; Job 3:11.

89. Job 38:4.

90. McCabe, *God Matters*, 43.

91. *Žižek!*, directed by Astra Taylor (Zeitgeist Films, New York, 2006), DVD.

92. McCabe, *God Matters*, 44.

93. Žižek and Milbank, *Monstrosity of Christ*, 43.

94. Eagleton, *Reason, Faith, and Revolution*, 17.

95. McCabe, *Law, Love and Language*, 91. Here, McCabe is, once again, indebted to Wittgenstein. For a further elaboration of the theological implications of the idea that the body is "intrinsically communicative," see Terry Eagleton, *The Body as Language: Outline of a New Left Theology* (London: Sheed and Ward, 1970). In his contribution to the present volume, Oliver Davies argues for a similarly embodied account of language, drawing interesting connections between Turner's later medieval work and contemporary linguistic theory.

96. Žižek and Milbank, *Monstrosity of Christ*, 55, 297.

97. McCabe, *God Matters*, 44–45.

98. Job 3:23.

99. Negri, *Labor of Job*, xvii; Timothy S. Murphy, "Editor's Introduction: Books for Burning," in *Books for Burning* by Antonio Negri (London: Verso, 2005), ix.

100. Negri, *Labor of Job*, xviii.

101. Ibid., 68; original emphasis.

102. McCabe, *Law, Love and Language*, 147; Augustine, *The City of God against the Pagans*, ed. R. W. Dyson (Cambridge: Cambridge University Press, 1998), 1072.

103. Negri, *Labor of Job*, xx–xxi.

104. Ibid., 47.

105. Ibid., 59, 87.

106. Ibid., 69, 74.

107. Eagleton, *On Evil*, 134.

108. Badiou, *Saint Paul*, 28.

109. Negri, *Labor of Job*, 75.

110. Ibid., 96–97; original emphasis. Cf. Job 42:5.

111. Negri, *Labor of Job*, 96; original emphasis.

112. Friedrich Nietzsche, *Twilight of the Idols / The Anti-Christ*, trans. R. J. Hollingdale (London: Penguin Books, 1990), 148.

113. Roland Boer, "Commentary: Negri, Job, and the Bible," in *Labor of Job*, 121–22, 125. It is worth noting that Boer has produced an exhaustive, five-volume study of Marxism and theology, particularly focused on the ways in which biblical narratives informed the Marxist tradition. See Roland Boer: *Criticism of Heaven: Marxism and Theology* (Leiden: Brill, 2007); *Criticism of Religion: On Marxism and Theology II* (Leiden: Brill, 2009); *Criticism of*

Theology: On Marxism and Theology III (Leiden: Brill, 2011); *Criticism of Earth: On Marx, Engels and Theology* (Leiden: Brill, 2012); and *In the Veil of Tears: On Marxism and Theology V* (Leiden: Brill, 2014).

114. Boer, "Commentary: Negri, Job, and the Bible," 124. Boer cites Karl Marx, "A Contribution to the Critique of Hegel's Philosophy of Right: Introduction," in *Early Writings*, 251.

115. Denys Turner, "Marxism, Liberation Theology and the Way of Negation," in *The Cambridge Companion to Liberation Theology*, ed. Christopher Rowland (Cambridge: Cambridge University Press, 1999), 207. Turner is quoting from Marx, "Economic and Philosophical Manuscripts," 357–58. See also Denys Turner, "Feuerbach, Marx and Reductivism," in *Language, Meaning and God: Essays in Honour of Herbert McCabe*, ed. Brian Davies (London: Geoffrey Chapman, 1987), 92–103.

116. Marx, "Contribution," 244; and Marx, "Economic and Philosophical Manuscripts," 358.

117. Eagleton, *Why Marx Was Right*, 1.

118. Turner, "Marxism," 214.

119. Ibid.

120. O'Regan makes a similar point in his contribution to the present volume when he outlines a "new protocol" for the conversation between Christianity and Marxism, which he says would now consist of "a profound affinity of grammar rather than some freestanding morality which both Christianity and Marxism might be thought to share."

121. On the "dictatorship of the proletariat," see Eagleton, *Why Marx Was Right*, 196–210.

122. Turner, "Marxism," 212. For an extended discussion of the prevalent influence of this doctrine of God in the medieval period, see Denys Turner, *The Darkness of God: Negativity in Christian Mysticism* (Cambridge: Cambridge University Press, 1995).

123. Turner, *Marxism and Christianity*, x.

124. McCabe, *God Matters*, 10.

125. Turner, *Marxism and Christianity*, 247.

126. Eagleton, *Why Marx Was Right*, 63.

127. Turner, *Marxism and Christianity*, 250.

128. McCabe, *God Matters*, 14.

129. See McCabe, *Law, Love and Language*, 133.

130. Terry Eagleton, Introduction to *The Gospels: Jesus Christ*, ed. Giles Fraser (London: Verso, 2007), xxx.

131. Ibid.

132. McCabe, *Law, Love and Language*, 143–45.

133. Ibid., 146.

134. Ibid.

135. Ibid., 149. For an allied discussion of the Eucharist, see Robin Kirkpatrick's essay in the present volume, in which he argues that Dante understood the Eucharist to be not unlike our common experience of eating together: "easy, intimate, and vernacular."

136. McCabe, *New Creation*, 73; original emphasis. On "transubstantiation," see also McCabe, *God Matters*, 116–29.

137. Turner, *Thomas Aquinas*, 240–41; original emphasis.

138. Catherine Pickstock, "Liturgy and the Senses," in Milbank et al., *Paul's New Moment*, 131. See also her *After Writing: On the Liturgical Consummation of Philosophy* (Oxford: Blackwell, 1998).

139. Francesca Aran Murphy, *God Is Not a Story: Realism Revisited* (Oxford: Oxford University Press, 2007), esp. 85–131.

140. Ibid., 132–75.

141. On the intellectual complacency of Russell's refusal to recognize the rational validity of the "creation question," see McCabe, *God Matters*, 5; and Denys Turner, "How to Be an Atheist," in *Faith Seeking* (London: SCM Press, 2002), 3–22. For further discussion of this theme with continued reference to Turner's essay, see Karmen MacKendrick's contribution to the present volume.

142. Matt. 19:24.

143. Cf. Murphy, *God Is Not a Story*, 132–42.

144. Gustavo Gutiérrez, *On Job: God-Talk and the Suffering of the Innocent*, trans. Matthew J. O'Connell (Maryknoll, NY: Orbis Books, 1987), 94.

145. Ibid., 86–87.

146. Ibid., 90–91.

147. For a meditation on the difficulties of saying "Thank you" and the power of the practice of gratitude to unite the atheist and the theist, see Vittorio Montemaggi's contribution to the present volume, which immediately follows this essay.

REVELATIONS
OF
LOVE

FIFTEEN

How to Say "Thank You"

Reflecting on the Work of Primo Levi

VITTORIO MONTEMAGGI

·

It is not always easy to say "Thank you." Difficulties in this regard can stem from our pride and our self-centeredness. So caught up are we in our estimation of ourselves, our actions and our surroundings, that we fail to acknowledge in gratefulness (either inwardly or openly or both) just how dependent we are on others. Difficulties can also stem from a genuine recognition precisely of how inestimable our dependence on others is—so much that our capacities of thought and language accurately to express our gratitude for this are stretched beyond their limit. I regularly fail on account of difficulties of both kinds. But it is failure of the second kind that I feel most characterizes my relationship with Denys Turner and his work. And this is so, not least, because of the way in which, both in person and through his writings, Turner has helped me to appreciate just how important it is for theological reflection to take seriously at all times the possibility of its failing in the first of the two senses above. For ultimately it is only on such grounds that the second kind of failure can be fully and joyfully embraced in our attempts truthfully to live our relationship with the divine.

The main aim of this essay, then, is to say "thank you" to Turner; and one of its primary methodological assumptions is that it will in this respect inevitably fail, the value of the gift received far outweighing that of what I feel I can give in return. The reference to "methodological assumptions" is here deliberate and literal. Indeed, one of the presuppositions underlying the present reflections is that there can be real *scholarly* value in trying to read and write in a spirit of gratefulness, and in recognizing our possible failures in this regard. This is particularly the case when we are dealing with the interpretation of texts by which we are invited to engage with fundamental questions concerning human existence, and even more so with texts of this sort which in turn invite us to make reflection on gratefulness itself a part of our explorations of such questions. For one way of approaching fruitfully interpretation of texts of this kind is to proceed in gratitude for the opportunity they give us to find out or understand more deeply fundamental things about ourselves, and in recognition that gratitude might be one of those things in life that is better understood for being practiced than for being talked about.

One text that calls for this kind of response is Julian of Norwich's *A Revelation of Love*, which invites us to reflect on the all-embracingness of divine love and to participate in this love by gratefully embracing the world it creates—a world which brings with it not only goodness but also all of our individual and collective failures, and which we are nonetheless called joyfully to be part of, in gratitude for it as the "behovely" gift of God, our divine Father and Mother. The text I would like to start with, however, is not strictly speaking Julian's own but Turner's reading of it in his recent *Julian of Norwich, Theologian*.[1] In fact, and to be more precise, I would like to begin from thinking about the relationship between Turner's text and Julian's. For the form of this relationship seems characterized, precisely, by a profound sense of gratefulness: gratitude for the common journey toward the divine that we share with Julian and for the possibility that Julian's text opens up for us to pursue it with her.

In the very first paragraph of his book Turner states, "Because I did not know what I really thought about the theology of Julian of

Norwich's *A Revelation of Love*, I decided to write a book about it."[2]
A rather disarming statement, especially if we consider how it might
be seen to reflect Julian's own theological procedure. Having her
"shewings" as its starting point, and the Short Text as a first stage of
written elaboration, Julian's theology, as presented to us in the Long
Text, is clearly *in via*. Indeed, Julian ends her book by telling us in
the last chapter that "it is not yet performed." We are not presented
with a finished, self-standing theological product but with the living
relationship between Julian and the truths she feels have been revealed to her directly by the Lord, a relationship that neither begins
nor ends with her Long Text but transcends this and gives it meaning
as a particular stage in Julian's journey from, in, and to the divine.
At the same time, as Turner points out, the incompleteness and
open-endedness of Julian's theological performance calls for our own
participation in the continuation of her book. Insofar as the journey
toward the divine is a common one, we are called to learn from each
other as to how it might be best pursued. We are thus invited to allow
Julian's journey to become part of our own and vice versa: "I have . . .
envisaged this whole essay of mine in the spirit of Julian's own invitation to take her thought forward in the same way that the Long Text
was extruded out of the Short. For such elaborations contain no intrinsic principle of finality and can be endlessly continued. In that
sense, in this work of mine, I am doing no more than Julian does in
her Long Text, though it goes without saying that mine is a secondary business of interpretation compared with her primary and constructive theological achievement."[3]

In the same spirit, and in the light of Turner's own book as "not
yet performed," I would like to take some of the perspectives opened
up in *Julian of Norwich, Theologian* as the starting point for reflecting on the work of Primo Levi. The choice might at first appear
surprising. For the world of the Italian author—a Jewish chemist,
atheist, and survivor of Auschwitz—would appear to be far removed
from that of the medieval theology explored by Turner in his book.
And certainly, in many significant respects, it is. But the exercise is,
I think, worth pursuing, not least for theological reasons. There is

much, I would like to suggest, that as theologians we can be grateful for in Primo Levi's work, and reflecting on this in the light of Turner's work can help bring this to light. The choice of reflecting in the present context on Primo Levi is, moreover, a personal one, for it was Turner who first encouraged me to pursue theological reflection in connection with the work of Primo Levi. In this respect, I would also like to acknowledge the debt owed to the theological possibilities opened up by David Burrell's comparative reading, "Assessing Statements of Faith: Augustine and Etty Hillesum."[4]

One immediate point of contact between Turner's book and the work of Primo Levi is the idea that if, as Turner proposes we do, we are to take seriously Julian's idea that sin and the world's evils are "behovely," we also have to accept that "[behovely], then, not 'amisse,' was the bureaucratic, cold efficiency with which the murder of 6 million Jews was planned and executed."[5] This is a startling claim. It does not simply say that it might in principle be possible to set up a theological framework that would allow one to say that the existence of God and the Shoah are not mutually exclusive. (Turner in fact argues against versions of this claim that are based on the so-called free will defense.) It says, rather more strikingly, that Auschwitz actually "fits" in the divine plan, for nothing that occurs could even in principle be "amisse," or fall outside the all-embracingness and power of divine love. This does not necessarily entail the notion that the Shoah was, qua sin and evil, caused by God. But it does entail the notion that God, as creator, was indeed the cause of each of the free human actions that made up the Shoah (and not simply of human freedom as understood more generally). This latter notion relies on the doctrine of evil as privation and on a "distinction between the cause of an action and the cause of its being sinful,"[6] but I will not presume at this stage to articulate further Turner's complex and compelling reasoning on this point.[7] For our present purposes it is sufficient to note that on Turner's reading it would be a mark of theological incoherence for us today to accept Julian's claims concerning the all-embracingness of divine love without also accepting that the Shoah too is part of "the true story of the divine love of Creation."[8]

Primo Levi's thought on this question could not appear to be more different. For Levi, God and Auschwitz are indeed mutually exclusive. This was not the original motivation for his atheism, for Levi had renounced belief already as a teenager, years before deportation: "I did try to find contact with God, but nothing ever came of it. I had been presented with a Ruler God, a punitive God who left me quite unmoved. After that short period of confusion, I cut myself off from him entirely, holding him at a distance like a sort of infantile phenomenon that had little to do with me."[9] But Auschwitz did confirm Levi in his conviction of the absence from the universe of a personal, loving and omnipotent God: "[Either] God is all-powerful or he is not God. But if he exists, and is thus omnipotent, why does he allow evil? Evil exists. Suffering is evil. Thus if God, at his bidding, can change good into evil or simply allow evil to spread on Earth, then God is bad. And the hypothesis of a bad God repels me. So I hold on to the simpler hypothesis. I deny him."[10] Levi's argument too would merit closer analysis than space permits here: especially the prioritizing of omnipotence, the equation of evil and suffering (which we know from some of Levi's other writings that he did not regard as absolute),[11] the strength with which, having prioritized omnipotence, Levi then rejects the idea of God on moral grounds (we also know from some of Levi's other writings that he held that the central ethical imperative is that of creating the least possible suffering, for oneself and for any other creature capable of suffering).[12]

For our present purposes, however, I would like to turn to another important aspect of Levi's atheism and its relationship to his experience of Nazi dehumanization: open-endedness. While Levi remains firm in his atheism throughout his life, the *question* of God never becomes a fully closed one:[13] "I never have been [a believer]. I'd like to be, but I don't succeed. . . . There is Auschwitz, and so there cannot be God. I don't find a solution to this dilemma. I keep looking, but I don't find it."[14] Moreover, throughout his works Levi shows a deep, rich, and increasingly intense relationship with the text of scripture and with the religious and cultural traditions of Judaism.[15] Levi's atheism is not predicated on a rigid rejection of the divine and of religion, as infantile in its closure to mystery as the version of belief Levi distances himself from as a teenager. Neither is it based on an equally infantile notion that scientific explanations can offer satisfactory answers to the fundamental questions concerning existence that drive philosophical and religious inquiry: "Science studies the great machine of the cosmos, it reveals to us bit by bit its secrets, but it gives no answers to mankind's big questions. . . . If you ask science about the 'aims' of life, it will reply: 'Nothing to do with me.' And leave it at that."[16] Levi's atheism seems, rather, predicated on a profound and *living* relationship with a question tied in deep and fundamental ways to his experience of surviving the atrocious suffering of the concentration camps. One of the deeper reasons for Levi's atheism is, in fact, that there cannot be a reason for his survival. He speaks more than once of the "blasphemy" proposed to him by a believer friend of his, that Levi had clearly been predestined to survive, perhaps so that he might write the important testimonial works that he did in fact write. Levi cannot and will not accept this, for if it were true it would mean that he could have been saved instead of someone else. Indeed, in the perverse dynamics and statistics of the camps, one's survival could literally and directly mean the death of another. And Levi had seen perish a great number of human beings worthier and more upright than many of those who survived.

> He [Levi's friend] told me that my having survived could not be the work of chance, of an accumulation of fortunate circumstances (as I maintained, and still maintain) but rather of Providence. I bore the mark, I was an elect: I, the non-believer, and even less of a believer after Auschwitz, was a person touched by Grace, a saved man. And why just I? It is impossible to know, he answered. Perhaps because I had to write, and by writing bear witness: wasn't I in fact then, in 1946, writing a book about my imprisonment?
>
> Such an opinion seemed monstrous to me. It pained me then as when one touches an exposed nerve, and kindled the doubt. . . . I might be alive in the place of another, at the expense of another; I might have usurped, that is, in fact killed.

The "saved" of the Lager were not the best, those predestined to do good; the bearers of a message. What I had seen and lived through proved exactly the contrary. Preferably the worst survived, the selfish, the violent, the insensitive, the collaborators of the "grey zones," the spies. It was not a certain rule (there were none, nor are there certain rules in human matters), but it was, nevertheless, a rule. I felt innocent, yes, but enrolled among the saved and therefore in permanent search of a justification in my own eyes and those of others. The worst survived—that is, the fittest; the best all died. . . .

My religious friend had told me that I survived so that I could bear witness. I have done so, as best I could, and I also could not [not] have done so; and I am still doing so, whenever the opportunity presents itself; but the thought that this testifying of mine could by itself gain for me the privilege of surviving and living for many years without serious problems, troubles me, because I cannot see any proportion between the privilege and its outcome.[17]

Levi addresses this same question in forceful terms at the end of "October 1944," the chapter of *Se questo è un uomo* (If This Is a Man/Survival in Auschwitz) in which he speaks of the "great selection" of that month. After describing how the inmates return to their bunks after the selection, Levi tells us:

Silence slowly prevails and then, from my bunk on the top row, I see and hear old Kuhn praying aloud, with his beret on his head, swaying backwards and forwards violently. Kuhn is thanking God because he has not been chosen.

Kuhn is out of his senses. Does he not see Beppo the Greek in the bunk next to him, Beppo who is twenty years old and is going to the gas chamber the day after tomorrow and knows it and lies there looking fixedly at the light without saying anything and without even thinking any more? Can Kuhn not fail to realize that next time it will be his turn? Does Kuhn not understand

that what has happened today is an abomination, which no pro-
pitiatory prayer, no pardon, no expiation of the guilty, which
nothing at all in the power of man can ever clean again?

If I was God, I would spit at Kuhn's prayer.[18]

How can one thank God for the gift of life when that life means the
death of another? Moreover, given that "part of our existence lies in
the feelings of those near to us,"[19] how can one thank God for the
gift of life when part of oneself is dying with the other?[20]

The way that Levi speaks of Kuhn's prayer at the end of "October
1944" clearly implies his atheism, especially in the reference to "the
power of man." Yet the reference to God with which the chapter
closes carries with it all the force of a compelling theological statement, a statement, that is, which seems to want to direct us toward
better comprehension of what might be required of us to speak truthfully with and about God. This suggestion is reinforced by the way in
which Levi speaks of the same episode later in life, which makes it
clear that at the end of "October 1944" Levi is speaking not only of
Kuhn and his prayer but also about himself.

> I . . . entered the Lager as a non-believer, and as a non-believer
> I was liberated and have lived to this day; actually, the experi-
> ence of the Lager with its frightful iniquity has confirmed me in
> my laity. It has prevented me, and still prevents me, from con-
> ceiving of any form of providence or transcendent justice. Why
> were the moribund packed in cattle cars? Why were the chil-
> dren sent to the gas? I must nevertheless admit that I experi-
> enced . . . the temptation to yield, to seek refuge in prayer. This
> happened in October of 1944, in the one moment in which I lu-
> cidly perceived the imminence of death. Naked and compressed
> among my naked companions with my personal index card in
> hand, I was waiting to file past the "commission" that with one
> glance would decide whether I should immediately go into the
> gas chamber or was instead strong enough to go on working. For
> one instant I felt the need to ask for help and asylum; then, de-
> spite my anguish, equanimity prevailed: you do not change the

rules of the game at the end of the match, nor when you are losing. A prayer under these conditions would have been not only absurd (what rights could I claim? and from whom?) but blasphemous, obscene, laden with the greatest impiety of which a non-believer is capable. I rejected that temptation: I knew that otherwise were I to survive, I would have to be ashamed of it.[21]

Seen in this light, Levi's atheism seems to be predicated on what we might call an ethically motivated rejection of idolatry. (As Levi puts it elsewhere, "You cannot invent your own God for your own personal use. It would not be honest.")[22] In this sense, perhaps, the fact that Levi searches but is not able to find a satisfactory idea of God in which to believe need not be seen as some kind of theological failure as much as the consequence of a radical commitment not to idolatrously fall short of a belief in God that could be true to what the concentration camp had revealed to him about the human condition. In this respect, it is important to note that Levi does not agree with the view that the collapse of human solidarity found in the camps— human beings putting their own survival before that of others— presents us with an honest picture of human nature. Levi believes, rather, that what is revealed by the breakdown of human solidarity in the camps is the imperative to do all that is in our power to do to prevent the creation of contexts in which our "social instincts are reduced to silence."[23] In this sense, the impossibility of believing in God, for Levi, can be seen to stem, in significant measure, from a commitment to believing *only* if this could be done in such a way that it would in no way mean for him to put his own needs and his own life before those of others.

To speak of the relationship between belief, atheism, and idolatry along the above lines clearly brings us into the sphere of another prominent aspect of Turner's work, which finds concise and compelling expression in his Cambridge inaugural lecture, *How to Be an Atheist*,[24] as well as constituting a central feature of his *Faith, Reason and the Existence of God*.[25] And indeed I will turn to this aspect of Turner's work below, and especially to his reflections on the importance of wonder. But in order to lead to this, allow me first to build on what has been said so far by tracing another connection between Turner's *Julian of Norwich, Theologian* and the work of Primo Levi.

One of the texts written by Levi that most forcefully gives voice to the deep and lacerating tensions he lived with, in, and through the guilt of survival is his poem "The Survivor":

to B.V.

Since then, at an uncertain hour
Dopo di allora, ad ora incerta
That agony returns:
And till my ghastly tale is told,
This heart within me burns.
He sees again the faces of his companions
Livid in the first light of day,
Gray by cement dust,
Indistinct in the fog,
Tinged with death in their restless sleep.
At night they pound their jaws
Under the oppressiveness of dreams
Chewing a turnip that isn't there.
"Stand back, away from here, submerged people,
Leave. I did not supplant anyone,
did not usurp anyone's bread.
No one died in my stead. No one.
Return to your fog.
Non è mia colpa if I live and breathe,
And eat and drink and sleep and dress clothes."

4 February 1984[26]

Levi's poem is a paralyzing text.

It is also a remarkable text, crafted with a disarming self-consciousness of its literary and metaliterary character. It begins with the words of Coleridge's Ancient Mariner[27] and ends with a line from Dante's *Inferno* (33.141) which speaks of how the demon which is now Branca d'Oria eats, drinks, sleeps, and dresses in clothes. In explicitly denying any guilt on his part at being alive, against the claims made by the memory of his suffering companions, the survivor equates his existence to that of a traitor whose treachery is so extreme that his soul is already in hell while his body on earth is governed by a demon. Furthermore, the initial citation of Coleridge presents this as the obsessively irreducible burden carried by the survivor, determining the character of his very desire to speak. The poem does not tell us, of course, of the extent to which the survivor's voice might be identified with Levi's own—but it is difficult not to hear in the shift from the third to the first person in line 14 the irruption of Levi's own fraught experience of survival. And this—especially if seen in the light of the Dantean citation—brings us back to *Julian of Norwich, Theologian*.

Indeed, Turner's book can count among its many merits that of presenting us, in chapters 3 and 4, with reflections on Dante's *Commedia* that represent one of the sharpest and most illuminating contributions available to our understanding of the theology of Dante's poem, and especially of its first *cantica*, the *Inferno*.[28] I have argued elsewhere for the theological significance of reflecting on the relationship between Dante and Levi.[29] What I would like to do at present is reflect briefly on some of the theological implications of a comparison between Levi's work and Dante's theology as presented to us in Turner's book on Julian. And here, like Denys, I also need to register my great debt to the theological readings of Dante's poem found in the work of Robin Kirkpatrick, especially in his recent translation of and commentary on the *Commedia*.[30]

At the heart of Turner's reading of Dante is the notion that hell is a place sinners *choose* to inhabit in and through their self-centeredness. I quote at length:

It is a place where sinners, by choice, inhabit their sins and live their lives structured by sin's distorted perceptions of love. That love they have to reject, as being an invasion of some imagined personal space, independent of God, as a violation of their personal freedom and autonomy. But this self-deceived self-affirmation shows up in the refusal of the damned to accept that there can be any narrative other than their own, for they deny that there is, after all, any *divina commedia*. The damned all have their own stories to tell, and *Inferno* tells them. Each of them, from Francesca da Rimini to Ugolino, know that those stories which they each tell of their fates recount not just why they were sent there to hell in the first place—that is, their specific sin—but also why they are held there without term in a condition of sinfulness, for the grip of hell on them is but the grip with which they hold onto their stories, without which they cannot imagine for themselves an identity or reality. They need their stories, stories of their own telling, and they need the misrepresentations that those stories tell. Hell is but the condition consequent upon their ultimate refusal to abandon that need. Hell, then, is the condition not of those who have sinned, for many who have sinned more grievously than Francesca and Paolo are not in hell but in a place of Redemption in purgatory. Hell is the condition of those who do not repent of their stories, who refuse the offer of their revision by the divine love, and insist on living by means of the story that sin tells, the story of the attempt to achieve a self-made significance independently of the story of the divine love.[31]

This, I think, is one of the most accurate statements available concerning the theology of Dante's *Inferno*. But what happens if we try to read it in the light of the dynamics of the way in which Levi places in hell the survivor of his poem, and perhaps himself? Levi's survivor too, in a sense, places himself in hell on the basis of an unrelentingly held narrative centered on his own self, arguably kept in hell by his own generation of it. The poem is clearly not written from a theological perspective. Yet, like the end of "October 1944," it does seem to carry with it the force of a theological statement, raising in the present context the following question: How are we, theologically, to compare Levi's poem with the reading of Dante just quoted? One could perhaps say that as fraught and lacerating as the survivor's con-

dition is, it should nonetheless be seen as an instance of mispercep-
tion that keeps the survivor from God. Indeed, one could offer a
theological rationale for this: unless one were to hold some such
view, then one would in effect be legitimating a sphere of human existence in which the center and meaning of human existence is not
seen as lying in and with God, but with the individual self.

The matter, however, is more complex than this. It is made so by
the fact that what Levi's poem presents us with is a record of lived
experience, the experience of living, and having lived for four decades, with the guilt and shame of being alive instead of someone
else. We are presented, that is, with a text that is an integral part of
its author's living relationship with fundamental truths about *his*
human condition revealed to him in and through unspeakable suffering. The dynamics are not altogether different from those of the
relationship between Julian's "shewings" and her Long Text. The
poem's metaliterary dimension, moreover, suggests that its author intends for us to be drawn into an intertextual conversation the performance of which has (to use Turner's phrase) "no intrinsic principle
of finality." As with Julian's text, we are called by Levi's to share in a
conversation concerning some of the deepest facets of human existence, a conversation the importance of which is not confined by the
contours of any particular, individual moment of it. In other words,
as with Julian so with Levi, we are called to share in a communal reflection concerning nothing other than fundamental truths about the
human condition, and we are asked to do so on the basis of our interaction with writings which can be seen as records of a life lived in
the light of an extraordinary experience which we did *not* share with
their authors.[32] On what authority, then, could we shape our contribution to such reflection in the form of theological judgment or explanation?[33] That is, on what grounds could we offer any kind of
judgment or explanation as to the self-centeredness of Levi's survivor
that might somehow compare him to the characters of Dante's infer-
nal invention? Or, by the same token, on what grounds could *we* offer
any kind of judgment or explanation as to whether and how the
god-centeredness of Julian's text is genuinely divine? How, in other
words, might it be possible for us to determine and compare the

honesty or authenticity of Levi's and Julian's texts and, in turn, assess them from a theological point of view?[34]

The above are not meant purely as rhetorical questions but as carrying something of the kind of tension compellingly highlighted in Julian's text—and thoroughly explored in Turner's reading of it— between the all-embracing mystery of divine love revealed to her and her doctrinal belief in damnation. (Another way of phrasing this question would be to ask what the theological coherence is of Dante's *Inferno* as seen from the perspective of the all-embracing love of the *Paradiso*.)[35] I will not presume to answer them. I would, however, like to suggest that one of the things the theologian can be grateful for in Levi's writings is their forceful reminder of the danger that, as theologians, we regularly run, in thinking about human suffering, of turning into one of Job's friends, presuming we can speak for God and provide theological judgment or explanation where none is actually possible.[36] Through a radical kind of humility and through his radical commitment to telling us, and himself, how *not* to be grateful for one's life,[37] Primo Levi reminds us just how mysterious the gift of life actually is, and how radical a failure it is to structure our belief in such a way that makes us neglect our responsibility not to place our life over that of others. This reminder is particularly urgent for Christian believers, whose failures in this respect toward Jews throughout the centuries have been the cause of unspeakable suffering, as well as a sadly significant part of the historical process that led to the creation of a culture where the un-Christian horrors of Nazi and Fascist anti-Semitism were possible.

Thus approached, Levi's atheism can, predicated as it is on a radical commitment to avoid the self-centered idolatry of placing one's needs before those of others, be seen as presenting the theologian with a fruitful reminder of the importance of *listening*;[38] listening to the other in an attempt to understand rather than judge,[39] and in an attempt to discern as much as possible the extent to which we fail, caught up as we are in our own estimation of things, to recognize in gratitude what others might have to offer us on our common journey.[40] Indeed, should God speak to us out of the whirlwind, we might eventually find ourselves dependent, like Job's friends, on the prayers of those we had presumed to explain. Arguably, it is only on the basis of this kind of humility that it might be possible truly to accept in gratitude the whole of God's creation, and to say of all that exists, including Auschwitz, that it is "behovely."

Levi too believes one should accept in gratitude one's place in the cosmos, respectful of the fact that the mystery in which it originates lies beyond our capacities of thought and language. We have seen above some of the things Levi says about both religious and scientific versions of the presumption of explaining the universe and our place in it. It is significant, in this respect, how he combines the two in speaking about Darwin and his ideas concerning the origin of beauty.

> Darwin had many enemies: he has some still. They were the upholders of religion, and they attacked him because they saw in him a destroyer of dogmas. Their myopia is incredible: in Darwin's work, as in his life, a deep and serious religious spirit breathes, the sober joy of a man who extracts order from chaos, who rejoices in the mysterious parallel between his own reasoning and the universe, and who sees in the universe a grand design. . . . [I]n sharp and almost amusing polemic, directed against the absurd thesis that animals and plants are created beautiful to be admired by human beings, Darwin attains the harmonious beauty of strenuous and rigorous reasoning. Denying man a privileged place in creation, he reaffirms with his own intellectual courage the dignity of man.[41]

We seem to find here an echo of God's words to Job out of the whirlwind, in which Job is confronted with the grandeur of creation, that it was not brought into existence and fashioned simply for the sake of human beings and that the mystery of its origin lies hidden in God.[42] It is also interesting to note the admiration with which Levi speaks of how in Darwin such recognitions coincide with "a deep and serious religious spirit."

Elsewhere, Levi speaks of and invites us to wonder at the mystery of human consciousness, and of the interconnectedness of the whole of existence.[43] At the end of *The Periodic Table*, for example, he tells the story of an atom of carbon, which after centuries of peregrinations and molecular transformations comes to be part of the neural processes which guide his writing hand. He speaks of this final adventure of his atom as "the most secret," and with

> the humility and restraint of him who knows from the start that his theme is desperate, his means feeble, and the trade of clothing facts in words is bound by its very nature to fail.
>
> It is again among us, in a glass of milk. It is inserted in a very complex long chain, yet such that almost all of its links are acceptable to the human body. It is swallowed; and since every living structure harbors a savage distrust toward every contribution of any material of living origin, the chain is meticulously broken apart and the fragments, one by one, are accepted or rejected. One, the one that concerns us, crosses the intestinal threshold and enters the bloodstream: it migrates, knocks at the door of a nerve cell, enters, and supplants the carbon which was part of it. This cell belongs to a brain, and it is my brain, the brain of the *me* who is writing; and the cell in question, and within it the atom in question, is in charge of my writing, in a gigantic and miniscule game which nobody has yet described. It is that which at this instant, issuing out of a labyrinthine tangle of yeses and nos, makes my hand run along a certain path on the paper, mark it with these volutes that are signs: a double snap, up and down, between two levels of energy, guides this hand of mine to impress on the paper this dot, here, this one.[44]

On another occasion, in speaking of the virtues of the work of François Rabelais and of the unexpected affinity he feels with the French author, Levi highlights the significance of the fact that "gigantic above every other thing is Rabelais's and his creatures' capacity for joy. This boundless and luxuriating epic of satisfied flesh unexpectedly reaches heaven by a different route: because the man who feels joy is like the man who feels love, he is good, he is grateful to his Creator for having created him, and therefore will be saved."[45]

We seem to be very far here from Levi's harsh critique of the idea that it might be possible to thank God for having survived death in the concentration camp. Yet we are not very far from the awareness of human suffering and the need to relieve it.

> He [Rabelais] is close to us, chiefly because in this boundless painter of terrestrial joys we perceive the permanent, firm consciousness matured through many experiences that not all life is here. It would be difficult to find a single melancholy page in all of his work, and yet Rabelais knows human misery; he is silent about it because, a good physician also when he writes, he does not accept it, he wants to heal it:
>
> > *Mieux est de ris que de larmes escrire*
> > *Pour ce que rire est le proper de l'homme.*[46]

It is clearly important not to take all the various extracts from Levi's writings referred to above as aimed at presenting a coherent conceptual system. Yet, taken together, they do present us with compelling material for theological reflection. Indeed, I considered above some of the theological implications of that which I referred to as Levi's radical commitment to the rejection of the idolatry of a self-centered prioritization of one's own perspectives over others and the world. What could be suggested now, in the light of the last few passages quoted, is that in fact, at least on Turner's own definition of the term, it might overall be slightly problematic to refer to Levi unambiguously as an "atheist."[47] For Levi certainly does not "find *that the world is* to be a platitudinously dull fact."[48] Indeed, Levi's own work seems in many respects to betray "amazement of intellect, and a sort of primal gratitude of spirit, that there is anything at all, rather than nothing, and that there is any*one* at all, rather than no one, for whom it exists."[49] Needless to say that, in many other respects, the perspectives opened up for us by Levi's work differ greatly from the theology articulated in Turner's. But in this respect—a rejection of idolatry centered on the recognition that we cannot explain but can wonder at the "why" of our existence and that of the cosmos—they are at one. Once again, we find in Levi's writings theological implications to be gratefully received, in this instance the recognition that a certain kind of atheist might be closer to a certain kind of believer than either would respectively be to other, more idolatrous, kinds of atheists and of believers. In a culture that seems in more ways than one increasingly to idolize the very contrast between atheism and belief, this could be a rather important idea to entertain.[50]

One of the main things, then, that, as theologians, we can be grateful for in Levi's work is the possibility it presents us for reflecting afresh, and profoundly, on the ways in which we fail to be as truly open-minded as the mystery of creation calls us to be. At the same time, Levi importantly reminds us—through his painful testimony of the camps and of the guilt and shame of survival—that no genuine relationship with the divine can take the form of neglect of the life, needs, and suffering of others. This should, indeed, be one of the central considerations governing all our attempts to think of, speak about, and relate to the divine, accompanied, as it should be, by the willingness to *listen* to what, beyond our self-centeredness, we might gratefully learn from others and the world. That it might be possible for the atheist and the believer constructively to converge on a fundamental rule of theological grammar might appear surprising.[51] As Levi might put it, however, "it is strange but beautiful that this imperative is reached even when starting from radically different presuppositions."[52]

NOTES

Infinite thanks are due to Eric Bugyis and David Newheiser for their guidance and support and to the participants in "The Trials of Desire and the Possibility of Faith" conference for inspiring exchanges, both formal and informal. I am especially grateful to Bernard McGinn, whose detailed response to the present essay as delivered at the conference opened up extremely fruitful perspectives. I also wish to express warm gratitude to the students in my classes at the University of Notre Dame, Primo Levi: Literature, Ethics, and the Pursuit of Knowledge; Religion and Literature: The Example of Primo Levi; Religion and Literature: In the Light of Job; and Between Religion and

Literature: Meaning, Vulnerability, and Human Existence, for illuminating discussions on the questions addressed here. I am further extremely grateful, for illuminating conversations, to Scott Annett, Ann Astell, Zygmunt Barański, Damiano Benvegnù, Tracy Bergstrom, Piero Boitani, Malaika Bova, Theodore Cachey, Florencia Cano, Jacob Blakesley, Giorgio Capannoli, John Cavadini, Catherine Charlwood, James Cherry, Carlo Cogliati, Ian Cooper, Christian Coppa, George Corbett, Maggi Dawn, Sabrina Ferri, David Ford, Ben Fulford, Innocenzo Gargano, Christopher Gleason, Robert Gordon, Kevin Grove, Geoffrey Hartman, Douglas Hedley, Claire Honess, Lina Insana, Charles Leavitt, Giovanna Lenzi-Sandusky, David O'Connor, Cyril O'Regan, Giuseppe Mazzotta, Giuliano Milani, Christian Moevs, Susannah Monta, Anna Montanari, Daragh O'Connell, Alicia Ostriker, the late Émile Perrau-Saussine, Catherine Pickstock, Tamara Pollack, Russell Re Manning, Tzvi Novick, Riccardo Saccenti, Chiara Sbordoni, Juan Manuel Schvartzman, Regina Schwartz, Janet Soskice, Giovanni Stanghellini, Margie Tolstoy, Matthew Treherne, Giles Waller, Henry Weinfield, John Welle, and Anna Williams. I wish to add a special note of gratitude for the inspiration provided by conversation on Levi and the Shoah with the late Father Theodore Hesburgh, C.S.C., in connection with the development of the Primo Levi Collection at Notre Dame.

1. Denys Turner, *Julian of Norwich, Theologian* (New Haven: Yale University Press, 2011).

2. Ibid., ix.

3. Ibid., xviii.

4. David Burrell, "Assessing Statements of Faith: Augustine and Etty Hillesum," in *Faith and Freedom: An Interfaith Perspective* (Oxford: Blackwell, 2004). In connection with the present essay's reflections on gratitude as openness to creation as mystery, see also the essay by David Burrell in this volume.

5. Turner, *Julian of Norwich*, 61.

6. Ibid., 63.

7. See, e.g., Turner, *Julian of Norwich*, 60–65. See also Herbert McCabe, "Evil," in *God Matters* (London: Continuum, 2005).

8. Turner, *Julian of Norwich*, 66.

9. "God and I," in Primo Levi, *The Voice of Memory: Interviews, 1961–1987*, ed. Marco Belpoliti and Robert Gordon, trans. Robert Gordon (New York: New Press, 2001), 274.

10. Ibid., 275–76.

11. See, e.g., "Versamina," in Primo Levi, *The Sixth Day*, trans. Raymond Rosenthal (New York: Summit Books, 1990).

12. See, e.g., "Against Pain," in Primo Levi, *Other People's Trades*, trans. Raymond Rosenthal (New York: Summit Books, 1989).

13. See also C. Fred Alford, *After Auschwitz: The Book of Job, Primo Levi and the Path to Affliction* (Cambridge: Cambridge University Press, 2009). Alford's book has the merit of arguing for the importance of Levi's engagement with the question of God and of suggesting through this that it would deserve closer theological inquiry. (In other respects, however, the book offers an exceedingly one-dimensional reading of Levi's work, focusing exclusively on the trauma of the Holocaust. See my review in *Journal of Religion* 90, no. 4 [2010].)

14. Ferdinando Camon, *Conversation with Primo Levi*, trans. John Sheply (Marlboro: Marlboro Press, 1989), 63.

15. Four prominent examples of this are the poem "Shemà" which opens *If This Is a Man*, the chapter "Argon" in *The Periodic Table*, the essay "Ritual and Laughter" in *Other People's Trades*, and his novel *If Not Now, When?* See also Nancy Harrowitz, "Primo Levi's Jewish Identity," in *The Cambridge Companion to Primo Levi*, ed. Robert Gordon (Cambridge: Cambridge University Press, 2007).

16. Levi, "God and I," 277.

17. "Shame," in Primo Levi, *The Drowned and the Saved*, trans. Raymond Rosenthal (New York: Vintage, 1989), 82–83. See also "God and I," 275; and Camon, *Conversation with Primo Levi*, 62–63.

18. Primo Levi, *"If This Is a Man" and "The Truce,"* trans. Stuart Woolf (London: Abacus, 1987), 135–36.

19. Levi, *If This Is a Man*, 178.

20. See also, in this respect, Levi's references to John Donne's "no man is an island" in Levi, "Shame," 85–87.

21. "The Intellectual in Auschwitz," in Levi, *The Drowned and the Saved*, 145–46.

22. Levi, "God and I," 273.

23. Primo Levi, "The Drowned and the Saved," in *If This Is a Man*, 93.

24. Denys Turner, *How to Be an Atheist: Inaugural Lecture Delivered at the University of Cambridge, 12 October 2001* (Cambridge: Cambridge University Press, 2002). Also in Denys Turner, *Faith Seeking* (London: SCM, 2002).

25. Denys Turner, *Faith, Reason and the Existence of God* (Cambridge: Cambridge University Press, 2004).

26. Primo Levi, "Il superstite," a poem from the collection *Ad ora incerta*; my translation. See also "The Survivor," in Primo Levi, *Collected Poems*, trans. Ruth Feldman and Brian Swann (London: Faber and Faber, 1992), 64.

27. For a detailed analysis of Levi's relationship with Coleridge's poem, see Lina Insana, "Source Text and Subtexts: Translation and the Grey Zone,"

in *Arduous Tasks: Primo Levi, Translation and the Transmission of Holocaust Testimony* (Toronto: University of Toronto Press, 2009), 56–92.

28. Turner, *Julian of Norwich*, 88–93, 109–15.

29. Vittorio Montemaggi, "Primo Levi and the Tragedy of Dante's Ulysses," in *Christian Theology and Tragedy*, ed. Kevin Taylor and Giles Waller (London: Ashgate, 2011), 53–73. The reader is referred to this essay also for further bibliographical reference in connection with the questions addressed here.

30. Dante Alighieri, *The Divine Comedy*, trans. Robin Kirkpatrick, 3 vols. (London: Penguin, 2006–7). In connection with my reflections here on openness in theological discourse, see also the essay by Robin Kirkpatrick in the present volume.

31. Turner, *Julian of Norwich*, 92.

32. One also has to recall Levi's caution that he, like other survivors who count among the "saved," is *not* a true witness to the utter dehumanization of the camps. See Levi, "Shame," 83–85. It is important to note, too, that this passage immediately follows that in which Levi speaks of his friend's "monstrous" suggestion that Levi's survival was willed by God.

33. One could consider here also how this question might resonate with Levi's words at the beginning of his famous essay on the extreme complexity of judgment and explanation in connection with the question of morality as related to the concentration camp.

> [The] *desire* for simplification is justified, but the same does not always apply to simplification itself, which is a working hypothesis, useful as long as it is recognized as such and not mistaken for reality. The greater part of historical and natural phenomena are not simple, or not simple in the way that we would like. Now, the network of human relationships inside the Lagers was not simple: it could not be reduced to the two blocs of victims and persecutors. Anyone who today reads (or writes) the history of the Lager reveals the tendency, indeed the need, to separate evil from good, to be able to take sides, to emulate Christ's gesture on Judgment Day: here the righteous, over there the reprobates. The young above all demand clarity, a sharp cut; their experience of the world being meager, they do not like ambiguity. In any case, their expectation reproduces exactly that of the newcomers to the Lagers, whether young or not; all of them, with the exception of those who had already gone through an analogous experience, expected to find a terrible but decipherable world, in conformity with that simple model which we atavistically carry within us—"we" inside and the enemy outside, separated by a sharply defined geographic frontier.

Primo Levi, "The Grey Zone," in *The Drowned and the Saved*, 39. From the point of view of Christian theology, Levi's warning might further be taken as a reminder of the urgency not to idolize our talk about Christ, presuming that our understanding of Christ might render our theological discourse invulnerable to apophatic negation. For reflection on the relationship between apophaticism and Christology, see the essay by Philip McCosker in the present volume.

34. I am extremely grateful to Bernard McGinn for suggesting to me the categories "honesty" and "authenticity" as fruitful ones for a comparative reading of Levi and Julian. For the related questions of medieval conceptions of mystical experience and of the construction of authorial personae in medieval texts, see, respectively, the essays by Bernard McGinn and Katie Bugyis in the present volume.

35. Or, as David Ford puts it in referring to the final cantos of the *Inferno* as a test case for theological reflection on hell, "in the face of such frozen, eternal despair, how is joy possible for anyone, anywhere?" See David F. Ford, "Tragedy, Theology and the Discernment of Cries," in Taylor and Waller, *Christian Theology and Tragedy*, 240.

36. The Book of Job is, in fact, a centrally important text for Primo Levi. See Primo Levi, *The Search for Roots: A Personal Anthology*, trans. Peter Forbes (Chicago: Ivan R. Dee, 2002), 3–21. It is of particular interest to note how in introducing the Book of Job to his readers, Primo Levi tells us that "Job the Just, degraded to an animal for an experiment, comports himself as any of us would, at first he lowers his head and praises God ('Shall we receive good at the hand of God, and shall we not receive evil?'), then his defences collapse. Poor, bereft of his children, covered in boils, he sits among the ashes, scraping himself with a potsherd, and contends with God. It is an unequal contest: God the Creator of marvels and monsters crushes him beneath his omnipotence" (11). Particularly striking in the present context is the idea that Job behaves "as any of us would." One might perhaps be tempted to object, on the grounds that it is conceivable that someone (perhaps ourselves) might behave in a different way. But perhaps Levi is saying something different, namely, that if one does not behave as Job does, then one has not yet suffered as Job does: the protest before God as integral part of the suffering condition of Job and the presumption to think otherwise as only possible from outside that condition of suffering. While Levi himself does not refer to it, God's final approval of Job and reproach of his friends in chapter 42 could, indeed, be seen theologically to support this kind of reading.

37. On the question of life, and the denial of life, see also the essay by Karl Hefty in the present volume.

38. See also the exploration of the importance of the art of listening in Levi's work found in Robert Gordon's essay, "Storytelling," in Robert Gordon, *Primo Levi's Ordinary Virtues: From Testimony to Ethics* (Oxford: Oxford University Press, 2001), 237–54.

39. As Moni Ovadia puts it, "Primo Levi has taught us that understanding is more important than judging." *Vai a te stesso* (Turin: Einaudi, 2008), 74 (my translation). I am grateful to Giorgio Capannoli for pointing me to this text.

40. One could fruitfully consider here how this openness to the other might enter into dialogue with an emphasis on particularity such as found in the poetry of Gerald Manley Hopkins, and as explored in the essay by John Hare in the present volume. I am also extremely grateful for the discussion on particularity as it developed during our conference. In connection with this question, and in specific relation to a Christian understanding of prayer, one could turn once again to Turner's work: "Jesus told the parable of a man who had a devil cast out of his soul. No doubt delighted and relieved the man tidied up his soul, swept it out quite clean, put everything back in order, whereupon the devil cast out returned with seven devils to occupy him, and the last condition of the man 'was worse than the first' (Matt. 12.45; Luke 11.26). So much so for the vanity of human hopes and plans. I think that the story could be thought of as a story of the person who looks for the Spirit in himself, as the place of privileged access. So I say again: the Spirit is the love which binds us together in bonds of charity; that is why if you cannot find the Spirit in every other person, whatever you find in yourself, it will not be the Spirit of Jesus" ("Waiting for the Spirit," in Turner, *Faith Seeking*, 114–15).

41. "Why Are Animals Beautiful?," in Levi, *The Search for Roots*, 25.

42. On beauty, awe, and mystery, see also the essay by A. N. Williams in the present volume.

43. For further theological reflection on the relationship between self, mind, body, and world, see the essay by Oliver Davies in the present volume. On the interconnectedness of all things, as seen in the light of the mystery of the relationship of the cosmos to the divine, see the essay in the present volume by Mary-Jane Rubinstein.

44. Primo Levi, "Carbon," in *The Periodic Table*, trans. Raymond Rosenthal (New York: Everyman's Library, Alfred A. Knopf, 1995), 241.

45. Levi, "François Rabelais," in *Other People's Trades*, 136.

46. Ibid., 136–37.

47. On the nature of belief, see also the essay by Karmen MacKendrick in the present volume.

48. Turner, "How to Be an Atheist," in *Faith Seeking*, 22.

49. Ibid., 22. I take it, of course, that the "for" in this last sentence does not mean to intend that all that is was created for human beings but is rather in line with the wonder at the mystery of consciousness also expressed by Levi in "Carbon."

50. On the related question of the relationship between religion, theology, and ideology, see the essay by Ludger Viefhues-Bailey in the present volume. See also, in the present volume, the essay by Terry Eagleton.

51. On the question of theological grammar, as seen from a Christian perspective and in specific relation to the work of Denys Turner, see the essay by Cyril O'Regan in the present volume.

52. Levi, "Against Pain," 196.

SIXTEEN

Sitit Sitiri

Apophatic Christologics of Desire

PHILIP McCOSKER

FROM "APOPHATIC RAGE" TO "CHRISTOLOGIA NEGATIVA"

The predilection for apophatic or negative theology in theological writing of recent decades is undeniable. One might even say that the kinds of theological tendencies which are gathered under the—variously defined—umbrella of "apophaticism" have defined much recent theology and constitute one of its most interesting areas of growth.[1] It is my contention, however, that theology's rediscovery of apophaticism is in its adolescence. By this I mean to say that it is reaching an exciting, yet murky, stage of its development.

A major developing gain of second order reflection on apophaticism is the fact that we are now talking about apophaticisms in the plural. We have now realized that apophaticism comes in various shapes and sizes. Denys Turner's book *The Darkness of God* broke crucial ground in this regard.[2] There he brilliantly and captivatingly argues that a variety of apophaticisms can be read as the various parsings of the confluence of two sources, the one biblical, Moses's encounter with God on Mount Sinai, and the other philosophical, the allegory of the cave, yielding various construals of the dialectical metaphors of darkness and light, ascent and descent, so important to theologians with the apophatic bug. It is important to note that he does not intend to suggest that these two sources do *in fact* account for all the apophaticisms that there are but rather, simply, that these two sources *could* be used to understand many of them; they are a useful heuristic tool for analyzing those texts which he looks at.[3] In this way it is more of an analytical approach than a primarily historical one, a possible taxonomy rather than a definitive or historical one, its aim pedagogical and eye-opening. Similarly, this essay contrasts some possible partial readings of three theologians to highlight different possible ways of interlinking apophasis and desire with Christology. The readings I present—especially of Bonaventure and Meister Eckhart—are thus intentionally heuristic rather than exhaustive.

Significant for our purposes is the fact that Turner refuses to posit a diremption between apophatic and kataphatic theology. He argues, rather, that these should not be seen as exclusive opposites, and therefore alternatives, but rather as complementary (in some complicated way) in any good theology. So he argues that Julian of Norwich's riotous affirmations are ultimately aiming in the same direction as Meister Eckhart's radical negations, for instance: both are ways of embodying and bringing to the fore the limitations of human language when aimed at that unique subject, God, albeit in different ways. Attention to different kinds of difference and opposition, especially in connection with issues of inclusion and exclusion, is one of the greatest gifts Turner gave me in preparing my doctoral thesis.[4] It is worth noting at the outset that for the first systematic theoretician of opposition, Aristotle, *apophasis* and *kataphasis* are the very words he uses for his definition of mutually exclusive and collectively exhaustive opposition, namely, contradiction.[5] As we shall see, the noxious temptation to construe the relation between God and creation as one of contradiction—"apophatically" in the Aristotelian sense—is never far away.

Turner's analytic taxonomy of apophaticisms is complemented by other possible ways of parsing the plurality of apophatic theologies.

There are taxonomies which focus on textual[6] or linguistic strategies,[7] yet others which have a more historical or genealogical approach,[8] especially genealogies of different Dionysianisms,[9] as well
as the very useful, more expansive and textured aetiological taxonomy
of Bruce Milem.[10]

What is striking about these taxonomies of apophaticism is that
they are rarely *theologically* driven. Rarely is the structure and dyna-
mism of a particular kind of apophaticism described as doctrinal or
in theological terms. What I mean is that different kinds of apophaticism have not been linked with various parsings of a particular theological doctrine, other than the doctrine of God *tout court*. This is
what I am going to try to do in a tentative and exploratory way in this
essay. If Christ is our way to the knowledge of God, and that God is
in some way not immediately available to us, but only through some
complex concurrence of veiling and unveiling, then is it not likely
that Christology would be a fertile locus for accounts of apophaticism and more precisely of the relation of apophaticism to kataphati-
cism? Such Christological modulations of apophaticism may also
affect how one might conceive of desire in relation to what is created
and what is uncreated.

There are various possible ways of exploring the apophatics of
Christology. One route is conciliar, arguing, following the lead of Walter Kasper, that the definition of Chalcedon, supposedly the summit
of Christological reflection, in fact "does not express any metaphysical
theory about Christ, but contents itself with a *christologia negativa*
which safeguards the mystery."[11] Thus theologians such as Gregor
Maria Hoff and Sarah Coakley have emphasized the "apophatic" nature of Chalcedon in various ways. Coakley notes that Chalcedon
does not define its terms, or their interrelations, and that it leaves a
whole series of questions unanswered, describing the Christological
union ultimately in the paradoxical string of alpha-privative adverbs:
expressing its positive contribution negatively, and by negating the
positive views it deems heretical in its anathemata.[12] Hoff adds some
other functional aspects of this Chalcedonian apophaticism: the bish-
ops did not want to produce a definition at all, and when they did
so they produced an "aporetic configuration" which was capable of

being fleshed out in several different ways (aporia and plurality being significantly linked).[13] In this way one could well agree with Jaroslav Pelikan that, pace the Gospel writers, the most significant question for the conciliar tradition is in fact not "Who do you say that I am?" (e.g., Mark 8:29) but rather "Who do you say that I am not?"[14]

Other than this conciliar route one might consider a more properly biblical route for considering apophatic Christology. Denis Edwards has pursued this line in a little-known article in which he looks at the sayings of Jesus, in particular the proverbs and parables, and notes the central role which mystery plays not only in his teaching but also in his life and death. He argues that the concerns of the historical Jesus, construed as "surrender in trust into God's future, letting God be God," significantly overlap with those of the apophatic tradition.[15]

A further route might be to try to bring the postmodern fascination with apophaticism into dialogue with Christology. This is a route taken by Lieven Boeve.[16] He wishes to avoid any and every Christolatry by emphasizing Jesus Christ as a central locus of revelation and reference in the mediation of God to the world: Jesus always exceeds and points beyond himself. This he does by emphasizing that Christianity is an "open narrative," a concept he develops in dialogue with postmodern thinkers of difference reacting to the hegemony of grand, totalizing, master narratives of modernity. Christ as the revelation of the *deus semper maior* is an open wound in such narratives, showing us that he himself and the God he reveals constitute an open, because living, narrative. As such our speech about God cannot be absolute because it must remain necessarily open. Boeve goes on to read the Chalcedonian definition in this way, emphasizing that its metaphors must be kept in the tension between expression and inexpressibility to avoid becoming dead.[17]

APOPHATIC CHRISTOLOGICS OF DESIRE

In what follows I wish to begin to sketch out a further path, not exclusive of these earlier attempts at exploring Christological apophaticism, yet distinctive in emphasis. Taking a cue from a passage at the end of Turner's *The Darkness of God*, I want to see whether the paradoxical, aporetic doctrinal skeletons of Chalcedon and possibly other councils can be linked up with the apophatic "rhythm of affirmation, negation and the negation of the negation,"[18] seeing, with Turner, the "apophatic" tradition in its fullness not simply as a strategy of negation, but as a way of coordinating affirmations and denials (and hence a creaturely logic of either/or) within a wider theological emphasis on God as the negation of negation (and hence a creatorly logic of both/and). Can this shape be expressed (weakly or strongly), or even lost, Christologically? And can we then say something about the workings of desire in these contexts: might desire have a Christologic? Can such a logic fail?[19] To do so we will look at a small sample of writings from the mystical theologians so fond of the apophatic and so productively engaged by Turner in his recent writings: Bonaventure, Meister Eckhart, and Maximus the Confessor.[20] These will enable us to make some comments relating apophatic Christologies to the trials of desire, the overall theme of this book.

Bonaventure

At first blush it would seem that Bonaventure should prove to be a model of the mutual dependency of apophaticism and Christology. Christ lies at the heart of his account of mystical ascent in his *Itinerarium Mentis in Deum*. Christ crucified forms an *inclusio* framing the beginning and end of that *Itinerarium*. As he begins his meditation on the pilgrimage of the believer to God, Bonaventure calls on the "pater luminum" who is the source of all illumination, and focuses our mind on the image of Christ crucified: "With Christ I am nailed to the cross. I live, not now I, but Christ lives in me" (Gal. 2:20). Significantly for our purposes Bonaventure situates the pilgrim as a person of desires: "No one is in any way disposed for divine contemplation that leads to mystical ecstasy unless like Daniel he is a man of desires."[21] Those desires, at least in this initial phase, are generated both negatively, by groaning in our hearts (Ps. 37:9), and positively, by "flash of insight" which turns the mind "most directly and intently towards the rays of light." A dialectic of desire, one might say.

Thereafter, once the journey into the stages of ascent is commenced, the first three chapters, the first three wings of the seraph, consider ascent to God via the traces to be found in creation, in the universe, the sense world, and in the *imago Dei* within us. A journey from without to within and thence "upward" to God. This relies on what has been called Bonaventure's "semiotic ontology" whereby, dependent on a strong doctrine of *creatio ex nihilo*, and hence of an understanding of God's transcendence such that the creator God, characterized by infinity of power and radical difference from all which he creates, is immanent in what he creates by very virtue of that creatorly transcendence. As Bonaventure says, God "is in" the vestiges: "est in eis." It is only because there is a causal link between God and the world (of a very peculiar kind) that the latter can begin to ponder the former; as cause God "contains" the creation as it were enfolded within himself. According to Bonaventure, humans are able to perceive intimations of that "enfoldedness" in the "unfoldedness" of creation. In this way, for Bonaventure, creation is a symbol, a sign, and a sacrament of the creator, all of which combine, in a precisely paradoxical way, continuity and discontinuity. It is the discontinuity between creator and creature which enables any continuity. It is God's difference which enables all creaturely differences. God does not exclude creation here, precisely to the contrary.

Toward the end of the text Bonaventure considers God's name in Exodus 3:14 as "Ego sum qui sum." For Bonaventure "being itself is so certain that it cannot be thought not to be."[22] Bonaventure gets to its certainty by a "top-down" method: since being is better than nonbeing, pure being must be thought to be the best, and therefore exist, for nonbeing and mixed being are only known through higher being, or being in potency only through being in act: repeated "knowings" lead one up to the highest, pure, being: "purus actus."[23] This pure being is beyond particular *and* universal being: it is "extra omne genus."[24] This means, paradoxically, that it contains all genera without displacing any. Because we are used to considering and seeing entities which are in one or more earthly genera we tend not to note the all-encompassing genus, the "supreme Being," and when we do glimpse it, it is as if we "see nothing" (*nihil videre*).[25] God can be all or nothing depending on one's point of view.

GOD'S SHEER UNITY enables a series of nonexclusive paradoxes unfolding from it: "for Being itself, is first and last; it is eternal and most present; it is utterly simple and the greatest; it is most actual and most unchangeable; it is most perfect and most immense; it is supremely one and yet all-inclusive."[26] Because it is first, it must also be last, that is, beginning and consummation. God's supreme unity is the cause of all essences, and his power is consequently infinite. Bonaventure notes that in this divine paradox of excessing unity, God is "utterly simple and the greatest," so that he is "the same time . . . center and circumference." Again, because of this peculiar unity God is outside *and* inside everything, like "an intelligible sphere whose center is everywhere and whose circumference is nowhere."[27] Although, and because, immutable, God gives rise to movement in all else. God's unity and immensity means that he is "within all things, but not enclosed; outside all things, but not excluded; above all things, but not aloof; below all things, but not debased."[28]

This inclusive paradoxicality continues when Bonaventure considers God with the lens of Dionysian self-diffusive good as revealed by Jesus and the Trinity. Just as before this "superexcellent goodness" leads to further paradoxes in Bonaventure's view: "supreme communicability with individuality of persons, supreme consubstantiality with plurality of hypostases, supreme configurability with distinct personality, supreme co-equality with degree, supreme co-eternity with emanation, supreme mutual intimacy with mission."[29] Mereological considerations are not appropriate to God, for "whatever is possessed is given, and given completely"—and vice versa, one might add.[30]

More significantly for our purposes, Bonaventure then instructs us to compare the paradoxes of the considerations of the two cherubim in turn with the "superwonderful union of God and man in the unity of the Person of Christ": in this conjunction lies "the perfection of the mind's illumination," and the mind can rest, for it has seen the exaltation of humanity in the union of the trinitarian paradoxes and those of Christ: "the first and the last, the highest and the lowest, the circumference and the center, the Alpha and the Omega, the caused and the cause, the Creator and the creature, that is, the book written within and without [Rev. 5:1; Ezek. 2:9]."[31]

This perfection and rest that are attained near the end of the text allow the *transitus* to be effected, and Christ is the way, door, ladder, and vehicle for this.[32] More precisely, however, and in an *inclusio* with the beginning of the text, it is Christ *crucified* as contemplated by Francis who is the Passover: where he leaves us is precisely where we go to follow him to the Father: to the cross.[33] In doing so we are to leave behind all intellectual activity, and "the height of our affection must be totally transferred and transformed into God."[34] Here, as Bonaventure's text closes, darkness and silence fall, cognitive operations fail (even more). Most significantly, at the end, Bonaventure's Christological paradoxicality fails him in the *transitus*: he tells us that we must "leave behind" all that is human.[35] In the end we are to seek "God not man," and not—by implication—both.[36] Bonaventure seems to give in here, at the very last point, to a logic of contradiction and exclusion. Our desire for God trumps or displaces our creaturely desires and the latter are, by implication, cut off from the former. Bonaventure's careful Chalcedonian apophasis and erotology lurches, at the last, in a noxious miaphysite direction. One might say the cross trumps the resurrection and ascension.

This is at least a *possible* reading of Bonaventure's *Itinerarium*.[37] An apparently Chalcedonian Christologic, based on a radical and therefore inclusive understanding of God's transcendence/difference, appeared to be governing his account of the ascent of the soul to God but is then trumped at the end by a Christologic which is less than (or even anti-) Chalcedonian. In the end a miaphysite tendency seems to win out, and this can be mapped onto our map of desires: at the summit of ascent for Bonaventure it seems, ironically given his excellent doctrine of creation and sense of creation reflecting the creator, that our creaturely desires must be supplanted and displaced by a pure and exclusive desire for God, with all that this implies.

Meister Eckhart

Arguably the outworking of this failure to maintain Chalcedonian balance is to be seen clearly in the work of another apophatic author Denys Turner has frequently promoted in his writings: Meister Eckhart. Turner has been keen to bring to the fore Eckhart's ability— through his particular emphasis on God's radical transcendence as *unum indistinctum*—to purify and cleanse lesser theologies of idolatrous clutter.[38] And this Eckhart does magnificently. But surprisingly frequently in Eckhart's sermons, especially the German ones, there is a one-sidedness to this doctrine of God which turns out to displace the creaturely and human to the point where it *appears* to imply a lopsided Christology. Just as Bonaventure seems, at least on one possible reading of the end of his *Itinerarium*, to drop the human and the creaturely and imply an ultimate zero-sum between God and the creaturely, so too does this same sense emerge from many of Eckhart's texts.[39]

Indeed, one could adduce many texts to bring to the fore this kind of tendency. There is a real sense for Eckhart in which God and creatures—again surprisingly given his understanding of the nature of God—cannot coexist. So, for instance, he tells us "light and darkness cannot co-exist, or God and creatures: if God shall enter, the creatures must simultaneously go out."[40] So if we are to become one with God we must lose our identity: "if God and your soul are to become one, your soul must lose her being and her life."[41] In order to be united with God we are to become nothing: "Since it is God's nature not to be like anyone, we have to come to the state of being nothing in order to enter into the same nature that He is. So, when I establish myself in Nothing and Nothing in myself, uprooting and casting out what is in me, then I pass into the naked being of God."[42] In undergoing this we leave behind the world and the creaturely: "Man has a twofold birth: one into the world, and one out of the world, which is spiritual and into God."[43] Eckhart emphasizes the point: "you must be pure of heart, for that heart alone is pure that has abolished creatureliness."[44] And in case there were any doubt as to the zero-sum game, Eckhart tells us point-blank: "Where the creature stops, God begins to be."[45] Yet again: "Do you know why God is God? He is God because he is without creature."[46] Consequently, "that man alone is pleasing to God who is detached and removed from all transient beings."[47]

Where does this leave our relations with, and desires for, creaturely realities, especially other persons, our friends and loved ones?[48] Eckhart gives us an idea: "For you should know that there, in the unity, there is neither Conrad nor Henry. I will tell you how I think of people: I try to forget myself and everyone and merge myself, for them, in unity."[49] He underlines again that "spiritual and material things cannot be united."[50] Our creaturely identities and all that goes with them appear to be impediments for Eckhart in the path to union with God. "You should wholly sink away from your youness and dissolve into his Hisness, and your 'yours' and His 'His' should become so completely one 'Mine' that with Him you understand His unbecome Isness and His nameless Nothingness."[51] Although it is true that many of these texts are drawn from German vernacular sermons which Eckhart may have largely preached to Beguine communities,[52] and that he may be exaggerating his position to correct some exaggeration in his congregation's thought or practice, as Oliver Davies argues when he says that his words are frequently aiming to achieve "cognitive transformation within his audience," it nevertheless seems that this particular dynamic is so widespread that it cannot all be solely rhetorical.[53]

Where, you might well ask, is the Christologic here? Again, as with the very end of Bonaventure's *Itinerarium*, it seems, by implication, that there is a miaphysite trumping of humanity by divinity in the background of these texts by Eckhart, a zero-sum game between divinity and humanity which sits ill with a Chalcedonian insistence on the preservation of the integrity of both natures in the incarnate Christ.[54] By extension the logic of desire here is that one should, insofar as one is to desire anything given Eckhart's emphasis on nothingness and the impeding nature of anything individuating, solely desire union with God and not anything creaturely. Creaturely realities, by the logic seen above, cannot lead to God. Here the trial of desire is to suppress or switch off our creaturely desires and faculties.

It would be wrong to allege that Eckhart does not have a Christology, or that it cannot be parsed so as to be seen to be more consonant with the aporetic conciliar tradition, but nevertheless the dynamic identified in the texts above sits ill alongside such a Christology and indicates a failing Christologic of desire, however much one might point to other texts in Eckhart where a "functional" Christology of divinization is arguably more present.[55]

Maximus the Confessor

Maximus's Christology stands at the peak of the patristic struggles for an articulation of the mysterious identity of the Christian savior. A few texts by the martyred monk are suggestive here, starting with *Ambiguum* 10 in which Maximus is meditating on the Transfiguration of Jesus. Strikingly, Maximus maps the relation of affirmations, negations, and apophasis onto Christology: we get an astonishing sense of the Christologic of apophaticism here, and hence of a Christologic of desire.[56] For Maximus the more Christocentric one is, the more apophatic one is.[57]

The text is an extended commentary on a snippet from Sermon 21 by Gregory of Nazianzen, itself a paean of praise to Athanasius. Maximus is worried that Nazianzen's text might suggest that we can reach God by reason alone without the practical ascetical struggle which targets all which "hides" God, that by passing "through" matter and the fleshly we might be blessed by an "ascent from here." In dwelling on the detail of the Matthaean and Lucan accounts which emphasize that both Jesus's face and garments were transfigured, Maximus makes a number of points, but most significantly a distinction between what he calls the "two universal modes of theology."[58] The first is that which is "pre-eminent and simple and uncaused" and which "through sole and complete denial truly affirms the divine, and fittingly and solemnly exalts its transcendence through speechlessness": the dazzling radiance of Christ's face in the transfiguration leads the disciples and us to acknowledge God's transcendence of all. Christ is himself here the knowable revelation of the unknowable God. Second, there is that knowledge which "follows" and "is composite, and from what has been caused magnificently sketches out [the divine] through affirmation." By this latter kind of knowledge we can know "that the accumulated mighty works of the sensible order" are the work of the creator, and we "form conjectures concerning the knowledge of God and say that he is all that we can deduce from the fact that he is the cause of all that he has made."[59]

Again a little later in the text Maximus reiterates that the light from Christ's face "conquers the human blessedness of the apostles by a hidden apophatic theology" by which they realize that "the blessed and holy Godhead is by essence beyond ineffability and unknowability and countlessly raised above all infinity, leaving not the slightest trace of comprehension to those who are after it . . . since the uncreated is not naturally contained by creation, nor is the unlimited comprehended by what is limited."[60] Likewise "the affirmative mode[,] . . . starting from the beauty and magnitude of the creatures, introduces the explanation that the God of all is the fashioner, this is shown through the radiant garments of the Lord, which the Word shows to be the manifestation of creatures."[61]

Christ here in his transfiguration is seen to point in two "directions" at once: to the transcendence of God above all concepts and speech but at the same time to his immanence as creator in all that he has created and which depends on him.[62] Maximus tells us that God has, in his *philanthropia*, made himself a "type and symbol of himself" in order to "lead all creation to himself."[63] Maximus's interpretation of the presence of Moses and Elijah at the transfiguration fits into this in a number of possible ways. Maximus suggests that Moses represents the Law he received, and therefore represents the scripture. The presence of the effulgent Logos is to be found in the scriptures: the Logos in the *logoi* of the sacred texts. But not only in scripture: Elijah represents, at least in part, the revelation of God in the works of nature. In this way the written and natural law bespeak the God who as Logos speaks through them and is continually embodied.[64] Note that it does not seem that Maximus is here proposing various alternative routes to God, as it were, through Christ, or scripture, or nature. Rather the situation of the explanation within a meditation on the transfiguration shows that it is Christ who reveals the theophanic nature of God's economy so that we can perceive it in its many all-encompassing aspects. God cannot be excluded from anything.

So far we might take from this that Maximus is highlighting a Chalcedonian conjunction of divine and human, uncreated and created in Christ, as especially made manifest at the transfiguration, which should lead us to affirm the integrity and validity of both in our quest for God: we do not see here Maximus leaving the human or creaturely behind in a progressive abstraction and dialectical progress to God, as some receptions of the Dionysian impulse have suggested and a dynamic I tried to highlight in Bonaventure and Eckhart above. So far, so Chalcedonian. But we can go further, I believe, and see in faint outline another Christological structure in Maximus's thought too, a Constantinopolitan supplement to this Chalcedonian logic.

For Maximus it is God who takes the initiative in all this. It is by his *philanthropia* that we encounter Christ, and thereby God in this world, in the embodiments of the Logos in the *logoi* of scripture and nature, and indeed in virtuous action. For Maximus our knowledge of God, which is participatory, involves us being grasped by God. A "soul can never attain the knowledge of God unless God Himself in His condescension takes hold of it and raises it up to Himself. For the human intellect lacks the power to ascend and to participate in the divine illumination, unless God Himself draws it up."[65] This is what God is doing in the whole economy, and it is this encounter with God in Christ which reveals the continual embodiment of God in the *logoi* of creation. Maximus argues for a Christological apophatic epistemology here. In following the pattern of Christ's life we must bury our intellect: "all intelligible realities need burial[,] . . . the total quiescence of the things which act upon them through the intellect." All realities, he says, "need the cross." Once this is achieved, then "the Logos, who exists alone in himself, appears as if risen from the dead. He encompasses all that comes from him."[66] We see here how Maximus's account of our knowledge of God follows a narratival Christologic as well as the Chalcedonian logic outlined above (narrative and metaphysics are definitely not exclusive, as some appear to think), whereby the creaturely is safeguarded and seen as revelatory in the light of the divine. But we also see here how the priority of the Logos in "encompassing" our knowledge and concepts, in encompassing the creaturely, reveals the deeper Christological parsing of Chalcedon by Constantinople, where it is clarified that Christ's human nature does not have its own hypostasis but is rather anhypostatic qua human, and enhypostatic in the Logos. The Chalcedonian symmetry is ultimately predicated on the Constantinopolitan asymmetry. Such a combination of creaturely realities, logics, and desires, within the divine life, must be based on a radical conception of God's transcendence which grounds a strong doctrine of creation. We have seen how this can be seen to break down on possible readings of some texts by Bonaventure and Eckhart above.

If we translate all this onto the landscape of desire we could say that for Maximus our seeking of God depends on and springs from God's seeking of us. Our desire for God is a function of his desire for us: *sitit sitiri*, God thirsts to be thirsted for, desires to be desired.[67]

One can see an illustration of this dynamic within a text encapsulating the belief which led to Maximus's several exiles, torture, and eventual martyrdom, but a belief which his defense ultimately inscribed into Christian orthodoxy, namely, the doctrine of Christ's two wills. In his *Opusculum* 6, dating from about AD 641, Maximus emphasizes not only that Christ is "made known" in two natures, as Chalcedon had insisted, but also exists *as* those two natures: "he maintains all the while the difference between the two natures from which, in which, and which he is by nature."[68] Moreover, in this text Maximus sees the clearest instantiation of the consequences of this, namely, the insistence on Christ's two wills, dyotheletism, in the agony in the garden of Gethsemane. For Maximus Christ's "Not what I will" is an essential element in the cosmic drama of redemption. It is vital for Maximus that the subject who speaks the phrase is the "man whom we consider as Savior" and that thus there is "harmony between the human will of the Savior and the divine will shared by him and his Father." The human will has been deified and actively assents to the Father's redemptive *philanthropia*. By following Christ's virtuous example as presented by Maximus we are enabled to participate in this redemption. But, crucially, our doing so involves us doing so as full, integral humans, including all our desires. We are to turn our desires to God's desire for us by imitating Christ's deployment of his human will and desire in assenting to the Father's philanthropic plan of redemption.[69]

CONCLUSION

I have undertaken some readings of a few texts from mystical and apophatic theologians and their attendant Christologies to see if I could pick out various logics of desire, in tandem with the theme of this volume. Thus I traced in Bonaventure's *Itinerarium* a valiant attempt to maintain the paradoxical balance of the Chalcedonian aporetic Christologic which frames and centers Bonaventure's description of the stages of ascent of the *mens* to God and which depends on a radically apophatic understanding of God's transcendence. Christ, and Christ crucified, frames the text. However, I argued that this paradoxical balance was ultimately and surprisingly lost at the end of the text when Bonaventure tells us we should desire God and not man. Here we saw Bonaventure's paradoxical apophatic ascent undone by a final trumping of the creaturely by God. Here creaturely desires must be left behind; we are to seek God alone. God and creation appear, at the last, to be exclusive of each other.

I went on to see this dynamic maximized and set in full relief in some of Meister Eckhart's German sermons. A full displacing, zero-sum dynamic was seen at play here when Eckhart time and again emphasizes that God and the creaturely cannot mix and that consequently we must desire to minimize, even do away with, all that is creaturely and individuating, so as to enable God to enter in. We, and all that goes with us, including our desires, clearly get in the way. So again it turns out to be a matter of desiring God alone and not the creaturely. In Eckhart's case Chalcedonian Christology is arguably sidelined, so his is a Christologic of desire only negatively, by being an undone Christologic of desire: Chalcedon, at least on the basis of the few texts we looked at here, is very much in the background and plays little role in his ascetical theology. This is ironic given the nature of Eckhart's doctrine of God which appears to set him up to argue for the nonexclusion of God from any aspect of creaturely life. Eckhart's thus seems to be a Christologic of desire manqué.

Finally, I turned to Maximus the Confessor, finding both a Christological parsing of negative theology through the lens of the transfiguration and a full Christologic of desire found in the garden of Gethsemane: the full safeguarding of the integrity of the human nature of Christ, and therefore our own, within the divine philanthropic plan of redemption. I argued that this Chalcedonian emphasis on symmetry as evidenced in Maximus's championing of dyotheletism is significantly predicated on the asymmetry of divine initiative, the latter, however, crucially not displacing the former. Truly in Maximus's Christology we see that our desiring of God is a result of, and a response to, God's saving desire for us. It is only by being fully human that we can journey to God.[70]

I am tempted to make a few further, even more rash, comments about the historical trajectory I have sketched. I started with Bonaventure in the thirteenth century and then moved on with Eckhart to the fourteen century and ended up with Maximus in the seventh. Could one argue that the varying integrations and coordinations of the range of theological subdisciplines we have been looking at more or less in tandem here—humanity, divinity, creation, christology, desire, and negative theology—have become harder and harder over time, and that what I have traced, however incompletely, is one aspect of the fragmentation of the theological whole? One might provide as evidence of such a reading the way in which these theological areas became increasingly treated separately, for instance, in the way in which John of the Cross's magnificent apophaticism found in *The Dark Night*, advising us to "desire . . . satisfaction in nothing[,] . . . to be nothing[,] . . . [to have] the knowledge of nothing,"[71] needs to be supplemented by the account of the incarnation and redemption found in his *Romanzas*?[72] Elsewhere, in sixteenth-century France, we come across the immolationist sacrificial spirituality of Charles de Condren, radicalizing Pierre de Bérulle's ideas of the multiple creaturely *néant* and his spirituality of *annéantissement*, which advocates one of his correspondents to desire nothing, to "stop being so that He [the Son] can be."[73] Thereafter we see the kind of logic behind these views appearing in Christological form in the radical kenotic Christologies of the nineteenth-century kenoticists, which, after some divagations following on from the initial debates between Johannes Brentz and Martin Chemnitz in the seventeenth century to do with Lutheran construals of the *communication idiomatum*, and then via the multiple construals of kenosis in Gottfried Thomasius and Johannes Ebrard, end up with W. F. Gess arguing that in order to become incarnate the Son must "give up all divine attributes."[74] Could there be a clearer statement of a zero-sum between God and the creaturely? Such views make the Christological views of the late John Hick, one of Turner's predecessors at Birmingham, seem rather less avant-garde than has been supposed.[75] Once we get to our present circumstances, it has become novel, even sexy, to talk about desire in theology or indeed about negative theology precisely because of that fragmentation.[76] What was once theologically integral has become marginal and attractive precisely because apparently marginal. If this is right, then it may go some way to explain why we have found the better integration of our themes in the earlier, less fragmented theology of Maximus.

Rooting out idolatrous conceptions of God has been one of the many beneficial lessons I have learned from Denys Turner so far. I hope that in trying to pick out some of the possible consequences of such views of God in these Christologics of desire I may have gone a tiny bit of the way to reciprocating that gift, with much gratitude and indeed love.

NOTES

1. I take the phrase "apophatic rage" from Martin Laird, "'Whereof We Speak': Gregory of Nyssa, Jean-Luc Marion and the Current Apophatic Rage," *Heythrop Journal* 42 (2001): 1–12.

2. Denys Turner, *The Darkness of God: Negativity in Christian Mysticism* (Cambridge: Cambridge University Press, 1995).

3. Ibid., 11.

4. For more on different differences and oppositions, see my *Christ the Paradox: Expanding Ressourcement Theology* (Cambridge: Cambridge University Press, 2016), chap. 1 passim.

5. See Aristotle, *Categories*, 10–11, but also *Metaphysics*, 5.

6. William Franke, *On What Cannot Be Said: Apophatic Discourses in Philosophy, Religion, Literature, and the Arts*, 2 vols. (Notre Dame: University of Notre Dame Press, 2007).

7. Michael Sells, *Mystical Languages of Unsaying* (Chicago: University of Chicago Press, 1994).

8. Deirdre Carabine, *The Unknown God: Negative Theology in the Platonic Tradition: Plato to Eriugena* (Leuven: Peeters, 1995); and Deirdre Carabine, "*Apophasis* East and West," *Recherches de théologie ancienne et médiévale* 55 (1988): 5–29.

9. Jan Miernowski, *Le Dieu néant: Théologies négatives à l'aube des temps modernes* (Leiden: Brill, 1998).

10. Bruce Milem, "Four Theories of Negative Theology," *Heythrop Journal* 48 (2007): 187–204. A structurally similar taxonomy is given in Paul Rorem, "Negative Theologies and the Cross," *Harvard Theological Review* 101 (2008): 451–64.

11. Walter Kasper, *Jesus the Christ*, trans. V. Green (London: Burns & Oates, [1974] 1976), 238.

12. Sarah Coakley, "What Does Chalcedon Solve and What Does It Not? Some Reflections on the Status and Meaning of the Chalcedonian 'Definition,'" in *The Incarnation: An Interdisciplinary Symposium on the Incarnation of the Son of God*, ed. S. T. Davis, D. Kendall, and G. O'Collins (Oxford: Oxford University Press, 2002), 143–63.

13. Gregor Maria Hoff, "Chalkedon im Paradigma Negativer Theologie: Zur aporetischen Wahrnehmung der chalkedonensischen Christologie," *Theologie und Philosophie* 70 (1995): 355–72.

14. Jaroslav Pelikan, "'Who Do You Say That I Am'—Not? The Power of Negative Thinking in the Decrees of the Ecumenical Councils," in *Who Do You Say That I Am? Confessing the Mystery of Christ*, ed. John Cavadini and Laura Holt (Notre Dame: University of Notre Dame Press, 2004), 17–31.

15. Denis Edwards, "Negative Theology and the Historical Jesus," *Australasian Catholic Record* 60 (1983): 167–85.

16. Lieven Boeve, "Christus Postmodernus: An Attempt at Apophatic Christology," in *The Myriad Christ: Plurality and the Quest for Unity in Contemporary Christology*, ed. T. Merrigan and J. Haers (Leuven: Peeters, 2000), 577–93.

17. See also, in a similar vein, William Greenway, "Chalcedonian Reason and the Demon of Closure," *Scottish Journal of Theology* 57, no. 1 (2004): 56–79.

18. See Turner, *Darkness of God*, 268.

19. Desire has recently become a topic of Christological interest. See, e.g., Jan-Olav Henriksen, *Desire, Gift, and Recognition: Christology and Postmodern Philosophy* (Grand Rapids, MI: Eerdmans, 2009), esp. 27–38. In fact he is partly dependent on the earlier work of the monk of Downside Abbey, Sebastian Moore: *Jesus the Liberator of Desire* (New York: Crossroad, 1989). It will be clear that my approach here differs from Henriksen's considerably. For yet another different approach, see Catherine Keller, "Forces of Love: The Christopoetics of Desire," in *Who Is Jesus Christ for Us Today? Pathways to Contemporary Christology*, ed. Andreas Shuele and Günter Thomas (Louisville, KY: Westminster John Knox, 2009), 115–33. For a different argument about the colocation and entanglement of creaturely desires and desire for the creator, see Sarah Coakley, *God, Sexuality and the Self: An Essay "On the Trinity"* (Cambridge: Cambridge University Press, 2013).

20. I use "mystical theology" in the loose sense adopted by Denys Turner as signifying a theology which unites speculative *and* experiential concerns. See Turner, *The Darkness of God*, 168.

21. *Itinerarium* Prologue.

22. *Itinerarium* V.3.

23. *Itinerarium* V.3.

24. *Itinerarium* V.4.

25. *Itinerarium* V.4.

26. *Itinerarium* V.7.

27. *Itinerarium* V.8. On the origins and multiple appearances of this image, see Sarah McNeil Powrie, "The Infinite Sphere: The History of a Metaphor in Theology, Science and Literature (1100–1613)" (PhD diss., University of Toronto, 2006) and its bibliography.

28. *Itinerarium* V.8.

29. *Itinerarium* VI.3.

30. *Itinerarium* VI.3.

31. *Itinerarium* VI.7.

32. *Itinerarium* VII.1.

33. *Itinerarium* VII.2–3.

34. *Itinerarium* VII.4.

35. *Itinerarium* VII.5.

36. *Itinerarium* VII.6 ("Deum, non hominem").

37. In kind response to this essay Oliver Davies rightly noted that a fuller reading of these texts would take into account their different natures, audiences, and purposes: Eckhart's German sermons are not the same genre as Maximus's scriptural meditations or other *opuscula*. While I agree entirely that such performative concerns should ideally be taken into account, I do not think doing so would alter the fundamental doctrinal point I am after.

38. See, e.g., Denys Turner, *Faith, Reason and the Existence of God* (Cambridge: Cambridge University Press, 2004), 162–68.

39. For a fascinating analysis of von Balthasar's ambivalence toward Eckhart which makes a similar point to mine, see Cyril O'Regan's rich study, "Balthasar and Eckhart: Theological Principles and Catholicity," *The Thomist* 60 (1996): 203–39. O'Regan traces the origin of the difficulty I am highlighting to Eckhart's promotion of *intelligere* over *esse* with a consequent rejection of analogy.

40. Texts from Meister Eckhart's German sermons are quoted from *Sermons & Treatises*, ed. M. O'C. Walshe, 3 vols. (Shaftesbury: Element, 1987), giving the volume number followed by the page number, here I, 17.

41. Walshe, I, 52.

42. Walshe, I, 66.

43. Walshe, I, 67.

44. Walshe, I, 116.

45. Walshe, I, 118.

46. Walshe, I, 220.

47. Walshe, II, 201.

48. I do not agree with the interpretation of Eckhart's spirituality of "abandon" as the other side of the same metaphysical coin as Thomas's spirituality of desire given by Giuseppe Barzaghi. See his "Desiderio e abbandono: Tommaso d'Aquino e Maestro Eckhart: le due face di un'unica metafisica," in *Metafisica e desiderio*, ed. Claudio Ciancio (Milan: Vita e Pensiero, 2003), 173–201. For Thomas's understanding of desire, see Gianmarco Stancato, *Le concept de désir dans l'œuvre de Thomas d'Aquin* (Paris: Vrin, 2011). Despite its title Nicholas Lombardo's *The Logic of Desire: Aquinas on Emotion* (Washington, DC: Catholic University of America Press, 2011) is actually rather more about the overall framework of desire for Thomas than desire itself. His reflections on boredom at the end of the book are most suggestive.

49. Walshe, II, 226.

50. Walshe, II, 263.

51. Walshe, II, 333.

52. On Eckhart's vernacular preaching, see Bernard McGinn, "Meister Eckhart and the Beguines in the Context of Vernacular Theology," in *Meister Eckhart and the Beguine Mystics* (London: Continuum, 1994), 1–14.

53. Oliver Davies, *Meister Eckhart: Mystical Theologian* (London: SPCK, 1991), 196. I am very grateful to Oliver Davies and Bernard McGinn for their spirited defense of Eckhart in discussion.

54. Eckhart does not achieve the Chalcedonian balance of Hadewijch of Antwerp when she is addressed in her tenth vision thus: "Behold, this is my bride, who has passed through all your honours with perfect love, and

whose love is so strong. . . . Behold, Bride and Mother, you . . . have been able to live me as God and Man!" (in *Hadewijch: The Complete Works*, ed. Columba Hart [New York: Paulist, 1980], 288). For a description of this phase in Hadewijch's account of ascent, see Bernard McGinn, "Suffering, Emptiness and Annihilation in Three Beguine Mystics," in *Homo Medietas: Aufsätze zu Religiosität, Literatur und Denkformen des Menschen vom Mittelalter bis in die Neuzeit. Festschrift für Alois Maria Haas zum 65. Geburtstag*, ed. Claudia Brinker-von der Heyde and Niklaus Largier (Bern: Peter Lang, 1999), 155–73, esp 160–61.

55. Eckhart's Christology is a controverted part of Eckhartian scholarship, with many scholars attempting to defend him from Christological crossfire. See Richard Schneider, "The Functional Christology of Meister Eckhart," *Recherches de théologie ancienne et médiévale* 35 (1968): 291–322; Richard Woods, "'I am the Son of God': Eckhart and Aquinas on the Incarnation," *Eckhart Review* 1 (1992): 27–46; Édouard-Henri Wéber, "Le Christ selon Maître Eckhart," in *Christ among the Medieval Dominicans*, ed. Kent Emery and Joseph Wawrykow (Notre Dame: University of Notre Dame Press, 1998), 414–29; Bernard McGinn, "Was Eckhart Christologically Challenged?," *Eckhart Review* 8 (1999): 29–47; and Bernard McGinn, *The Mystical Thought of Meister Eckhart* (New York: Crossroad, 2001), 115–27. I should emphasize again that I am not claiming to give anything like a full account of Eckhart's theology but simply to highlight a particular logic found in some portions of his German sermons.

56. For another use of Maximus to think through desire Christologically, see Aaron Riches, "Deification as Metaphysics: Christology, Desire, and Filial Prayer," in *Belief and Metaphysics*, ed. Conor Cunningham and Peter Candler (London: SCM, 2007), 245–71.

57. For Maximus's apophaticism, see the very suggestive article by Iain McFarland, "Developing an Apophatic Christocentrism: Lessons from Maximus the Confessor," *Theology Today* 60 (2003): 200–214; as well as J. Williams, *Denying Divinity: Apophasis in the Patristic Christian and Soto Zen Buddhist Traditions* (Oxford: Oxford University Press, 2000), chap. 5; Andrew Louth, *Maximus the Confessor* (London: Routledge, 1996), 51–54; and Ysabel de Andia, "Transfiguration et théologie négative chez Maxime le Confesseur et Denys l'Aréopagite," in *Denys l'Aréopagite et sa posterité en Orient et en Occident: Actes du Colloque International, Paris, 21–24 septembre 1994*, ed. Ysabel de Andia (Paris: Institut d'Études Augustiniennes, 1997), 291–326.

58. *Ambiguum* 10.31b, in Andrew Louth, *Maximus the Confessor* (London: Routledge, 1996), 131.

59. Ibid., 131–32.

60. Ibid., 132–33.

61. Ibid., 133.

62. On these themes in Maximus, see Adam Cooper, *The Body in Maximus the Confessor: Holy Flesh, Wholly Deified* (Oxford: Oxford University Press, 2005), chaps. 1–3. One could say this pointing-in-two-directions-at-once is the "shape" of analogy.

63. *Ambiguum* 10.31c, in Louth, *Maximus the Confessor*, 132.

64. Famously Maximus tells us that "the Word of God and God wills always and in all things to accomplish the mystery of his embodiment" (*Ambiguum* 7, in *On the Cosmic Mystery of Jesus Christ: Selected Writings from St Maximus the Confessor*, ed. Paul Blowers [Crestwood: St Vladimir's Seminary Press, 2003], 60).

65. *Centuries on Theology*, I.31, in *The Philokalia*, trans. and ed. G. E. H. Palmer, Philip Sherrard, and Kallistos Ware (London: Faber and Faber, 1981), 2:120.

66. Ibid., I.67: *Philokalia*, II, 127.

67. The phrase "*Deus sitit sitiri*" (God thirsts to be thirsted for) is often attributed loosely to Augustine but is in fact to be found in Gregory of Nazianzen, *Oration* 40.26. Often found in eucharistic contexts in churches, I first came across it on an altar frontal at St. Aloysius, Woodstock Road, Oxford.

68. *Opusculum* 6, in *On the Cosmic Mystery*, 174.

69. For more on Maximus's complex treatment of desire and other human passions, see two excellent articles by Paul Blowers: most recently his "The Dialectics and Therapeutics of Desire in Maximus the Confessor," *Journal of Early Christian Studies* 65 (2011): 425–51; and his earlier "Gentiles of the Soul: Maximus the Confessor on the Substructure and Transformation of the Human Passions," *Journal of Early Christian Studies* 4 (1996): 57–85.

70. For a similarly Maximian but differently focused account of desire, see Eugene Rogers, *Sexuality and the Christian Body* (Oxford: Blackwell, 1999), e.g., 227–36 passim.

71. John of the Cross, *Ascent of Mount Carmel* 1.13.11, in *The Collected Works of St John of the Cross*, ed. Kieran Kavanaugh and Otilio Rodriguez (Washington, DC: Institute of Carmelite Studies, 1991), 150. For interesting reflections on these verses in connection with the theme of idolatry, see Michael Buckley, *Denying and Disclosing God: The Ambiguous Process of Modern Atheism* (New Haven: Yale University Press, 2004), 108–19. For an analysis of John's erotology, see Christopher Hinkle, "Love's Urgent Longings: St John of the Cross," in *Queer Theology: Rethinking the Western Body*, ed. Gerard Loughlin (Oxford: Blackwell, 2007), 188–99.

72. There are obviously exceptions, the most obvious being Nicholas of Cusa who integrates Christology and apophaticism magnificently. See Peter

Casarella, "*His Name Is Jesus*: Negative Theology and Christology in Two Writings of Nicholas of Cusa from 1440," in *Nicholas of Cusa on Christ and the Church*, ed. Gerald Christianson and Thomas M. Izbicki (Leiden: Brill, 1996), 281–307; and now Knut Alfsvåg, *What No Mind Has Conceived: On the Significance of Christological Apophaticism* (Leuven: Peeters, 2010), chap. 6.

73. See his letter to Sœur Angélique de Jésus: "Laissez-vous à lui, sans vous regarder et sans écouter vos dispositions ni votre état, et sans désir d'être ou d'avoir, et sans prendre vie ni être dans les dispositions soit de Dieu ou de péché ou de nature qui se passent en vous; mais laissez être le Fils de Dieu en vous en tel état qu'il lui plaira et en telle manière qu'il voudra, et vous, cezzez d'être afin qu'il soit" (*Lettres du Père Charles de Condren [1588–1641]*, ed. Pierre Auvray and André Jouffrey [Paris: Cerf, 1943], 25–26). For more on de Condren's ideas of sacrifice and destruction, see Vincent Carraud, "De la destruction: Métaphysique et idée du sacrifice selon Condren," in *Il Sacrificio*, ed. Jean-Luc Marion, Stefano Semplici, and Pierluigi Valenza, Archivio di filosofia 76/1–2 (Pisa: Fabrizio Serra, 2009), 331–48.

74. On all this, see T. R. Thompson, "Nineteenth-Century Kenotic Christology: The Waxing, Waning, and Weighing of a Quest for a Coherent Orthodoxy," in *Exploring Kenotic Christology: The Self-Emptying of God*, ed. C. Stephen Evans (Oxford: Oxford University Press, 2006), 74–111; and my "Emptying Kenosis," *Reviews in Religion and Theology* 14, no. 3 (2007): 380–88.

75. See his in/famous essay "Jesus and the World Religions," in *The Myth of God Incarnate*, ed. John Hick (London: SCM, 1977), 167–85, here 178. In fact Hick was not the first to use the analogy of circles and squares to talk of Christ's two natures, Baruch Spinoza was. See his "Letter to the most noble and learned Henry Oldenburg" (dated ca. 11 or 12/1675), Letter 73, in *Spinoza: The Letters*, ed. Samuel Shirley (Cambridge: Hackett, 1995), 333.

76. Desire is a popular topic in contemporary theology. Most frequently it is treated in an undifferentiated way. For interesting reflections which start to treat desire's polyvalence in a nuanced way, see the useful philological work of Giles Pearson, *Aristotle on Desire* (Cambridge: Cambridge University Press, 2013), and the suggestive heuristic essay by Christopher Cordner, "Two Conceptions of Love in Philosophical Thought," *Sophia* 50, no. 3 (2011): 315–29.

SEVENTEEN

Our Love and Our Knowledge of God

JOHN HARE

This essay is about Scotus's view of individuation as it connects to our relation to God. I want to tie this theme in Scotus to some thoughts about the darkness of God, which I interpret to mean God's incomprehensibility.[1] I will end with some brief remarks about the influence of this view of individuation in the nineteenth and twentieth centuries, especially in Kierkegaard and Barth, because I do not want to leave the impression that the issues here are exclusively medieval.

Famously, Scotus holds that what individuates one substance from another of the same species is a "thisness," or haecceity, not, as in Aristotle (in *Metaphysics* Z, 8) and Aquinas, the matter.[2] Two cows, Beulah and Marigold, are the same in species, let's say bovinity, but Beulah has in addition the individual perfection of Beulahhood and Marigold has the individual perfection of Marigoldity. These individual perfections are perfections of the common species, just as the species is a perfection of a common genus. Scotus thinks that what makes us individuals should not be something *less* perfect than what makes us members of the same species.

I should add something else by way of personal confession. My original access to Scotus was through the poet Gerald Manley Hopkins. I lived for a year in his rooms at Balliol College and I read all of his poetry. I was struck especially by his poem "As Kingfishers Catch Fire" and the lines, "Each mortal thing does one thing and the same: / Deals out that being indoors each one dwells; / Selves—goes itself; / *myself* it speaks and spells. / Crying *What I do is me: for that I came*."[3] Hopkins was influenced here by Scotus, and recognized his debt.

Now I am not a metaphysician. But this idea about the individuation of substances has implications for moral theology, and these are what I want to explore. First of all, there are implications about the relation between intellect and will. An individual essence can be the object of will and of its activity of loving, while being as universal belongs to the intellect and its activity of understanding. Scotus agrees with the maxim *nihil volitum quin praecognitum*, nothing is willed except what is previously cognized. But something can be different *as loved* from what it is *as understood*. I will move away from cows to people, so that I do not have to talk about loving cows. Suppose Beulah and Marigold are human beings. They have the same species essence but different individual essences, which are not (at least in our current lives) clearly accessible to us. I like very much the picture in the Book of Revelation, where we are told that God has a name for each of us, written on a white stone, which God will give to us when we go to heaven, but which now God knows and we do not.[4] It is perhaps like the name "Peter," which Christ gave to Simon, a name that meant "rock," when Peter was by no means yet a rock. We live, as it were, into the name. My point, though, is that the intellect can cognize Beulah and Marigold under their common species, human, which it has abstracted from perception, but it cannot yet clearly cognize the individual essence. I will make a qualification to this claim in a moment, under the heading "intuitive cognition." But it is possible to love what one has not understood. It is possible, for example, to love God in Godself without understanding God in Godself, and it is possible to love oneself as oneself without understanding oneself as oneself. Our love can attach itself to an object as particular in a way that is not yet accessible to the intellect.

This is how Scotus understands what Paul says in 1 Corinthians 13, that of the three that stand, Faith, Hope and Love, the greatest is Love. For Scotus, the greatest of the three is still Love, even in heaven. He is not denying that in heaven we will have both intellect and will, but he thinks the seeing is introductory to the most important thing, the loving. I am not going to enter into the vexed question of how to compare the views of Aquinas on this matter, because it would take the rest of the essay to treat adequately.[5] I will say just that Scotus has a more substantial notion of will, which is where the ranking of the two affections (for advantage and for justice) takes place, and which is therefore the appropriate site for freedom and for the possibility of defection (though not necessarily the opportunity), even in the presence of the beatific vision. Scotus thinks this is what happened in the fall of Lucifer.[6] This difference in notion means that we cannot simply contrast the statements of the two thinkers about will as though they meant the same thing by the term.

I am going to proceed by looking briefly at three topics in Scotus in their relation to the theme of this essay, particular happiness, intuitive cognition, and the nature of theology as practical science. I then come to the main point, which is to discuss one way of thinking about the darkness of God that comes out of these Scotist themes about our knowledge and our love of God. There are other ways, indeed other ways in Scotus, to think of the darkness of God. For example, the infinity of God, as contrasted with our finitude, is an important theme for him, and he belongs firmly on the Neoplatonist side of the important divide between Plato and the Neoplatonists. Plato is still Pythagorean, in that he tends to put infinity or indefiniteness (to apeiron) in the second of the two Pythagorean columns of fundamental principles, along with evil. It is not until Plotinus that to apeiron belongs to the One. But that is a topic for another time, and for now I want to emphasize the modest point that there is a way of thinking about God's darkness in terms of the individuation of substances, and it should not be lost just because there are other ways of thinking about this darkness.

So now the three Scotist topics. Scotus holds that the best state of human beings is to be "co-lovers" of God (condiligentes), entering into the love that is between the three persons of the Trinity.[7] This has a different theological content from the description of the best state of human beings that one might find in Aristotle, for example.

When Scotus talks of "happiness in particular," he implies that it is more perfect than happiness in the universal, as the particular adds perfection to the universal. I want to suggest a meaning for the phrase "particular happiness," though it goes somewhat beyond the texts of Scotus. Suppose it is true that the best state for each of us is to be a co-lover, but it is also true that the best state for each of us is something unique, a haecceity into which we are called. What this suggests is that there are different ways of loving God, different as each one of us is different from each other human being.

I will give one example, and I will return to it in the second half of this essay. The example comes from the interlinked stories of the woman with the hemorrhage and Jairus, the ruler of the synagogue, as told with slightly different details in Mark and Luke.[8] Jairus's twelve-year-old daughter is sick, in fact dying. He comes to Jesus for help, but Jesus makes him wait while he listens to the whole story of the woman, who for twelve years has been going from doctor to doctor and who has come to Jesus, hoping just to touch his garment and be cured from her issue of blood. Jesus makes her become public and tell her story (and so, reveal her uncleanness) to the whole crowd. He then calls her (the only place he does this in the Gospels) "my daughter," and heals her. He takes Jairus, however, away from the crowd, away even from the rest of his disciples, with just Peter, James, and John, away from the mourners outside the house, and he heals the daughter. I think that because of the way the stories are told, we are supposed to see that Jesus is taking these two people through opposite temptations, the woman through the temptation of hiddenness into public accountability and Jairus through the temptation of control into personal obedience. The point is that we are called through different temptations because we start out as different and we have been formed by different circumstances. The love of God into which each of us is called is reached through facing these different temptations, not by avoiding them. I think we get a preliminary sense through these different, unique trajectories of our different, unique destinations. Hopkins, at the end of the poem I quoted earlier, says this: "The just man justices; / Keeps grace: that keeps all his goings graces; / Acts in God's eye what in God's eye he is— /

Christ. For Christ plays in ten thousand places, / Lovely in limbs, and lovely in eyes not his / To the Father, through the features of men's faces."

The second topic I said I would discuss is Scotus's treatment of intuitive cognition. Here again I am going to have to pass over many of the details. The question is what kind of cognitive access we have to the haecceity which is our final end. Scotus says that the object of intellect is being. This is true in the next life as well as in this one, and Scotus is notoriously committed to the view that God has being in the same sense as we do. I will not discuss this view of his here, except to note that it does not imply that we know God's *essence* just by knowing that God is. In fact, to the contrary, God's individual essence is inaccessible to us in this life, for Scotus, and only imperfectly accessible to us in the next.[9] Because the objects of our intellect include in principle the being and essence of God, we are not in principle confined in our intellects to the essences of material beings. But on his view of haecceity, the singular has more perfection, and so more being, than the general or the universal. The intellect therefore has, in principle, the capacity to contemplate this singular being, though he says that the intellect cannot contemplate it *as* singular (a nature itself is, for Scotus, prior to the question of its singularity or universality). When the intellect operates this way, contemplating a singular being, it can in principle do so intuitively, and not merely by abstraction from phantasms. I said, however, that this capacity is a capacity in principle. In this present life, Scotus says, our intellect understands only things whose species are displayed in the phantasm. He does, however, hold out for an *uncertain* operation of intuitive cognition even in our present life. Abstractive cognition, he says, we frequently experience within ourselves; but with respect to intuitive cognition, "even though we do not experience it within ourselves with as much certainty, such cognition is possible."[10] I do not want to put much reliance on this point, since there are texts that cast doubt on this doctrine. But there is at least a suggestion that we may have direct though uncertain cognitive access even during our present life to singular natures, though not to these natures *as* singular. One of these singular natures is our own haecceity. I go through this in order to suggest, though again this goes beyond the texts of Scotus, that we may get hints in this life of the name or nature into which we are being called.

The last of the three preliminary topics I want to address is the nature of theology as a practical science. Scotus here departs from the tradition of Aristotle. A science is practical or theoretical, he says, in virtue of its object, and the object of theology is "God as one who should be loved . . . according to rules from which action can be chosen."[11] The will does not necessarily aim at happiness specified as our entering into the love that is between the members of the Trinity, and theology has the task of making it clear that this is our proper end, and making clear how we are to achieve it. I want to draw from this passage a reflection about the kind of priority of the practical that Scotus is proposing. A theologian in this life does not, he is saying, contemplate God as God is in Godself but rather God as one to be loved by us. The contrast with Aristotle is striking. Aristotle, on one common interpretation, holds that God's activity consists in the contemplation of God alone, and that God does not *act* at all. Human beings have a godlike bit, the *nous*, and by contemplating God we become like God in this way. Our chief good is the activity of this *nous*. When we rank theoretical and practical wisdom, on this view, we should see theoretical activity as the end at which practical activity aims, in the same way as health is the end at which medicine aims.[12] A life focused on practical activity, for example, the life of a statesman, is a second-best kind of life. This is a reading of the doctrine at the end of the *Nicomachean Ethics*, and I will leave aside questions about the consistency of this view with other parts of the *Ethics*.[13] This difference between Scotus and Aristotle relates to another fundamental difference, that Aristotle does not have, on my view, a doctrine of will.[14] For Scotus will is a superior faculty to intellect, and we are aiming at the best state of this best faculty, which is the state of loving God. If I am right about Scotus's view of individuation, however, we should add that this loving that we are headed toward is not the same loving for each of us. This thought takes us to the second half of this essay, whose aim is to draw conclusions about the darkness or incomprehensibility of God from the premises discussed so far. I will end with some remarks about Kierkegaard and Barth.

One of Scotus's favorite images for our status in this life is the picture of pilgrimage. We are *viatores*, or *in via*, on the way. In one respect this is an excellent image for my purposes here. It implies that we have not yet arrived at our destination, and that we are not yet complete or perfect. We are looking forward, as Abraham (Heb. 11:10) looked for the city with foundations, whose architect and builder is God. But in another respect the image of a pilgrimage is an obstacle or impediment to the point I am trying to make. Consider someone on a pilgrimage to Santiago. Even if she has not been there yet, she knows just where she is going and how to get there. She has the reports of other pilgrims, about what was the best accommodation, let us say, in Toulouse. The stages by which she reaches the destination and the destination itself are *shared*, and because they are shared with previous pilgrims, knowledge about them is accessible to her. What I want to stress, by contrast, is that our destination, our particular way of loving God, our name on the white stone, is *not* known to us.

Consider again Jairus, the ruler of the synagogue, and the woman with the flow of blood. Suppose you had asked them earlier about the path they were going to be asked to travel. Would Jairus have known that his daughter was going to get sick unto death and that he was going to have to ask an itinerant rabbi for a miracle? Would the woman have known she was going to have a flow of blood and that after fruitlessly pursuing doctors in secret for twelve years, she was going to have to tell her story to a large crowd of people? My point is that we are shaped by how we respond to our circumstances, and these circumstances are to a very large extent not known to us in advance.

We can put this point more schematically. We are in time. For Scotus, God is *not* in time. This is not a point of dispute with Aquinas. I think they are right, though it would take a long time to justify this claim. When God gives us the name on the white stone, this is a name that God has already been calling us by, even though we did not yet know it. Jesus called Simon "Peter" even though he was not yet a rock. When Simon received the name, he did not know that he was going to be tested three times before the crowing of the cock. He did not know that Jesus was going to take him, on the beach after the resurrection, three times through the question, "Do you love me?" I think Jesus was taking Peter, as he took Jairus and the woman, *through* a temptation rather than bypassing it, but in this case the way, the *via*, was *back* and through. The love into which he was entering was a love to be shaped by suffering, and finally by loss of independence. "You will stretch out your hands, and someone else will dress you and lead you where you do not want to go."[15] Peter's case is interesting partly because he is given two things we are not. In terms of the picture of pilgrimage, he is given at least a provisional name, and so destination, and he is given one of the way stations. For us, being in time means that the future, by which we are to be shaped, is unknown.

I want to tie this point to something Karl Barth says about the conditions on our agency placed by the fact that we are recipients of divine command. Barth is, like Scotus, a divine command theorist. Just as Scotus denies that the second table of the law brought down by Moses from Sinai is natural law strictly speaking, because it is not "known from its terms," so Barth denies any deducibility of the divine command from human nature. But this does not mean that we cannot learn some things about ourselves from the fact that we are commanded. Barth suggests we can learn four things—that we are individual centers of agency, that we are in time, that we are free, and that we are language users.[16] Though I am taking this point further than Barth himself does, I want to say that these four features of our agency put constraints on what we can take to be a divine command. Each feature gives us something like a rebuttable presumption against taking some candidate prescription to be a divine command. Thus being language users gives us a rebuttable presumption against taking a command to lie to be God's command, because the general permission of lying is inconsistent with the practice of communication through speech. The fact that we are centers of agency *in time* puts constraints of a different kind. I will mention two. The first is that we choose by connecting present experience with past experience. We characteristically do not choose moment by moment, without comparing the situation in which we choose to situations we have known before. Sometimes this point is put in terms of a narrative that is required for the intelligibility of individual choices. Thus Charles Taylor says, "But this is to state another basic condition of making sense of ourselves, that we grasp our lives in a narrative."[17] I think, though there is lot more to be said about this, that because we do not know what route God has chosen for each of us to our final end, we should assume the pilgrimage is not complete before a full life span, and therefore a killing would be a premature termination. I say this because the fact that we do not know the route does not imply that we know nothing about the route. Divine command theorists have to have something to say to the objection from arbitrariness, that God could command just anything, for example, flying a plane loaded with passengers into a skyscraper and killing thousands of innocent people. Robert M. Adams says we may only take something as a divine command if it could be the command of a *loving* God who intends the good of the creation.[18] But what we have here is a constraint, not a deduction. Scotus says the divine commands cannot be deduced from our nature, though they *fit* our nature exceedingly well, because they take us toward our end.[19] We do not, moreover, get *obligation* from such fittingness, because obligation requires an obligator. There is probably an infinite number of good ways to act and be, and only the members of this set that God requires are obligatory.

For the present essay the more important constraint from our being centers of agency in time comes not from our connection, known to us, to the past but from our connection, unknown to us, to the future. Let me gather together some of the pieces. Theology gives us, Scotus tells us, as its object God as one to be loved. But how God is to be loved is different for each of us, depending on the shape that we acquire through our different lives. Perhaps the love of God by God's people as a whole is completed by each of our different loves. But this individual shape that we will acquire is unknown to us, and so the loving of God that we will do is unknown to us, and so the object given us by our theology is unknown to us and is now incomprehensible to us. Here we have a way of thinking about the darkness of God.

This connects with how we should think about God's relation to the evil we experience. We get what I am going to call, following Kant, a response to the problem of evil from within practical reason.[20] We do not get what Kant calls "a theodicy proper," proposing for each case what God's reason for allowing it is, or even (as in Plantinga's free will defense, which he distinguishes from theodicy) what it might possibly be.[21] Rather, we assume that we are under the moral law, and therefore we have what Kant calls a "moral faith" that we are under a providential ordering of the cosmos, such that the good in it is more fundamental than the evil, even though we do not see and indeed often could not see, in any way that would justify the permission of the evil, what that good is. This is Kant's response to the story of Job. God speaks out of the whirlwind, and lays before Job's eyes "the wisdom of his creation, especially its inscrutability," revealing not just glimpses of the beautiful side of creation "but also harmful and fearsome things" like Behemoth and Leviathan.[22] The inscrutability resides in God being what Kant calls "noumenal," beyond our categories that help us make sense of our lives in space and time. The darkness of God, on the picture I have been presenting, is a consequence of our being in time and God not so being. And the recognition of this kind of darkness is a prerequisite for the kind of comfort that moral faith can provide. Here is Hopkins again: "I cast for comfort I can no more get / By groping round my comfortless, than blind / Eyes in their dark can day or thirst can find / Thirst's all-in-all in all a world of wet. / Soul, self; come, poor Jackself, I do advise / You, jaded, let be; call off thoughts awhile / elsewhere; leave comfort root-room; let joy size / At God knows when to God knows what; whose smile / 's nor wrung, see you; unforeseen times rather— as skies / Betweenpie mountains—lights a lovely mile."[23] I know that explaining poetry in prose is a fool's game. But here is Hopkins's suggestion. God knows the time, the "when," and we do not, and God knows the destination, the "to-what," and we do not; and it is only when we call off thoughts a while elsewhere and stop groping around, trying to find light where there is only dark, or sweet water where there is only salt, only then do we leave comfort root-room, and let joy grow. God's smile is not wrung, not forced, but at the times God chooses, once we acknowledge this incomprehensibility, God's smile can "light a lovely mile."

I want to close with Kierkegaard and Barth, but just before this it is worth saying that scripture provides a precursor of the kind of idea I have been proposing, at Isaiah 40:28–31: "Hast thou not known? Hast thou not heard, that the Creator of the ends of the earth, fainteth not, neither is weary? There is no searching of his understanding. He giveth power to the faint; and to them that have no might he increaseth strength. Even the youths shall faint and be weary, and the young men shall utterly fall: But they that wait upon the Lord shall renew their strength; they shall mount up with wings as eagles; they shall run, and not be weary; and they shall walk, and not faint." There are two basic ideas in this passage, and it is easy to miss the connection between them. The prophet starts with God being beyond our limitations and incomprehensible to us; God does not suffer from our limitations of getting tired and weary, and there is no searching by us of God's understanding. But the prophet immediately proceeds to explain that if we acknowledge that we, unlike God, do grow faint and weary, and if we *wait* upon God, God will renew our strength. Note that all the images of our status before God in this passage are images of motion, of being *in via*, walking, running, and mounting up like eagles. I want to suggest that there is a connection between the two basic thoughts of the passage. The recognition of God's unlikeness to us, God's not getting weary and God's not being understandable, comes before our receiving this divine assistance.

Kierkegaard has, in *Works of Love*, a similar progress of thought to the one I have been suggesting from Scotus.[24] Kierkegaard has three of the themes I have been discussing, the emphasis on particularity, the primacy of love, and therefore the hiddenness or darkness of God. I will start with particularity. Kierkegaard says that what makes us different from other animals is that we have what he calls distinctiveness, and especially distinctiveness before God (230), so that "within the species each individual is the essentially different or distinctive." "One human being, honest, upright, respectable, God-fearing, can under the same circumstances do the very opposite of what another human being does who is also honest, upright, respectable, God-fearing." Each one of us has a particular call and a particular election (364). Without this, he says, we have no God-relation. We have distinctiveness when we have the courage to be ourselves before God (271). Scotus in the same way says that "granted that all the circumstances are the same in regard to an act of killing a man except the circumstances of its being prohibited in one case and not prohibited in another, God could cause that act which is circumstantially the same, but performed by different individuals, to be prohibited and illicit in one case and not prohibited but licit in the other."[25] The comparison of these two texts is not exact, because Scotus has a technical sense for "circumstances" that is not quite the same as Kierkegaard's. But I think the particularism is clear in both cases. Second, the priority of love over understanding is a better-known theme in Kierkegaard. In *Concluding Unscientific Postscript*, truth or faith is an objective uncertainty held fast in an appropriation process of the most passionate inwardness.[26] Johannes Climacus, the pseudonymous author, is emphasizing the priority from the perspective of our salvation of our passion, our appropriation, over any kind of theoretical knowledge.

But for present purposes the most important shared theme is the third. Love, and so God, has to be hidden. There is a wrong way to hold this thought, because love is known and revealed by its fruits. But Kierkegaard in *Works of Love* emphasizes that there is no particular kind of work that we can know from the outside is done from love, because whether or not it is done from love depends on the individual's God-relation (13). Kierkegaard has the wonderful image of the hidden spring (9). "Where does love come from, where does it have its origin and its source, where is the place it has its abode from which it flows? Yes, this place is hidden or is secret." If you try to force your way in, because of curiosity, you will forfeit the joy and blessing of it. "Just as the quiet lake originates darkly in the deep spring, so a human being's love originates mysteriously in God's love." "The quiet lake, however calm its surface, is actually flowing water." In this passage, the individual is pictured as the lake, and the hiddenness of the spring is related back to the particularity of the individual. "The divine authority of the Gospel does not speak to one person about another, does not speak to you, my listener, about me, or to me about you—no, when the Gospel speaks, it speaks to the *single* individual. It does not speak *about* us human beings, you and me, but speaks *to* us human beings, to you and me, and what it speaks about is that love is to be known by its fruits" (14).

Barth was strongly influenced by Kierkegaard, and many of the same themes appear. This is especially true at the time of the second edition of the *Commentary on Romans*, but it remains true in *Church Dogmatics*, even though the explicit references to Kierkegaard are fewer in the later work. I want to emphasize one theme in Barth's treatment of divine command, namely, the particularity of the command, and therefore its inaccessibility to general or natural human reason. In the first half volume of the section of *Church Dogmatics* on the Doctrine of God, Barth repeats the Kierkegaardian claim that God cannot be known *in abstracto* but only in the overflow of the divine life to God's creatures. This is shown, in relation to human beings, by God's election of us, by God's covenant with us, which then forms the *terminus a quo*, or the context in which the divine command operates. This command, though it comes to all human beings, comes to them in the particular circumstances of each person. "For as God is not only the God of the general but also of the particular, of the most particular, and the glory of the latter is His, so is it with His command."[27] He goes on, "[The command] is not a generalized thing to which particularized expression must accrue from elsewhere. . . . The divine decision, in which the sovereign judgment of God is expressed on our decisions, is a very definite decision. This means that in the demand and judgment of His command God always confronts us with a specific meaning and intention, with a will which has foreseen everything and each thing in particular." The Ten Commandments, for example, brought down by Moses from Sinai, are on this view not commands at all, in the paradigm sense, but are to be seen as propaedeutic, prescriptions that we are to think through beforehand in order that we might be ready for the divine command addressed to each of us in our particular circumstances.[28]

Along with this emphasis on particularity comes, as with Kierkegaard, an emphasis on the inaccessibility of the command to the categories of natural law. I have already tried to show that Barth has his own categories, within which to give us some constraints on what we should take to be divine command. To these we should add the constraints that come from his view that the imperative is always grounded in an indicative, namely, in the fact that we *are* called and reconciled and redeemed, and so in the electing, atoning, and covenanting work that God has already done for us. But Barth is, like Kierkegaard, always alert to the danger of our presumption, and our claims to understand God separately from the moment-by-moment special and sovereign work of the Holy Spirit. He was working in a context in which he thought this kind of presumption had visible political consequences. There is thus in Barth a kind of inscrutability or darkness to God's decision, given in the divine command, in terms of our preceding rational categories, and this conclusion follows from Barth's particularism.

Just a word by way of conclusion. I have tried to trace a certain way of thinking about the darkness of God that starts from premises about the particularity of God's relation to us, and the primacy of love in that relation. I spent most of the time on Scotus, but I have tried at the end to relate this way of thinking to a pattern of thought conspicuous in the nineteenth and twentieth centuries, especially in Kierkegaard and Barth. I do not by any means want to say this is the only, or the best, way to think about the darkness or incomprehensibility of God. But it forms, I believe, one important tradition of reflection about the limitations of our intellects.

NOTES

This essay is written out of a deep respect and affection for Denys Turner and an anticipated sense of loss for the time when he is no longer my colleague. He and I taught a course together twice at Yale Divinity School, on the moral theology of Aquinas and Scotus. Denys supported Aquinas, by and large, and I supported Scotus, though neither of us was, of course, unreasonably partisan. The class went very well, both times, and was most illuminating about what the real differences are, as opposed to what much of the usual secondary literature says they are.

1. This incomprehensibility is relative. Scotus also thinks that God "can be understood and known distinctly by the intellect of the pilgrim at least abstractively." *Reportatio* I-A, prol., q. 2, 185. I am merely pointing out a limitation to this comprehension.

2. See *ST*, Ia, 14, 11. See also Eleonore Stump, *Aquinas* (New York: Routledge, 2003), 47–50. I am not attempting to justify the attribution of this view to Aristotle or Aquinas.

3. Gerard Manley Hopkins, "As Kingfishers Catch Fire," in *The Norton Anthology of Poetry*, 4th ed., ed. Margaret Ferguson et al. (New York: W. W. Norton, 1996), 1064; original emphasis. See *Gerard Manley Hopkins*, ed. W. H. Gardner (Baltimore: Penguin Books, 1953), 128: "But just then when I took in any inscape of the sky or sea I thought of Scotus."

4. Rev. 2:17.

5. See *ST*, Ia, 82, 3, "Hence the love of God is better than the cognition of God, whereas, conversely, the cognition of corporeal things is better than the love of corporeal things. Still, absolutely speaking, the intellect is more noble than the will." The translation is by Alfred J. Freddoso, www3 .nd.edu /~afreddos/summa-translation/TOC.htm.

6. I say "though not necessarily the opportunity" because of the case of the blessed in heaven.

7. *Ordinatio* IV, suppl. dist. 49, q. 9, a. 1 and 2.

8. Mark 5 and Luke 8.

9. *Ordinatio* I, dist. 3, 25–30.

10. *Quodl.* Q.6, 18–19.

11. *Lectura* prol., pars 4, qq. 1–2.

12. *Nicomachean Ethics* VI, 13, 1145a5f.

13. I have dealt with this question at greater length in *God and Morality* (Oxford: Blackwell, 2007), 43–51.

14. But see Anthony Kenny, *Aristotle's Theory of the Will* (London: Duckworth, 1979).

15. John 21:18.

16. Karl Barth, *Church Dogmatics*, iii, 55–56, ed. G. W. Bromiley and T. F. Torrance (London: T & T Clark, 2009), 4–8 (328–32).

17. Charles Taylor, *Sources of the Self* (Cambridge, MA: Harvard University Press, 1989), 47.

18. Robert M. Adams, *Finite and Infinite Goods* (Oxford: Oxford University Press, 1999), 249–76.

19. *Ordinatio* III, suppl. dist. 37.

20. Kant, *On the Miscarriage of All Philosophical Trials in Theodicy*, 8:264, in *Religion and Rational Theology*, trans. and ed. Allen W. Wood and George di Giovanni (Cambridge: Cambridge University Press, 1996). I have given an account of Kant's views in this short work in "Kant, Job, and the Problem of Evil," in *Contemporary Moral Theory and the Problem of Evil*, ed. Jim Sterba (Bloomington: Indiana University Press, forthcoming).

21. Alvin Plantinga, *God, Freedom, and Evil* (New York: Harper and Row, 1974).

22. Kant, *Miscarriage*, 8:266. See Job 40–41.

23. Gerard Manley Hopkins, "My Own Heart Let Me More Have Pity On," in *The Norton Anthology of Poetry*, 1066.

24. Søren Kierkegaard, *Works of Love*, ed. and trans. Howard and Edna Hong (Princeton: Princeton University Press, 1995).

25. *Ordinatio* III, suppl. dist. 37.

26. Søren Kierkegaard, *Concluding Unscientific Postscript*, trans. and ed. Howard and Edna Hong (Princeton: Princeton University Press, 1982), 203.

27. Karl Barth, *Church Dogmatics*, II, 2, 663, trans and ed. G. W. Bromiley et al. (Edinburgh: T & T Clark, 1957). Barth consistently speaks of God with male pronouns.

28. I have been persuaded here by John Webster, *Barth's Moral Theology* (London: T & T Clark, 1998). Other important sources are Gerald McKenny, *The Analogy of Grace* (Oxford: Oxford University Press, 2010); David Clough, *Ethics in Crisis* (Aldershot: Ashgate, 2005); and Nigel Biggar, *The Hastening That Waits* (Oxford: Clarendon Press, 1993).

EIGHTEEN

Eckhart, Derrida, and
the Gift of Love

DAVID NEWHEISER

Love, like God, is elusive. In both cases, the experience is evanescent—
it may suddenly evaporate, leaving one to wonder whether it was love
(or God) all along. For this reason, to dispassionate observers faith
and love can both seem unhinged. We recoil from the idea that the
beloved is simply the means to an end, a tool for our use, but if love
does not calculate costs and benefits, it cannot ensure the lover's
well-being. Insofar as love is absorbed in its beloved, it is blind to
risks that it cannot exclude.

Like love, Christian commitment is a perilous thing. It is therefore understandable that some critics demand that people do without
it. In light of the evil wrought in God's name, it can seem safer to remain within the confines of sensible, scientific rationality, avoiding
beliefs that go beyond the available evidence. However, if (as some
say) God is love, it may be difficult to reject the one without excluding the other. In fact, despite its danger, not everyone has relinquished love; since safety is not always the decisive consideration,
perhaps faith remains possible as well.

This essay plays upon a surprising affinity between Meister Eckhart and Jacques Derrida. These authors differ in obvious respects:

Eckhart was a Dominican friar, while Derrida was a modern philosopher who is often taken for an atheist.[1] I will argue that they nevertheless develop congruent accounts of love. In my reading, both Derrida and Eckhart interpret love as a gift that is entirely free of economic exchange. Because the calculation of costs and benefits is a constant feature of human consciousness, they both conclude that the gift of love cannot be identified with certainty.

Although Eckhart and Derrida do not reject the pleasure that comes from believing that one is loving (or beloved), they suggest that love allows no complacency. In their view, since what seems like love may be a means to obtain satisfaction, lovers should preserve an alert circumspection. By the same token, although calculated self-protection is doubtless important, they argue that it is extrinsic to love. In their view, lovers should not expect to balance love against prudential restraint: although both demands are indelible, they operate at different levels, and so they cannot be reconciled. Like faith, a love that exceeds economy is irreducibly dangerous, but Eckhart and Derrida suggest that its danger must be endured if we hope for something beyond calculation.

THE ARGUMENT that follows is deeply indebted to Denys Turner, though I suspect he may be uneasy with the result. Where many representatives of Christianity insist on a constricted dogmatism, Turner articulates a subtle and expansive vision of faith. He argues that, rather than remain locked in oppositional dependence upon its enemies, Christian thought must incorporate a relentless self-criticism. In this way, Turner suggests that Christian discourse is characterized by a delicate fragility, unable to ensure itself according to the dictates of dispassionate rationality. In this way, he productively complicates the distinction between atheism and Christian thought.[2]

My reading of Eckhart and Derrida inhabits the space opened by Turner's work. However, Turner has accused Derrida of spreading insidious nonsense, often by comparing him unfavorably to Eckhart.[3] I will argue that Turner misreads both authors, but the larger point is that his polemic against "postmodernism" stems from a misguided attempt to preserve Christian thought from the appearance of atheism. Whereas he claimed in 1999 that "atheism is in any case a crucial dimension of faith,"[4] in 2004 Turner defends the view that Christian discourse is secured by its knowledge of God.[5] The latter argument is motivated by his intention "to challenge on its own terms the atheological rationalism of our modern times."[6] On Turner's own terms this seems like a mistake, for he himself has shown that atheological rationalism misunderstands what is at issue.[7]

In what follows I side with the Turner who says that "God is not a thing and we cannot know him"[8] against the one who affirms "the possibility of a purely rational and certain knowledge of God."[9] When the early Turner distinguishes Christian thought from atheism, he insists that "to produce that distinction requires . . . a theology which has been unnerved by the closeness of the engagement in which it must associate with Marx's atheism and has thereby problematized its own very possibility as a discourse."[10] Like this Turner, I think the most compelling response to the critics of religion comes from acknowledging the affinity between Christian mystical theology and sophisticated forms of atheism.

As I will argue, Eckhart and Derrida agree that a love which exceeds quotidian calculation lies (like God) beyond our grasp, but neither of them claim that it must therefore be relinquished. They thus suggest that humans do not require the unreliable reassurance promised by the claim that the knowledge of God is certain. The gift of love, as Derrida and Eckhart describe it, exemplifies the way in which faith remains possible for those who hesitate to embrace unjustified certainty. Together they describe a form of affirmation that presses forward without guarantees, stretching into the unknown, emboldened by an unpredictable love.

AFFIRMATION AND APORIA

Derrida claims that "deconstruction . . . is not negative, even though it has often been interpreted as such despite all sorts of warnings. . . . It never proceeds without love."[11] In light of his well-known writing on *différance*, dissemination, and the trace, this claim might seem strange; after all, some have concluded that his project is purely corrosive. Derrida claims that even his earliest work on the indeterminacy of textual meaning already carries ethical and political significance (despite its abstraction),[12] but the situation becomes even more difficult with his late reflections on justice and democracy, concepts that Derrida argues are incapable of realization. Despite his insistence on affirmation, it is difficult to locate an affirmative moment in Derrida's thought, for he allows for no stable space that would be free from the play of meaning and the pull of an impossible responsibility.

Derrida's discussion of the gift exemplifies this difficult situation. Beginning from the intuitive point that the donee ought not simply return a gift to the donor, Derrida develops a radical claim. He writes that "if there is gift, the given of the gift . . . must not come back to the giving. . . . It must not circulate, it must not be exchanged, it must not in any case be exhausted, as a gift, by the process of exchange."[13] This seems reasonable enough, for on the face of it a gift goes beyond simple exchange—which is to say, it is somehow gratuitous. However, Derrida goes on to argue that even the return of something different from the gift (including something as simple as thanks) is enough to pull the gift back within the ambit of economy. He writes, "As soon as the donee knows it is a gift, he already thanks the donator, and cancels the gift. As soon as the donor is conscious of giving, he himself thanks himself and again cancels the gift by re-inscribing it into a circle, an economic circle."[14] Since any recognition would represent an exchange for the gift, the gift cannot appear as such—neither to the donor nor to the donee, for consciousness in either case would constitute a symbolic transaction.

On this view, even the greatest generosity is not enough to ensure the gift, and yet Derrida claims nevertheless that "there is no gift without the intention of giving."[15] The gift ought to be intentional—we should know what we do, what we give, and why—and yet conscious intentionality would annul the gift's gratuity. Derrida writes, "It is a matter . . . of responding faithfully but also as rigorously as possible both to the injunction or the order of the *gift* ('give') as well as to the injunction or the order of meaning (presence, science, knowledge)."[16] We must address both these demands, and this aporia is paradigmatic of Derrida's ethics. As he explains, "To give in the name of, to give to the name of, the other is what frees my responsibility from knowledge—that is, what brings responsibility unto itself, if there ever is such a thing."[17] Some conclude that Derrida offers only instability, but he argues that this is where responsibility and the gift begin.

Although the gift does not lie within our power, Derrida argues that we may nonetheless pursue it. He writes, "If the gift is another name of the impossible, we still think it, we name it, we desire it. We intend it. And this *even if* or *because* or *to the extent that* we *never* encounter it, we never know it, we never verify it."[18] The impossibility of the gift serves as the condition of our pursuit of it; indeed, because the gift can never be identified, our desire can never be sated. Nor does this entail mere futility, for the impossibility that Derrida has in view is not that which is simply not possible but rather that which is "more impossible than the impossible if the impossible is the simple negative modality of the possible."[19] Whereas the not-possible simply negates what is possible, the impossible Derrida has in mind cannot be excluded, for it is unconstrained by the present conditions of possibility. Derrida explains, "The possibility of the impossible, of the 'more impossible' that as such is also possible ('more impossible than the impossible'), marks an absolute interruption in the regime of the possible that nonetheless remains, if this can be said, in place."[20] The known constraints to possibility retain their validity, and yet their authority is not absolute since what may come is not limited by what we know.

BECAUSE ONE cannot know whether the call to give has been fulfilled, Derrida leaves no room for satisfaction. However, he is clear that this ought not entail a resigned passivity, for although the impossible remains beyond our achievement, its coming cannot be precluded. On the contrary, he argues that such impossibility is the stuff of passion; he writes, "Perhaps there is nomination, language, thought, desire, or intention only there where there is this movement still for thinking, desiring, naming that which gives itself neither to be known, experienced, nor lived."[21] When regulated by the strict economy of presence and possibility, desire and thought lack the scope they require, and so Derrida claims that it is only in the face of the impossible that they are given range and motility. It is here that the affirmative exigency of deconstruction emerges: although there is an aridity to Derrida's thought, this ascesis is intended to open the possibility of a passionate love.

Whereas some suppose that love connotes a wholesome intimacy, Derrida writes that "a certain departure, a certain separation, an interruption of the bond, a radical un-binding remains[,] . . . the condition of the social bond as such. I mean that of love."[22] In Derrida's account, responsibility requires the recognition that the other remains beyond one's grasp, and love must acknowledge this irreducible distance. Derrida goes so far as to suggest that the separation between oneself and another constitutes the possibility of a relational bond; he reflects, "Why would love be only the ardent force of an attraction tending towards fusion, union, and identification? Why would the infinite distance which opens respect up . . . not open love up as well?"[23] Because respect requires the recognition that the beloved is other, love must resist the impulse to consume its object. Commenting at one point that "love is narcissistic,"[24] Derrida acknowledges that we are never free from the impulse to appropriate, just as one can never ensure the escape from economy. But the gift of love may nonetheless come—this is the possibility Derrida describes in relation to the divided desire of God.

Meister Eckhart describes God as "the quiet desert, into which distinction never gazed, . . . a simple silence, in itself immovable,"[25] and he counsels that we should be similarly empty. Taking up this figure, Derrida observes that "the at times oracular tone of apophasis . . . often resounds in a desert."[26] This renunciation might seem simply barren, but Derrida notes that it pulls in two directions. It may, he says, "correspond with the most insatiable desire of God," while, on the other hand, it "can remain readily foreign to all desire, in any case to every anthropotheomorphic form of desire."[27] The willingness to let go of everything for the sake of God implies an impressive passion, but divine distance interrupts narcissistic desire. Derrida writes, "Isn't the desert a paradoxical figure of the *aporia*? No marked out or assured passage, no route in any case, at the very most trails that are not reliable ways, the paths are not yet cleared, unless the sand has already re-covered them."[28] According to Derrida we are caught between conflicting demands—renunciation and desire—that must both be endured in order to preserve a difficult affirmation.

Derrida comments in relation to Eckhart, "Unless I interpret it too freely, this *via negativa* does not only constitute a *movement* or a *moment* of deprivation, an asceticism or a provisional kenosis. The deprivation should remain at work (thus give up the work) for the (loved) other to remain the other."[29] This ascesis is not simply provisional, for it knows no limit, and yet it is the condition for love. Derrida writes, "Isn't it proper to desire to carry with it its own proper suspension . . . ? To go toward the absolute other, isn't that the extreme tension of a desire that tries thereby to renounce its own proper momentum, its own movement of appropriation?"[30] The divided desire of God articulated by Eckhart describes the aporia that all love must endure, moving toward the other while suspending the impulse to violate a responsible distance, resisting the reversion to economic exchange. Derrida comments, "To surrender to the other . . . would amount to giving oneself over in going toward the other, to coming toward the other but without crossing the threshold, and to respecting, to loving even the invisibility that keeps the other inaccessible."[31] Although the two movements are at odds, it is the very impossibility of their coincidence that opens the possibility of love.

UNSETTLING INDISTINCTION

As others before him had done, Eckhart argues that because God is beyond the created realm, none of the categories of creaturely thought are adequate to describe the divine. However, since every difference is distinguished against the background of some similarity, Eckhart concludes that the thoroughgoing distinction between God and creation entails that no difference between them can be identified.[32] Eckhart writes that because "no difference at all is or can be in the One,"[33] it follows that "indistinction belongs properly to God, distinction to creatures."[34] That is, whereas creatures are characterized by their distinction from each other, God is distinguished by the fact that no distinction can be drawn. But Eckhart goes further still: "God, so far as he is God, is not the perfect end of created beings. . . . So therefore let us pray to God that we may be free of God."[35] Because any object that we could discern would not be God, Eckhart surmises that God ought not serve as the object of human action and intention.

The conceptual ascesis signaled in this striking expostulation finds its counterpart in an ethical movement by which we are brought into divine indistinction.[36] Eckhart argues that, just as identifying an object of knowledge separates the individual from God, positing a reason for loving God makes the reason the object of a love which is therefore no longer directed toward God. He says, "You love a cow because of the milk and cheese and because of your own advantage. This is how all those people act who love God because of external riches or because of internal consolation. They do not love God rightly; rather they love their own advantage."[37] According to Eckhart, loving God for the sake of any benefit simply consecrates self-love. A century before Eckhart Bernard of Clairvaux writes, "God is not loved without reward, even though he should be loved without thought of reward."[38] But where Bernard moderately claims that "true love . . . has its reward in what it loves,"[39] Eckhart suggests that a love that would exceed narcissistic reappropriation must be further disoriented, lacking any object whatever.

In Eckhart's view, because nothing we could imagine (however wholesome) can orient the love of God, Bernard's claim that the love of God is guaranteed a reward, albeit as its unintended consequence, still promises too much. Eckhart writes, "Those people are all businessmen who . . . perform their works for God's glory . . . because they want to give one thing in return for another, and thus they want to make a business deal with our Lord."[40] While it might seem from this that Eckhart (like Bernard) simply requires love to be free of selfish concern, in fact he is clear that love must be free of intention altogether. He says, "As long as a person in any of his works seeks anything at all of all that which God can or shall give, he is like these businessmen. If you want to be so completely free of making business deals that God permits you in this temple . . . you should be as empty as that nothing is empty which is neither here nor there."[41] Because God cannot be specified or described, any recompense that (with Bernard) we might take to be internal to the love of God would offer something else instead, constituting the object of an intention that still aims too low.

Such a love is beyond our grasp since any act of grasping is enough to annul it; instead, it is a gift modeled after God's own gratuitous love. Eckhart writes, "God seeks nothing of his own. In all his works he is empty and free and works them out of genuine love. This is how the person acts who is united with God. He, too, is empty and free in all his works and he does them only for the glory of God, seeking nothing of his own."[42] Just as God gives God's love irrespective of desert or recompense, the human lover ought to be equally empty, and it is in this mutual emptiness that the final distinctions fade. Eckhart says, "All things that are in time have a why. . . . But if someone asked a good man: 'Why do you love God?'—'I do not know, because of God.'"[43] Such love is submerged in God alone: "It knows nothing but love. . . . It cannot properly form any other word but 'love.'"[44] Eckhart's gift of love is deprived of words, caught in a love that cannot be grasped, identified, or experienced.[45]

AS DERRIDA observes, Eckhart's negativity is the place of aporia. Since any active seeking and any intentionality reinscribes love within economy, uncalculated emptiness is required—"to be deprived of God for God's own sake,"[46] as Eckhart puts it. The paradox is that this entails that even the "for God's sake" must be relinquished. Just as Eckhart's prayer that God free us of God undercuts itself, here the only way to God is to submit to the deprivation of every intention, but this intended deprivation still intends too much. Eckhart explains, "A man who would possess this poverty ought to live as if he does not even know that he is not in any way living for himself or for the truth or for God. Rather, he should be so free of all knowing that he does not know or experience or grasp that God lives in him."[47] Since intending to live for God is a sort of self-assertion, the truly empty soul will not even aim for God; she persists without a why, in a certain sort of silence. But such silence is deeply unsettling, for there are conflicting demands at work—intend to love, love without intention—that cannot be resolved.

This tension is neatly illustrated by Eckhart's claim that "if a man . . . could remain free of all activities, interior or exterior, he ought to be on his guard in case this very state itself may become a form of activity."[48] On the one hand, Eckhart claims that we must attempt to free ourselves from activity since intentionality divides us from the divine indistinction; on the other hand, this very attempt displaces the state toward which we are straining. Any means to God inevitably misses God, who admits of no mediation. As Eckhart says, "whoever is seeking God by ways is finding ways and losing God."[49] Nevertheless, the necessary emptiness requires that the relinquishing of ways be relinquished as well.

The aporia of detachment from activity corresponds to Eckhart's reflections on silence. Whereas he suggests that we enter "the quiet desert, into which distinction never gazed," emptying ourselves in order to become one with "a simple silence, in itself immovable,"[50] he nevertheless proliferates speech. Once again, it is not a matter of choosing between two possibilities, speech and its exclusion; both the inadequacy of speech and its necessity remain in force. Derrida provides one way to understand this dynamic. He writes, "*There is something secret*. But it does not conceal itself. Heterogeneous to the hidden, to the obscure, to the nocturnal, to the invisible, to what can be dissimulated and indeed to what is nonmanifest in general, it cannot be unveiled."[51] Derrida has in mind a silence so deep that it can neither be hidden nor revealed, but since it eludes every identification it cannot be excluded either. He explains, "My saying, the declaration of love or the call to the friend, the address to the other in the night, the writing that does not resign itself to this unsaid—who could swear that they are consigned to oblivion simply because no said can speak them exhaustively?"[52] Such silence breathes through speech, running beside or beneath it without emerging into conscious identification, but for this reason it cannot be said with certainty not to occur.

Like Derrida, Eckhart is clear that the aporia he describes does not exclude the affirmation of language and love. Much as Derrida argues that the injunction to give must remain in place even though the gift is beyond our achievement, Eckhart says, "'Love God above all things and your neighbor as yourself,' and this is a command from God."[53] Since love is free of intention, this command is not something we can fulfill, but he continues: "It is not just a commandment; rather, it is also what God has given and what he has promised to give."[54] Eckhart insists that our inability to calculate or contain such an occurrence does not entail its bare impossibility; like Derrida, he admits that what exceeds predictable possibility may nonetheless come. He specifies that "what God has given and what he has promised to give is simply marvelous, incomprehensible, unbelievable,"[55] for a comprehensible gift would be no gift at all. But an unbelievable belief, an incomprehensible love, and a discourse that continues under the sign of relentless negativity need not be abandoned.

ALTERITY AND AFFECTION

Both Eckhart and Derrida argue that the gift is free from economy, and they both conclude on this basis that it excludes intentionality too. Where Eckhart is clear that such a gift characterizes love, Derrida's account of love centers on the renunciation required to respect the beloved's distance. Derrida writes, "A logic of the gift . . . reorientates friendship, deflecting towards what it should have been—what it immemorially will have been. This logic calls friendship back to non-reciprocity, to dissymmetry or to disproportion, to the impossibility of a return to offered or received hospitality."[56] Whereas any concern for return remains on the level of economic circulation, in Derrida's account the gift breaks the movement of reappropriation out of respect for alterity. Similarly, for Eckhart the uncalculated gift becomes the model of our relationship with the God who remains beyond our grasp. For both of them, the aporia of the gift is the condition for the affirmation of love.

Although it might seem that Derrida and Eckhart describe loves directed toward different objects, any neat distinction between Derrida's love (of any other at all) and Eckhart's (of God) is complicated by divine indistinction. Derrida writes that "if God is completely other . . . then every other (one) is every (bit) other. *Tout autre est tout autre.*"[57] As Derrida notes, the French phrase is apparently tautological; by playing upon the fact that the French "tout autre" refers both to an otherness which is total and to otherness of every kind, the phrase problematizes the difference between the divine and everything else. This echoes Eckhart's argument that if God is entirely different from creatures, no distinction between God and creatures can be drawn, but Denys Turner insists that Derrida and Eckhart are actually at odds. Turner writes, "Derrida's principle, 'every other is completely other,' is not only a straightforward logical absurdity, it is also an ethically offensive one."[58] He complains that Derrida's generalized alterity "could not be true of any finite relation,"[59] and so he concludes that "I love my 'loved ones' . . . not as a '*wholly* other,' for that is to love them into a vacuous non-entity"[60]—something, he says, Eckhart knows full well.

However, Turner's reading of Derrida is not supported by the texts in question. Turner argues that "Derrida's collapsing of all 'otherness,' whether created or uncreated, into a uniformly 'total' otherness, is logically incoherent nonsense,"[61] but Derrida made the same point forty years earlier: "That the other appears as such only in its relationship to the same, is a self-evidence."[62] Derrida is therefore aware that an undifferentiated otherness is no different from total sameness; his "tout autre" complicates one sort of distinction without obliterating distinction altogether. Although Turner complains that "it is hard to know what [Derrida] could possibly mean,"[63] context makes clear that the passage in question is a focused intervention into an existing debate.

Derrida borrows the language of "wholly other" from Kierkegaard and Levinas. Where Turner takes "tout autre est tout autre" as an abstract statement of principle, Derrida's aim is to show that, whereas these authors take total otherness as distinctively divine, they themselves suggest that divine and human alterity cannot be so neatly distinguished. Derrida writes, "Levinas's thinking stays within the game . . . between the face of God and the face of my neighbor, between the infinitely other as God and the infinitely other as another human."[64] Like Kierkegaard, Levinas maintains a distinction between the wholly Other God (*tout autre*) and everything else (*tout autre*) such that it remains possible to discriminate between religious comportment (toward God) and ethical comportment (toward other others). In response, Derrida's tautological "tout autre" suggests that, if God is totally other, then God cannot be neatly distinguished from everything else.[65]

Where Turner pits Eckhart against Derrida, Eckhart also blurs the division between ethical and religious action. For Eckhart, religious acts are problematic because (as we have seen) seeking God by means of particular practices makes the means more important than God. He says, "When people think that they are acquiring more of God in inwardness, in devotion, in sweetness and in various approaches than they do by the fireside or in the stable, you are acting just as if you took God and muffled his head up in a cloak and pushed him under a bench."[66] This sentiment is surprising, for it undermines the privilege of piety, and Eckhart goes so far as to say that "if a man were in ecstasy, as Saint Paul was, and knew that some sick man needed him to give him a bit of soup, I should think it far better if you would abandon your ecstasy out of love and show greater love in caring for the other in his need."[67] Where Turner pits Eckhart against Derrida's "tout autre," it is here that the two authors converge most clearly.

In an ironic inversion of Turner's argument, Eckhart agrees with Derrida that the gift of love is indiscriminate. He says, "For so long as you think better of your own people than you do of the man whom you never saw, you are going quite astray, and you have never had a single glimpse into this simple ground."[68] As we have seen, Eckhart takes God's love as the model of our own, but for this reason the gift of love cannot distinguish (since to calculate is unloving economy). Thus, he says, "if you like one person more than another, this is wrong. If you like your father, your mother, and yourself more than some other person, this is wrong."[69] This does not entail that the distinction between stranger and mother must be ignored at all times, nor does Derrida's "tout autre . . . " obliterate alterity altogether. Observing distinctions of this kind is entirely appropriate; the point is simply that love, as such, requires a sort of indifference.[70] Derrida is therefore closer than Turner to Eckhart, for Derrida appreciates that Eckhart's negative theology issues in an ethics of indistinction.[71]

ALTHOUGH TURNER misreads both Eckhart and Derrida, the substance of his concern is compelling, for the familiar loves we experience are directed and distinguished: we love the ones who are close to us, and we love them better than strangers and enemies. When Eckhart insists that "a man ought gladly to be robbed of all that he has for the love of God, and out of love he should wholly abandon and deny love's consolations,"[72] one may worry whether love can endure such a stringent demand. However, Derrida and Eckhart both allow for the mundane experiences that sustain quotidian love. Although the ideal they describe is stringent, Eckhart admits that "a saint never became so great that he could not be moved,"[73] and Derrida affirms upon the death of a friend "that I love Jean-François, that I miss him, like the words I cannot find, beyond words."[74] Since even the cessation of activity remains one action too many, the exclusion of emotion would not be empty enough. On the contrary, the ascesis Eckhart and Derrida describe does not preclude the humane practice of life.[75]

Instead of rejecting the rhythms of everyday existence, Eckhart invites a "being-at-home"[76] that moves within everyday life while acknowledging that ultimate significance is not in our power. Eckhart explains, "A man cannot learn this by running away, by shunning things and shutting himself up in an external solitude; but he must practice a solitude of the spirit, wherever or with whomever he is."[77]

Just as the silence required by divine indistinction does not extinguish speech, Eckhart suggests that there may be a sort of disjunction in society. He says, "You stand in the midst of things, but they do not reside in you; and those are careful who go about unimpeded in all their daily pursuits. . . . Such people stand in the midst of things, but not *in* things."[78] Rather than require an arcane spiritual exercise, this dispossession operates within the imperfect practice of everyday life. Eckhart's ethics of indistinction does not demand particular activities; it functions instead to hold open a space within the everyday for something more.

Likewise, although Derrida argues that love is in a sense indiscriminate, he is clear that it need not displace lived relationships, for it operates within them. Because, he says, "the logic of the gift . . . calls friendship back to the irreducible presence of the other,"[79] the aporia of the gift serves to intensify, not preclude, attention to particular others. Insofar as such attention distinguishes an object and interprets the give-and-take of encounter, it does not fulfill the conditions for the indiscriminate gift, but this does not mean we must dispense with it: Derrida acknowledges that calculation must continue. He writes, "Justice and gift should go beyond calculation. This does not mean that we should not calculate. We have to calculate as rigorously as possible. But there is a point or a limit beyond which calculation must fail, and we must recognize that."[80] Calculation is necessary, not only because it is structurally unavoidable, but also because prudence is important in the realm of politics and personal relationship. On Derrida's account, mundane considerations remain in force; his account of the gift is meant not to demand a specific change in lifestyle but rather to point to the coming of the incalculable within life itself.[81]

For this reason, the frequently repeated claim that Derrida rejects Eckhart's religiosity is misguided. The discussion of Derrida's relation to Eckhart often centers on Derrida's suggestion that "what I write is not 'negative theology' . . . in the measure to which 'negative theology' seems to reserve . . . some hyperessentiality, a being beyond Being."[82] Derrida's concern is that Eckhart (et al.) retain an ultimate affirmation concerning what is ostensibly inconceivable, which leads John Caputo to conclude (as many do) that this represents Derrida's final judgment. Although Caputo says that "the Meister is a salient example of the recognition that . . . language keeps unsaying what it says," he adds that "to be sure, Eckhart did all of this in the name of a super-essential being"[83]—which is to say, Eckhart's negativity is disingenuous after all. However, this fails to account for the fact that Derrida makes this claim in a modality ("in the measure to which") which indicates that other readings are possible.[84] Derrida finds in Eckhart "a principle of multiplication of voices and discourses, of disappropriation and reappropriation of utterances."[85] As we have seen, Derrida claims that the very ambivalence of Eckhart's negative theology describes the condition of love; by emphasizing this complexity, Derrida undermines the claim that a hyperessentialist reading can account for Eckhart's corpus as a whole.

Caputo's claim that "deconstruction differs from the Christian mystical theology . . . of Meister Eckhart as an indeterminate differs from a determinate affirmation of the impossible"[86] is wrong on both counts. On the one hand, insofar as Eckhart categorically denies that any speech or activity is adequate to God, he requires an indeterminacy as rigorous as that of Derrida. On the other hand, it is absurd to valorize Derrida in this fashion, for Derrida is clear that the required indeterminacy cannot be attained.[87] Whereas Caputo suggests that Derrida dwells in the pure indeterminacy of "religion without religion" while Eckhart is sullied by his association with a particular tradition, Derrida acknowledges that determinate affirmations can and should continue. Since both authors work within a tradition that significantly inflects their work, the differences between them should not be elided.[88] Nevertheless, their differing commitments do not preclude the reading I have developed, for they both recognize that such calculations are inevitably provisional. Both of them articulate the character of love as best they can, but they both agree that the gift of love opens within the calculated practices that it invariably exceeds.[89]

ELUSIVE LOVE

If I am right that Eckhart and Derrida develop congruent accounts of love, it remains to be seen whether their construal of love is viable. John Milbank describes a trenchant objection: "As against a logic which would associate a purity of love with unilateral action, it seems not insignificant that within romantic love an asymmetry of giving, where only one partner gives presents and favors, suggests not at all freedom and gratuitousness, but rather an obsessive admiration that subsists only at a willfully melancholic distance."[90] Indeed, if one attempted to directly realize the love Derrida and Eckhart describe, the result would be lamentable—not unilateral but a-lateral, free of any direction at all, destabilized by an apparent insanity. Milbank concludes that "a good, a sensible gift, always does receive something back: if not the gratitude of another and delight in her pleasure . . . then at least the self-awareness that we have sought to do so."[91] Such an economy is reasonable and recognizable from daily life, and it has the advantage of avoiding the danger entailed by the denial of calculation.

As Milbank suggests, there is something insane in the insistence that love must be unknowing, for the absence of reciprocity is often pure abuse. Derrida writes, "For an event to happen, the possibility of the worst, of radical evil, must remain a possibility, something that may indeed happen. Otherwise the good event . . . could not happen either."[92] On Derrida's account, the gift holds a space open for alterity, one that he argues is essential to preserving the possibility of love, and indeed this is risky. But Milbank is wrong to say that "for Derrida, the desire to give is the ethical impulse as such. But . . . it cannot ever be realized in any act. It cannot *be*."[93] In the first place, it is not the desire to give which is basically ethical for Derrida, it is the gift itself. (The gift, as we have seen, cannot be reduced to the desire to give, for it eludes all intentionality.) In the second place, Derrida's claim that the gift cannot be achieved by action does not entail that it cannot be. Derrida explains, "I tried to precisely displace the problematic of the gift, to take it out of the circle of economy, of exchange, but not to conclude, from the impossibility for the gift to appear as such . . . to its absolute impossibility."[94] Indeed, the gift is a key figure for Derrida for the coming of the impossible, which intervenes in excess of intentional action.[95]

It is for this reason that Derrida may say, "This principle of ruin at the heart of the most utterly new . . . could never be eluded or denied. And yet. At the heart of this acquiescence . . . an empty space would be left . . . [f]avorable to friendship and like friendship, the friendship that would then deserve its just name."[96] The unforeseeable newness of an indiscriminate gift is certainly risky, but it is by enduring this danger that a space opens for a love and friendship that goes beyond economy. For his part, Eckhart is clear that a love that is more than self-interest offers no respite: "Thus," he says, "a person must be killed and be completely dead, and must be nothing in himself."[97] Self-abnegation is not the whole story, for the avoidance of abuse remains urgently important, and yet for these authors love itself cannot exclude danger. As Derrida says, "What is it that makes us tremble in the *mysterium tremendum*? It is the gift of infinite love."[98]

BECAUSE IDENTIFYING the gift (before or after the fact) entails economic calculation, the gift is divided against itself and beyond our achievement, but Eckhart and Derrida both argue that the impossible may nonetheless come. Both of them are clear that the aporia they articulate heightens responsibility; for both of them, the failure of discourse does not entail the interdiction of speech. We are obligated to continue speaking and giving as best we can, and the fact that our efforts are insufficient opens the prospect of something better than what we are able to realize of ourselves. Love represents such a beyond—and so, despite its darkness, it remains alluring.

One might wonder what the stringent formality of this account has to do with the mutual pleasure, give-and-take, push-and-pull, of experienced love. Love is a fragile thing and must be carefully nourished, and it offers consolations aplenty after all. Derrida and Eckhart do little to illuminate these everyday rhythms, and that is a weakness of their account. (Whatever else it may be, love-making is an art that is patiently learned, one that requires a sustaining sensitivity to the well-being of oneself and another.) Denys Turner is right to note that it is perverse to insist that we love everyone indiscriminately, for such a love would be unsustainable and unreal. John Milbank is right that a unilateral gift would risk the worst abuse, both in its neglect of self-protection and in its potentially obsessive neglect of the beloved himself. Lovers, then—which indeed we all are—will remain unsatisfied.

This dissatisfaction is demanded by the logic of my argument. If love is as elusive a thing as I have suggested, then no single account of it can be adequate. If, as Derrida says, genuine giving is not aware of itself, a love free of narcissistic reappropriation could neither be identified nor delineated. If, as Eckhart argues, love must be free of intentionality, then even the best account of its indistinction would remain too definite. Both authors claim that love cannot attain self-satisfaction, but in this they implicitly admit that their own accounts fail. Their interpretation of love could not claim final authority, for it remains in the domain of provisional calculation. By the same token, the gift of love that they describe is not an ideal to be realized directly, as if it could overrule love's familiar forms. Since such love cannot be manifest, it can only come within, underneath, and alongside experienced passions.

This is not the whole story, nor could it be. Because love is many-splendored and blind, there are many stories to be told. The point of this particular telling is to hold open the prospect of a love that is absorbed in its beloved, unconcerned with personal gain. Although all we see is economy, lovers still hope that there may be something more. Although we reasonably desire a love that is wholesome and safe, some of us suspect that love is more than a mutually convenient arrangement. Similarly, even though Christian commitment remains dangerous and unjustified, some still decide to run the risk. Although interpreting love as gift raises the specter of violence, to deny this danger would leave loveless self-interest. The choice remains open, and it is not certain which is better. Nevertheless, in a spirit of hope, some may perhaps be inspired to keep faith with unsettling love.

NOTES

An earlier version of this essay appeared in *The Heythrop Journal*, DOI: 10.1111/j.1468–2265.2012.00754.x. © 2012 The Authors. The Heythrop Journal © 2012 Trustees for Roman Catholic Purposes Registered. Published by Blackwell Publishing Ltd., 9600 Garsington Road, Oxford OX4 2DQ, UK and 350 Main Street, Malden, MA 02148, USA.

1. My argument in this essay entails that it is misleading to call Derrida an atheist, without qualification. As Derrida himself notes in relation to Eckhart (among others), "If on the one hand apophasis inclines almost toward atheism, can't one say that, on the other hand or thereby, the extreme and most consequent forms of declared atheism will have always testified to the most intense desire of God?" ("*Sauf le nom [Post-Scriptum]*," in *On the Name* [Stanford: Stanford University Press, 1995], 36).

2. For instance, Turner writes at one point that "in the heart of every Christian faith and prayer there is, as it were, a desolation, a sense of bewilderment and deprivation, even panic, at the loss of every familiar sign of God" (Denys Turner, "Marxism, Liberation Theology and the Way of Negation," in *The Cambridge Companion to Liberation Theology*, ed. Christopher Rowland [Cambridge: Cambridge University Press, 1999], 216).

3. Turner accuses Derrida of nihilism (*How to Be an Atheist: Inaugural Lecture Delivered at the University of Cambridge, 12 October 2001* [Cambridge: Cambridge University Press, 2002], 324), of "logophobia" ("Tradition and Faith," *International Journal of Systematic Theology* 6, no. 1 [January 2004]: 25), and of reducing Dionysius the Areopagite to "a dismembered torso" ("How to Read the Pseudo-Denys Today?," *International Journal of Systematic Theology* 7, no. 4 [October 2005]: 428). Because Turner rarely cites Derrida, it is hard to tell what he takes to justify his interpretation, and in fact each of these claims is false.

4. Turner, "Marxism, Liberation Theology," 216.

5. Turner claims that "the theist cannot be allowed to retreat to a position of theological post-modernism, a position of endless deferral, according to which there is only postponement, only penultimacy, an endlessly contingent 'otherness,' no rest in any ultimate signifier which could stabilize the whole business of signification upon a foundational rock of fixed and determinate reference" (*Faith, Reason and the Existence of God* [Cambridge: Cambridge University Press, 2004], 235). Leaving aside the fact that Turner's understanding of "post-modernism" is problematic, the idea that "theism" must be stabilized upon a referential foundation is a departure from the perspective Turner describes in his earlier work: "A theological discourse which can qualify as truly cognitive is that which knows itself to be the decentred

language of a decentred world, a discourse which is above all a moment of 'unknowing' in a contingent, semantically unstable world. . . . It is time that theology returned to an old and radical biblical theme, the criticism of idolatry. It will not do this while it stabilises itself upon the myths either of God or of man at the centre of the universe and of its order" ("De-centring Theology," *Modern Theology* 2, no. 2 [1986]: 142–43).

6. Turner, *Faith, Reason and the Existence of God*, xii.

7. See Turner's comment in his conversation with Terry Eagleton, above, that "one of the ways, it seemed to me, that Marxism played into something very, very important for Christians and that was Marx's rejection of atheism. . . . Atheism and theism are playing on the same tennis court, and they are just opponents on the same mistaken territory." (Cf. Denys Turner, "Marx, Matter and Christianity," *New Blackfriars* 65, no. 764 [1984]: 70–72.)

8. Turner, "De-centring Theology," 142.

9. Turner, *Faith, Reason and the Existence of God*, 11.

10. Turner, "Marxism, Liberation Theology," 214. In an earlier essay he had gone even further, claiming that "to know God we must do justice to Marx" (Denys Turner, "Atheism: Is it Essential to Marxism?," *Journal of Ecumenical Studies* 22, no. 3 [1985]: 566).

11. Jacques Derrida, "The Almost Nothing of the Unpresentable," in *Points . . .* , ed. Elisabeth Weber (Stanford: Stanford University Press, 1995), 83.

12. See Jacques Derrida, *Rogues* (Stanford: Stanford University Press, 2005), 39.

13. Jacques Derrida, *Given Time: I. Counterfeit Money* (Chicago: University of Chicago Press, 1994), 7.

14. Jacques Derrida and Jean-Luc Marion, "On the Gift: A Discussion between Jacques Derrida and Jean-Luc Marion," in *Questioning God*, ed. John D. Caputo, Mark Dooley, and Michael J. Scanlon (Bloomington: Indiana University Press, 2001), 59.

15. Derrida, *Given Time*, 123.

16. Ibid., 30.

17. Jacques Derrida, *The Politics of Friendship* (New York: Verso, 1997), 69.

18. Derrida, *Given Time*, 29; original emphasis. Compare the early Turner, who writes, "Love is both necessary and impossible. . . . Love is necessary in the clear sense that to refuse to love is to refuse to recognise the revolutionary demands which 'the facts' make on us; but impossible, because what love demands in the conditions of capitalist exploitation is made impossible by those conditions" (Denys Turner, "Marxism, Christianity and Morality: Replies to Francis Barker and Brian Wicker," *New Blackfriars* 58, no. 683 [1977]: 198).

19. Derrida, "*Sauf le nom*," 43.

20. Ibid.

21. Derrida, *Given Time*, 29.

22. Jacques Derrida, "Abraham, the Other," in *Judeities*, ed. Bettina Bergo, Joseph Cohen, and Raphael Zagury-Orly (New York: Fordham University Press, 2007), 5.

23. Derrida, *Politics of Friendship*, 255.

24. Derrida, *Points . . .* , 199.

25. Meister Eckhart, "Sermon 48," in *Meister Eckhart: The Essential Sermons, Commentaries, Treatises, and Defense*, ed. Edmund Colledge and Bernard McGinn (New York: Paulist Press, 1981), 198.

26. Derrida, "*Sauf le nom*," 80.

27. Ibid., 37.

28. Ibid., 53–54.

29. Ibid., 74.

30. Ibid., 37.

31. Ibid., 74.

32. See Denys Turner, "The Art of Unknowing: Negative Theology in Late Medieval Mysticism," *Modern Theology* 14, no. 4 (October 1998): 477–79.

33. Meister Eckhart, "Commentary on Exodus," in *Meister Eckhart: Teacher and Preacher*, ed. Bernard McGinn (New York: Paulist Press, 1986), 63.

34. Ibid., 79.

35. Meister Eckhart, "Sermon 52," in Colledge and McGinn, *Meister Eckhart*, 200; translation modified. As Michael Sells argues, the interpolated quotation marks around "God" in the English translation undercuts the radicality of Eckhart's German (*Mystical Languages of Unsaying* [Chicago: University of Chicago Press, 1994], 188–92).

36. Amy Hollywood comments, "Detachment, then, is both an epistemological and an ethical movement; to know God is to share in the divine being, marked by equality and justice" (*The Soul as Virgin Wife* [Notre Dame: University of Notre Dame Press, 2001], 157).

37. Meister Eckhart, "Sermon 16b," in McGinn, *Teacher and Preacher*, 278

38. Bernard of Clairvaux, *On Loving God*, in *Bernard of Clairvaux: Selected Works*, ed. Gillian R. Evans (New York: Paulist Press, 1987), 187.

39. Ibid.

40. Meister Eckhart, "Sermon 1," in McGinn, *Teacher and Preacher*, 240.

41. Ibid.

42. Ibid.

43. Meister Eckhart, "Woman, the Hour Is Coming," in Reiner Schürmann, *Wandering Joy* (Great Barrington: Lindisfarne Books, 2001), 54.

44. Meister Eckhart, "Sermon 71," in McGinn, *Teacher and Preacher*, 322.

45. Eckhart says, "Whoever sees anything or if anything comes to your attention, it is not God" (ibid., 323). In his contribution to this volume, John Hare writes that (according to Kierkegaard) "love, and so God, has to be hidden." Eckhart and Derrida agree, but for them this hiddenness runs so deep that it is not simply inaccessible from the outside, as Hare suggests—for them, it remains elusive even while one is experiencing it.

46. Meister Eckhart, "The Book of 'Benedictus,'" in Colledge and McGinn, *Meister Eckhart*, 217.

47. Eckhart, "Sermon 52," 201.

48. Meister Eckhart, "Counsels on Discernment," in Colledge and McGinn, *Meister Eckhart*, 280.

49. Meister Eckhart, "Sermon 5b," in Colledge and McGinn, *Meister Eckhart*, 183–84.

50. Eckhart, "Sermon 48," 198.

51. Jacques Derrida, "Passions," in *On the Name*, 26; original emphasis.

52. Derrida, *Politics of Friendship*, 70.

53. Meister Eckhart, "Sermon 30," in McGinn, *Teacher and Preacher*, 294.

54. Ibid.

55. Ibid., 292.

56. Derrida, *Politics of Friendship*, 63.

57. Jacques Derrida, *The Gift of Death* (Chicago: University of Chicago Press, 1995), 77–78.

58. Turner, *Faith, Reason and the Existence of God*, 167.

59. Ibid.

60. Ibid.

61. Ibid., 166. He repeats the claim in "Atheism, Apophaticism, and Différance," in *Théologie negative*, ed. Marco Olivetti (Roma: Biblioteca dell'Archivio di Filosofia, 2002), 225–41.

62. Jacques Derrida, "Violence and Metaphysics," in *Writing and Difference* (Chicago: University of Chicago Press, 1978), 129.

63. Turner, *Faith, Reason and the Existence of God*, 154.

64. Derrida, *Gift of Death*, 83–84.

65. Derrida elaborates, "If every human is wholly other, if everyone else, or every other one, is every bit other, then one can no longer distinguish between a claimed generality of ethics . . . and the faith that turns towards God alone, as wholly other, turning away from human duty" (ibid., 84). Against this background, the early Turner seems strikingly Derridean: he writes, "It

is somewhere within that desolation and negativity that the nexus is to be found which binds together the Christian rediscovery of justice with the poor and the rediscovery of the God who demands that justice. For in that bond of action and experience—'praxis'—is the discovery that, as the liberation theologians say, 'knowing God is doing justice'" ("Marx, Liberation Theology," 216).

66. Eckhart, "Sermon 5b," 183–84.

67. Eckhart, "Counsels on Discernment," 259.

68. Ibid., 182.

69. Eckhart, "Sermon 30," 294.

70. Turner claims that Derrida "[casts] all 'distinction' into the great logical stew-pot of 'radical alterity' or some such impressive nonsense about 'every other [being] completely other'" and is therefore guilty of "that contemporary fashion in antiessentialism which results, as it were, in an absolutisation of relativism, an ideology of alterity" ("Theology in the University," in *Fields of Faith: Theology and Religious Studies for the 21st Century*, ed. David Ford, Ben Quash, and Janet Martin Soskice [Cambridge: Cambridge University Press, 2004], 32). This reading of Derrida is misguided. To take one example among many, Derrida claims that, because hospitality is unconditional, it cannot distinguish friend from enemy, and yet he acknowledges that such distinctions remain necessary. This is not an absolute relativism, nor does it obliterate distinction altogether: although Derrida thinks hospitality is indiscriminate, he is clear that the judgment of particular cases must continue. Derrida writes, "When we control a border, when we try to discriminate, when we try to find criteria to discriminate between the enemy and the friend . . . it is a way of limiting hospitality, hospitality as such, if there is such a thing. I'm not sure there is pure hospitality. But if we want to understand what hospitality means, we have to think of unconditional hospitality, that is, openness to whomever, to any newcomer" ("Discussion with Richard Kearney," in *God, the Gift, and Postmodernism*, ed. John D Caputo and Michael J. Scanlon [Bloomington: Indiana University Press, 1999], 132–33).

71. In fact, the early Turner comes close to this position. He writes that "what Marx and the Christian traditions of negative theology have in common is their rejection of a describable God. . . . All, as it were, demand that we should love in divine darkness, in a world deprived of any ultimate meaning which is at our disposal" ("Marx, Liberation Theology," 214).

72. Eckhart, "Counsels on Discernment," 259.

73. Meister Eckhart, "Sermon 86," in McGinn, *Teacher and Preacher*, 343.

74. Jacques Derrida, *The Work of Mourning* (Chicago: University of Chicago Press, 2001), 215. See Martin Häglund's illuminating reflections on love and mortality in Derrida (*Radical Atheism: Derrida and the Time of*

Life [Stanford: Stanford University Press, 2008], 114 ff.). Although Häglund's reading of Derrida is generally sound, his argument suffers from clumsy generalizations concerning "the" (ostensibly univocal) "entire religious tradition" (113).

75. I take this to be the implication of a point that Turner repeats throughout his oeuvre: if apophatic theology requires that theological statements be subject to negation, this strategy is inseparable from an equally robust demand for theological affirmation. (See, e.g., Denys Turner, *Eros and Allegory: Medieval Exegesis of the Song of Songs* [Kalamazoo, MI: Cistercian Publications, 1995], 55.) Just as negations alone are inadequate to divine transcendence, both Derrida and Eckhart suggest that the ascesis of intention required by love is not the last word: instead they describe a tension I have elsewhere described as eschatological.

76. Eckhart, "Sermon 86," 341.

77. Eckhart, "Counsels on Discernment," 253. In his contribution to this volume, Philip McCosker writes, "Insofar as one is to desire anything given Eckhart's emphasis on nothingness and the impeding nature of anything individuating, [one should] solely desire union with God and not anything creaturely. Creaturely realities, by the logic seen above, cannot lead to God." McCosker's claim that Eckhart places divinity and humanity in competition is a worrying objection, but my reading suggests that the points where Eckhart appears to do so may be read as an unusually rigorous attempt to chasten acquisitive desire without obliterating creaturely desire altogether. After all, I have argued that Eckhart considers ethical comportment toward creaturely realities to be integral to human relation with God.

78. Eckhart, "Sermon 86," 340.

79. Derrida, *Politics of Friendship*, 63.

80. Jacques Derrida, "The Villanova Roundtable: A Conversation with Jacques Derrida," in *Deconstruction in a Nutshell*, ed. John D. Caputo (New York: Fordham University Press, 1997), 19.

81. Mark Jordan's reflections concerning a negative theology of marriage exemplify the significance of this critical gesture (*Blessing Same-Sex Unions: The Perils of Queer Romance and the Confusions of Christian Marriage* [Chicago: University of Chicago Press, 2005], 39, 49, 113–16). Jordan trenchantly argues that the obscurity of divine manifestation in human relationship precludes the simplifications that beset the debate over same-sex unions. By the same token, Jordan resists privileging psychological analysis in the evaluation of same-sex relationships, which echoes one implication of my argument—that love exists in excess of its therapeutic effects.

82. Jacques Derrida, "How to Avoid Speaking: Denials," in *Derrida and Negative Theology*, ed. Harold Coward and Toby Foshay (Albany: State University of New York Press, 1992), 77.

83. John Caputo, *More Radical Hermeneutics: On Not Knowing Who We Are* (Bloomington: Indiana University Press, 2000), 253.

84. Mary-Jane Rubenstein claims that "Derrida goes on to say—without footnote, qualification, or parenthetical remark—'No, what I write is not negative theology'" ("Dionysius, Derrida, and the Critique of 'Ontotheology,'" *Modern Theology* 24, no. 4 [2008]: 726). However, Derrida immediately qualifies the suggestion that negative theology is hyperessentialist with this "in the measure to which . . . " For this reason, Rubenstein is also wrong to claim that according to Derrida "negative theology . . . ultimately services an ultra-positive theology" (726). In fact, Derrida discusses negative theology in more than thirty separate publications from 1964 to 2003, and in almost all of them the concern regarding hyperessentialism does not appear.

85. Derrida, "How to Avoid Speaking," 113. Although Caputo sometimes acknowledges that negative theology is not univocal (e.g., John Caputo, *The Prayers and Tears of Jacques Derrida: Religion without Religion* [Bloomington: Indiana University Press, 1997], 8), he nevertheless claims that "negative theology is always a higher, more refined way of affirming that God exists, or hyperexists" (7). Apart from the fact that these two claims are contradictory, the latter statement represents an exaggeration that mars Caputo's frequently helpful interpretation of Derrida.

86. John Caputo, "Apostles of the Impossible," in Caputo and Scanlon, *God, the Gift, and Postmodernism*, 198.

87. Likewise, Ian Almond incorrectly identifies "the fundamental difference between the reasons why Eckhart and Derrida put their concepts of God/sign under erasure, the former choosing to do so . . . because of an inarticulable presence, the latter because of an ineluctable absence" (Ian Almond, "Negative Theology, Derrida and the Critique of Presence: A Poststructuralist Reading of Meister Eckhart," *Heythrop Journal* 40, no. 2 [1999]: 163). Almond is wrong on both counts: Derrida's account of love is oriented by the presence of the other while Eckhart nowhere claims that God's presence can be achieved.

88. In his contribution to this volume, Oliver Davies warns against "the uncritical assimilation of ancient texts into contemporary forms of understanding." In this essay I emphasize the affinity between Eckhart and Derrida because I think that affinity illuminates the matter of love, but this does not rule out other readings that (with other purposes in mind) would emphasize their many differences.

89. In her contribution to this volume, Karmen MacKendrick writes, "Apophasis . . . says yes as much as it says no, affirms as much as negates." Where MacKendrick focuses on faith, here I have glossed the affirmative dimension of apophatic negativity in relation to love.

90. John Milbank, "Can a Gift be Given? Prolegomena to a Future Trinitarian Metaphysic," *Modern Theology* 11, no. 1 (January 1995): 124.

91. Ibid., 125.

92. Jacques Derrida and Alexander Garcia Düttmann, "Perhaps or Maybe," *Responsibilities of Deconstruction, Warwick Journal of Philosophy* 6 (Summer 1997): 9.

93. Milbank, "Can a Gift be Given?," 130; original emphasis.

94. Derrida, "On the Gift," 59.

95. In his contribution to this volume, Denys Turner associates "Derridean deconstruction" with sophistic irony, claiming that "the postmodern mind looks every gift horse in the mouth: it receives nothing with 'fine delight,' and if its thought is fathered by anything it is fathered by a cynicism preciously refined." I have argued that Derrida might seem like a cynic on the basis of a careless reading of two or three isolated texts, but the evidence indicates overwhelmingly that his project is predicated on an (admittedly difficult) affirmation. If I am right that for Derrida the impossibility of identifying the gift is the condition under which it is possible that there should be anything beyond economy, his account of the gift of love is not cynicism, it is its antidote.

96. Derrida, *Politics of Friendship*, 66.

97. Meister Eckhart, "Sermon 29," in McGinn, *Teacher and Preacher*, 290.

98. Derrida, *Gift of Death*, 55.

Afterword

How to Fail, or "The fine delight that fathers thought"

DENYS TURNER

As I reviewed the essays in this book, by some present and former colleagues, collaborators, and students, all friends, who have contributed so much to the joys of the academic life (and there have been many such joys), I asked myself what I could contribute, by way of thanks, especially to the editors of this volume, Eric Bugyis and David Newheiser, as I confronted the task of tail-ending it. The answer came quite quickly and spontaneously: I could write on the one subject on which I am fully confident of excelling them all, being an expert in it, namely, "how to fail." For I do know about failure in a personal way, having over the years become quite good at it, indeed having made a career of it, and, in the end, I have concluded that instruction in the arts of failure was something I had become skilled even at teaching to others. Thus have I made a success out of at least one thing that it might serve some purpose to pass on to younger generations.

Over the forty-odd years of university life I have taught in University College, Dublin, studied for the DPhil in Oxford, and carried on academically at Bristol, Birmingham, Cambridge, and now Yale universities, and I think in those years I have accumulated enough good reasons why I should give due thought to the matter of how to fail. Just to take the present instance: we here in Yale are members of an institution which sets great store by its being successful, as no doubt you are in yours. And it goes along with how much it seems to matter to us that ours is thought of as an importantly good university—how important does importance seem to us!—that we will probably have thought there was a good deal of personal success attached to our getting here at all, whether to professorial appointments, to post-docs, on to PhD programs, or whatever. And for sure it did take some doing. But this pressure to be successful didn't stop with our getting here, because now that we have made it, we feel just as much pressure to go on being successful, at any rate more than in many another institution, because, as we are rather fond of repeating, ours are "world-class" institutions—which simply means that we are all the more afraid that we might fail than if we were somewhere else that is but ordinarily excellent. So why not learn how to do it, and lose our fear of its just happening to us, catching us unprepared for it? At least, then, we would be in some degree of control over the outcome.

And that might be good for us. Because success in the university world is tied in with a stress more than usually intense: some of it imposed upon us by the expectations of others, much of it, I guess, internalized from those expectations, and a great deal of it self-generated by personal feelings of inadequacy. In short, in our elite institutions the price of failing is set very high, because we know we are supposed to be the best, as good as they get.

"But are we?" we wonder. I do not think that all of us, all the time, feel very successful: and that's not putting it even half as strongly as, in truth, I might have. I remember a colleague was with me in Cambridge when I heard that I had been elected to the Norris-Hulse Professorship there. I said to him over lunch, "One day some-one is going to rumble me"—by the way, just in case you are imagining that in fearing a rumbling I anticipated being knifed by Cambridge dons in a street fight (as, I gather from *West Side Story*, you might suppose I meant), in English English, to "rumble" someone is to un-mask their claims to intelligence, or skill, or expertise, or knowledge or such. So what I meant was, "One day someone is going to work out that intellectually I am a fraud." To which my colleague replied, "To tell the truth, most of us academics feel the same a good deal of the time." And I know there is a cultural difference here that might seem to suggest that this is an anecdote illustrative merely of that peculiarly English form of arrogance that takes on the rhetorical mask of self-deprecation, whereas Americans are more upfront in their self-belief and sense of self-worth and wouldn't dream of saying so downbeat a thing about themselves. But that's not been my expe-rience of the brightest American academics I know: I have not met a PhD student in Yale yet, however brilliant, who has not at some point confessed to a quiet suspicion that we, the professors, must have made some sort of mistake in admitting him or her to the PhD pro-gram. Speaking for myself, I have always been of the view that I am a great deal more skilled at persuading committees to appoint me to a job than I am at doing the job when they have done so. And I know that I am not alone among academics in thus feeling more plausible than real.

It is true, I think, whether over here or over there, that it's much the same: many of us have a capacity for self-doubt which perversely afflicts us even, or perhaps all the more, when being offered praise for, say, a particularly good lecture or seminar presentation, on re-ceipt of a favorable book review or an unexpectedly fulsome appre-ciation of a term paper. It is just then that we think to ourselves: "Oh well, he's only saying it's good to encourage me. He doesn't really mean it." And if we are perverse enough to feel that way when what we have done is well thought of, perhaps we are more perverse still in that as often as we doubt ourselves when praised, we react with hostile defensiveness when we have done badly and are criticized for it. It's all very odd. But there is something about academics that causes in them an insecurity that is quite wildly unstable, the appear-ance of a controlling discipline disguising how close they steer to the manic; and I think I have an idea as to what it is. In due course I will try to explain.

Of course I do know that while this perverse self-doubt is not ex-clusive to them, academics are possessed by demons all of their own which from within their own particular mentality powerfully abet the external pressures. They come allied with our very strengths, for they have to do with the very nature of intellect itself, and with the stresses we place it under, often, I suppose, too one-sidedly. I was once standing in a queue for coffee after an unusually clear-minded paper at a philosophy conference and overheard one philosopher say to another, "Thank God for that sort of lucidity, else you can see nothing." "Thank God for opacity," said his companion, "else there is nothing to see." Smart-ass he may have been, but the respondent was right. Intellect uprooted and unrestrained is an imperious, all-seeing eye, it's what Jeremy Bentham called a *panoptikon*, this being his design for a prison in which there is nowhere to hide, every in-mate being always and everywhere visible to the scrutiny of their wardens, the wardens themselves being invisible to the inmates. And if intellect is allowed to see with too abandoned an intensity it will see through everything, dispelling all the densities of the given, leav-ing nothing to be simply contemplated in which the mind can rest, but in a fierce excess of lucidity will see only the other side of every-thing and discover nothing to be there, only its "otherness," as the postmodernists say—or, more impressively, its "alterity." And this, at its worst, is intellect in its self-destruct mode, that manifestation of thought which corrodes its own sources, paralyzing spirit in an ex-cess of self-reflection.

I once entertained the fancy of a perfectly mad, because per-fectly lucid, academic: it was that of a centipede furnished with in-tellect. I am no entomologist, as you might guess, but I suppose that a centipede must have a pretty complex nervous system to cope with the business of getting one hundred legs to cooperate in the business of walking. Schopenhauer was pretty cynical and pessimistic, as no doubt you know; and he said that when you think about it, walking on two legs is problem enough, being the precarious condition of just about not falling flat on your face.[1] Then it's best not to think about it, you'll say. Quite so. But imagine the entanglement of the poor centipede's legs were it to be cursed with an intellect requiring it to think out how to do it step by step as it went along. Too much thought can thus paralyze, and when I consider the predicament of the all-too-knowing centipede I think of the uprooting of feeling which an excessive one-sidedness of thought can afflict us with too, being what Hegel called the "unhappy consciousness."[2] He was referring to that excess of self-consciousness which inhibits, because it empties out, the spontaneities of feeling which are the very ground of selfhood, and action, and relationship. And I think also of the words with which the Angel admonishes the questioning Gerontius in John Henry Newman's eponymous *Dream*: "it is thy very energy of thought which keeps thee from thy God."[3]

You may take it that I haven't said these things in order to offer any encouragement to the cultural forces of anti-intellectualism, which in any case need little enough encouragement in our society and times. Merely I wanted to draw your attention to an ideology prevailing within our universities, namely, to their obsession with critique and their neglect of, maybe at its worst contempt for, the contemplative. Perhaps as universities we have responded too cravenly to the political and financial pressures on us to judge our worth by measures of crude process and gross outcomes, a curious combination, I might add, of a postmodernist cynicism dissolving all activity into process without purpose, and a utilitarian calculus, which knows nothing of outcomes except those that can be measured or graded. What gets neglected in all this illusory palaver of assessment and measurement is the sources of our intellectual endeavors, where that place is to be found from which what we do, when we do it well, derives. What and where are the wellsprings of spirit from which emerges the quality of "the intellectual life"? In any case, do we know anymore how to speak of intellect except as the tool of the technological? How may we speak without embarrassment of intellect as engaging in a form of life, as a way of becoming and being truly and fully alive, fully human? It is hard to know even where to start, because we seem to have lost any grip on what could possibly be meant by such an expression.

Except that the words of Gerard Manley Hopkins come to mind in one of his later poems. He addressed it to "R. B.," Robert Bridges, one of his few friends who in his lifetime got the hang of his poetry. In that poem Hopkins wrote of "The fine delight that fathers thought."[4] And it is with very particular poignancy that those words come to mind in connection with my theme here, because Hopkins was in his own estimation, particularly in 1885, three years before his death, in a year of deep depression, a failure; a failure, because, he said, he had lost the feel for that "fine delight" on which his poetry drew. He'd become that self-aware centipede. Untethered from its creative sources, Hopkins's all too reflective mind turned back on them and devoured them. Not a word of his was published until thirty years after his death, and throughout his life as a Jesuit priest Hopkins's spirit was crushed between the creative compulsions of the poet and the scruple that writing poetry was itself too much of a vocation to be compatible with his pastoral calling. In that year of 1885 the two collided head-on, resulting in a sequence of sonnets that Bridges simply described as "terrible." And yet, terrifyingly depressed, as are his depletions of spirit, paradoxically the spiritual desolation finds words for itself in some of his finest poetry:

> . . . Only what word
> Wisest my heart breeds dark heaven's baffling ban
> Bars or hell's spell thwarts. This to hoard unheard,
> Heard unheeded, leaves me a lonely began.[5]

I really don't know, and it doesn't much matter, whether it is right to describe Hopkins's state of mind in those months in 1885 as that of the clinically depressed or better as the spiritual condition known as the "dark night of the soul." In any case, why could it not be both? For sure, all the symptoms of a clinical condition are there in those last sonnets, in the wild, overworked, convoluted excesses of stylistic compression of "Spelt from Sybil's Leaves," on the one hand, and in the tendency, just occasionally, to slip into a self-indulgent sadness, not so far from a maudlin self-pity, on the other. I think, though, that his loneliness as poet did have its root in a more general spiritual, and not merely psychological desolation, and his obsessively burdened selfhood in something like that Hegelian hyperactive self-awareness that is the "unhappy consciousness."

> I am gall, I am heartburn. God's most deep decree
> Bitter would have me taste: my taste was me;
> > . . . I see
> The lost are like this, and their scourge to be
> As I am mine, their sweating selves; but worse.[6]

And when in his despair he yearns to hit rock bottom, he knows all too well that there isn't one, it can always get worse.

> No worst, there is none. Pitched past pitch of grief,
> More pangs will, schooled at forepangs, wilder wring . . . [7]

It is mind in overdrive that does the damage, not mind as such, but the mind that has become disengaged, alienated from its fathering in "fine delight," for such a mind

> . . . has mountains; cliffs of fall
> Frightful, sheer, no-man-fathomed. . . .
> . . . Here! creep,
> Wretch, under a comfort serves in a whirlwind: all
> Life death does end and each day dies in sleep.[8]

This is mind in self-destruct mode, the mind that like the snake of the classical myth endlessly circles back upon itself, devouring its own tail, depleting its own energies as it feeds on the very sources of their power. Yet though the Hopkins of these "terrible" sonnets—"self, poor jackself," as he describes himself—may have become overwhelmed, overloaded with an excess of selfhood, still there is a strange paradox in all this, for the Hopkins haunted by depression is none other than the poet who writes so creatively of his consequent loss of creativity. Hopkins, as it were, outwits his failures of feeling by the creative success of his poetic reflection upon the failure itself; and so his poetry taunts its own failure, and there is a sort of irony in the way in which he doubles back on his depression and recycles it as poetry, tense and brittle as the language thereby becomes, the depression redeemed by the poetry it gives birth to. Poised as he is on that cusp which Dryden knew barely to divide great wits from its alliance with madness, in Hopkins, depressive immobility and creative frenzy are held in uneasy tension, never finally resolved one way or the other; if they feed off one another, neither is ever finally consumed.

Where, then, in Hopkins is that "fine delight that fathers thought"? Oh, it is there alright, even in those wild, mad reversals of mood that overwhelm him in that period of manic depression. It is there in some friendships, he says, and he admits that it is "not but in all removes I can / Kind love both give and get,"[9] and to the end he delights in what he calls the "instress" of nature and persons, that impress of the divine which he finds in the "freshness deep down things," in the individuation of every one of a million leaves on just one tree. For each leaf in its contingent "thisness" reflects back that existential balance teetering precariously on the edge that divides being from nothingness, so that only love holds it short of falling over into annihilation, just as that same love shows in the care for each leaf's difference. For Hopkins, as for his medieval theological mentor, Duns Scotus, any sort of God, savage, cruel, or indifferent, could have produced a world governed merely by the repetitive generality of causal law; but only an infinite "mastering" love can account for the individuation, the uniqueness, whether of persons or of leaves. For unlike the "otherness" of the postmodern, which postpones and distances you from the immediacy of a thing, the "thisness" of a leaf arrests your attention and draws you into it. Of course, then, that "fine delight" is there too in Hopkins, for even when it is lost to him as mood it is still there as faith. For if, in the all-consuming Heraclitean fire

> Flesh fade, and mortal trash
> Fall to the residuary worm; / world's wildfire, leave but ash:
> In a flash, at a trumpet crash
> I am all at once what Christ is / since he was what I am,
> and This Jack, joke, poor potsherd / patch, matchwood, immortal
> diamond,
> Is immortal diamond.[10]

Is his a special case? I think not, not in part, not at least in that vulnerability of his to an alienated self-destructiveness, to the madness that to great wits is near allied. For that condition of a self so self-absorbed as to have almost a Dantean hellishness about it, the condition of being doubled self-punishingly over upon oneself, forced to live with one's "sweating self," though guiltless otherwise; is not this, even if not always with the same intensity, still too often routinized into the grim, disappointed selfhood to which many academics feel at least sometimes prone, driven by an excess of intellect overworked and unrestrained? But unrestrained by what? Unrestrained, because untethered from that "fine delight that fathers thought," the fine delight being endlessly dissipated by the excess of thought that it fathers. But what is this "fine delight"?

It is found in response to the opacity of things, to their density, which consists in their character of being given, and of being, as Hopkins saw, ultimately loved: after all, as I said, it is love that underlies Hopkins's Scotist individuation. Let me explain. What I have been trying to describe to you thus far negatively is a perverse mentality, a mind-set which consists in a kind of pure irony, too often the default mode of the academic: and how we love it! This is an irony that sees nothing because it sees through everything, and ultimately sees through even itself, the very excess of thought leading to those depletions of meaning. It is a practical mentality, a depressive disease of soul from which Hopkins from time to time suffered personally. But it is also a theory, a philosophy, that Hopkins was far from sharing, and in its form as a philosophy it is an ancient story as well as a contemporary one, a story of societies as much as of persons.

It is the story of the sophists of ancient Greece who, Plato thought, were but retail dealers, shopkeepers of the mind, who valued nothing, including knowledge itself, except for what it will exchange with. Sophists are the ultimate relativists; they are dissipaters. Inheritors of a culture in disarray in consequence of decades of civil war in the Peloponnese, they saw nothing in it but the collapse of moral discourse into a merely arbitrary rhetoric, unsecured in anything but sectional interest: and so they thought, as Plato has Thrasymachus say, that words get their fixity to their objects from the power of the strongest to secure them there, and in no other way. In a world where words can mean whatever you like, it's the most powerful who make them mean what they like, as Humpty Dumpty says to Alice— you would almost think that Lewis Carroll knew a hundred years ahead of time that if you insist on Derridean deconstruction you will but create space to be filled by a Nietzschean will to power. And let me risk your postmodern ire: our casual postmodernist who is now a commonplace is but the sophist *redivivus*, a moral and intellectual relativist who, for want of intellectual challenge, hardly bothers any more to disguise the character of his skepticism as dogma, his deconstruction having become the regnant orthodoxy.

And for all that the French think they invented deconstructive irony, they have hardly anything to say, except in tones of mournful seriousness, which the delightful Hume had not already said with cheerful casualness two centuries before them. Hume is the one who not only sees through it all, but knows that to see through it all is precisely the point, because it is to that end that the European Enlightenment has finally brought us, namely, to the dissipation of all opacities, all densities, to the point where all seeing is reduced to that of the X-ray that can see nothing in anything for it can only see through things, "rumble" them (in the English sense). Hume took his cue from Descartes who, of course, had very different outcomes in mind than those of the Scottish skeptic. But the Humean worm is already chomping away in the Cartesian apple; differing in so much else as they do, Descartes and Hume share the common assumption that were there any selfhood to be known it should be presented in its immediacy to our powers of introspection. Well, it should be, they agree, and Descartes thinks it is, the "I am" is there, he tells us in the "I think." But, as Hume admonishes, before you theorize a priori, just try it empirically: don't think, just take a look, look into yourself and tell me what you see there, other than "a bundle . . . of different perceptions,"[11] a stage, as you might say, with no theater, a play but no stage, the burning glare of self-reflection dissolving all impression of substance into mere process, all light and no opacity. As to that merely postulated Cartesian selfhood, then, there is nothing there at all that answers to it in experience, for the self-absorbed gaze has dissolved any self to be glimpsed. And when the postmodernists today make a theoretical meal of Hume's self-dissolving trick, they generalize its power to such universal effect as to remove every ultimate in the name of an endlessness of the penultimate; nothing is anything except what it is other than. Nothing new there either. After all, there were ancient Greeks who conceived of the world as nothing but an endless pile of tortoises stacked upon one another, each supporting and supported by another, none supporting the lot; it's "tortoises all the way down," as Bertrand Russell might have put it, or as William James is thought to have said of Hume's self-dissolving selfhood, it is "like a hank of self-suspending onions hung from a string which does not exist."

That is the name of our game, I mean, of our university game, and it is what we do best: we dissolve, we dissipate. That dissipation of enchantment for which the Enlightenment so enthusiastically aimed has done its work thoroughly and with finality, and the work of dissipation having been at last completed, we are left with the dissipating itself as objectless method, there being nothing left any more to dissipate. For our Binsey poplars, Hopkins's "aspens dear," are already hewn down to make way for yet more tarmac.

> O if we but knew what we do
> When we delve or hew
> Hack and rack the growing green![12]

It was industrialization reaching out to the then village of Binsey, now an Oxford suburb, at which Hopkins protested when he wrote his "Binsey Poplars," and though I bet you would not have credited Hopkins the middle-class Jesuit priest with saying it, I assure you I quote from one of his letters: "Horrible to say, in a manner I am a Communist."[13] And for sure, you shouldn't assume that it takes a Marx to identify the inner connection between philistinism and capitalism as being constituted by the conversion of every form of use value into exchange value. Of course, Marx knew that that conversion was but the economic form and foundation of a culture no longer capable of understanding the nature of gift, of the world, whether of nature or of persons, as gifted, which was pretty much Hopkins's objection too. I suppose you could say that the postmodern mind is simply the theoretical form of what Marx predicted for societies themselves, in which, like everything else, even intellect itself and its "fine delight" in the gift of creation is recycled as commodity in exchange. For the postmodern mind looks every gift horse in the mouth: it receives nothing with "fine delight," and if its thought is fathered by anything it is fathered by a cynicism preciously refined. For which reason, it can be sourly ironic, but it cannot laugh, it can be grimly witty, but it lacks humor, for, as Chesterton might have put it (and probably did), it takes nothing seriously enough to be able to find anything genuinely funny.

And now we get to the point. See how fine a line it is that separates the cultured philistinism of the ironic from the mind-world of those who shudder in awe in the presence of creation—a fine line it is, but it is of the greatest consequence that we should know where to draw it; they are easily confused because of course it belongs also to our monotheistic traditions that the world is in a way pointless. But the pointlessness of the creature is not that of the endlessly ironic never quite managing to disappear over the edge of an endlessly retreating horizon. It has the delightful pointlessness of a kind of cosmic joke. For the world, we say, is created, as jokes are created, out of nothing. You spoil a joke by anticipating its punch line; good jokes explode out of the blue—just as it is no joke if you have to explain it. And to creation itself—that is, to the ultimately mysterious fact that there is anything at all—there is nothing anticipated, its "out of the blue" is that "out of nothing." And as good jokes serve no purpose except to delight, neither does creation, for, as Thomas Aquinas says, it was out of sheer pleasure at the thought of it that God created all things, not *"propter suam utilitatem,"*[14] not, that is to say, because there was anything in it for him, nor for any further reason at all, but simply as play: for as Wisdom says, "it is my delight to play with the children of men."[15] It was just that God, as it were, was tickled at the thought of us and laughed us into being. Well, then, as irony is to joy and laughter, so is the cynical pointlessness of the postmodern to the pointlessness of the cosmic joke: that is to say, as opposites often do, irony and delight stand in that degree of proximity to one another that a mirror image stands to what it images, everything the same but in horizontal inversion.

For me it is just here that Thomas Aquinas is still worth reading. Differing in so much as he does with Hopkins's Scotus, all three track their different routes to a creating source of wonder, of "fine delight." For Thomas that wonder tracks back to the act of existence itself: *"esse est creari"* he says, "to be is to be created." That is to say, if you want to get to the heart of the matter, it lies there in what it is for something to be, in its *esse*, thus eliding the infinitive form of the Latin verb into a noun and vice versa, for its being is act and its act is to be. For Thomas, where the creative work of God is visible is not, as in Scotus, first in a thing's being this as distinct from that, nor in its being this kind of thing rather than that kind of thing; nor is the creative act of God visible even in the world's being just this actual world as distinct from its being one of the other indefinite number of worlds that could have been but isn't. The *esse* of anything at all is its standing not over and against alternatives of any kind but over and against there being nothing at all. And "nothing at all" isn't an alternative of any kind.[16]

Of course, here the mind can only boggle. Try this for a proposition: it was in the cards that there might have been nothing. But that doesn't mean that there is a state of affairs called "nothing" and before there was anything that is what there was in the cards, as if "nothing" refers to what all things are made out of; "made out of nothing" means that all things are made and there is no "out of" in their making. Simple. But also impossibly simple. As I say, you have to steady your nerve here and stop trying desperately to think impossible thoughts as if they were possible. What you have to do instead is stop still and be simply and unanxiously amazed. That, I know, is a hard saying for academics, for we will only with reluctance allow anxiety to relax its grip on our chronically dialectical minds. But the medieval theologian distinguished a destructive and unhinged *curiositas* from *contemplatio*—and note that *curiositas* is but the abstract noun derivative from the Latin *cura*, meaning, among other things, "anxiety," "worry." Thomas, however, knows where and when sheer amazement has to take over from dialectics, *admiratio* from *inquisitio*, that is, where and when you have got to that point where the mind's jaw simply drops and the words trail away into silence. And by the way, I have the idea that that is exactly what the poet is trying to get you to do, so that poetry, like all philosophy, as Thomas (following Aristotle) said, begins in amazement and is composed so as to sustain you there, in amazement unresolved. Note: Aristotle never says, and Thomas firmly denies it, that philosophers or even theologians are the sort of intellectual killjoys who, knowing their disciplines to arise out of amazement, see it as the goal of their explanations to put an end to the wonder it arises from, which is, of course, roughly Richard Dawkins's view of the goal of knowledge. If anything, philosophy and theology serve only to intensify the astonishment from which they arise, an astonishment that is purely and simply existential: there might have been nothing at all.

And that means there is another thought that you have to let go of, namely, that had there been nothing at all anything would have been missing. For something to be missing there would have to be something it is missing from, and "created out of nothing" means it exists but there couldn't be any antecedent state of affairs to generate expectations of anything at all, let alone this. Think poetry again: the point about a poem being that no one needed it, no one was waiting for it, but then it appears, "out of the blue" again. If Shakespeare hadn't written Sonnet 30, there wouldn't have been a sonnet-thirty-shaped gap to be filled so that you would miss it. You couldn't have anticipated these words before Shakespeare wrote them:

Then can I drown an eye, unused to flow
For precious friends hid in death's dateless night,
And weep afresh love's long since cancell'd woe . . .[17]

But once written those lines seem necessary because now we couldn't
do without them. Sonnet 30 is wholly surprising, ex nihilo, at once
pure gift and also perfectly apt because it creates the space it so perfectly fills. It is at once pure contingency because beforehand we
couldn't have known that we wanted it, and absolutely necessary
because now we could not imagine being without it. And that's what
we mean when we say that the world we have got is wholly surprising
because that there is anything at all must be, like Sonnet 30, or like
a joke, both wholly unexpected and just so. Hence the proper response to it is, as to jokes, to roar with laughter, or, as one does upon
reading Sonnet 30, to smile with pleasure at the poem's wholly un-
called for beauty. So we say, those of us for whom all that exists is a
creature, a creation, that existence, mine, and yours, and everything
else's, is an absolute surprise, which tickles our fancy just as it tickled
the divine fancy to pull it all off. And having done so out of delight
at the thought, the creator contemplated what he had done and, as
jokes go, thought his was a good one, as Genesis says. Well, then,
that, as Thomas would have read the words, was the "fine delight"
that fathered the thought of us and all that there is; and our "fine delight" is, as Hopkins said it was, in response to that "freshness deep
down things" which survives even the brutal axing of Binsey's poplars.

   That's Thomas. Thomas, of course, is by no means the only medieval theologian who thought of intellect as being fathered by just
that "fine delight." In fact, Hopkins's "fine delight" is above all a
Franciscan thing, and Scotus was not the only follower of that crazy
troubadour, Francis, for whom thought is either the child of "fine
delight" or else a perversely corrupt tool of violence and tyranny
which will grub up Binsey poplars without scruple. It's the same for
Bonaventure: intellect is the mirror of the divine creative light; intellect is, he says, the light in which we see things—or as we might say,
intellect is our power to see the joke of creation, its gratuitousness,

its being pure grace.[18] But, he adds, the light in which we see the world cannot itself be one of the things seen: for if, as in consequence of lunatic, postmodern urgings we might, we attempt to turn our minds back on themselves as if to see the light itself, then of course Hume is right, we seem to see nothing, for light can only be seen through, and we are right away back with the paralyzed self-reflectivity of the centipede. Light can't be what you see, because if it were we could see nothing in it. Light is visible only as refracted off opaque objects, as if to say: we can know the uncreated divine laughter only in the joke that is the creature, or, as Hopkins said, in that "freshness deep down things." And that joke is you, and it's me, and it's all creation: for deep down we too are fresh, individuated— Scotus's "this." In fact you might say that like existence itself, I too am God's gift to the human race, because I am just this person, gratuitously made thus; but then, as I might say, so are you, because you are just that person, gratuitously made other. Now that that is so really is funny, it is the wonderfully jokey one-offness of the pure Franciscan Scotus, it's his *haecceitas*, the pure immediately given "thisness" of the other, the exact reversal of the postmodern "otherness" that always escapes from under the finger of "this"; and it is pure Jesuit Hopkins, it's what he calls "instress," it's his Christ who "plays in ten thousand places / Lovely in limbs, and lovely in eyes not his / To the Father through the features of men's faces."[19] Personally I don't care whether it's Thomas's creation ex nihilo or Scotus's *haecceitas*, either way it's the same: it is only such thought as is fathered by this "fine delight" that knows its way through into that "freshness deep down things"; nor do I care whether it's written in verse or in prose, either way it's poetry.

Does all this seem to be a Hopkins made a little too hearty, too innocently affirmative? Well, maybe it is for those for whom the world answers only to the self-referentially ironic, responds to no rhetoric that does not cleverly subvert its own sources of meaning, for whom the poet, indeed the intellectual, is but the snake condemned endlessly to devour its own tail. But you cannot accuse the Hopkins from whom was wrung those terrible sonnets of an uncritical self-assurance personally; nor can you fairly accuse of historical optimism the poet who, not out of anachronistic Romantic nostalgia, but out of an avowedly Marxist rage, tells of how

> Generations have trod, have trod, have trod;
> And all is seared with trade; bleared, smeared with toil;
> And all wears man's smudge and shares man's smell: the soil
> Is bare now, nor can foot feel, being shod.[20]

It is this Hopkins, his Victorian world, like ours, "seared" and "bleared," who nonetheless asks "What do then? how meet beauty?" and answers:

> . . . Merely meet it; own,
> Home at heart, heaven's sweet gift; / then leave, let that alone.[21]

This, then, is the Hopkins for whom when all is said and done you should just stop saying it and doing it, you should just for once give over to simple awe; and as for beauty, "merely meet it." For even the "achieve of, the mastery" of the Windhover, its "Brute beauty and valour and act, oh air, pride, plume, here / Buckle!" They do buckle, every mortal beauty gives way, Hopkins glosses in his subtitle, "to Christ our Lord," that is, to

> . . . the fire that breaks from thee then, a billion
> Times told lovelier, more dangerous. O my chevalier![22]

There Hopkins leaves us. And there we too should leave off.

Well, shortly I will do so—I mean, this year I retire after forty-eight years of academic teaching, and I thought before I leave off I would try to say something I have never attempted before and speak to you about poetry, and the contemplative life, and about what we think we are at in universities, and a whole slew of things that I want to get off my chest before I give up altogether and forgo the luxury that those forty-eight years have afforded me, that is, the luxury of a captive audience. And now that time is running out for saying things, it's in a way fortunate that I find there to be less and less that

I want to say, because so many things that once seemed important seem less so now. To put it simply, as a man famously said to a woman doing the washing up, only one thing is necessary, and that isn't the washing up, which can wait. Well, I suppose that lying behind these remarks is the thought that in universities too there is the restlessness (or as you call it in Latin, *negotium*) of those who with Martha wash the dishes, and there is the idleness of Mary (in Latin, it is her *otium*) who sitting at the feet of the wise man just listened and did nothing to help her sister. Now, I guess all of you are likely, in proportions which (alas) are likely to vary on a gender basis, to be regularly engaged in both washing up and sitting idly at wisdom's feet simply listening. And since you have all been doing both for some years now I am sure that you are very aware of many differences between the two, and perhaps you know of this one in particular. As to washing up: the more of it that you have done, the less there is to do, the gap between the "done" and the "to do" lists decreases. But as to wisdom, the opposite is the case, because for the wise the more they learn, the bigger the gap gets between what they know and what they discover they don't know.

Now, to say as simply as I can what I have been talking about, it's this: if what you want is success, do the washing up. There may be a lot of it, but you'll get there, and when you get there you'll know it, and there is of course a kind of satisfaction to be had in finishing the job: at any rate, it will get you tenure. But if you want to engage in the conversation along with the contemplative Mary, then you had better be prepared to be led deeper and deeper into a sort of unknowing, into an ever widening, ever deepening, and always dizzying gap between what you know and what you know you don't know. But it's there, in the space cleared by means of failure—not, that is, by that depressed, skeptical, self-subverting failure of a deconstructive strategy, but by that fine failure of unknowing delight that "fathers thought" and "Leaves yet the mind a mother of immortal song."[23] Anything else is just business "about many things." And I don't care how academic they are; it is not among those "many things" that is to be found the "one thing necessary."

Well, I did say that I would explain how to fail. I have no idea how far I have succeeded. All I can say for sure is that it has taken me forty-seven years to get around to writing about the subject, because it has taken that long to get around to failing with any degree of adequacy. And having at long last made some headway with failure it seems to be time to go, and leave you to it, to continue learning how to do it for yourselves and to persist, as Thomas Aquinas puts it, *contemplata aliis tradere*, that is (roughly translated), to persist in passing on the skills of failure to others. Maybe you in your turn will be faster off the blocks than I have been. It would be difficult to be slower.

NOTES

Four people are to blame for this feeble attempt to write about poetry: Elena Lloyd-Sidle, who invited me to Chicago to present a paper of which this is a lightly revised version, and I am very grateful to her for permission to allow it to be included in this volume; Ashley Makar, who is simply the best poet I know and helped me with many comments on an earlier draft; Juliette Jean-freau, whose very beautiful presentation at the Institute for Sacred Music at Yale on Hopkins's "The Windhover" inspired me to try my prosaic hand at poetry before it's too late; and Courtney Palmbush, my chief editor and critic, who is writing about poetry and every now and then sends me verse to read just so I don't entirely forget what good writing is like.

1. I believe, but cannot any longer track down the precise reference, that something like this is to be found somewhere in his *Parerga und Parali-pomena*.

2. G. W. F. Hegel, *Phenomenology of Spirit*, trans. A. V. Miller (Oxford: Oxford University Press, 1976), 525 ff.

3. John Henry Newman, *The Dream of Gerontius* (London: Longmans, Green, and Co., 1907), 27.

4. Gerard Manley Hopkins, "To R. B.," in *Poems and Prose*, ed. W. H. Gardner (Harmondsworth: Penguin Classics, 1985), 68.

5. Hopkins, "To seem the stranger lies my lot," in *Poems and Prose*, 62.

6. Hopkins, "I wake and feel the fell of dark," in *Poems and Prose*, 62.

7. Hopkins, "No worst, there is none," in *Poems and Prose*, 61.

8. Ibid.

9. Hopkins, "To seem the stranger lies my lot," in *Poems and Prose*, 62.

10. Hopkins, "That Nature is a Heraclitean Fire and of the comfort of the Resurrection," in *Poems and Prose*, 66.

11. David Hume, *Treatise of Human Nature*, ed. L. A. Selby-Bigge (Oxford: Clarendon Press, 1967), I, iv, vi, 252.

12. Hopkins, "Binsey Poplars," in *Poems and Prose*, 39.

13. Hopkins, *Poems and Prose*, 173.

14. Thomas Aquinas, *Summa theologiae,* vol. 8: *Creation, Variety and Evil,* ed. Thomas Gilby, O.P. (Cambridge: Cambridge University Press, 2006), Ia, q. 44, a. 4, ad. 1.

15. Prov. 8:31.

16. See my *Faith, Reason and the Existence of God* (Cambridge: Cambridge University Press, 2004), chap. 9.

17. William Shakespeare, "Sonnet 30," in *The Oxford Shakespeare: The Complete Sonnets and Poems*, ed. Colin Burrow (Oxford: Oxford University Press), 441.

18. Bonaventure, *Itinerarium Mentis in Deum*, ed. Philotheus Boehner, O.F.M., and Zachary Hayes, O.F.M. (St. Bonaventure, NY: Franciscan Institute, 2002), chap. 5.

19. Hopkins, "As kingfishers catch fire," in *Poems and Prose*, 51.

20. Hopkins, "God's grandeur," in *Poems and Prose*, 27.

21. Hopkins, "To what serves mortal beauty?," in *Poems and Prose*, 58.

22. Hopkins, "The Windhover: To Christ Our Lord," in *Poems and Prose*, 30.

23. Hopkins, "To R. B.," 68.

Contributors

ERIC BUGYIS is Lecturer in Religious Studies at the University of Washington, Tacoma, teaching courses on philosophy of religion, critical theory, and Christian thought. Among his recent publications is "Postsecularism as Colonialism by Other Means," *Critical Research on Religion* (2015). He holds a PhD in religious studies from Yale University. Bugyis is currently writing a book on the natural theology of Herbert McCabe.

KATIE ANNE-MARIE BUGYIS is Assistant Professor in Religious Studies at St. Martin's University. Among her published works are "Envisioning Episcopal Exemption: The Life of Christina of Markyate," *Church History* (2015); "Through the Looking Glass: Reflections of Christ's 'trewe louers' in Nicholas Love's The Mirror of the Blessed Life of Jesus Christ," in *Devotional Culture in Late Medieval England and Europe: Diverse Imaginations of Christ's Life*, ed. Stephen Kelly and Ryan Perry (2015); and "Handling 'The Book of Margery Kempe': The Corrective Touches of the Red Ink Annotator," in *New Directions in Medieval Manuscript Studies and Reading Practices: Essays in Honor of Derek Pearsall's 80th Birthday*, ed. Kathryn Kerby-Fulton, John Thompson, and Sarah Baechle (2014). Her current book-length project seeks to uncover the liturgical and pastoral ministries performed by Benedictine women religious in England during the central Middle Ages.

DAVID BURRELL, C.S.C., is the Theodore M. Hesburgh C.S.C. Professor Emeritus of Philosophy and Theology in the College of Arts and Letters at the University of Notre Dame and is currently serving in Notre Dame University Bangladesh. His publications include *Knowing the Unknowable God: Ibn-Sina, Maimonides, Aquinas* (1986), *Faith and Freedom: An Interfaith Perspective* (2004), *Deconstructing Theodicy: A Philosophical Commentary on Job* (2008), *Aquinas: God and Action* (2008), and *Towards a Jewish-Christian-Muslim Theology* (2011).

OLIVER DAVIES is Professor of Christian Doctrine and coordinator of the Transformation Theology Project at King's College, London. Among his publications are *Meister Eckhart: Mystical Theologian* (1991), *A Theology of Compassion: Metaphysics of Difference and the Renewal of Tradition* (2001, 2003), *The Creativity of God: World, Eucharist, Reason* (2004), and *Theology of Transformation: Faith, Freedom, and the Christian Act* (2013). He is currently co-convener of a project on public theology in China and the West and is exploring the potential of neuroanthropology for the development of theology and the study of religions.

TERRY EAGLETON is Distinguished Professor of English Literature at Lancaster University, England. He has written around fifty books and is himself the subject of at least two monographs. Eagleton is a leading literary critic and according to the *Independent* in 2007, "the man who succeeded F. R. Leavis as Britain's most influential academic critic." Some of his recent publications are *Reason, Faith and Revolution* (2009), *On Evil* (2010), *Why Marx Was Right* (2011), and *Culture and the Death of God* (2014), all with Yale University Press.

JOHN HARE is Noah Porter Professor of Philosophical Theology at Yale Divinity School. His best-known book, *The Moral Gap* (1996), develops an account of the need for God's assistance in meeting the moral demand of which God is the source. Among his other publications are *Plato's Euthyphro* (1981; 2nd rev. ed. 1985), *God's Call* (2001), *Why Bother Being Good?* (2002), and *God and Morality: A Philosophical History* (2007).

KARL HEFTY holds an Arthur J. Ennis O.S.A. Postdoctoral Fellowship at Villanova University. His current research examines approaches to the theological category of revelation within phenomenology. Trained in theology and the philosophy of religion at the University of Chicago and the University of Cambridge, he also works in the areas of Greek and Latin patristic thought (in particular, Augustine) and in the history of medieval philosophy. Previously Hefty was a lecturer in Greek thought and literature at the University of Chicago, where he was also a junior fellow at the Martin Marty Center for the Advanced Study of Religion. His publications include the English translation of Michel Henry's *Incarnation: A Philosophy of Flesh*.

ROBIN KIRKPATRICK is Professor of Italian and English Literature at the University of Cambridge and has written a number of books on Dante and on the Renaissance. He is particularly interested in the relationship between Italian and English literature from 1300 to 1600 and in the modern period. His verse translation of the *Commedia* with notes and commentary was published by Penguin Classics in 2006–7.

KARMEN MacKENDRICK is Professor in the Philosophy Department at Le Moyne College, Syracuse, New York. Her multidisciplinary research interests center on questions of language, corporeality, and temporality, primarily in relation to theology and religious studies. She is the author of several books, including *Word Made Skin: Figuring Language at the Surface of Flesh* (2004), *Divine Enticement: Theological Seductions* (2013), and *The Matter of Voice* (forthcoming), all with Fordham University Press. She is currently engaged in projects on humility and on absence and exile.

PHILIP McCOSKER is Departmental Lecturer in Modern Theology in the Faculty of Theology and Religion, University of Oxford, and Director of the Von Hügel Institute, Fellow of St Edmund's College, and Affiliated Lecturer in the Faculty of Divinity, University of Cambridge. His research interests include historical and systematic theology, philosophical theology, Christology, structures of doctrinal integrations more widely, mystical theologies, apophaticisms, and the paradoxicality of theology. He is the author of *Christ the Paradox: Expanding Ressourcement Theology* (forthcoming); coeditor, with Denys Turner, of *The Cambridge Companion to the "Summa Theologiae"* (forthcoming); and editor of *What Is It That the Scripture Says? Essays in Biblical Interpretation, Translation, and Reception in Honour of Henry Wansbrough OSB* (2006). He is the editor of the journal *Reviews in Religion and Theology*.

BERNARD McGINN is the Naomi Shenstone Donnelley Professor Emeritus of Historical Theology and the History of Christianity in the Divinity School and the Committees on Medieval Studies and General Studies at the University of Chicago. He has written extensively in the areas of the history of apocalyptic thought and, most recently, in the areas of spirituality and mysticism. His current long-range project is a seven-volume history of Christian mysticism in the West under the general title *The Presence of God*, five volumes of which have appeared: *The Origins of Mysticism* (1991), *The Growth of Mysticism* (1996), *The Flowering of Mysticism* (1998), *The Harvest of Mysticism in Medieval Germany* (2005), and *The Varieties of Vernacular Mysticism* (2012), all published by Crossroad-Herder.

VITTORIO MONTEMAGGI is Assistant Professor of Religion and Literature in the Department of Romance Languages and Literatures and Concurrent Assistant Professor in the Department of Theology at the University of Notre Dame. He received degrees in theology and European literature. His work has centered on the relationship between language, truth, and love. To date, his published work has focused primarily on Dante's *Commedia* and its relationship with the works of Gregory the Great, Shakespeare, Primo Levi, and Roberto Benigni.

DAVID NEWHEISER is Postdoctoral Research Fellow at the Australian Catholic University. His work addresses ethical and political questions in light of classic Christian thought and contemporary continental philosophy. His current book project, *The Darkness of Hope*, draws on Dionysius the Areopagite and Jacques Derrida in order to argue that religious commitment is characterized by a hope that presses forward without the assurance of safety.

CYRIL O'REGAN is Huisking Professor of Theology at the University of Notre Dame, where he specializes in systematic and historical theology. He has specific interests in the intersection of continental philosophy and theology, religion and literature, mystical theology, and postmodern thought. Among his publications are *The Heterodox Hegel*

(1994), *Gnostic Return in Modernity* (2001), *Gnostic Apocalypse: Jacob Boehme's Haunted Narrative* (2002), *Theology and the Spaces of Apocalyptic* (2009), and *The Anatomy of Misremembering: Von Balthasar's Response to Philosophical Modernity*, vol. 1: *Hegel* (2014). O'Regan is finishing up the second volume of *The Anatomy of Misremembering*, this time on Balthasar's response to Heidegger. He is also working on two separate books, which are part of his project on the return of Gnosticism in modernity, one on German Idealism, the other on Romanticism.

MARY-JANE RUBENSTEIN is Professor of Religion at Wesleyan University and a member of the core faculty in the Feminist, Gender, and Sexuality Studies Program. She is the author of *Strange Wonder: The Closure of Metaphysics and the Opening of Awe* (2009) and *Worlds without End: The Many Lives of the Multiverse* (2014), both with Columbia University Press.

DENYS TURNER is Horace Tracy Pitkin Professor of Historical Theology at Yale Divinity School. Prior to coming to Yale, he was the Norris-Hulse Chair of Divinity at the University of Cambridge. He is the author of *Marxism and Christianity* (1983), *Eros and Allegory: Medieval Exegesis of the Song of Songs* (1995), *The Darkness of God* (1995), *Faith Seeking* (2002), *Faith, Reason and the Existence of God* (2004), *Julian of Norwich, Theologian* (2011), and *Thomas Aquinas: A Portrait* (2013), as well as many articles and papers on political and social theory in relation to Christian theology and on medieval thought, especially the traditions of "mystical theology."

LUDGER VIEFHUES-BAILEY is Distinguished Professor of Philosophy, Gender, and Culture at Le Moyne College, Syracuse, New York. His work analyzes how discourses of religion and sexuality codetermine each other, integrating philosophical modes of analysis with those pertaining to gender and cultural studies. He is the author of *Beyond the Philosopher's Fear: A Cavellian Reading of Gender, Origin, and Religion in Modern Skepticism* (2007) and *Between a Man and a Woman? Why*

Conservative Christians Oppose Same-Sex Marriage (2010). His current book project, *No Separation: How Religion Makes the Secular Nation State*, is forthcoming from Columbia University Press.

A. N. WILLIAMS taught at Yale Divinity School and the University of Cambridge. She published in the fields of patristic, medieval, and systematic theology. She is the author of *The Ground of Union: Deification in Aquinas and Palamas* (1999), *The Divine Sense: The Intellect in Patristic Theology* (2007), and *The Architecture of Theology: Structure, System, and* Ratio (2011).

Index

483

CPSIA information can be obtained
at www.ICGtesting.com
Printed in the USA
BVHW031458061118
532329BV00001B/32/P